Empirical
Post
Keynesian
Economics

Empirical Post Keynesian Economics

Looking at the Real World

Edited by
Richard P. F. Holt
and **Steven Pressman**

M.E.Sharpe
Armonk, New York
London, England

Library of Congress Cataloging-in-Publication Data

Empirical post Keynesian economics : looking at the real world / edited by
Richard P.F. Holt and Steven Pressman.
   p. cm.
Includes bibliographical references and index.
  ISBN-10: 0-7656-1328-X (cloth: alk. paper); ISBN-10: 0-7656-1329-8 (pbk.: alk. paper)
  ISBN-13: 978-0-7656-1328-8 (cloth: alk. paper); ISBN-13: 978-0-7656-1329-5 (pbk.: alk. paper)
  1. Economics. 2. Keynesian economics. I. Holt, Richard P.F., 1953– II. Pressman, Steven.

HB171.E55 2005
330.15'6—dc22   2005030807

Printed in the United States of America

The paper used in this publication meets the minimum requirements of
American National Standard for Information Sciences
Permanence of Paper for Printed Library Materials,
ANSI Z 39.48-1984.

BM (c)   10   9   8   7   6   5   4   3   2   1
BM (p)   10   9   8   7   6   5   4   3   2   1

Dedicated to two brothers,
Murray Forbes and Sandy Forbes;
and a third brother, Alan Pressman.

Contents

List of Tables, Figures, and Appendices

Tables

Figures

Appendices

Empirical Post Keynesian Economics

RICHARD P.F. HOLT AND STEVEN PRESSMAN

Empirical Analysis and Post Keynesian Economics

Introduction

Post Keynesian economist Alfred Eichner (1976, 1983) argued that developing a complete economic paradigm must follow a certain historical trajectory. It must first provide a theoretical explanation of how real economies work, then it must supply a considerable amount of empirical evidence to support its theoretical analysis.

Eichner believed that the neoclassical model of economics failed both theoretically and empirically; in essence, it was not a complete paradigm.

Eichner found it particularly ironic that while neoclassical economics wanted to be seen as a "hard" social science, it did not focus on developing scientific propositions about the "nature of the observable world." Instead, neoclassical economics worked at developing individual and social-optimization models, and then proving theorems that followed from its initial axioms, all the while holding to the assumption that the real world works according to the axioms of its theory.

Moreover, Eichner believed neoclassical theory had not held up well when empirically tested. Eichner (1985, 181) argued that many of the key ideas at the core of neoclassical theory had failed to meet the test of experience. This included the notions of indifference curves, isoquants, and positively sloped supply curves in the industrial sector of the economy; the marginal physical product of capital; and the Phillips Curve. While some of these concepts have been modified, serious problems remain with the neoclassical approach. It has been impossible to derive indifference curves from empirical data (Mishan 1961), for example. Even worse, the psychological literature on framing effects (Tversky and Kahneman 1981, 1986) and the literature on preference reversal (Tversky and Thaler 1990, Tversky et al. 1990) seem to falsify the economic notion of indifference curves and neoclassical views about human preferences. Eichner (1976) himself tested the notion of positively sloped supply curves, and found that most industrial firms operate under conditions of increasing returns rather than diminishing returns.

For Eichner, a clear difference between neoclassical and Post Keynesian economics is that Post Keynesians desire to "explain the real world as observed empirically." But, to do this, Post Keynesians need to empirically test their theoretical model. This was a point that Eichner stressed numerous times (1978, 1983, 1985). It is also a general argument about economics that has been made many times, probably most persuasively by Wassily Leontief (1971) in his presidential address to the American Economic Association in 1970.

As Post Keynesian economists, we are interested in developing a complete Post Keynesian model, one that provides an alternative to the neoclassical model, and then testing that model. In a previous work (Holt and Pressman 2001), we argued that the Post Keynesian paradigm has progressed substantially since the writings of Eichner. Post Keynesian economics now has a distinct methodological approach (see Dow 2001) along with a well-developed theoretical base. There is a good deal of scholarly literature that summarizes the key Post Keynesian theoretical contributions in greater detail and contrasts them with neoclassical theory (Arestis 1992, 1996; Davidson 1972, 1994; Eichner and Kregel 1975; Lavoie 1992); there are examples of Post Keynesian literature geared toward students (Eichner 1978, Holt and Pressman 2001), and John King (2002) has provided a good summary of the history of Post Keynesian economics, including an excellent summary of its main theoretical and methodological foundations.

None of this denies that theoretical, methodological, and pedagogical issues are still being debated and discussed among Post Keynesians, but this is what you would expect to see from a vibrant and dynamic economic theory. This sort of discussion goes on within every economic paradigm or perspective, including in the dominant neoclassical paradigm. These internal debates—which revolve around refining the paradigm and solving its inherent puzzles—do not detract from the more important point that most of the key methodological and theoretical work has been done, and that the foundation of Post Keynesian economics is well established. For this reason, it is time for Post Keynesians to take their work beyond methodology and theory, which dominated much of the discussion of the past fifty years or so, and enter a new stage, one that focuses on public policy and empirical analysis.

Although we believe that both these areas are important for the next stage of Post Keynesian thought, this book is concerned with empirical analysis. Empirical analysis is important because it is only through empirical work and testing that one is able to evaluate the accuracy of economic theory, and it is only through empirical work that one may test the policy implications that derive from the theory. In this introductory chapter, we first briefly discuss the different stages through which Post Keynesian economics has already gone. Then we identify a new stage that still needs to be developed, one that focuses on the empirical implications of Post Keynesian economics. Next we summarize the empirical work and findings in the main chapters that comprise this book. Finally, we conclude with some thoughts about future empirical work that needs to be done.

Different Stages of Post Keynesian Thought

Eichner (1985) identified two overlapping stages in the development of Post Keynesian economics. A first stage, stretching from the late nineteenth century to the 1960s, mainly involved a theoretical critique of neoclassical economics. This critique begins with Marx and Veblen, both of whom Eichner classifies as Post Keynesians of sorts. Veblen, with great wit, demolished the neoclassical idea of rational and autonomous economic agents. For Veblen ([1899] 1908), consumption behavior was social in nature. Spending was determined by the desire to keep up with one's neighbors, and even surpass their levels of consumption. Cars were not bought because they provided the individual with the greatest possible utility, but because (given budget constraints) they were more lavish and more expensive than the cars driven by one's friends and neighbors. The same thing was true of homes, of clothing, and of most consumer items. Marx, like Veblen, saw behavior as determined in large part by social factors—in particular by one's economic class—and, like Veblen, saw economic power as a main factor driving capitalist economies.

Many years after Veblen and Marx, there were the incisive critiques of Piero Sraffa and Joan Robinson. Sraffa's (1926) *Economic Journal* article on increasing returns showed that supply and demand analysis could not apply in a world of increasing returns. His *Production of Commodities by Means of Commodities* (1960) made the more general criticism that the neoclassical theory of value and distribution was circular in its reasoning. He then sought to develop a theory of value and distribution that went back to the classical notion of an economic surplus and the importance of economic power in determining the distribution of that surplus, and, as a result, of economic growth. Robinson (1953–54) raised the question of how it is possible to measure capital and thus its return. Since there was no way to measure aggregate capital (outside of having the rate of return on capital and using this to measure capital), neoclassical theory could not explain either value or distribution. This led to the famous "Cambridge controversy," which Harcourt (1972) documented so ably and with great wit. Robinson (1974, 1980) also stressed the importance of historical time in economic analysis rather than equilibrium analysis, and criticized the use of equilibrium analysis by mainstream economists.

A second stage in Post Keynesian economics, according to Eichner, stretches from the 1930s (but mainly the 1960s) to the present (or at least to 1985, when Eichner was writing). During this stage, Post Keynesians were primarily concerned with developing a theoretical alternative to neoclassical economics. John Maynard Keynes, Michal Kalecki, and Nicholas Kaldor were among the key actors in this stage of the development of Post Keynesian economics.

Keynes ([1936] 1964) developed a monetary theory of production in *The General Theory*. He explained how a money-using economy could easily fall into prolonged bouts of high unemployment. He also explained the economic policies that were needed to remedy that problem. Kalecki (1990–97) explained the importance of markup pricing, and what determined the markup. He also explained how the markup affected income distribution, investment, and the business cycle (see Sawyer 1985).

Kaldor (1956) set forth a nonmarginalist, Post Keynesian theory of distribution. He explained how aggregate spending propensities lead to a division of output between capital and labor. This explanation for distribution did not depend on the marginal returns to aggregate capital and labor, and so did not depend on the suspect notion of aggregate capital. More recently, the work of Luigi Pasinetti (1962) has built on the work of Kaldor to develop the mathematical structure of a theory of distribution that was not neoclassical in nature. At a broader and more abstract level, Vivian Walsh and Harvey Gram (1980) highlighted the differences between the classical and neoclassical theories of general equilibrium.

Eichner (1985, 177) noted that this theoretical perspective stands in sharp contrast to neoclassical theory. It focuses on "production rather than just distribution, income effects rather than just substitution effects, [and] a monetarized rather than just a barter economy." Post Keynesian models were also more concerned with how economies move through time and recognized that this process may change the ultimate economic outcome. In these models, investment or capital accumulation determines prices (because the markup is determined, in part, by the need for internal funds for investment), income distribution, and the rate of economic growth.

The consequences of this approach to economics are fundamentally different from the consequences of neoclassical economics on a number of important issues. For example, while neoclassical economists see income distribution as the outcome of the marginal productivities of individuals, Post Keynesians see income distribution as the outcome of power relationships in the economy. And while rational expectations and real business-cycle macroeconomics see government policy as ineffective in changing macroeconomic outcomes, Post Keynesians see macroeconomic policy as necessary for economic stability and full employment. For Post Keynesians, there is no presumption that market outcomes are always optimal, and no presumption that macroeconomic policy is at best ineffective and at worst harmful, as viewed by many neoclassical economists (Holt and Pressman 2001).

Eichner, however, argued that these developments and advances did not go far enough. For Eichner (1983,10), a third stage is needed in Post Keynesian economics. At this important stage, the Post Keynesian theoretical paradigm must be tested and validated. As the historian of science Thomas Kuhn (1962) noted, in any mature science most of the theoretical issues have been addressed. Certainly there are anomalies and puzzles that need to be explained, and some people will work on these issues, but most practitioners need to engage in empirical work to articulate and confirm the paradigm by establishing its scope and precision (Kuhn 1962, 36). This empirical work informs the doctoral dissertations and the refereed publications needed to advance professional careers and to sustain the paradigm. Until this stage is reached, Post Keynesian theory is inadequate, according to Eichner. Only at this stage will economics in general, and Post Keynesian economics in specific, become scientific. At the empirical stage, Post Keynesians must focus on several things.

First, Post Keynesians need to compare the conclusions of their theory with reality and see if there is correspondence. In addition, Post Keynesian theory needs to be tested against other theories to determine which is closer to accurately describing the real world. Similarly, other (i.e., neoclassical) theories must be tested against Post Keynesian theory rather than against a null hypothesis. Theories have consequences, and, at some point, those consequences have to be examined. While it is certainly true that observations are often "theory-laden" (Hanson 1958), and that what you see is determined, to some extent, by how you see the world, still, it is possible to see things from different perspectives when contrasting views are clearly elucidated. This is most obvious in the famous duck/rabbit analogy—an optical illusion which can appear as either a duck or a rabbit—originally presented by Wittgenstein in the *Philosophical Investigations* and then used by Hanson to argue for theory-laden perceptions. As Hanson himself points out, the duck/rabbit can be seen sometimes as a duck and sometimes as a rabbit, and people can be led to see both perspectives. Thus, theory-laden perception does not invalidate empirical work.

The ability to compare and contrast things from two different theoretical perspectives is made easier in a discipline like economics, where many key, theoretical terms are quite well defined. Thus, Post Keynesians and neoclassicists can pretty much agree on definitions of saving and investment, for example. They can also agree that in a simple economy with no government and no foreign trade, savings must equal investment. This is, in fact, a basic national income accounting identity. Where these two schools differ is not here, but in how they see the causal nexus between the two. For neoclassicists, savings causes investment; it provides the funds needed to build new capital equipment. In contrast, Post Keynesians hold that investment determines savings. Investment can be financed by borrowing from banks, which does not require savings because banks create money by lending. Investment, in turn, generates jobs and incomes. Some of this income will be spent, and the rest will be saved; thus, at the end of the process, savings come to equal investment.

Given perspectives that are similar in some respects, but different in a number of crucial areas, it should be possible to test for the causal nexus in a number of different ways. There are Granger causality tests. It should also be possible to look at historical episodes, where either savings incentives were increased or investment incentives were increased, and to trace the rise (or fall) of savings and investment in the economy over time. On the Post Keynesian view, savings incentives, by lowering spending, should lower investment demand. Investment incentives, however, should expand the economy and increase savings. In the neoclassical perspective, the reverse is true. What we have here is a testable proposition and an alternative hypothesis. Despite different ways of looking at the world, these different theoretical frameworks are distinguishable and testable.

Second, empirical work is important because it helps to delineate the scope of a theory. For example, Keynes was at times in favor of the gold standard and at other times opposed. His arguments were primarily about the effects of fixed exchange rates on aggregate spending. If fixed exchange rates sometime increase spending and sometimes reduce it, we need to know the conditions under which fixed exchange rates might increase spending and employment, and the conditions under which flexible rates are better for expanding effective demand.

Third, empirical work is needed to delineate elasticities. If theory holds that tax cuts stimulate spending (rather than savings to pay for the future taxes needed to repay the resulting large deficit, as Barro [1974] argues), we still need to know how much additional spending takes place and how much spending gets crowded out as a result of tax cuts. Similarly, it is important to know the value of both regional and national multipliers. Only empirical work can answer these questions for us.

Fourth, theoretical and methodological arguments are not likely to be noticed by neoclassical economists. In part, this stems from the methodological precepts of Friedman (1953), who argued that the only thing that matters for economics is the validity of its predictions. Although Friedman's methodology has been subjected to much critical examination, its instrumentalism is generally accepted, and Friedman's 1953 essay on positivist economics has become a ready response to alternative theoretical viewpoints and to theoretical arguments raised against neoclassical theory (see Boland 1979, Caldwell 1982). Consequently, the only way to engage neoclassical theory is to present empirical evidence refuting its predictions and supporting the Post Keynesian perspective.

Solid empirical work also lets Post Keynesians appeal not just to economists but to other social scientists, to policy makers, and to the general public. It may even convince some people who are not economists of the importance and creditibility of Post Keynesian theory

To take just one important and recent real-world example of how empirical work can change minds in the profession, consider the neoclassical view of unemployment and the minimum wage. The standard neoclassical analysis holds that minimum wages above the equilibrium wage cause involuntary unemployment, and that higher minimum wages would cause unemployment to rise. The work of David Card and Alan Krueger (1994, 1995) has demonstrated that, contrary to neoclassical expectations, a higher minimum wage does not increase unemployment. As a result of their empirical work, the case for increasing the minimum wage grew stronger. The U.S. Congress, in fact, raised the national minimum wage shortly after the Card and Krueger results became known, and their results are generally thought to have been important in generating the political support for this action.

Another well-known example is the case of social security and the savings rate. Martin Feldstein (1974) found that empirical results supported the neoclassical hypothesis that social security depresses individual savings. Yet, Dean Leimer and Selig Lesnoy (1982) found that Feldstein's own data set (when properly analyzed) did not support his conclusion. There is also the work of Rick Mishkin (1982, 1983), which refuted the now classical work of Robert Barro (1978, 1981). Mishkin showed, contrary to the rational expectations conclusion of Barro, that both anticipated and unanticipated changes in the money supply can affect the level of output. Many other examples can be given where empirical results have markedly changed theoretical beliefs (see Goldfarb 1997).

Post Keynesians need to contribute to such a list. But they also must be aware that those who are doing cutting-edge work in the profession are slowly moving away from deductive reasoning as the key method used in economic analysis to a more complex approach where inductive and deductive method are used simultaneously. Within the economic profession there is an awareness of and frustration with the limitations of mainstream economics. This has led to important work in chaos and complexity theory, and work that assumes the bounded rationality and heterogeneity of agents. Some Post Keynesians have argued that the only way change will occur within the profession is by dramatic external shock like the Great Depression or a financial collapse that significantly challenges the foundation of the theoretical perspective of economics. This may be so, but it also might be possible to make changes by working within the profession (Colander et al. 2004). This is part of the reason why it is important for Post Keynesians to test their theory by empirical analysis, and to use new empirical methods that are being developed in order to challenge mainstream economic theory. For example, Post Keynesians can go beyond the use of traditional statistical and econometric testing and use more recent econometric work that deals with the limitations of classical statistics. This type of work can be helpful for Post Keynesians who want to look at economic processes based on path-dependent concepts such as hysteresis and cumulative causation. Other areas would include evolutionary game theory, computer simulations, and experimental and behavioral economics. Post Keynesians should be open to these different types of methods that emphasize more or a transdisciplinary approach to understanding economic behavior and systems and their policy implications.

We do not deny that Post Keynesians have done empirical research. Nor do we deny that Post Keynesian hypotheses have been tested. Indeed, a good deal of empirical research has been done in the Post Keynesian tradition, and has been published in professional journals such as the *Journal of Post Keynesian Economics,* the *Cambridge Journal of Economics,* the *International Review of Applied Economics,* and the *Review of Political Economy,* to cite a few. We should also mention that there has been a tradition of empirical work in Post Keynesian economics since 1945 at Cambridge University's Department of Applied Economics (DAE). Under the tutelage of four directors—Richard Stone (1945–55), Brian Reddaway (1955–70), Wynne Godley (1970–87) and David Newberry (since 1988)—the DAE has emphasized the limitation of neoclassical theory in understanding the real world and has carried out important empirical work in the Keynesian tradition. They have published from Stone's work establishing national income accounts, Godley's work in economic forecasting and Newberry's work on economic transition in Eastern Europe and his work on environmental economics.

There has also been the important empirical work by such Post Keynesians as Geoff Harcourt, who has advocated throughout his long career that Post Keynesians do more empirical work (Harcourt 1999, 2000). James K. Galbraith (1998) has done extensive work showing the importance of low rates of unemployment for greater income equality. Another strand of Post Keynesian empirical work, stemming from Kaldor and from Thirlwall's laws, has focused on export-led growth (McCombie and Thirlwall 1994). And Steven Pressman (2002, forthcoming, and in chapter 2) has shown that government spending and tax policies that redistribute income are the key determinants of national poverty rates and income equality. But, alas, these works have tended to be the exceptions rather than the rule. To be more optimistic, one might argue that this recent empirical work indicates the beginning of the third stage of Post Keynesian thought that Eichner called for.

Summary of the Empirical Work

This book continues these efforts. It is broken down into three broad areas, following traditional macroeconomic concerns with different types of aggregate spending —consumption, business investment, and foreign trade. Although no section explicitly deals with governmental spending, each chapter addresses policy issues, and in each chapter the presence of government and the need for government spending and good government policy should be obvious.

Part I focuses on consumer behavior. For Keynes, consumption was determined mainly by current income; but this was not the entire story. Keynes recognized a number of objective and subjective factors that also determined aggregate consumption. Within neoclassical economics, the theories of consumption that moved beyond the simple Keynesian consumption function have focused almost exclusively on expectations as a determinant of consumption. Post Keynesians, however, like Keynes, have been interested in other factors affecting consumption, such as income distribution and the availability of credit, which the four chapters in Part I look at. The first two chapters concern income distribution, the following two, credit availability.

In Chapter 2, Steven Pressman focuses on the income received by the very bottom of the income distribution, or the problem of poverty. He uses the Luxembourg Income Study, an international database of individual and household income, to examine the impact of income redistribution on the poor. Pressman finds that poverty rates would be extremely high throughout the world and over time without government redistribution. He next looks at the causes of the phenomenon of poverty, testing the neoclassical explanation against the Post Keynesian one. Neoclassical explanations focus mainly on human capital factors and economic incentives. For neoclassical theory, government redistribution toward the poor should reduce market incentives and thus reduce the market incomes of the poor.

Its net effect is therefore likely to be minor or negative. In contrast, for Post Keynesians, government redistribution generates incomes that are spent and that contribute to economic growth. Pressman looks at just one period (the 1990s), when social spending came under great pressure in many countries and when many countries adopted significant welfare reforms, and seeks the causes of rising poverty in the 1990s. He finds little support for the neoclassical explanations of greater poverty and a bit more support for Post Keynesian explanations.

In Chapter 3, James K. Galbraith and Enrique Garcilazo look at the relationship between pay inequality and unemployment in Europe. What drives their analysis is the insight that pay inequalities influence job search. To get at this problem, they employ European panel data at multiple geographic levels from 1984 to 2000. This allows them to separate the regional, national, and continental influences on European unemployment. With their own set of inequality measures derived from REGIO, Eurostats' harmonized regional statistical database, they find that greater pay inequality in Europe is associated with more, not less, unemployment, and that the effect is stronger for women and young workers. There are modest country fixed effects for Spain and the United Kingdom, but strong effects are found only for small countries. Moreover, these are all negative, which may be due to considerable past emigration in some cases, and to strategic wage bargaining in others. Apart from this, there are few distinctive effects at the national level, indicating that national labor market institutions are not the decisive cause of high European unemployment. Rather, the results of Galbraith and Garcilazo show a striking pan-European rise in unemployment immediately following the ratification in 1992 of the Treaty on European Union, otherwise known as the Maastricht treaty.

The next two chapters look at credit availability and consumption. Two issues are important here. First, a lack of credit may reduce spending. Second, excessive credit may lead to excessive spending, and then a debt crisis, which is solved by reducing consumption. In this way, the consumer debt cycle may lead to business fluctuations.

In Chapter 4, Gary Dymski and Carolyn Aldana present an empirical study on racial discrimination and segregation in housing markets. Access to credit is important if consumers are going to be able to purchase homes, and then fill their homes with all kinds of goods and services. Anything that limits access to credit will reduce consumer spending and will adversely affect the overall economy. Dymski and Aldana begin with a reflection on racial and gender discrimination in Post Keynesian economics. They argue that investigation of these relations follows logically from the socio-economic emphasis of central contributors to the Post Keynesian and institutionalist tradition, most notably John Kenneth Galbraith, who examined the economic impact of unequally distributed social power. Further, in a world where flows of jobs, capital, and credit are insufficient to permit broad-based prosperity, social differences (such as differences in race or gender) can influence access to scarce economic resources. This leads to a vicious cycle— racial discrimination worsens economic inequality, which undercuts the possibilities for prosperity identified by Keynes. The study's empirical results provide evidence for the persistence and intransigence of African-American disadvantage in residential credit markets across the United States. With few exceptions, they show that African-Americans are at a disadvantage in home-loan markets due to a combination of structural inequality, racial animus, and market power. The chapter also demonstrates the presence of a "racial U-curve" in lending markets; the idea is that the degree of minority disadvantage in urban credit markets depends on the degree of racial competition in credit and other markets.

Chapter 5 continues with the theme of credit and access to credit, but with a twist. Rather than looking at whether everyone has access to credit, Robert Scott looks at consumers who have too much access, that is, too much credit card debt, a problem that suggests curtailed future consumption. Indeed, if this problem afflicts enough consumers, the macroeconomic consequences could be severe. To examine this issue, Scott develops a model to investigate the determinants of credit card default by consumers. Using a unique data set collected by Ohio State University, he uses a random number generator to mix up the data set and divides it in two. Scott uses half the data set to perform exploratory data analysis (EDA) and develop a final model of credit card default. The other half of the data set was saved for when the final model was developed and a more formal econometric test could be performed.

The EDA technique allows for a Post Keynesian treatment of the data. Instead of assuming a specific model, EDA permits data mining and thus a more realistic model. The dependent variable in Scott's analysis is default, and it is measured as a count variable. The independent variables were discovered by two methods—an exhaustive review of the literature and through EDA. Once all the independent variables were identified, a full model was specified (with all variables included). Then Scott ran a one-step backward regression, removing all stand-alone variables with a p-value equal to 3 or higher. The vector variables were tested using the likelihood-ratio test; but only one vector (education) was removed. At the end of the EDA process, a streamlined model was left. This final model was tested using the withheld portion of the data. It was found that two variables were significant in both the final EDA regression and the regression with the withheld data—income and the number of credit cards that individuals had charged to the maximum limit.

Scott's results show that the credit card industry is using loose lending practices to pull consumers into debt traps, and then charging them high interest rates, late fees, and over-limit fees. Relying on Hyman Minsky's financial-instability hypothesis, Scott finds that the lending practices of credit card companies cause instability in the macroeconomy due to the needless fluctuation of consumer incomes, and thus consumption, created by the debt trap. One solution to this problem in the United States would be to have the Treasury Department's Office of the Comptroller of the Currency regulate credit card companies and require them to apply stricter lending policies.

Part II of the book moves from the arena of consumer spending to the arena of business investment. This is the area of spending that has received the most attention by Keynes, neoclassical economists, and Post Keynesians. Investment is important both because its volatility drives business cycles and because investment is recognized as a key factor affecting both productivity and income growth. Yet, much of the debate among Post Keynesians about investment spending has focused on risk versus uncertainty or on whether we can say much about investment beyond the fact that "animal spirits" are the key determinant of investment.

Ever since the beginning of the Industrial Revolution in Britain, in the eighteenth century, innovation and investment have been crucial elements in economic explanations of the dynamics of capitalism. Classical economics recognizes that innovation, embodied in the form of new machines through fixed capital investment, is essential for economic development. Keynes recognized the importance of investment to both full employment in the short run and to economic growth and development in the long run. Focusing more on uncertainty and expectations, Keynes never carefully examined the relationship between stabilization and growth. Nor did he focus much on the relationship between innovation and growth. Although these issues have been explored by several Post Keynesians, including Alfred Eichner, John Kenneth Galbraith and Michal Kalecki, they still need further development within a Post Keynesian framework.

In Chapter 6, Jerry Courvisanos sets up a theoretical linkage between innovation and investment in historical time, without reference to any static equilibrium model. In this way, the relationship between instability of cycles and trend growth can be clearly identified. Courvisanos employs a Kaleckian theoretical framework, and then develops a model of innovation and investment from this framework. This is followed by an empirical investigation of the important linkages between innovation and investment that have been missed when examined through static analyses of these relations. His statistical analysis is based on Australian industry-sector data (1984–98) on R&D and capital expenditure in panel data form and in evolutionary industry life-cycle form. One conclusion from this empirical work is that Post Keynesians need to reexamine the way strategies are formed and developed in both the private and public sectors in order to better understand the role of innovation in the investment-planning process.

In Chapter 7, Tony Laramie, Doug Mair, and Anne Miller address the two basic problems that confront Post Keynesians who seek to engage in empirical work. The majority of present-day Post Keynesians are committed to critical realist methodology. But critical realists are rather skeptical of econometrics, particularly its assumption of closed economic systems. Laramie, Mair, and Miller attempt to econometrically estimate Kalecki's investment theory taking into account critical realist reservations. They do this by adapting the behavioral and institutional version of Kalecki's investment theory developed by Courvisanos (1996), which also forms the foundations for Chapter 6. This approach argues that profits, financial gearing, and capacity utilization tangibly influence the complex psychological pressures that affect business investment decisions. Businesses have conventional norms regarding profits, financial gearing, and capacity utilization. These conventions, in turn, affect the investment decisions of firms. These norms can be interpreted as "demi-regularities" and provide the conditions for closure and make possible the use of econometrics.

However, Laramie, Mair, and Miller do recognize that econometrics needs to be used carefully. As such, they meticulously follow the procedures recommended by Adrian Darnell and J. Lynne Evans (1990). Their chapter sets out the rules by which they have followed the falsification procedure proposed by Darnell and Evans. The auxiliary hypotheses that surround Kalecki's hypothesis that investment decisions are principally determined by what happens to profits are carefully tested, as are the Gauss-Markov assumptions about the stochastic equation to be estimated. The results obtained confirmed that movements in profits and capacity utilization have been the principal determinants of investment decisions in the United Kingdom over the period 1980 to 1996.

In Chapter 8, Michelle Baddeley summarizes the theoretical literature on fixed assets in investment under uncertainty. She begins by examining some of the limitations of Dale Jorgenson's neoclassical theory of investment when applied to a world of uncertainty, and then explains how uncertainty has been introduced into the analysis of orthodox investment models using James Tobin's q approach. The chapter argues that using stock-market-based measures of the future prospects of investment decisions (like Tobin's q) is unlikely to be reliable in a world replete with speculation and financial instability. By contrast, Keynesian, Kaleckian, and Minskian approaches all take account of the impacts of uncertainty, financial constraints, and financial instability on entrepreneurial activity—via psychological factors, such as animal spirits, and via more objective factors, such as risk.

These different approaches lead Baddeley to construct two empirical models of investment for the United Kingdom and the United States. The empirical models are tested against each other using non-nested testing techniques. The empirical results support a range of models, but the overall finding in this chapter is that financial instability and uncertainty have negative impacts on investment activity. This suggests that strong institutions, designed to moderate financial instability, will have substantial benefits in terms of boosting investment activity.

In Chapter 9, Lawrance Evans provides an empirical investigation of the relationship between U.S. stock returns and the buyback of corporate equities prevalent during the last two decades of the twentieth century. The efficient markets hypothesis (EMH) and the Modigliani-Miller theorem both imply that reducing the supply of corporate equity should have no bearing on market valuations. The former theory maintains that the excess demand curve for equity is horizontal at the full-information price, while the latter extends EMH theory to suggest that the market value of the firm is independent of the manner in which it decides to finance investment or to distribute profits. However, simple supply and demand theory suggests that, similar to the markets for money and real estate, supply changes generate price-pressure effects irrespective of fundamentals. Correspondingly, more complex speculative market theories, which place adaptive expectations at the center of the equity price determination process, suggest that supply changes can influence market valuations through various channels.

Evans provides considerable empirical evidence from vector autoregressive and ordinary least square techniques to support his contention that the decline in the amount of outstanding corporate equity facilitated the movement of U.S. stock-market returns to levels unjustified by fundamentals. Because the relationship between equity supply and stock market returns is unique to the 1982:4–2000 period, there appears to be more support for Post Keynesian expectation theories, such as the Minskian theory advanced by Robert McCauley et al. (1999), rather than simple price pressure (supply and demand) theories. Nevertheless, the marginalization of supply dynamics in the conventional theories of the recent stock market boom renders them either highly implausible (those informed by EMH) or incomplete.

Part III of the volume focuses on international economic relations. In Chapter 10, Özlem Onaran and Engelbert Stockhammer bring into the picture the issue of exports, foreign trade, and international economic relationships. Their analysis focuses on a major structural change that occurred in Turkey. Following pressure from the International Monetary Fund and the World Bank, Turkey moved from an import-substituting industrialization strategy to an export-led growth strategy in 1980. Onaran and Stockhammer empirically examine the economic consequences of this change. In particular, they seek to determine whether this change has had the intended economic effects, and seek to shed some light on the contentious question of whether economic growth is profit led or wage led.

Beginning with Kaldor (1967), many Post Keynesians have focused on expanding exports as a means to growth. For Kaldor, this meant an economic policy that sought to develop the national manufacturing sector so that it would benefit from economies of scale and be more productive. This would ensure that the domestic economy could export more goods to other countries, further generating efficiencies and foreign demand. In contrast, for many countries (especially less-developed countries today) the attempt to expand exports follows a very different path. These nations have sought to sell more abroad by lowering domestic wages. Lower wages have two effects, which tend to work against one another. First, lower wages reduce the costs of production, so that goods can be produced more cheaply and thereby sold to other countries. With lower wages, profits will also increase, and so capital will accumulate, firms will hire more labor, and the economy will expand. On the other hand, lower wages mean less income going to domestic workers and lower effective demand within the country. This should reduce profits, and thereby investment.

Onaran and Stockhammer seek to disentangle these mechanisms using the structural change that took place in Turkey as a sort of controlled experiment. They set forth and then estimate a Post Keynesian open-economy model in a structural vector autoregression form. This lets them estimate empirically the relationship between distribution and growth, and allows them to evaluate whether accumulation and employment are profit or wage led. Their findings support the Post Keynesian position that accumulation, growth, and employment have not been profit led in Turkey, and that the structural reforms imposed in Turkey in the 1980s did more harm than good.

Finally, in Chapter 11, Frederico Jayme investigates whether external restrictions affect long-term economic growth in Brazil using Thirwall's model. An examination of this model is useful in attempting to understand the pattern of Brazilian economic growth from 1955 to 2002, since Thirwall's demand-pull approach demonstrates that increasing returns are essential to analyzing economic development. The results of this chapter support Thirlwall's law that exports, income elasticities of imports, and GDP have a long running relationship. Indeed, the time period covered, and selected sub-periods, show there has been co-integration between exports and GDP.

Conclusion

As we noted earlier, Alfred Eichner believed that there was a need for a paradigm shift in economics. He argued that the neoclassical model failed to "explain the real world as observed empirically" (1976). Eichner saw Post Keynesian economics —concerned with understanding how economies work in the real world—as an alternative paradigm. In order to provide an alternative to the neoclassical model, he insisted that Post Keynesians do empirical testing of their model. This book follows the advice of Eichner by adding significant empirical work to the Post Keynesian corpus. Besides presenting this important empirical work, we have also tried to show that there is a difference in the empirical approach that Post Keynesians take compared to neoclassical economists.

Unlike their neoclassical colleagues, Post Keynesians do not believe that explanation and prediction are the same, mostly because of the role of uncertainty and the nonergodic behavior found in a modern, money-using, entrepreneurial economic system. This has created a lot of discussion and debate among Post Keynesians concerning the validity and importance of empirical work, particularly econometrics as presented by neoclassical economists. Just because econometric and empirical work has been misused by neoclassical economists, it does not mean that Post Keynesians should not pursue empirical work and testing, especially where the role of empirical work is more descriptive than predictive. In many ways, this different approach in doing empirical work also reflects a major methodological difference between Post Keynesians and other schools of thought.

A lot more empirical work still needs to be done. Our hope is that this volume will inspire more Post Keynesians to focus on empirical work and that it will provide some models for other Post Keynesians doing empirical research. Carrying out such work will strengthen and help complete the Post Keynesian paradigm. It will also help to usher in a new stage in the development of Post Keynesian economics.

References

Arestis, P. 1992. *The Post Keynesian Approach to Economics.* Aldershot, UK: Edward Elgar.
———. 1996. "Post Keynesian Economics: Towards Coherence." *Cambridge Journal of Economics* 20(1): 111–35.

Barro, R. 1974. "Are Government Bonds Net Worth?" *Journal of Political Economy* 82(6): 1095–1117.

———. 1978. "Unanticipated Money, Output and the Price Level in the United States." *Journal of Political Economy* 86(4): 549–80.

———. 1981. *Money, Expectations and Business Cycles.* New York: Academic Press.

Boland, L. 1979. "A Critique of Friedman's Critics." *Journal of Economic Literature* 17(1): 503–22.

Caldwell, B. 1982. *Beyond Positivism: Economic Methodology in the Twentieth Century.* London: George Allen and Unwin.

Card, D., and A. Krueger. 1994. "Minimum Wages and Employment: A Case Study of the Fast-Food Industry in New Jersey and Pennsylvania." *American Economic Review,* 84(4): 772–93.

———. 1995. *Myth and Measurement: The New Economics of the Minimum Wage.* Princeton, NJ: Princeton University Press.

Colander, D., R. Holt, and B. Rosser, Jr. 2004. *The Changing Face of Economics: Conversations with Cutting Edge Economists.* Ann Arbor, MI: University of Michigan Press.

Courvisanos, J. 1996. *Investment Cycles in Capitalist Economies: A Kaleckian Behavioural Contribution.* Cheltenham, UK: Edward Elgar.

Darnell, A., and J. Evans. 1990. *The Limits of Econometrics.* Aldershot, UK: Edward Elgar,.

Davidson, P. 1972. *Money and the Real World.* London: Macmillan.

———. 1994. *Post Keynesian Macroeconomic Theory.* Aldershot, UK: Edward Elgar.

Dow, S. 2001. "Post Keynesian Methodology." In *A New Guide to Post Keynesian Economics,* eds. R. Holt and S. Pressman. London and New York: Routledge,.

Eichner, A. 1976. *The Megacorp and Oligopoly: Micro Foundations of Macro Dynamics.* New York: Cambridge University Press.

———. 1985. *Toward a New Economics: Essays in Post Keynesian and Institutionalist Theory.* Armonk, NY: M.E. Sharpe.

Eichner, A., ed. 1978. *A Guide to Post Keynesian Economics.* Armonk, NY: M.E. Sharpe.

———. 1983. *Why Economics Is Not Yet a Science.* Armonk, NY: M.E. Sharpe.

Eichner, A., and J. Kregel. 1975. "An Essay on Post Keynesian Theory: A New Paradigm in Economics." *Journal of Economic Literature* 13(4): 1293–1314.

Feldstein, M. 1974. "Social Security, Induced Retirement, and Aggregate Capital Accumulation." *Journal of Political Economy* 82(5): 905–26.

Friedman, M. 1953. "The Methodology of Positivist Economics." In *Essays in Positive Economics.* Chicago: University of Chicago Press, 3–43.

Galbraith, James K. 1998. *Created Unequal: The Crisis in American Pay.* New York: Free Press.

Goldfarb, R. 1997. "Now You See It, Now You Don't: Emerging Contrary Results in Economics." *Journal of Economic Methodology* 4(2): 221–44.

Hanson, N.R. 1958. *Patterns of Discovery.* London: Cambridge University Press.

Harcourt, G. 1972. *Some Cambridge Controversies in the Theory of Capital.* New York: Cambridge University Press.

———. 1999. "'Horses for Courses': The Making of a Post Keynesian Economist." In *The Makers of Modern Economics,* Vol. IV, ed. A. Heertje, 32–69. Cheltenham, UK: Edward Elgar.

———. 2000. "Harcourt, G.C. (born 1931)." In *A Biographical Dictionary of Dissenting Economists,* 2nd ed., eds. P. Arestis and M. Sawyer. Cheltenham, UK: Edward Elgar.

Holt, R., and S. Pressman, eds. 2001. *A New Guide to Post Keynesian Economics.* London and New York: Routledge.

Kaldor, N. 1956. "Alternative Theories of Distribution." *Review of Economic Studies* 23(2): 83–100.

————. 1967. *Strategic Factors in Economic Development.* Ithaca: New York State School of Industrial and Labor Relations.

Kalecki, M. 1990–97. *Collected Works of Michal Kalecki.* Edited by J. Osiatynski. Oxford, UK: Clarendon Press.

Keynes, J.M. 1964 [1936]. *The General Theory of Employment, Interest and Money.* New York: Harcourt, Brace and World.

King, J. 2002. *A History of Post Keynesian Economics since 1936.* Cheltenham, UK: Edward Elgar.

Kuhn, T. 1962. *The Structure of Scientific Revolutions.* Chicago: University of Chicago Press.

Lavoie, M. 1992. *Foundations of Post Keynesian Analysis.* Aldershot, UK: Edward Elgar.

Leimer, D., and S. Lesnoy. 1982. "Social Security and Private Savings: New Time-Series Evidence." *Journal of Political Economy* 90(3): 606–29.

Leontief, W. 1971. "Theoretical Assumptions and Nonobservable Facts." *American Economic Review* 61(1): 1–7.

McCauley, R.; J. Rudd; and F. Iacono. 1999. *Dodging Bullets: Changing US Corporate Capital Structure in the 1980s and 1990s.* Cambridge, MA: MIT Press.

McCombie, J., and A. Thirlwall. 1994. *Economic Growth and the Balance-of-Payments Constraint.* London: Macmillan.

Mishan, E. 1961. "Theories of Consumer Behavior: A Cynical View." *Economica* 28: 1–11.

Mishkin, F. 1982. "Does Anticipated Money Matter? An Econometric Investigation." *Journal of Political Economy* 90 (February): 22–51.

————. 1983. *A Rational Expectations Approach to Macroeconomics.* Chicago: University of Chicago Press.

Pasinetti, L. 1962. "Rate of Profit and Income Distribution in Relation to the Rate of Economic Growth." *Review of Economic Studies* 29(4): 267–79.

————.2002. "Women and Poverty in Developed and Transitional Economies." *Journal of Economic Issues* 35(1): 17–40.

Pressman, S. Forthcoming. "The Decline of the Middle Class: An International Perspective," *Journal of Economic Issues.*

Robinson, J. 1953–54. "The Production Function and the Theory of Capital." *Review of Economic Studies,* 21(2): 81–106.

————. 1974. "History versus Equilibrium." *Thames Papers in Political Economy.* London: Thames Polytechnic.

————. 1980. "Time in Economic Theory." *Kyklos* 33(2): 219–29.

Sawyer, M. 1985. *The Economics of Michal Kalecki.* London: Macmillan.

Sraffa, P. 1926. "The Laws of Return under Competitive Conditions." *Economic Journal* 36(144): 535–50.

————. 1960. *Production of Commodities by Means of Commodities.* Cambridge: Cambridge University Press.

Tversky, A., and D. Kahneman. 1981. "The Framing of Decisions and the Psychology of Choice." *Science* 211(4481): 453–58.

————. 1986. "Rational Choice and the Framing of Decisions." *Journal of Business* 59(4): S251-S278.

Tversky, A., P. Slovic, and D. Kahneman. 1990. "The Causes of Preference Reversal." *American Economic Review* 80(1): 204–17.

Tversky, A., and R. Thaler. 1990. "Preference Reversals." *Journal of Economic Perspectives* 4(2): 201–211.

Veblen, T. 1908 [1899]. *The Theory of the Leisure Class.* New York: Macmillan.

Walsh, V., and H. Gram. 1980. *Classical and Neoclassical Theories of General Equilibrium.* New York: Oxford University Press.

Part I

Empirical Studies of Distribution, Inequality, and Consumption

2

STEVEN PRESSMAN

What Can Post Keynesian Economics Teach Us About Poverty?

Introduction

This chapter looks to Post Keynesian economics in order to help us understand what happened to poverty in the 1990s. Its perspective is both empirical and international. It uses standardized income data across nations and it looks at how poverty changed in a set of seventeen countries during the 1990s. It then compares neoclassical and Post Keynesian attempts to understand these changes.

For many reasons, the 1990s provide a good test case for studying the causes of poverty. The distribution of income became more unequal in most countries beginning in the late 1980s and the inequality continued to grow through the early twenty-first century. Many countries enacted significant welfare reform in the 1990s. For example, in the United States, Aid to Families with Dependent Children (AFDC), popularly referred to as "the welfare program," was dismantled in 1996 when President Clinton signed a welfare reform act that required welfare recipients to look for work and limited welfare benefits to a maximum of five years for any individual. In other countries, social spending came under attack throughout the 1990s as conservative governments replaced liberal, social democratic governments. In addition, the European Union's Maastricht treaty of 1992 limited the ability of countries to run large annual budget deficits and to incur large amounts of governmental debt; there was thus great pressure to reduce government expenditures.

Due to these political and economic forces, replacement rates for unemployment insurance and sick pay declined in many, but not all, countries throughout the world. For example, in Belgium, the Netherlands, New Zealand, Sweden, and the United States, the decline was large and significant—around ten percentage points for unemployment insurance. However, in other countries there was virtually no change in the replacement rates for major social-insurance programs (see Allan and Scruggs 2004).

These very different experiences across nations provide an opportunity to examine the impact of such changes on national poverty rates, and to test various theories about the impact of government spending programs on poverty. The

21

following section presents Post Keynesian and neoclassical theories of poverty and inequality. The next section briefly describes the Luxembourg Income Study (LIS), the main database for the empirical work that follows. The next uses the LIS to see how governments of different countries affect the income of those at the bottom of the income distribution, and to examine how these two variables changed during the 1990s. The final section then tests the neoclassical and Post Keynesian theories of poverty using the LIS data, and is followed by a summary of our findings and conclusions.

But first a few remarks on Post Keynesian economics and empirical work. Within the Post Keynesian camp, there has been a great deal of criticism of empirical work, especially concerning statistical analysis. This criticism has come from several different but inter-related directions.

First, and perhaps most important of all, Keynes himself raised doubts about statistical analysis. In reviewing Tinbergen's (1939) book on business cycles, Keynes ([1939] 1973) pointed out that there were problems with the econometric approach that Tinbergen was using and advocating. In brief, the problem was that econometrics could not tell us anything important about the real world. Keynes claimed that econometrics can only give quantitative precision to what is already known qualitatively about economic relationships. Tinbergen (1940) replied that regression coefficients can help test theories and that they might suggest new economic theories. He then went on to develop macroeconomic models to study economic fluctuations and to test theories about the business cycle. But Keynes and most Post Keynesians have remained skeptical of this claim, and also have maintained a healthy skepticism about what macroeconometric models can do. Believing that human behavior frequently changed, and that an economic world populated with real humans was not predictable, they have generally rejected macroeconometric forecasting.

Second, Post Keynesians have held that key assumptions made in doing econometric work (e.g., that the future would be like the past) were not correct, and that inferences about future economic relationships and performance based on past experience were not valid. As Paul Davidson (1982–83, 1991, 1996) has pointed out, a good deal of mainstream empirical work, and most all macroeconomic modeling and forecasting involves the assumption that the world is ergodic. An ergodic process is one for which time and space averages are equal; what happens at one point in time gives important information about what is likely to happen at other points in time. This stationarity implies that averages remain the same over time, and that rational agents can discover these averages. For Davidson and most Post Keynesians the world is non-ergodic in many respects and at many times. This means that we cannot always assume that relationships that held in the past will also continue to exist in the future. As a result, our predictions about the future are flawed. Another way of saying this is that the world is uncertain, that expectations are uncertain, and that our expectations about other people's expectations are even more uncertain. When there is a major structural change, economic relationships will change. If we do not know when and how expectations change, do not know when economic relationships will change, and do not know when our macroeconomic models are going to be any good, we will not be able to use the past to help understand or predict the future.

Finally, critical realism (see Lawson 1994, 1997) has repudiated empirical work and econometrics because this work fails to get underneath empirical regularities and discover the underlying mechanisms that drive economic relationships. Instead of seeking out surface regularities in the macroeconomy, Lawson advises Post Keynesians to adopt a critical realist methodology, which involves seeking to uncover underlying causal structures in surface phenomenon. The practical result of this critique is that empirical and econometric work has been looked down on and ignored. Lawson (1997) takes a strong stand against using econometrics in any empirical analysis because the conditions necessary to use it are never met. That is, there is never a closed system or a sort of controlled experiment that one could perform using econometrics. We always leave out relevant variables, relationships change over time, we never know the functional specification of the relationship that exists in the real world, and so on.

It should be noted, as an ironic aside, that these criticisms are not dissimilar to the famous "Lucas Critique" of Keynesian macroeconomics. Lucas (1976, Lucas and Sargent 1978) criticized the use of large-scale macroeconomic models to evaluate the consequences of different economic policies. His criticism was that these models all assume macroeconomic relationships will remain unchanged in the face of any change in policy. But this assumption will not, in general, hold true according to Lucas and Sargent (1978, 52), because "a change in policy *necessarily* alters some of the structural parameters . . . in a highly complex fashion." Without knowing which economic relationships remain the same, which change, and how they change, an econometric model is of no value in assessing alternative policies. This, they claim, is the reason for the poor track record of econometric forecasting models, especially their failure to predict or explain the stagflation of the 1970s.

But, more importantly, it needs to be noted that all of these criticisms apply to inferential statistics, but do not apply to descriptive statistics.[1] Descriptive statistics involves using statistics to describe the real world. It makes no assumptions about the world continuing to exist this way in the future; it makes no assumptions that human behavior will not change in the future; and it makes no assumptions that what is being described actually gets to the bottom of some underlying mechanism that drives economies. Rather, descriptive statistics merely seek to present a picture of the world as it exists at one point in time or at several points in time. This approach to empirical work seems perfectly consistent with the Post Keynesian economics, which prides itself on seeking to understand the real world. Certainly, the first step in understanding the real world is to describe its properties, its characteristics and it key relationships.

A good deal of empirical work in economics falls under the rubric of descriptive statistics. At the first and most simple level, descriptive statistics involves actually gathering data. To understand the business cycle, for example, we need data on gross domestic product and on unemployment, and on other variables that we will use to define the cycle and its various stages. This involves going out into the world and gathering some data. It also involves figuring out how to best go about measuring the things we are most interested in studying.

Second, once we have accumulated data, we need to describe the properties of that data. Descriptive statistics help us in this endeavor. It gives us information on the mean and the distribution of data. It lets us compare these means and distributions across time and space. We can look at means and variances across different time periods in one country, or we can look at means and variances at one point in time at two different places—for example, in two different areas within one country, or among two different groups of people within one country at one point in time, or among two countries in one time period.

Once we have these simple descriptive statistics, we can also look at some of the possible reasons for the differences we find in the real world. For example, might the differences in unemployment for two countries be the result of differences in the labor force participation rates of women (or young people or minorities, who generally have higher rates of unemployment)? Shift-share analysis, which enables researchers to control for changes in various socio-demographic variables, lets us describe the impact of such factors on the data that we have generated.

This sort of empirical work does not succumb to the criticisms of empirical work generally made by Post Keynesians. It makes no pretense about underlying causal mechanisms, nor does it purport to give a full account of why unemployment differs from one country to the next. Rather, it describes the impact of socio-demographic factors on the national rate of unemployment.

Finally, even correlation analysis and simple regression analysis can be used to describe the data and the relationships among various variables in the data. The simple regression model merely measures how much of the variance in the dependent variable can be explained by the variance due to a set of independent variables. A regression provides the best summary of the relationship between two (or more) variables, and its output (a regression equation) is a line which lies as close as possible to the given data points. It also provides some information regarding the extent to which changes in the independent variables are associated with changes in the dependent variable, and the extent to which this relationship is likely to be due to chance. No inferences need be made about whether changes in one variable cause changes in another variable. This issue is the province of theory. Theory tells us about these causal connections. Moreover, no inference is made about whether these relationships are likely to continue into the future. We are not predicting anything about the future. All we are doing is describing the data and the relationship among a set of existing data points.

The empirical work that follows is of the descriptive variety. It begins with measurement, calculating the rate of poverty in different countries at different points in time, and it describes changes in poverty rates over time. It then seeks to empirically understand some of the possible reasons for these changes. Using shift-share analysis, it looks at the extent to which socio-demographic variables and human capital factors can explain differences in poverty rates over time and across countries. It also examines the main Post Keynesian explanation of poverty and inequality. Finally, it employs simple regression analysis where shift-share analysis is not possible due to a lack of sufficient data.

Two Views of Poverty and Anti-Poverty Policy

Standard economic theory looks toward supply-side factors as the main determinants of income, and therefore, poverty. From the perspective of neoclassical economics, governments need to support free markets and competition because this will encourage work effort and efficiencies in production. This, in turn, will tend to raise productivity, increase incomes, and lower poverty rates.

In addition, according to the neoclassical approach, we need to get incentives right. This means that governments should intervene as little as possible in the market economy. Government support for the poor, according to the neoclassical perspective, may create perverse incentives that make poverty even worse. Redistribution may reduce work effort, leading to lower productivity by workers and thus lower incomes (Boskin 1987, Gilder 1981, Wanniski 1978); redistribution may also reduce labor force participation and generate welfare dependence as people come to prefer government handouts to working (Butler and Kondratas 1987, Murray 1984). The end result of both these processes is likely to be less income earned by many households, thereby pushing these households into poverty.

Once the right institutional structure has been developed, neoclassical economics argues, the rest is pretty much up to the individual. Individual income is a function of the marginal productivity of workers. Someone who is more valuable to a firm will be paid more money than someone who contributes less to firm revenues.

Human capital theory (Becker 1993, Mincer 1974, Schultz 1961) has taken this idea one step further, seeking to explain wage differentials based on education and experience. The key insight of human capital theory is that more educated workers will be more productive and receive higher pay. Likewise, more experienced workers will be more valuable to the firm and should also receive more income than less experienced workers. Human capital theory usually relies on age as a proxy for experience since work experience usually rises as one gets older. Another important proxy for experience is gender, since women generally acquire less human capital because of child bearing and child-rearing responsibilities.

Post Keynesians have been skeptical of this standard approach. They have questioned the marginal productivity theory of distribution for logical reasons (Harcourt 1972, James K. Galbraith 2001), and they have voiced concerns regarding the macroeconomic consequences, or the income effects, of getting the incentives right. Instead, Post Keynesians have focused on economic power as an explanation for income differentials (Palley 1998, 2003). More economic power for capital tends to reduce wages at the expense of profits and increase inequality. At the same time, greater power for capital affects government redistribution efforts, as the state reduces its support to the poor while at the same time lowering the taxes it collects from the wealthy.

More positively, Post Keynesians have advanced two different views on the causes of poverty. The first, stemming from the work of Hyman Minsky (1965, 1968) and James K. Galbraith (1998), focuses on unemployment as the key determinant of inequality and poverty. According to these authors, higher unemployment leads to greater inequality and increased poverty, while lower rates of unemployment tend to reduce inequality and poverty. Minsky (1965) also argues that when unemployment is low, labor markets will be tight. This will increase the wages of low-income workers and will also draw more workers into the labor market (thus increasing their incomes). Both of these forces should generate greater income equality, and should lower poverty rates, especially when poverty is defined in relative terms.

In addition, it is important to note that high unemployment can put severe fiscal stress on governments, forcing them to cut back on unemployment and social assistance benefits. In contrast, with a booming economy and low unemployment rates, the government faces a more favorable fiscal position, which enables it to be more generous in providing social transfers. So, in addition to reducing poverty before any fiscal redistribution, low unemployment makes it easier for the government to reduce inequality and poverty given a certain distribution of factor income (Huber and Stephens 2001, ch. 7).

This dovetails with the second strand of the Post Keynesian approach to poverty. John Maynard Keynes and John Kenneth Galbraith both argue that government redistribution is necessary to improve inequality and lower poverty rates. These efforts work directly to reduce poverty by supplementing the income of low-income earners. They also work indirectly to lower poverty because of the impact of greater equality on effective demand and employment. The importance of income distribution as a determinant of consumption, and therefore economic growth, has received some empirical support (Pressman 1991, Brown 2004).

In a 1930 paper, Keynes (1981) addressed the issue of poverty, and called for higher profit taxes on businesses. He wanted this money used for three redistribution programs: (1) family or child allowances, (2) more liberal social-insurance and pension programs, and (3) increases in "useful" form of state expenditure. Under this last category Keynes included greater state spending on health, education, recreation, travel, and housing. Most of these, he thought, would lead to a healthier, happier, and better-educated work force, thus increasing worker productivity.

The General Theory (Keynes [1936] 1964) also contains a strong redistributive theme that is too frequently ignored. Greater income equality puts more money into the hands of people in lower income classes. These people have higher propensities to consume than do wealthy individuals. Redistributing income to the lower classes thus raises aggregate consumption. Conversely, "the transfer of income from [low-income] wage-earners to other factors is likely to diminish the propensity to consume" (ibid., 95).

Tax policy also affects income distribution, for it is the distribution of disposable income that determines aggregate consumption. Keynes supported the use of tax policy to equalize incomes. "If fiscal policy is used as a deliberate instrument for the more equal distribution of incomes, its effect in increasing the propensity to consume is, of course, all the greater" (ibid.). Towards this end, he advocated high tax rates on unearned income, capital gains, and inherited wealth (all forms of income that are received disproportionately by the wealthy) in order to spur greater spending and generate faster growth.

But it is not just Keynes who took up the theme of redistribution. John Kenneth Galbraith (1958) argued that governmental redistribution is necessary to solve the problem of poverty. Moreover, the opportunity cost of such redistribution should not be that great. In a wealthy country, Galbraith maintained, the lost private goods are not as important as the public goods and the poverty reduction that comes from government fiscal efforts. Years of favoring private production and neglecting the provision of public goods have created a situation of private affluence and public squalor. A much-quoted passage (ibid., 98f.) describes this contrast:

> A family which takes it mauve and cerise, air-conditioned, power-steered and power-braked automobile our for a tour passes through cities that are badly paved, made hideous by litter, blighted buildings, billboards, and posts for wires that should long since have been put underground. . . . They picnic on exquisitely packaged food from a portable icebox by a polluted stream and go on to spend the night at a park which is a menace to public health and morals. Just before dozing off on an air mattress, beneath a nylon tent, amid the stench of decaying refuse, they may reflect vaguely on the curious unevenness of their blessings.

For Galbraith, the solution to this problem is both higher taxes and more public spending.

The Luxembourg Income Study

The Luxembourg Income Study (LIS) began in April 1983, when the government of Luxembourg agreed to develop, and make available to social scientists, an international microdata set containing a large number of income and socio-demographic variables on developed and developing countries. Until that time, most cross-national studies of income distribution and poverty were plagued with problems because the national data they employed defined key terms differently. For example, transfer income and in-kind benefits can be treated differently by different nations when they gather and report income data. Likewise, different nations can have different notions of what constitutes a family or household (e.g., do you actually have to be married to count as a family?).

One goal in creating the LIS database was to employ common definitions and concepts so that variables are measured according to uniform standards across countries. As a result, researchers can be confident that the cross-national income data and socio-economic variables that they are analyzing have been made as comparable as possible.

By 2005, the LIS contained information for thirty nations—Australia, Austria, Belgium, Canada, the Czech Republic, Denmark, Estonia, Finland, France, Germany, Greece, Hungary, Ireland, Israel, Italy, Luxembourg, Mexico, the Netherlands, Norway, Poland, Romania, Russia, the Slovak Republic, Slovenia, Spain, Sweden, Switzerland, Taiwan, the United Kingdom, and the United States. Data for each country was originally derived from national household surveys similar to the U.S. Current Population Reports, or (in a few cases) from tax returns filed with the national revenue service. Data sets for additional countries are in the process of being added to the LIS.

Currently five waves of data are available for individual countries. Wave 1 contains data sets for countries for one year in the late 1970s or early 1980s. Wave 2 contains data sets for the mid-1980s. Wave 3 contains data sets for the late 1980s and early 1990s. Wave 4 contains country data sets for the mid-1990s. Wave 5, with data sets centered around the year 2000, began to come online in 2002. Finally, historical data from the late 1960s and/or early to mid-1970s is available for a few countries.

LIS data is available for more than 100 income variables and nearly 100 sociodemographic variables. Wage and salary incomes are contained in the database for households as well as for different household members. In addition, the data set includes information on in-kind earnings, property income, alimony and child support, pension income, employer social-insurance contributions, and numerous governmental transfer payments and in-kind benefits such as child allowances, Food Stamps, and social security. There is also information on five different tax payments. Demographic variables are available for factors such as the education level of household members; the industries and occupations where adults in the family are employed; the ages of family members; household size, ethnicity, and race; and the marital status of the family or household head.[2]

This wealth of comparable information permits researchers to do cross-national studies of poverty and income distribution, and to empirically address questions about the causes of poverty and changing income distribution, with the knowledge that the cross-national data they are using is as comparable as possible.

This data also provides a basis for performing something like a "natural experiment." Countries differ in the benefits they provide to their citizens and the degree to which they reduce income inequality. The effort that individual countries have made in these areas also differs over time. Similarly, the human capital that is accumulated by households differs across nations, as does the distribution of human capital. Likewise, countries differ in where they are in the business cycle. These factors, too, change over time. Controlling for these differences will enable us to shed some light on both Post Keynesian and neoclassical views on the causes of poverty. More specifically, it will let us generate some empirical evidence that can support or cast doubt on these theories when applied to the question of why national poverty rates changed dramatically during the 1990s.

Poverty in the 1990s

In what follows, the focus of our analysis will be the household. Looking at households is better than looking at persons since many individuals (e.g., children and spouses) are poor only to the extent that they are members of a poor household. Also, looking at households is preferable to looking at families because single individuals and unrelated individuals living together are included in household data but not in family data, and we are concerned about the poverty of all people, not just those who are members of families.

The actual measurement of poverty has been a matter of contention for many years, but for most international studies the preferred method is to adopt a relative definition of poverty. There are many reasons for this. As Amartya Sen (1979, 1981, 1983) has noted, poverty is about being able to appear in public without shame. Other authors have noted that humans are social animals, and so what is necessary for humans to live decently must be a social decision (Fuchs 1965, Rainwater 1974, Ruggles 1990). In addition, what we regard as being necessary for a decent life changes over time and by place (Atkinson 1998; Goodin et al. 1999, ch. 2; Iceland 2003). For example, private baths, telephones, and television sets were not necessities a hundred years ago in the United States; but in the early twenty-first century we generally expect all U.S. households to have these amenities. Similarly, decent child care was not an economic necessity in the United States fifty years ago, when two-parent, single-breadwinner families were the norm. Today, child care is needed by most U.S. families with children. Fisher (1995) approached this issue empirically, and has estimated that people's idea of what is minimally necessary to live increases by around 0.6 percent to 1 percent for every percentage-point increase in average incomes. For all these reasons, most scholars have concluded that a relative definition of poverty is more appropriate than an absolute definition when looking at developed nations. This is even more so when making cross-national comparisons, since the alternative is to rely on the suspect notion of purchasing power parity or to use current exchange rates whose values reflect the views of currency speculators rather than equivalent real incomes (Pressman 2002).

In what follows, we use the Organisation for Economic Co-operation and Development (OECD) definition of poverty, and examine the percentage of households receiving less than 50 percent of adjusted median household income. Income must be adjusted to take account of the different income needs of households of different sizes. A family of four needs more income than a single individual. But does it need four times more, or are there economies of scale in consumption? If there are no economies of scale, we look at per capita household income. If there are some economies of scale, we thus need to make adjustments. Also, we employ the recommended OECD adjustments for family size in studies of income distribution, and the household-size adjustments that are implicit in the Orshansky (1969) definition of poverty. That is, it is assumed that additional adults in the household need 70 percent of the income of the first adult, and that each child requires 50 percent of the income of the first adult.

This decision about adjusting for family size should make little difference in our overall results. Williams, Weiner, and Sammartino (1998) have found that for the United States, over the years 1980–95, the adjustment choice makes little difference when looking at overall trends in income distribution, although of course the levels will be different. Several studies employing the LIS (Pressman 2002, Smeeding, Buhmann, and Rainwater 1988) arrive at the same conclusion regarding the measurement of poverty and the measurement of income inequality using different algorithms when adjusting for household size.

Finally, we will focus here mainly on nonelderly households (where "nonelderly" means that the head of the household is less than sixty years old). This is necessary to make sure that our results are not heavily influenced by retirement systems. In most countries, eligibility for retirement benefits begins at around age sixty. And even in countries with higher eligibility ages, such as the United States, many households can collect public pension benefits (but in smaller amounts) before they reach the official retirement age. Thus, households with heads sixty and over tend to rely heavily on government transfers and tend to earn little income via work. Since they are significantly different from other households in numerous ways, it is better to control for differences in the size of the elderly population across nations and over time by focusing mainly on nonelderly households.

Table 2.1 begins by presenting some basic data on the size of the low-income population both before and after the government has affected household income.[3] These figures look at the entire population, not just the nonelderly population. The seventeen countries listed in Table 2.1 were chosen because these are the LIS countries for which both Wave 3 and Wave 5 data were available when this paper was being written. They include a wide array of nations: several former communist countries (Hungary, Poland, Russia, and part of Germany) that underwent wrenching transformation in the 1990s; several social democratic Scandinavian countries that have long histories of providing generous and universal social benefits (Finland, Norway, and Sweden); four European countries that have been identified (see Goodin et al. 1999) as being "Fordist" because firms typically provide good pay and benefits to their (usually male) workers (Germany, Italy, Luxembourg, and the Netherlands); three free-market capitalist nations (Canada, the United Kingdom, and the United States); two European nations at very different levels of economic development, but with strong national commitments to market outcomes (Spain and Switzerland); and two non-European/non–North American countries (Israel and Taiwan).

Table 2.1

Poverty in the 1990s (percent)

Country	Factor income poor (Wave 3)	Disposable income poor (Wave 3)	Factor income poor (Wave 5)	Disposable income poor (Wave 5)
Canada	32.5	11.7	33.0	11.4
Finland	35.2	4.9	39.8	4.1
Germany	32.5	5.9	41.4	7.8
Hungary	46.4	6.3	61.1	6.2
Israel	35.5	12.5	40.5	17.3
Italy	37.5	8.3	45.1	12.0
Luxembourg	35.4	2.9	41.6	7.0
Netherlands	40.6	6.2	37.2	8.3
Norway	33.5	4.6	35.7	5.6
Poland	47.5	7.9	47.7	8.7
Russia	40.9	17.3	52.9	16.9
Spain	38.3	9.1	40.4	11.3
Sweden	42.8	7.3	40.2	6.9
Switzerland	30.7	10.5	27.9	8.0
Taiwan	13.5	7.2	18.7	10.1
United Kingdom	39.3	11.7	43.6	11.1
United States	38.8	18.3	31.6	17.6
Averages	36.5	9.0	39.9	10.0

Source: Author's calculations from Luxembourg Income Study.

The basic story told in Table 2.1 is that factor income (FI) poverty is very high throughout the world, but that government tax and spending policies reduce poverty considerably. FI poverty rates were a bit more than 35 percent on (unweighted) average in the early 1990s, and climbed to 40 percent by the beginning of the new century.

This rise in FI poverty during the 1990s should not be unexpected given the well-known increase in inequality that occurred then. FI poverty rose in all countries in our sample, with only four exceptions (the Netherlands, Sweden, Switzerland, and the United States). In three countries (Germany, Hungary, and Russia), FI poverty increased substantially, no doubt the consequence of German reunification and of the economic transition to market-based economies.

The rise in disposable income (DI) poverty was less pronounced—one percentage point. Most of this increase is due to much higher DI poverty in three countries—Israel, Italy, and Luxembourg. On the other hand, a number of countries experienced declines in DI poverty, including some (Hungary and Russia) that experienced large increases in FI poverty.

As noted earlier, we need to control for the different sizes of the elderly population across nations because of key differences between this segment of the

Table 2.2

Nonelderly Poverty in the 1990s (percent)

Country	Factor-income poor (Wave 3)	Disposable-income poor (Wave 3)	Factor-income poor (Wave 5)	Disposable-income poor (Wave 5)
Canada	21.9	13.5	18.9	13.1
Finland	16.1	5.2	21.8	4.8
Germany	9.2	6.0	17.0	7.2
Hungary	27.3	6.6	46.2	7.7
Israel	23.1	11.7	28.8	16.7
Italy	16.4	9.0	21.8	13.9
Luxembourg	16.2	2.6	22.5	8.6
Netherlands	21.5	7.2	18.0	9.5
Norway	16.9	6.5	18.0	7.2
Poland	33.5	7.7	31.0	10.6
Russia	23.9	14.3	39.3	20.5
Spain	19.6	9.7	17.2	10.4
Sweden	26.1	9.5	22.2	8.8
Switzerland	15.2	11.9	9.0	7.2
Taiwan	9.3	5.7	8.1	6.4
United Kingdom	22.1	11.8	25.8	9.7
United States	21.2	18.7	19.1	16.2
Averages	20.0	9.3	22.6	10.5

Source: Author's calculations from the Luxembourg Income Study.

population and the rest of the population. Results for nonelderly households appear in Table 2.2, and they support the main findings of Table 2.1. FI poverty rates are both high and relatively stable across nations. During the 1990s, there was a rise in FI poverty of around 2.5 percentage points. Nonelderly DI poverty also increased during the 1990s, on average, and it increased a bit more than the increase in Table 2.1 (by 1.2 percentage points rather than 1 percentage point). In several nations, nonelderly DI poverty pretty much changed in line with nonelderly FI poverty. For example, in the United States, FI poverty fell by 2.1 percentage points and DI poverty fell by 2.5 percentage points, while in Luxembourg, FI poverty rose by 6.3 percentage points and DI poverty rose by 6 percentage points.

The first column of Table 2.3 summarizes the most important data in Table 2.2 by looking at the change in nonelderly DI poverty during the 1990s. It shows that while poverty rates rose on average in the 1990s, there was considerable variation across countries. In the United Kingdom and the United States, DI poverty fell substantially. In a few countries (Canada, Finland, and Sweden), DI poverty fell slightly. But in some cases (Israel, Italy, Luxembourg, and Russia), DI poverty rose considerably, by around 5 to 6 percentage points.

Table 2.3

The Impact of Human Capital and Demographics on Poverty in the 1990s (percent)

Country	Change in nonelderly disposable-income poverty from Wave 3 to Wave 5	Change in nonelderly disposable-income poverty due to age	Change in nonelderly disposable-income poverty due to gender	Change in nonelderly disposable-income poverty due to education
Canada	−0.4	−0.5	−0.4	−1.4
Finland	−0.4	−0.3	0	−0.6
Germany	+1.2	−0.6	+0.4	N.A.
Hungary	+1.1	0	0	−1.0
Israel	+5.0	−0.1	+0.1	N.A.
Italy	+4.9	0	+2.8	−1.6
Luxembourg	+6.0	+0.4	+5.4	−2.5
Netherlands	+2.3	−0.5	−0.4	N.A.
Norway	+0.7	−0.3	+2.0	−0.4
Poland	+2.9	−0.2	0	−0.9
Russia	+6.2	−0.2	0	+0.9
Spain	0.7	0.9	1.3	−2.5
Sweden	−0.7	−2.8	−0.1	−0.1
Switzerland	−4.7	−0.1	0.1	N.A.
Taiwan	+0.7	0	0	−1.0
United Kingdom	−2.1	−0.4	−0.1	N.A.
United States	−2.5	−0.7	−0.2	−1.4
Averages	+1.2	−0.3	0.6	−1.0

Source: Author's calculations from Luxembourg Income Study.

Why Did Poverty Rise in the 1990s?

As we saw above, neoclassical economics and Post Keynesian economics offer different analyses of poverty and different explanations for why poverty rates change. Neoclassical economics focuses on demographic factors and blames state intervention in the marketplace for causing poverty, while Post Keynesians look to the state to mitigate poverty by keeping unemployment low and income distribution relatively equal.

We begin by examining the neoclassical explanation for rising poverty in the 1990s. As noted above, human capital theory implies that if a nation's demographic distribution changes, poverty rates could rise. In particular, if households are more likely to be headed by a woman, or if more households are headed by younger individuals, then we would expect poverty rates to rise. Female-headed households (FHHs), by definition, are households without a male spouse present, so they will likely have just one adult breadwinner. They also have no fallback if the household head is unemployed as a result of economic conditions, health problems, or other reasons. In addition, women earn less than men, and human capital theory has attempted to explain why it is rational for women who expect to leave the labor market for some time after the birth of a child to invest less in human capital than a man who expects to remain in the labor force continuously throughout his life. Thus, for many reasons, FHHs have lower incomes and a greater chance of winding up in poverty according to human capital theory.

Similarly, for reasons noted earlier, income generally rises with age. Therefore, if household heads in one country were becoming younger over time, we would expect poverty rates in that country to rise, while if they were becoming older over time, we would expect poverty rates to fall.

Table 2.3 asks how much poverty rates would have changed in each country had there been no demographic or educational changes in the 1990s. These figures were derived by employing simple shift-share analysis. Column 2 shows the change in poverty due to the changing age structure of the population. For every nation, the population was divided into four age groupings (under 30, 30–39, 40–49, and 50–59). We then calculated poverty rates for each age group in Wave 5, and computed the aggregate poverty rate as the weighted average of these four poverty rates using national age distributions from the early 1990s (i.e., Wave 3) as our weights. The difference between the actual poverty rate and this computation represents the change in poverty due to a changing age distribution of the population (keeping everything else constant).

Column 2 indicates little support to the view that age changes can explain recent changes in poverty. Overall, the changing age distribution of the population tended to lower, rather than increase, DI poverty rates in the 1990s. This result should not be entirely unexpected given the recent aging of the population in most developed countries (Martin and Kats 2003). As birth rates have dropped in the developed world over the past several decades, fewer households are in lower age brackets and thus fewer households should earn relatively low incomes and wind up in poverty. In only a few countries can a changing age structure help explain changing national poverty rates: Canada, Finland, Sweden, the United Kingdom, and the United States.

Column 3 of Table 2.3 repeats our shift-share exercise, but it controls for the changing gender composition of households over time rather than their changing age distribution over time. Numerous studies of rising poverty in the United States have found that the growth of FHHs was responsible for a sharp increase in U.S. poverty rates during the 1960s, 1970s, and early 1980s (Pressman 1988, Lerman 1996, McLanahan, Sorensen, and Watson 1989, Eggebeen and Lichter 1991). However, with few exceptions, Table 2.3 shows that the change in poverty due to changes in the gender distribution of households during the 1990s is close to zero. One of the main reasons for this is that there was no worldwide surge in the percentage of FHHs during the 1990s. In fact, the fraction of FHHs fell in most countries. The only exceptions among our seventeen countries were Germany, where FHHs grew from 17 percent to 22 percent of nonelderly households; Italy, where FHHs grew from 10 percent to 13 percent of nonelderly households; Luxembourg, where FHHs grew from 15 percent to 17 percent of nonelderly households; Norway, which experienced the largest increase in FHHs (from 18 percent to 23 percent of nonelderly households); and Spain, where FHHs grew from 8.5 percent to 12 percent of nonelderly households. For Luxembourg and Spain, this growth of FHHs can explain almost all the rise in poverty during the 1990s. For Germany, Italy, and Norway, the rise of FHHs seems to be a significant contributing factor to higher overall poverty rates. Nevertheless, for most countries, it does not appear that changes in the gender composition of families can help explain why poverty rates changed during the 1990s.

Finally, human capital theory looks to changing education levels to explain changing poverty rates. As noted earlier, when the education level of the household head rises, incomes should go up and poverty levels should fall. In an earlier paper (Pressman 2002), I examined the impact of education on poverty rates by gender over the 1980s and early 1990s. That paper found that, with only one minor exception (the United States) in 1991, FHHs had the same education distribution as other households, and so education could not explain the gender-poverty gap. But this study was made difficult by the fact that education levels had not been consistently defined across countries and time in the LIS, nor by gender.

Recently, the LIS has dealt with this problem by setting out standardized educational levels for household heads. This new education variable follows the International Standard Classification of Education designed by the United Nations Educational, Scientific, and Cultural Organization (UNESCO 1997). It divides educational attainment into three broad categories (low, moderate, high) based on the learning experiences and competencies developed at each education level. Low educational attainment is a primary education or no educational degree; moderate education means the successful achievement of a secondary education; and the highest level requires a post-secondary education, either a college degree or some professional degree or certification.

Column 4 of Table 2.3 shows the national changes in poverty during the 1990s that can be attributed to changing education levels. Like our other calculations in Table 2.3, it employs shift-share analysis (using the three UNESCO education levels). In almost every case, education levels improved throughout the world during the 1990s. For example, in the United States, the distribution of education was 15 percent, 52 percent, and 34 percent for the three UNESCO education levels in the early 1990s. By 2000, the educational distribution of the United States was 12 percent, 50 percent, and 38 percent for the three education levels, respectively.

When smaller fractions of household heads have low levels of education, human capital theory would predict falling national poverty rates, which is not what we see. In addition, the data in column 4 of Table 2.3 provides little empirical support for the view that education was a major factor explaining changing poverty in the 1990s. In Luxembourg, for example, nonelderly DI poverty rose 6 percentage points, the second highest of all our fifteen LIS nations, while higher educational attainment by household heads in Luxembourg was reducing poverty on the order of 2.5 percentage points, the largest such decline of all our countries. Only in the United States does education seem to matter a great deal. In the United States, greater educational attainment reduced nonelderly poverty rates by 1.4 percentage points. This is a bit more than half of the 2.5 percent drop in nonelderly poverty.

Looking at the main human capital explanations for poverty as a whole, we find very little empirical support for this approach. Both education and age tended to push poverty rates down throughout the world in the 1990s, while poverty was actually rising. Only the changing gender composition of households seems to be important, though there are only a few countries where the rise in FHHs and the rise in national poverty rates seem to be related. Moreover, it is hard to really count changes in the gender composition of the population as a true human capital factor; rather, it is more a sociological phenomenon that concerns household living arrangements.

Looking at individual nations, the three human capital factors, in combination, provide a good explanation of changing poverty in only a few cases. In the United States, the total drop in poverty can almost be completely accounted for by the three human capital changes. In Luxembourg, the three human capital factors together can explain around half of the change in poverty. In Finland, human capital factors pushed poverty down by around twice the overall change in poverty, and so we may conclude that human capital factors account for around half of Finland's change in poverty over the 1990s. The story is similar in Norway, where the human capital variable pushed poverty rates up rather than down, and accounts for around half the national increase in poverty during the 1990s. But, for the other thirteen nations in our study, human capital changes provide little help in understanding why poverty rates changed. If we were to average these results, attributing around 5 percent explanatory power for each of the remaining countries, human capital factors can explain 15–20 percent of changing poverty rates in the 1990s.

These impressions are supported by the simple regression results in Table 2.4. The first two columns of this table regress the change in DI poverty over the 1990s due to education against the overall changes in DI and FI poverty. If education were an important factor, it should work through changing the market incomes (i.e., FI poverty) of households; this change would then filter through to DI poverty. There was a tendency for more education to reduce FI poverty, but this does not filter through to DI poverty. Moreover, educational attainment does not vary with either DI or FI poverty during the 1990s, and both regressions have very low R-squared values. It should be noted that these results do not mean that education level is not a determinant of poverty. All these results show is that, during the 1990s, changes in education levels (as defined above) offer little insight into why poverty rates changed.

The next two columns of Table 2.4 combine the two demographic factors from human capital theory; it regresses their combined contribution to reducing poverty

Table 2.4

Simple Regression Results on Human Capital Theory and Poverty

Dependent variable	Δ DI poverty	Δ FI poverty	Δ DI poverty	Δ FI poverty
Constant	1.67 (1.28)	1.67 (1.30)	1.02 (0.67)	2.75 (1.83)
Independent variable	+0.07 (0.92) Education	−0.93 (0.93) Education	0.77* (0.37) Age and gender	0.65 (0.95) Age and gender
R^2	0	0.09	0.23	0.03

Note: Standard errors are in parentheses.
*Indicates statistical significance at the 0.10 level.

on overall poverty changes. These columns show that changing human capital appears to have had little impact on poverty during the 1990s. As expected, changes in demographic factors (mainly changes in the gender composition of households) do lead to greater poverty. Surprisingly, although human capital factors seem related to DI poverty, they do not seem to be closely related to FI poverty. As noted above, if demographic variables were driving changes in poverty, they should work by changing FI poverty, which would then lead to changes in DI poverty. The fact that these human capital variables seem to affect DI poverty more than FI poverty indicates that something else was likely going on in the 1990s. Likewise, low R-squared values and the small demographic changes that we saw in Table 2.3 make the real world impact of these demographic factors rather negligible. This leads us to Post Keynesian explanations for rising poverty.

Table 2.5 looks at changes in unemployment and changes in poverty during the 1990s for our seventeen countries. As noted above, Post Keynesian theory holds that unemployment would affect national poverty rates, and that changes in unemployment would have a greater impact on FI poverty rates than on DI poverty rates. Yet, what we see is that unemployment fell on average while poverty increased on average. However, data from individual nations provides some support for the Post Keynesian view. Falling unemployment in Canada, the Netherlands, Spain, Switzerland, and the United States are associated with declines in FI poverty, while rising unemployment in Finland, Germany, Luxembourg, and Russia are associated with rising FI poverty.

Taking this analysis a bit further, the first two columns of Table 2.6 present regressions that examine the relationship between changes in national unemployment rates and changes in national poverty rates. These provide some support for

Table 2.5

Changes in Unemployment and in Nonelderly Poverty (percent)

Country	Change in factor-income poverty from Wave 3 to Wave 5	Change in disposable-income poverty from Wave 3 to Wave 5	Change in unemployment rate
Canada	−3.0	−0.4	−3.6
Finland	+5.7	−0.4	+3.1
Germany	+7.8	+1.2	+2.8
Hungary*	+18.9	+1.1	−2.8
Israel	+5.7	+5.0	−1.8
Italy	+5.4	+4.9	−0.4
Luxembourg	+6.3	+6.0	+1.3
Netherlands	−3.5	+2.3	−3.5
Norway	+1.1	+0.7	−2.1
Poland**	−2.5	+2.9	−0.1
Russia	+15.4	+6.2	+4.6
Spain	−2.4	0.7	−2.4
Sweden	−3.9	−0.7	−0.5
Switzerland	−6.2	−4.7	−1.7
Taiwan	−1.2	+0.7	+1.5
United Kingdom	+3.7	−2.1	−2.4
United States	−2.1	−2.5	−2.8
Averages	+2.7	+1.2	−0.6

Sources: Luxembourg Income Study (for poverty rate changes), ILO (for unemployment rates, except Germany 1990, which used the OECD estimate for West Germany).
*For Hungary, 1992 unemployment data rather than 1991.
**For Poland, 1993 unemployment data rather than 1992.

the Post Keynesian position. Both regression coefficients have the right sign and the right magnitudes. Both are positive and the regression coefficient is much larger in column 1, as we would expect. If unemployment affects poverty, it should influence FI poverty first and foremost; it should affect DI poverty much less because of government efforts to mitigate the negative impact of business cycles on household incomes. Since high unemployment usually creates budget problems and makes it harder to engage in additional spending, we would expect unemployment to affect DI poverty much less than FI poverty. As columns 1 and 2 of Table 2.6 show, the impact of unemployment on DI poverty is one-third the impact of FI poverty. Overall, changes in unemployment can explain between 15 percent and 20 percent of the changes in poverty. These results are not bad for small cross-national studies of this sort.

Finally, the last columns of Table 2.6 examine the Post Keynesian view on redistributive fiscal policy. We measure the extent to which fiscal policy is redistributive by calculating the percentage of FI-poor households that actually are

Table 2.6

Some Simple Regression Results on Post Keynesian Theory and Poverty

Dependent variable	ΔFI poverty	ΔDI poverty	ΔFI poverty	ΔDI poverty
Constant	3.41* (1.64)	1.54** (0.72)	3.10* (1.62)	1.12 (0.76)
Independent variable	1.17* (0.66) ΔUnemployment	0.50 (0.29) ΔUnemployment	0.23 (0.14) ΔFiscal Policy	−0.06 (0.06) ΔFiscal Policy
R^2	0.18	0.16	0.16	0.05

Note: Standard errors are in parentheses.
*Indicates statistical significance at the .10 level.
**Indicates statistical significance at the .05 level.

removed from poverty due to government transfers and taxes (and thus are not DI poor) for each country in each year. We then use the difference-of-difference approach to ascertain how these changes in fiscal policy have affected FI poverty and DI poverty. The last two columns of Table 2.6 show that changing fiscal policy efforts had little impact on either changes in FI poverty or changes in DI poverty. The regression coefficients are as expected—greater fiscal policy effort reduces DI poverty but increases FI poverty. This latter result may be due to either the conservative criticism against redistributive economic policies (they discourage work effort) or to the fact that increasing inequality and poverty force democratic governments to make greater redistributive efforts. Resolving this issue is left for future study. For now, we note that fiscal policy can explain between 5 percent and 15 percent of the changing poverty during the 1990s, and that the two Post Keynesian factors together (changing unemployment rates and changing fiscal policy efforts) can explain between 20 percent and 35 percent of the rise in poverty during the 1990s.

Summary and Conclusions

The chapter has examined the neoclassical and Post Keynesian approaches to poverty using LIS socio-economic data sets for the 1990s. Several conclusions were reached regarding the causes of rising poverty in the 1990s.

First, human capital variables can explain very little of the rise in poverty over the 1990s. Furthermore, the small explanatory power that human capital theory has comes from changing family structure, which is more a sociological variable than a real human capital factor. The more traditional human capital variables (age and education) are not helpful in explaining rising poverty in the 1990s.

Second, the Post Keynesian emphasis on unemployment is a bit better focused than the neoclassical emphasis on microeconomic human capital factors as a main cause of rising poverty in the developed world

Third, human capital and Post Keynesian theory, even when combined, still leaves a great deal unexplained about the rise in poverty during the 1990s. Therefore, we need to think about looking elsewhere for a more complete explanation. There has been a great deal of debate within the mainstream of the profession over whether globalization or technical change has been responsible for rising income inequality throughout the world. Certainly, when income inequality rises, poverty should rise too. In moving forward, it is worth considering this debate and thinking about what Post Keynesian economics can contribute to it.

In a previous paper (Pressman 1993), I found that those countries whose exchange rates became more volatile in the post–Bretton Woods era saw labor receiving small wage gains relative to national increases in productivity. I argued that this was likely because greater capital mobility was weakening the position of labor and reducing wages. This analysis fits in nicely with the Post Keynesian view that income distribution depends on power and political factors more than on economic factors. We can, of course, take this analysis one step further. If lower wages come at the expense of greater profits, then we should see rising income inequality and rising poverty, especially when poverty is defined in relative terms. If globalization (either through more volatile exchange rates or more outsourcing) hurt the position of labor relative to capital during the 1990s, this might explain the rise in income inequality and poverty. In addition, this line of argument is consistent with Paul Davidson's call (1982, 2002) for fixed or managed exchange rates, with Keynes's desire for a system of fixed exchange rates, and with his argument (Keynes [1933] 1982; see also Radice 1988, Wolf and Smook 1988) in the early 1930s that Britain should make all their manufactured goods at home. But this is an issue for future empirical research.[4]

Notes

1. The author thanks Robert Scott for this point.
2. For more information about the Luxembourg Income Study, and for information on how to access the LIS databases, see Smeeding, Schmous, and Allegraza (1985), and Smeeding et al. (1988), and the LIS homepage at www.lisproject.org.
3. See the Appendix for data years and original sources of the data.
4. An earlier version of this paper was presented at the 2004 Eastern Economic Association meetings in Washington, DC. The author thanks Stephanie Bell and the participants at the session for helpful comments and criticism. The author also thanks Ric Holt for his helpful comments and suggestions.

References

Allan, J., and L. Scruggs. 2004. "Political Partisanship and the Welfare State." *American Journal of Political Science* 48(3): 496–512.

Atkinson, A. 1998. *Poverty in Europe.* Oxford, UK: Basil Blackwell.

Becker, G. 1993. *Human Capital,* 3rd ed. Chicago: University of Chicago Press.

Boskin, M. 1987. *Reagan and the Economy.* San Francisco: Institute for Contemporary Studies.

Brown, C. 2004. "Does Income Distribution Matter for Effective Demand?" *Review of Political Economy* 16(3): 291–307.

Butler, S., and A. Kondratas. 1987. *Out of the Poverty Trap.* New York: Free Press.

Davidson, P. 1982. *International Money and the Real World.* London: Macmillan.

———. 1982–1983. "Rational Expectations: A Fallacious Foundation for Studying Crucial Decision-Making Processes." *Journal of Post Keynesian Economics,* 5(2): 182–97.

———. 1991. "Is Probability Theory Relevant for Uncertainty?" *Journal of Economic Perspectives* 5(1): 129–43.

———. 1996. "Reality and Economic Theory." *Journal of Post Keynesian Economics* 18(4): 479–508.

———. 2002. *Financial Markets, Money, and the Real World.* Cheltenham, UK: Edward Elgar.

Eggebeen, D., and D. Lichter. 1991. "Race, Family Structure, and Changing Poverty Among American Children." *American Sociological Review* 56 (December): 801–17.

Fisher, G.M. 1995. "Is There Such a Thing as an Absolute Poverty Line Over Time? Evidence from the United States, Britain, Canada and Australia on the Income Elasticity of the Poverty Line." Washington, DC: U.S. Census Bureau Working Paper (available at www.census.gov/hhes/poverty/povmeas/papers/elastap4.html).

Fuchs, V. 1965. "Toward a Theory of Poverty." In *The Concept of Poverty,* 71–91. Washington, DC: Chamber of Commerce of the United States of America.

Galbraith, James K. 1998. *Created Unequal: The Crisis in American Pay.* New York: Free Press.

———. 2001. "The Distribution of Income." In *A New Guide to Post Keynesian Economics,* eds. R.P.F. Holt and S. Pressman, 32–41. London and New York: Routledge.

Galbraith, John K. 1958. *The Affluent Society.* Boston: Houghton Mifflin.

Gilder, G. 1981. *Wealth and Poverty.* New York: Basic Books.

Goodin, R., B. Headey, R. Muffels, and H.-J. Dirven. 1999. *The Real Worlds of Welfare Capitalism.* Cambridge: Cambridge University Press.

Harcourt, G. 1972. *Some Cambridge Controversies in the Theory of Capital.* Cambridge: Cambridge University Press.

Huber, E. and J. Stephens, 2001. *Development and Crisis of the Welfare State.* Chicago: University of Chicago Press.

Iceland, J. 2003. *Poverty in America.* Berkeley: University of California Press.

Keynes, J.M. 1964 [1936]. *The General Theory of Interest, Employment and Money.* New York: Harcourt Brace.

———. 1973 [1939]. "Professor Tinbergen's Method." *Economic Journal,* 49, September 1939. Reprinted in *The Collected Writings of John Maynard Keynes,* Vol. XIV, 306–20. London: Macmillan.

———. 1981. *The Collected Writings of John Maynard Keynes: Vol. XX, Activities 1929– 1931: Rethinking Employment and Unemployment Policies.* London: Macmillan.

———. 1982 [1933]. "National Self-Sufficiency." In *The Collected Writings of John Maynard Keynes: Vol. XXI, Activities 1931–1939: World Crises and Policies in Britain and America.* London: Macmillan.

Lawson, T. 1994. "The Nature of Post Keynesianism and its Links to Other Traditions: A Realist Perspective." *Journal of Post Keynesian Economics* 16(4): 503–38.

————. 1997. *Economics and Reality.* London: Routledge.

Lerman, R. 1996. "The Impact of Changing U.S. Family Structure on Child Poverty and Income Inequality." *Economica* 63(250): S119–S139.

Lucas, R. 1976. "Econometric Policy Evaluation: A Critique." In *The Phillips Curve and Labor Markets*, eds. K. Brunner and A. Meltzer, 19–46. Amsterdam: North Holland.

Lucas, R., and T. Sargent. 1978. "After Keynesian Macroeconomics." In *After the Phillips Curve: Persistence of High Inflation and High Unemployment*, 49–72. Boston: Federal Reserve Bank of Boston.

Martin, G., and V. Kats. 2003. "Families and Work in Transition in 12 Countries, 1980–2001." *Monthly Labor Review* 126(9): 3–31.

McLanahan, S., A. Sorensen, and D. Watson. 1989. "Sex Differences in Poverty, 1950–1980." *Signs* 15(1): 102–22.

Mincer, J. 1974. *Schooling, Experience, and Earnings.* New York: National Bureau of Economic Research.

Minsky, H. 1965. "The Role of Employment Policy." In *Poverty in America*, ed. M. Gordon, 175–200. San Francisco: Chandler.

————. 1968. "Effects of Shifts in Aggregate Demand upon Income Distribution." *American Journal of Agricultural Economics* 50(2): 328–39.

Murray, C. 1984. *Losing Ground.* New York: Basic Books.

Orshansky, M. 1969. "How Poverty is Measured." *Monthly Labor Review* 92(2): 37–41.

Palley, T. 1998. "Macroeconomics with Conflict and Income Distribution." *Review of Political Economy* 10(3): 329–42.

————. 2003. "Income Distribution." In *The Elgar Companion to Post Keynesian Economics*, ed. J. King, 181–86. Cheltenham, UK: Edward Elgar.

————. 1998. "The Feminization of Poverty: Causes and Remedies." *Challenge* 31(2): 57–61.

Pressman, S. 1991. "Keynes and Antipoverty Policy." *Review of Social Economy*, 49(3): 365–82.

————. 1993. "The Macroeconomic Effects of Exchange Rate Volatility." In *The Political Economy of Global Restructuring*, ed. I. Rima, 91–103. Hants, UK: Edward Elgar.

————. 2002. "Explaining the Gender Poverty Gap in Developed and Transitional Economies." *Journal of Economic Issues* 36(1): 17–40.

Radice, H. 1988. "Keynes and the Policy of Practical Protectionism." In *J.M. Keynes in Retrospect: The Legacy of the Keynesian Revolution*, ed. J. Hillard, 153–71. Hants, UK: Edward Elgar.

Rainwater, L. 1974. *What Money Buys.* New York: Basic Books.

Ruggles, P. 1990. *Drawing the Line.* Washington, DC: Urban Institute Press.

Schultz, T. 1961. "Investments in Human Capital." *American Economic Review* 51(1): 1–17.

Sen, A. 1979. "Issues in the Measurement of Poverty." *Scandinavian Journal of Economics* 81(2): 285–307.

————. 1981. *Poverty and Famines.* Oxford, UK: Clarendon Press.

————. 1983. "Poor, Relatively Speaking." *Oxford Economic Papers* 35(2): 153–69.

Smeeding, T.; B. Buhmann; and L. Rainwater. 1988. "Equivalence Scales, Well-Being, Inequality and Poverty: International Comparisons Across Ten Countries Using the Luxembourg Income Study (LIS) Database." LIS-CEPS Working Paper No. 17.

Smeeding, T.M.; L. Rainwater; B. Buhmann; and G. Schmays. 1988. "Luxembourg Income Study (LIS): Information Guide." LIS-CEPS Working Paper No. 7.

Smeeding, T.M.; G. Schmous; and S. Allegraza. 1985. "An Introduction to LIS." LIS-CEPS Working Paper No. 1.

Tinbergen, J. 1939. *Statistical Testing of Business Cycle Theories,* 2 vols. Geneva: League of Nations.

————. 1940. "On a Method of Statistical Business Cycle Research: A Reply." *Economic Journal* 50(197): 141–54.

United Nations Educational, Scientific, and Cultural Organization (UNESCO). 1997. *International Standard Classification of Education.* (available at www.unesco.org/education/information/nfsunesco/doc/isced_1997.html).

Wanniski, J. 1978. *The Way the World Works.* New York: Simon and Schuster.

Williams, R., F. Weiner, and F. Sammartino. 1998. *Equivalence Scales, the Income Distribution, and Federal Taxes.* Washington, DC: Congressional Budget Office.

Wolf, B., and P. Smook. 1988. "Keynes and the Question of Tariffs." In *Keynes and Public Policy After Fifty Years, Vol. II, Theory and Method*, eds. O. Hamouda and J. Smithin, 169–82. New York: NYU Press.

Appendix 2.1

Data Years and Data Sources

Country	Wave 3	Wave 5	Source
Canada	1991	2000	Survey of Consumer Finances
Finland	1991	2000	Income Distribution Survey
Germany	1989	2000	German Social Economic Panel Study
Hungary	1991	1999	Hungarian Household Panel
Israel	1992	2001	Family Expenditure Survey
Italy	1991	2000	Bank of Italy Survey
Luxembourg	1991	2000	Luxembourg Social Economic Panel Study
Netherlands	1991	1999	Socio-Economic Panel (Sep)
Norway	1992	1999	Income and Property Distribution Survey
Poland	1992	2000	Household Budget Survey
Russia	1992	2000	Russian Longitudinal Monitoring Survey
Spain	1990	2000	European Community Household Panel
Sweden	1992	2000	Income Distribution Survey
Switzerland	1992	2000	Swiss Poverty Survey (1992); Income and Consumption Survey (2000)
Taiwan	1991	2000	Survey of Personal Income Distribution
United Kingdom	1991	1999	Family Expenditure Survey (1991); Family Resources Survey (1999)
United States	1991	2000	March Current Population Survey

3

James K. Galbraith and Enrique Garcilazo

Unemployment, Inequality, and the Policy of Europe: 1984–2000

Introduction

Unemployment happens to individuals. The unemployment rate, however, is a matter of place, and places are nested inside larger places. The local has properties the nation may not share. The nation has characteristics that may not apply to the continent. In an integrated economy, the forces that operate on unemployment rates may extend over many horizons, from the near neighborhood to the entire world.

Yet, the literature on unemployment in Europe tends to concentrate on national characteristics and national unemployment rates. The predisposition is to blame unemployment on labor-market "rigidities"—and then to search for particular culprits, generally in the fields of national unemployment insurance, job protections, and wage compression. Periodic movements to reform national labor markets sweep aside the careful qualifications found in empirical work such as Nickell (1997) and Blanchard and Wolfers (1999), and presuppose that greater wage flexibility is the established cure for European unemployment. Neither local conditions, nor the influence of economic policy at the continental level, play important roles in the policy debate.

In a recent paper, Baker et al. (2002) provide a comprehensive review of the national-institutions approach to explaining European unemployment. They find only one robust result, namely that coordinated collective bargaining and (perhaps) union density are associated with less unemployment in Europe. Of course, this interesting finding is inconsistent with the rigidities framework. As far as macroeconomic policy is concerned, while a handful of lonely voices argue that interest and growth rates dominate the determination of unemployment in Europe, these too tend to root the relevant decision making at the national level (e.g., Palley 2004). Meanwhile, the higher policy discussion accepts that European policy—especially monetary policy—mainly influences the price level, leaving unemployment to be governed by market forces and national institutions.

Here, we try a different approach. Instead of the nation, our smallest unit of analysis is the region. Data are generally available for up to 213 regional entities across Europe, embedded within fifteen countries. Our analysis employs 159 regions from thirteen European countries, due to data limitations. We specify just four regional "labor market" variables that, we find, account significantly for the variation in regional unemployment rates. Then the panel structure permits us to measure national fixed effects, and so to identify those countries with characteristics that affect unemployment rates after controlling for regional conditions. Next, the panel structure permits us to identify time effects, whose pattern gives a picture of the influence of transnational forces, such as the integration of Europe and the effect of European macroeconomic and monetary policies. In this way, we allow the data to separate for us the influences of factors operating at the regional, national, and international or continental levels.

We identify two regional factors that influence the demand for labor. First is the strength of economic growth at any given time—an obvious determinant of construction and investment jobs, and a consequence of the local effects of macroeconomic policies and regional fiscal assistance. The second is a measure, which we constructed, of the average wage rate of the region relative to the average for Europe as a whole. Our thinking is that regions with higher average wages should tend to have stronger tax bases, more public-sector employment, and more open (and therefore taxed) employment in services.

On the supply side, we also identify two factors. The first is the relative size of the population of very young workers—an obvious measure of the difficult to employ. The second is a measure of the inequality of the wage structure. To acquire this measure, we construct, for the first time, a panel of European inequalities at the regional level, comparable both across countries and through time.

Our hypothesis that regional pay inequalities should be considered as on the supply side of the labor market is an innovation. It is standard to treat local wage rates as a product of supply and demand, while ignoring the question of whether these forces operate at the regional, national, or higher levels. Instead, in this analysis we take regional wage structure as a datum facing individual workers, a datum that affects the length of employment searches: The greater the differential between high- and low-paid jobs in the local setting, the longer a rational person will hold out for a better-paying job, accepting unemployment if necessary.

This theoretical position is well-known in neoclassical development economics, going back to a classic article by Harris and Todaro (1970), which treats the urban-rural pay differential as an incentive to migrate from the countryside to the cities, despite the presence of urban unemployment. The general concept—that inequality creates an incentive to search—has not been applied to Europe or to any developed-country setting as far as we know. But there is no compelling reason why it should not be. In practice, we find that pay inequality is a strong determinant of cross-sectional variation in European unemployment, and the positive coefficient is consistent with the Harris-Todaro conjecture.

Once regional conditions have been accounted for, our fixed-effects model finds few significant differences in unemployment among larger countries. The only substantial large-country fixed effects are for the United Kingdom (a negative shift) and Spain (a positive shift). However, large negative shifts are found for a number of smaller countries, which have much lower unemployment rates than our model would otherwise predict. The countries for which this is true are widely separated and appear to have little in common apart from that they are small. We will present some hypotheses below that may help account for this phenomenon.

Finally, we replicate the estimates for subpopulations, including men, women, and very young workers. We find significant differences in the unemployment experiences of different subpopulations: the very young as against older workers, and men as against women. As a broad rule, it appears that the less migratory a population, the higher its unemployment rate and the larger the effect of local labor-market conditions on unemployment.

The time effects are striking for all population groups. They show a sharp rise in unemployment across all regions beginning in 1993. This is an interesting break point in view of the coming into force of the Treaty on European Union (the Maastricht treaty). The effect continues through the 1990s, and suggests that a substantial part of European excess unemployment—generally between two and three percentage points—reflects policy conducted at the European level since 1992. In this regard, the monetary policy of the European Central Bank and the convergence criteria for the euro come to mind as leading suspects.

Theoretical Considerations

Our hypothesis is that unemployment at the local level is governed principally by four factors: two each on the demand and supply sides. On the demand side, the growth rate of effective demand and activity strongly conditions the availability of jobs; in periods of strong growth, construction and investment jobs are notably abundant.

Relative income also matters for jobs. Richer localities offer more employment of all kinds—whether in the public sector (because they have more tax revenue) or in the private-services sectors (because they have more discretionary private income). In poor regions, surplus labor is more likely to work, if at all, in the cash economy and to report itself as unemployed.

On the supply side, labor-force demography clearly matters. Young people are both hard to employ and to keep employed. So much is uncontroversial.

Our other argument is that regions with more equal pay structures will, other things being equal, experience less unemployment. Because this is contrary to the standard view, it deserves a full explanation.[1]

A half-century ago Simon Kuznets (1955) argued that inequality would rise in the early stages of economic development and transition to industrial growth. New urban centers were places of concentrated income and wealth. It was the urban-rural income differential that would become significant as cities grew, tapering in importance as the rural population dwindled. This was the most significant single factor behind Kuznets's inverted-U curve.

In 1970, John Harris and Michael Todaro offered a model capturing these characteristics in a paper aimed mainly at development economists. In their model, workers migrate from a low-marginal-product rural sector to cities, where minimum wages are imposed, and accept a high probability of sustained unemployment in exchange for a low probability of getting one of those jobs and enjoying the resulting rise in income. The equilibrium condition is that the expected value of the gain is just equal to the cost incurred in leaving rural employment, and this condition entails substantial equilibrium unemployment. From this, a positive relationship between urban/rural pay inequality and equilibrium unemployment emerges.

While Harris and Todaro focused on East Africa, consider how their argument might apply in modern Europe. Modern advanced societies have an elite group of knowledge and finance workers, a core of manufacturing workers, and a large reservoir of workers in the services. Access to knowledge and finance jobs is restricted by cartels and credentialing. The same is not true for manufacturing workers, who nevertheless enjoy wage premiums due to industry-specific labor rents. Services workers with few skills enjoy few such advantages, and the pay in the services sector.is largely set by social minimums, which are governed, in substantial part, by political decision makers. Services workers are like the earlier generation of farm workers in many relevant economic respects, and they may be considered a reserve army of the underemployed.

So long as the differential between service and manufacturing wages is fairly small, or if it is possible to search for better jobs while working, services workers will not abandon current employment to seek for better; but, if there are large differentials and obstacles to on-the-job searches, they will. In that event, measured unemployment will rise. As in Harris and Todaro, equilibrium local unemployment is a positive function of local pay inequalities.

Supply and demand at the regional level do not exhaust the possible sources of variation in unemployment. Labor-market policies, and to some extent the rules for measuring who is unemployed and who is not, are set at the national level. These factors may be expected to introduce some variation in unemployment rates between countries.

Our analysis does not attempt to sort out the particular institutional factors behind differences in national unemployment rates, after controlling for local conditions. Rather, we seek to establish how much of the observed differences in unemployment can be attributed to national differences, and for which countries these differences are important. The introduction of country-fixed effects permits this measurement to be easily carried out.

Finally, the factors that work on the continental (or, indeed, global) level need to be considered. Where a rise or decline in unemployment is common across the full spectrum of regions of Europe, it is reasonable to attribute it to policies and institutional changes emanating at the European level (or higher, such as via changing global economic conditions). Time-fixed effects capture these movements. Because for the past twenty years Europe has been a laboratory for economic integration and rule-bound policy making, it will be interesting to see what pattern emerges, especially in relation to three specific events: the introductions of the Single European Act (1987), Maastricht (1993), and the euro (1999).

In our model, several significant forms of unemployment are subject to policy control, and so are involuntary in Keynes's (1936) sense of the term. These include, particularly, the growth rate, the degree of pay inequality at the regional level, and the contribution of European-level economic policy and institutional change to European unemployment. Other factors, including population structure and national institutional characteristics, would have to be considered as sources of frictional or even of voluntary unemployment. Therefore, the analysis should be of considerable interest in sorting out the empirical relevance of these old theoretical questions.

Our framework may be applied to different subsets of the population, which can be expected to have different degrees of responsiveness to the forces at work. Women move in and out of work more than men do. Young people face an inevitable transition from school to work. The choice for these groups is: What job to aim for? A worker who accepts a low-wage job may be typed as a low productivity worker, who thus cannot make the transition to higher pay as easily as can a worker who has never been employed. For this reason, young people especially have an incentive to resist taking bad employment. Youth unemployment in unequal regions should therefore be expected to be an especially serious problem.

Migration is a reinforcing consideration. Certain countries have larger emigrant populations than others. Within any given population, older male workers tend to be more mobile than either women or youth. If acceptable jobs are not available in their immediate surroundings, they can be expected to search elsewhere, disappearing from the regional unemployment statistics. For this reason, the unemployment of less mobile subpopulations should show higher sensitivity to regional conditions, and less mobile subpopulations should generally experience higher unemployment rates than more mobile subpopulations.

Data and Model

Use of the region rather than the nation as the unit of geographic analysis has two distinct advantages. The first is that regions are more numerous: 159 in "old Europe" alone. The second is that regions are also more homogeneous: the standard deviation of population size for regions is merely a tenth of what it is for countries. Table 3.1 illustrates this.

We propose a model in which regional unemployment rates depend on four regional factors: pay inequality (+), the youth proportion of the population (+), economic growth rate (–), and relative wages (–). The first two of these factors influence the supply of unemployed labor; the second two affect the demand for labor (or supply of jobs). In addition, we expect to find national differences in average unemployment rates and variations in unemployment common to all re-

Table 3.1

Population Differentials for Nations and Regions in Europe, 1984–2000

Variable	N	Mean	Standard deviation	Minimum	Maximum
Nations	169	28,128	25,164	355.9	80,759.6
Regions	1853	2,306	2,556	22.5	17,663.2

Note: Population in thousands.

gions in Europe. These may be measured by country-fixed effects and time-fixed effects, respectively.

The main empirical innovation presented in this chapter lies in nearly comprehensive measures of pay inequality measured across broad economic sectors at the level of European regions, the 159 regional entities, over seventeen years (1984–2000).

We employ the between-groups component of Theil's T statistic to measure pay incquality. The methodology has been proposed in Conceição and Galbraith (2000) and in Conceição, Galbraith, and Bradford (2001), building on Theil (1972). Theil's T statistics can be expressed as follows:

$$T = \frac{1}{n} \sum_{i=1}^{n} \frac{y_i}{\mu_Y} * \log\left[\frac{y_i}{\mu_Y}\right],$$

(1)

where y_i denotes the income of an individual region indexed by i, n is the number of individuals in the population, and μ is the average income.

One of the most attractive features of this statistic is its decomposition property. As long as a distribution of income and a distribution of individuals are grouped into mutually exclusive and completely exhaustive groups, overall inequality can be decomposed into a between-groups component and a within-group component. The between-groups measure is derived from group means for payroll and group population weights; the within-groups measure is a weighted average of the Theil inequality index for each group. Formal expressions for both components are included in the Appendix; this study takes advantage of the fact that that under some very general conditions the dynamics of overall inequality can be captured using only the between-groups component.

This between-sectors calculation provides a new source of information on the relative inequality of the pay structures in the regions of Europe, and because the sector categories are standardized, the measures are comparable across regional (and national) boundaries as well as through time. Our data come from Eurostat's harmonized regional statistical database, REGIO. We use compensation of employees (e2rem95) and employment (e2emp195) for 159 regional entities among sixteen major economic sectors. Regions are classified by NUTS (nomenclature of territorial units for statistics) level 2 except for the regions of Germany and United Kingdom, where data are only available at NUTS level 1. A list of economic sectors and regions is included in the Appendix.

The relative wage variable (RelWage) is the ratio of each region's average payroll per worker relative to the average payroll per worker of Europe as a whole. Average payroll is derived by dividing total compensation of employees by employment for each year. The remaining regional variables—growth of gross domestic product (GDP)and proportion of the population under twenty-four years of age—are constructed conventionally from REGIO.

We now turn to a regression analysis, with the following reduced form, two-way fixed-effects model:

$$UN = \alpha + B_1 Theil + B_2 RelWage + B_3 GDPG +$$
$$B_4 PopUn24 + D_i Country + D_j Time, \qquad (2)$$

where:

$$
\begin{aligned}
UN &= \text{\textit{Regional unemployment rate}} \\
Theil &= \text{\textit{Pay inequality across sectors for each region}} \\
RelWage &= \text{\textit{Average regional wages relative to the}} \\
&\quad \text{\textit{European average}} \\
GDPG &= \text{\textit{Growth rate of GDP at the regional level}} \\
PopUn24 &= \text{\textit{Proportion of the regional population under}} \\
&\quad \text{\textit{twenty-four years of age}} \\
Country &= \text{\textit{Dummy to capture fixed-country effects}} \\
Time &= \text{\textit{Dummy to capture fixed-time effects}}
\end{aligned}
$$

The model can be fitted for all of Europe using annual data from 1984 to 2000, with full information for a total of 1465 region-year observations. The coefficients on the regional variables are reported in Table 3.2. Different models reflect estimates for the whole population and its component parts: men, women, and older and younger workers (i.e., greater /less than twenty-five years of age). We report a linear version of the model; a log-log version gave similar results, and is thus not reported.

All the variables have the correct sign and all but three are significant at conventional significance levels. Coefficients are systematically higher for less-mobile populations, except that GDP growth rates matter less for women—no surprise. R^2 is in the range of 60 percent for all models.

Higher growth at the local level reduces unemployment. Larger numbers of young people are associated with higher unemployment. The data on unemployment and inequality at the European-regional level support our hypothesis of a positive relationship between these two variables, though at a moderate significance level. In areas with high levels of pay inequality and high numbers of young people, the two effects would appear to combine to yield significantly higher unemployment rates.

Table 3.2

Coefficient Estimates: Linear Model, 1984–2000

	Total		Male		Female		< 25 Years		> 25 Years	
	Beta	p-value	Beta	p-value	Beta	p-value	Beta	p-value	Beta	p-value
Theil	4.97	0.04	3.22	0.13	6.80	0.04	11.97	0.03	4.08	0.04
PopUn24	57.02	0.00	50.58	0.00	76.46	0.00	112.32	0.00	38.04	0.00
RelWage	−7.08	0.00	−4.95	0.00	−9.91	0.00	−6.37	0.00	−7.43	0.00
G–GDP	−4.48	0.02	−5.67	0.00	−2.35	0.39	−6.30	0.17	−4.69	0.00
R^2	0.61		0.59		0.65		0.62		0.58	
N	1,465		1,465		1,465		1,465		1,465	

Inequality across Europe (measured by the RelWage variable) also appears to affect local unemployment rates. If the regression were taken literally, it would imply that reduction in the inequality of incomes across Europe would reduce unemployment in the poor countries, but at the same time it would increase it in the rich countries. Therefore, this result is ambiguous in policy terms.

The regional variables taken together play a considerable role in explaining variance, but each level of analysis—regional, national, and European—has a role to play. Table 3.3 provides measures of the variance explained (for unemployment of all workers) when the model is specified without fixed effects, with one-way fixed effects, and with two-way fixed effects. Coefficient estimates on the regional variables are also shown; these are notably stable except that the effect of GDP growth is to some extent absorbed by the introduction of time effects, indicating that macroeconomic forces tend to be common across the European regions.

It turns out that country-fixed effects are relatively unimportant for large countries, with two exceptions. Taking France (with the closest to average unemployment for the period) as the base case and +/–3 percent as the threshold, only Spain has much higher unemployment *ceteris paribus* than one would otherwise expect. In the United Kingdom, on the other hand, unemployment is lower than otherwise expected. Germany, with a positive fixed effect just over 3 percent is a borderline case; most of the German fixed effect is surely due to the special circumstances following reunification.[2]

Apart from this, neither the large countries nor Scandinavia have large differences in unemployment rates apart from those captured by the regional variables. Whether the Spanish and U.K. cases can be traced to particular causes is a matter for later research; we would want to investigate closely the effect of the cash economy in Spain and that of credit institutions in the United Kingdom. However, neither value can be attributed to Spanish wage rigidity or British flexibility, since the inequality of pay structures is already taken directly into account at the regional level.

There are, however, large negative fixed effects for small countries (Austria, Ireland, Portugal, Greece, and, to a lesser extent, the Netherlands). Figure 3.1 provides a map of the country-fixed effects; Table A1 (in the Appendix) presents the coefficient estimates. This effect may possibly be explained in some cases by the existence of large emigrant populations, for example, the Portuguese in France are absent from the labor force measured in Portugal, and therefore do not figure in Portuguese unemployment.

Austria is a more difficult case to explain. But the Austrian result may be due to strategic wage setting, with Austrian workers close substitutes for Germans in competing sectors, but cheaper. In an exploration reported in the appendix, we find that Austrian wages are indeed systematically lower than German on average in manufacturing, but the sector averages are actually higher than German in nontraded sectors. Similarly, Irish manufacturing wages are lower than British; this could help account for the explosion of jobs that brought Irish unemployment down so sharply in the late 1990s. Austrian and Irish wages are set substantially by central

Table 3.3

Analysis of Variance Explained Under Different Specifications*

	Region only		Region and country		Region and time		All variables	
	Beta	p-value	Beta	p-value	Beta	p-value	Beta	p-value
Theil	4.03	0.18	4.81	0.04	5.39	0.09	4.97	0.04
PopUn24	50.20	0.00	48.64	0.00	54.23	0.00	57.02	0.00
RelWage	−2.82	0.00	−6.81	0.00	−2.21	0.00	−7.08	0.00
G-GDP	−11.83	0.00	−8.56	0.00	−9.49	0.00	−4.48	0.02
Regional	X		X		X		X	
Country			X				X	
Time					X		X	
R^2	0.16		0.57		0.21		0.61	

*Dependent variable is total unemployment.

Figure 3.1 **European Unemployment: Country Fixed Effects**

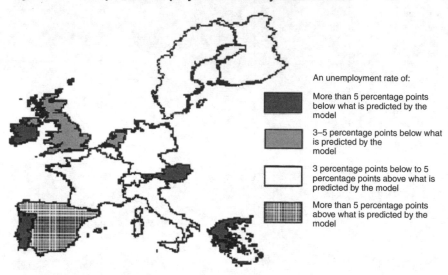

An unemployment rate of:

More than 5 percentage points below what is predicted by the model

3–5 percentage points below what is predicted by the model

3 percentage points below to 5 percentage points above what is predicted by the model

More than 5 percentage points above what is predicted by the model

bargaining, and it appears that in these countries wage competitiveness may be concentrated where it is useful.[3]

Figure 3.2 presents the time effects associated with the two-way panel. These estimates show a striking increase in the pan-European component of the unemployment rate from 1993 to the end of the decade, rising to a peak value of 4.6 points above the 1985 baseline in 1994, and settling above two full percentage points for most of the rest of the decade. This provides, in our view and based solely on the coincidence of timing, a very succinct measure of the employment penalty associated with the events of 1992, notably the signing of the Maastricht treaty and its introduction the following year. (Also in 1992, the exchange-rate mechanism of the European Monetary System collapsed. Gordon [1999] pins the responsibility for rising European unemployment at this time on the fiscal tightening required by Maastricht, however.) On a brighter note, excess youth unemployment in Europe has been reduced sharply since 1997, if these measures are correct.[4] Overall, it seems possible that the fixing of exchange rates and the introduction of the euro in 1999 had a good effect, as the pan-European component of unemployment declined toward the end of the decade. Table A2 in the Appendix reports the time effects and their significance levels.

Implications for European Unemployment Policy

These results, so different from those implied by the standard view, should be treated with caution. Much work remains to be done to establish the general validity of the models advanced here, and to corroborate specific explanations

Figure 3.2   **European Unemployment—European Time Effects**

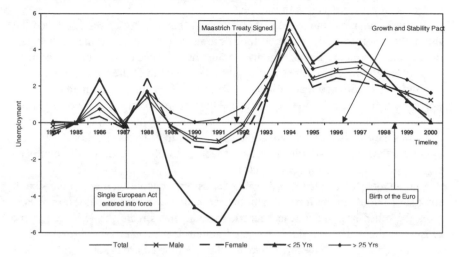

here suggested. Nevertheless, we feel that the hierarchical and panel structure of our model represents a useful advance over work that is tied to the national level of analysis. Something like our approach may be the wave of the future as economists come to grips with regional, national, and continental economic integration.

We draw a number of potential implications of this model for the design of unemployment policy in Europe. On the demand side, to state the least questionable inference, raising the growth rate of GDP reduces unemployment. That regional income convergence would do so is not readily determined from our information, since our variable measures relative wages. However, our model does suggest that income convergence would help the poorer regions, and that policies explicitly targeted to achieve regional income convergence would reduce the divergence in unemployment rates, if not necessarily their average level. Policies that promoted income equalization for individuals—such as, for instance, measures that raised the payout of nonwage incomes such as pensions in the poorer regions could, in principle, be expected to have this effect.

Targeted measures that provide prelabor-market opportunities for European youth would appear to help on the supply-side (and may already be doing so). Such opportunities would enable young people to time their entry into paid employment so as to escape being tarred as either relatively unproductive or as having started working life with a long stretch of unemployment. It may perhaps be noted that the United States does this very effectively, with high levels of university enrollment and military enlistment—and, unfortunately, incarceration—all targeted to keeping youth off the streets. As a result, youth unemployment in the

United States is not, except for certain relatively small populations, nearly as serious a social problem as it is in Europe.

Perhaps our most interesting implication is that that measures to reduce the inequality of European wages at the regional level—for example, industrial-development policies in poor regions—would help reduce chronic unemployment on average among Europeans. This is quite the opposite of the common view that Europe needs more pay inequality ("flexibility") rather than less. There is no support in our data for the idea that European unemployment is due to excessive solidarity in the European wage structure. It is possible, however, that some small countries have gamed the system at the expense of their larger neighbors; by exercising solidarity and discipline they have made themselves into attractive competitors for jobs in the traded-goods sectors.

Our analysis of country-fixed effects lends little encouragement to the search for magic bullets in the form of national labor-market institutional reforms. Perhaps the other large European countries should investigate the U.K. case very closely. Perhaps they should investigate Spain to learn what to avoid (except that, not being Spain, they have already avoided it). Perhaps there is something modest to be learned from Dutch labor-market policies; the Netherlands (with low emigration) has somewhat lower-than-expected unemployment. (On the other hand, Holland also has high rates of disability and part-time work, social accommodations to a shortage of work that other countries may prefer to shun.) Apart from that, there is little evidence that institutional differences among France, Germany, Italy, and the Nordic countries significantly inform their unemployment rates; most of the differences between these countries' experiences seem fully accounted for by regional variables.

Finally, our evidence points a reproving finger at the institutions and policy makers of the European Union. It appears from our evidence that European policy strongly contributed to a continent-wide increase in unemployment in the 1990s. In a word, Maastricht opened a half-decade that can be qualified as disastrous, and from which recovery is still incomplete. Thus, overcoming the high unemployment visited on Europe as a whole by the misgovernment of macroeconomic policy at the continental level under recent leadership emerges from this analysis as a high priority. Although some progress appears to have been made in the late 1990s, a return even to the by-no-means-optimal conditions of the mid-1980s remains quite far from complete.[5]

Notes

1. One might suppose the causation to run the other way: that regional pay inequality would be simply a positive function of local unemployment rates. However, while this is possible, two considerations suggest that it is not predominantly the case. First, unemployment rates vary much more than inequality measures over time. The effect of inequality on unemployment is therefore mainly cross-sectional (places with higher inequality experience higher unemployment on a chronic basis). Second, part of the greater inequality ob-

served in a regional pay structure is due to the scarcity of decently-paid middle-range jobs, and not exclusively to larger pay differentials per se, though in practice both may contribute. There is no compelling reason in neoclassical theory why higher unemployment rates should produce a gap in employment in the middle of the pay scale, as opposed to the bottom of it.

2. There is also an interesting negative effect for youth unemployment in Germany, which could be picking up the effects of the country's apprentice system.

3. We thank Richard Freeman and David Howell for jointly suggesting that we compare Austrian to German wages.

4. Richard Freeman suggests a link to large increases in university enrollment, especially in Spain. We are looking for evidence on this conjecture.

5. The research for this paper was supported by the Carnegie Scholars Program.

References

Baker, D., A. Glyn, D. Howell, and J. Schmitt. 2002. "Labor Market Institutions and Unemployment: A Critical Assessment of the Cross-Country Evidence." Working Paper, Center for Economic Policy Research, New School University.
Blanchard, O., and J. Wolfers. 1999. "The Role of Shocks and Institutions in the Rise of European Unemployment: The Aggregate Evidence." National Bureau of Economic Research (NBER), Working Paper 7282.
Conceição, P., and James K. Galbraith. 2000. "Constructing Long and Dense Time Series of Inequality Using the Theil Statistic." *Eastern Economic Journal* 26(1): 61–74.
Conceição, P., James K Galbraith, and P. Bradford. 2001. "The Theil Index in Sequences of Nested and Hierarchical Grouping Structures: Implications for the Measurement of Inequality through Time, with Data Aggregated at Different Levels of Industrial Classification." *Eastern Economic Journal* 27(4): 491–514.
Gordon, R.J. 1999. "The Aftermath of the 1992 ERM Breakup: Was There a Macroeconomic Free Lunch?" National Bureau of Economic Research (NBER), Working Paper 6964.
Harris, J.R., and M.P. Todaro. 1970. "Migration, Unemployment and Development: A Two-Sector Analysis." *American Economic Review* 60(1): 126–42.
Keynes, J.M. 1936. *The General Theory of Employment Interest and Money.* London: Macmillan.
Kuznets, S. 1955. "Economic Growth and Income Inequality." *American Economic Review* 65(1): 1–28.
Nickell, S. 1997. "Unemployment and Labor Market Rigidities: Europe versus North America." *Journal of Economic Perspectives* 11 (Summer): 55–74.
Palley, T.I. 2004. "The Causes of High Unemployment: Labor Market Sclerosis versus Macroeconomic Policy." In *Challenging the Market: The Struggle to Regulate Work and Income*, ed. J. Stanford. Toronto: McGill-Queens University Press.
Theil, H. 1972. *Statistical Decomposition Analysis: With Applications in the Social and Administrative Sciences.* Amsterdam and London: North Holland.

Appendix 3.1. Country- and Time-Fixed Effects

Table 3.1A

National Dummies—Linear Model, 1984–2000

	Model 1		Model 2		Model 3		Model 4		Model 5	
	Total	p-value	Male	p-value	Female	p-value	<25 Years	p-value	>25 Years	p-value
BE	1.54	0.02	−0.35	0.53	5.16	0.00	−2.44	0.10	2.30	0.0
DE	3.32	0.00	4.12	0.00	2.97	0.00	−7.59	0.00	3.93	0.00
GR	−5.20	0.00	−5.12	0.00	−3.64	0.00	1.45	0.42	−6.82	0.00
ES	5.04	0.00	3.70	0.00	8.96	0.00	9.71	0.00	2.86	0.00
IE	−9.70	0.00	−6.48	0.00	−14.57	0.00	−24.12	0.00	−7.47	0.00
IT	0.53	0.17	−0.24	0.48	3.46	0.00	9.28	0.00	−1.69	0.00
NL	−3.69	0.00	−3.16	0.00	−4.03	0.00	−13.00	0.00	−2.79	0.00
AT	−6.03	0.00	−4.90	0.00	−7.05	0.00	−17.09	0.00	−5.12	0.00
PT	−10.79	0.00	−8.25	0.00	−13.86	0.00	−16.81	0.00	−10.43	0.00
FI	0.90	0.24	3.26	0.00	−1.97	0.06	3.30	0.06	0.42	0.51
SE	−1.06	0.11	1.88	0.00	−4.41	0.00	−3.70	0.02	−0.95	0.08
UK	−4.10	0.00	−0.28	0.60	−9.09	0.00	−12.64	0.00	−3.50	0.00

Source: Country effect equation(2) from Eurostat data.

Inequality—Constructing the Theil Statistic

Table 3.2A

Time Dummies—Linear Model, 1984–2000

	Model 1		Model 2		Model 3		Model 4		Model 5	
	Total	p-value	Male	p-value	Female	p-value	<25 Years	p-value	>25 Years	p-value
84	-0.36	0.70	-0.17	0.83	-0.70	0.58	0.06	0.98	-0.50	0.51
86	1.11	0.18	1.60	0.03	0.36	0.75	2.35	0.22	0.75	0.28
87	-0.10	0.91	0.08	0.91	-0.30	0.79	-0.14	0.94	-0.22	0.74
88	1.76	0.03	1.38	0.06	2.38	0.04	1.70	0.37	1.72	0.01
89	-0.17	0.83	-0.14	0.84	-0.27	0.80	-2.90	0.12	0.56	0.40
90	-0.99	0.21	-0.83	0.23	-1.31	0.23	-4.59	0.01	0.04	0.96
91	-1.11	0.17	-0.98	0.17	-1.45	0.19	-5.51	0.00	0.19	0.78
92	-0.28	0.73	-0.09	0.90	-0.81	0.47	-3.44	0.07	0.84	0.22
93	1.86	0.04	1.96	0.01	1.53	0.21	1.28	0.54	2.53	0.00
94	4.57	0.00	4.31	0.00	4.70	0.00	5.72	0.01	5.09	0.00
95	2.32	0.00	2.46	0.00	1.95	0.07	3.33	0.06	2.95	0.00
96	2.74	0.00	2.88	0.00	2.45	0.02	4.39	0.01	3.30	0.00
97	2.76	0.00	3.04	0.00	2.23	0.04	4.37	0.02	3.34	0.00
98	2.06	0.01	2.03	0.00	1.97	0.07	2.63	0.14	2.74	0.00
99	1.55	0.05	1.65	0.02	1.31	0.23	1.22	0.51	2.36	0.00
00	0.83	0.33	1.25	0.10	0.21	0.86	0.05	0.98	1.64	0.02

Source: Time effect equation(2) from Eurostat data.

Inequality—Constructing the Theil

The Theil statistic is composed of two elements: a between-group inequality component and a within-group inequality component:

$$T \equiv T_B + \overline{T_W}, \tag{A1}$$

where:

> T = Total Theil
> T_B = Between-groups Theil component
> $\overline{T_W}$ = Within-group Theil component.
> The between-groups component can be represented by the following

two equations:

$$T_B = \sum_{i=1}^{n} \left(\frac{w_i}{\sum_{i=1}^{n} w_i} \right) \ln \left[\frac{w_i / \sum_{i=1}^{n} w_i}{e_i / \sum_{i=1}^{n} e_i} \right], \tag{A2}$$

$$T_B = \sum \frac{e_i}{\sum_{j=1}^{n} ej} \frac{\overline{w}_i}{\overline{w}_Y} \ln \left(\frac{\overline{w}_i}{\overline{w}_Y} \right). \tag{A2'}$$

The within-group component equals:

$$\overline{T_w} = \sum_{i=1}^{n} \left(\frac{w_i}{w} \right) \bullet T_w, \tag{A3}$$

$$T_w = \left(\frac{w_{ij}}{w_i} \right) \bullet \ln \left[\frac{w_{ij} / w_i}{e_{ij} / e_i} \right], \tag{A4}$$

If we index regions with the subscript i, and sectors with the subscript j, then

> w_{ij} = the total compensation received in region j and sector i
> e_{ij} = total people employed in region j and sector i
> $\overline{w}_i$ = average income of region i
> $\overline{w}_Y$ = average income of all regions

Table 3A.3

List of Regions-NUTS Level 1 for DE and UK, NUTS Level 2 for Remaining Countries

1	be1	Région Bruxelles-hoofdstad gewest	35	gr22	Ionia Nisia
			36	gr23	Dytiki Ellada
2	be21	Antwerpen	37	gr24	Sterea Ellada
3	be22	Limburg (B)	38	gr25	Peloponnisos
4	be23	Oost-Vlaanderen	39	gr3	Attiki
5	be24	Vlaams Brabant	40	gr41	Voreio Aigaio
6	be25	West-Vlaanderen	41	gr42	Notio Aigaio
7	be31	Brabant Wallon	42	gr43	Kriti
8	be32	Hainaut	43	es11	Galicia
9	be33	Liège	44	es12	Principado de Asturias
10	be34	Luxembourg (B)	45	es13	Cantabria
11	be35	Namur	46	es21	Pais Vasco
12	de1	Baden-Württemberg	47	es22	Comunidad Foral
13	de2	Bayern			de Navarra
14	de3	Berlin	48	es23	La Rioja
15	de4	Brandenburg	49	es24	Aragón
16	de5	Bremen	50	es3	Comunidad de Madrid
17	de6	Hamburg	51	es41	Castilla y León
18	de7	Hessen	52	es42	Castilla-la Mancha
19	de8	Mecklenburg-Vorpommern	53	es43	Extremadura
			54	es51	Cataluña
20	de9	Niedersachsen	55	es52	Comunidad Valenciana
21	dea	Nordrhein-Westfalen	56	es53	Illes Balears
22	deb	Rheinland-Pfalz	57	es61	Andalucia
23	dec	Saarland	58	es62	Murcia
24	ded	Sachsen	59	es63	Ceuta y Melilla (ES)
25	dee	Sachsen-Anhalt	60	es7	Canarias (ES)
26	def	Schleswig-Holstein	61	fr1	Île de France
27	deg	Thüringen	62	fr21	Champagne-Ardenne
28	def	Schleswig-Holstein	63	fr22	Picardie
29	deg	Thüringen	64	fr23	Haute-Normandie
30	gr11	Anatoliki Makedonia, Thraki	65	fr24	Centre
			66	fr25	Basse-Normandie
31	gr12	Kentriki Makedonia	67	fr26	Bourgogne
32	gr13	Dytiki Makedonia	68	fr3	Nord-Pas-de-Calais
33	gr14	Thessalia	69	fr41	Lorraine
34	gr21	Ipeiros	70	fr42	Alsace

Table 3A.3 *(continued)*

71	fr43	Franche-Comté	108	n113	Drenthe
72	fr51	Pays de la Loire	109	n121	Overijssel
73	fr52	Bretagne	110	n122	Gelderland
74	fr53	Poitou-Charentes	111	n123	Flevoland
75	fr61	Aquitaine	112	n131	Utrecht
76	fr62	Midi-Pyrénées	113	n132	Noord-Holland
77	fr63	Limousin	114	n133	Zuid-Holland
78	fr71	Rhône-Alpes	115	n134	Zeeland
79	fr72	Auvergne	116	n141	Noord-Brabant
80	fr81	Languedoc-Roussillon	117	n142	Limburg (NL)
81	fr82	Provence-Alpes-	118	at11	Burgenland
		Côte d'Azur	119	at12	Niederösterreich
82	fr83	Corse	120	at13	Vienna
83	ie01	Border, Midlands	121	at21	Kärnten
		and Western	122	at22	Steiermark
84	ie02	Southern and Eastern	123	at31	Oberösterreich
85	it11	Piemonte	124	at32	Salzburg
86	it12	Valle d'Aosta	125	at33	Tirol
87	it13	Liguria	126	at34	Vorarlberg
88	it2	Lombardia	127	pt11	Norte
89	it31	Trentino-Alto Adige	128	pt12	Centro (PT)
90	it32	Veneto	129	pt13	Lisboa e Vale do Tejo
91	it33	Friuli-Venezia Giulia	130	pt14	Alentejo
92	it4	Emilia-Romagna	131	pt15	Algarve
93	it51	Toscana	132	pt2	Açores (PT)
94	it52	Umbria	133	pt3	Madeira (PT)
95	it53	Marche	134	fi13	Itä-Suomi
96	it6	Lazio	135	fi14	Väli-Suomi
97	it71	Abruzzo	136	fi15	Pohjois-Suomi
98	it72	Molise	137	fi16	Uusimaa (suuralue)
99	it8	Campania	138	fi17	Etelä-Suomi
100	it91	Puglia	139	fi2	Åland
101	it92	Basilicata	140	se01	Stockholm
102	it93	Calabria	141	se02	Östra Mellansverige
103	ita	Sicilia	142	se04	Sydsverige
104	itb	Sardegna	143	se06	Norra Mellansverige
105	lu	Luxembourg	144	se07	Mellersta Norrland
106	n111	Groningen	145	se08	Övre Norrland
107	n112	Friesland	146	se09	Småland med öarna

Table 3A.3 *(continued)*

147	se0a	Västsverige	153	ukh	Eastern
148	ukc	Northeast	154	uki	London
149	ukd	Northwest (including	155	ukj	Southeast
		Merseyside)	156	ukk	Southwest
150	uke	Yorkshire and	157	ukl	Wales
		The Humber	158	ukm	Scotland
151	ukf	East Midlands	159	ukn	Northern Ireland
152	ukg	West Midlands			

Sensitivity Analyses

The REGIO data set permits us to extract annual data sets from 1984 to 2000 for the major countries of Europe. However, for a number of the small countries, including Greece, Austria, Ireland, and Portugal, full data are available only for the second half of the 1990s. This raises two questions: whether those years are representative of the whole period for these countries, and whether the panel analysis as a whole would be different if they were excluded.

Examination of the unemployment rates for the four countries suggests that the relatively low unemployment rates seen in Austria, Greece, and Portugal in the late 1990s are not wildly unrepresentative of their experience over the whole period, even though the absolute levels of unemployment do vary through time. The Irish case is very different, as Ireland passed from a high- to a low-unemployment country in the mid-1990s. It would thus be inappropriate to regard the low country-fixed effect found for Ireland as representative of institutions producing low unemployment throughout the period. It represents, rather, the exceptional experience of the late 1990s, when Ireland experienced a powerful economic boom.

To test the second question, we ran the full panel regression, with two-way fixed effects, on a panel excluding Greece, Austria, Ireland, and Portugal. The results for the whole population are given in Table 3.4A. Results for the male, female, young, and older subpopulations tell a similar story, and are available from the authors.

Table 3.4A

Sectorization Used to Calculate Regional Inequality

Sectors by NACE-CLIO (1984–94)	Sectors by NACE (1995–2000)
Fuel and power products	Agriculture, hunting, and forestry
Ferrous and non-ferrous ores and metals, other than radioactive	Fishing
Non-metallic minerals and mineral products	Mining and quarrying
Chemical products	Manufacturing
Metal products, machinery, equipment, and electrical goods	Electricity, gas, and water supply
Transport equipment	Construction
Food, beverages, tobacco	Wholesale and retail trade; repair of motor vehicles, motorcycles and personal household goods
Textiles and clothing, leather and footwear	Hotels and restaurants
Paper and printing products	Transport, storage, and communication
Products of various industries	Financial intermediation
Building and construction activities	Real estate, renting, and business
Recovery, repair, trade, lodging, and catering services	Public administration and defense; compulsory social security
Transport and communication services	Education
Services of credit and insurance institutions	Health and social work
Other market services activities	Other community, social, personal service
Non-market services persons	Private households with employed

Source: Eurostat.

Table 3.5A

Sensitivity Analysis—Model 1 (total unemployment) (excluding AU, IE, GR, PT)

	Model 1	
	Total	p-value
Theil	31.75	0.00
PopUn24	71.48	0.00
RelWage	−6.15	0.00
G-GDP	−6.92	0.00
BE	1.29	0.05
DE	4.54	0.00
ES	4.21	0.00
IT	0.32	0.43
NL	−3.47	0.00
FI	1.38	0.07
SE	−0.52	0.43
UK	−4.69	0.00
84	−0.36	0.70
86	1.11	0.18
87	−0.10	0.91
88	1.76	0.03
89	−0.17	0.83
90	−0.99	0.21
91	−1.11	0.17
92	−0.28	0.73
93	1.86	0.04
94	4.57	0.00
95	2.32	0.00
96	2.74	0.00
97	2.76	0.00
98	2.06	0.01
99	1.55	0.05
00	0.83	0.33
R^2	0.63	
N	1,240	

The model is substantially unaffected by the exclusion of the four small countries. All coefficients have the same sign and all remain significant. One difference is that the relationship between inequality and unemployment is stronger, and the significance of the coefficient estimate on the inequality variable rises eightfold, when the four small countries are not included. We take this as confirmation that the inequality-unemployment relation is not an artifact of the inclusion of the small countries in the late 1990s.

Wage and Employment Effects on Inequality

The between-groups component of Theil's T statistic is a compound measure influenced by both the relative wage rates between groups and the relative size of each group. A region with high inequality may have a large differential between the best and worst paid, or a marked bimodalism in the structure of employment, or some combination of both factors. It is worth noting that the line of causality traditionally argued to hold in economics, which runs from unemployment rates to the pay structure, does not imply anything in particular about the structure of employment. If there exists a large excess of unskilled workers, that should reduce the relative pay of unskilled workers, increasing inequality, but it would not necessarily change the technology employed in particular processes of production.

To provide an illustration of the roles of these two factors, we examine the structure of pay and employment in four European regions, two with high and two with low unemployment, in 2000. The following regions are included in the analysis: Andalucia and Extremadura, with high unemployment rates, and Navarra and Stockholm, with low unemployment rates:

- Extremadura (unemployment rate for 2000 = 24.4 percent)

- Andalucia (unemployment rate for 2000 = 25 percent)

- Navarra (unemployment rate for 2000 = 4.8 percent)

- Stockholm (unemployment rate for 2000 = 3.7 percent)

Table 3.6A

Summary Statistics for Average Wages Across Sixteen Sectors, 1995–2000

Variable/ average wage	Mean	Min	Max	N	p50
Extremadura	21.49	5.4	65.5	72	16.35
Andalucia	22.65	5.1	79.7	82	19.55
Navarra	25.93	7.5	52.1	72	26.00
Stockholm	35.59	16.7	64.0	88	36.15

Ranges for low-unemployment regions are much lower than for high-unemployment regions. We also find that low-unemployment regions have substantially larger shares of their employment near the mean, and less associated with the extremes of the distribution.

Table 3.7A

Ratio of Austrian to German Average Wages, by Major Sectors

	1995	1996	1997	1998	1999	2000
Mining and quarrying	1.04	1.01	1.01	1.06	1.09	0.98
Manufacturing	0.88	0.88	0.88	0.89	0.92	0.86
Electricity, gas, and water supply	1.22	1.19	1.21	1.26	1.22	1.14
Construction	1.04	1.03	1.06	1.11	1.27	1.20
Transport, storage, and communication	1.03	1.00	1.03	1.07	1.18	1.14
Financial intermediation	1.06	1.07	1.08	1.09	1.23	1.18
Real estate, renting, and business activities	0.99	0.96	0.94	0.90	1.09	0.95
Public administration and defense; compulsory social security	1.16	1.15	1.13	1.10	1.12	1.12

Evaluating the Strategic-Wage Conjecture

The conjecture that certain small countries with strong collective wage bargaining might generate domestic full employment at the expense of a larger neighbor can be evaluated directly for the case of Austria and Germany. The evidence is suggestive. As Table 3.7A shows, average wages in Austria are systematically higher than in Germany, except in two sectors: manufacturing and real estate. Manufacturing is, of course, by far the largest of these sectors. Is this the secret of Austrian unemployment rates consistently half of those of Germany?

Table 3.8A gives a similar analysis of relative wages in Ireland and the United Kingdom in the late 1990s; if the data are accurate, a similar story may apply. Indeed, it is striking how much higher average pay in such sectors as finance, health, and education appears to be in Ireland than in England. But manufacturing pay is lower, and this could well have given Ireland the edge in the location of new industry during the technology boom.

Coverage by Country and Year

Table 3.8A

Ratio of Irish to British Average Wages, by Major Sectors

	1995	1996	1997	1998
Mining and quarrying	0.71	1.05	0.86	0.87
Manufacturing	0.81	0.84	0.75	0.71
Electricity, gas, and water supply	0.74	0.65	0.70	0.63
Construction	1.32	1.27	1.17	1.11
Wholesale and retail trade*	1.35	1.39	1.32	1.29
Hotels and restaurants	1.15	1.05	0.97	0.90
Transport, storage, and communication	0.79	0.87	0.76	0.70
Financial intermediation	1.51	1.49	1.20	1.11
Real estate, renting, and business activities	1.19	1.13	1.07	1.02
Public administration and defense**	1.08	1.17	1.11	1.18
Education	1.27	1.30	1.17	1.10
Health and social work	1.52	1.48	1.39	1.22
Other community-, social-, personal-service activities	0.97	0.90	0.66	0.57

*Repair of motor vehicles, motorcycles, and personal and household goods.
**Compulsory social security.

Table 3.9A

Data Coverage by Country and Year (number of regions in parentheses)

Year	Observations	Coverage (number of regions in parentheses)
1984	35	be(8), it(20), uk(7)
1985	35	be(8), it(20), uk(7)
1986	56	be(8), es(17), it(20), pt(4)
1987	69	be(8), es(17), fr(20), it(20), pt(4)
1988	63	be(8), es(18), it(20), nl(12), pt(5)
1989	84	be(8), es(18), fr(21), it(20), nl(12)
1990	86	be(8), es(18), fr(21), it(20), nl(12)
1991	78	es(18), fr(21), it(20), nl(12), pt(7)
1992	78	es(18), fr(21), it(20), nl(12), pt(7)
1993	57	es(18), it(20), nl(12), pt(7)
1994	45	es(18), it(20), pt(7)
1995	133	de(16), gr(13), es(18), fr(21), it(20), nl(12), at(9), pt(7), fi(4), se(6), uk(7)
1996	139	de(16), gr(13), es(18), fr(21), it(20), nl(12), at(9), pt(7), fi(6), se(6), uk(11)
1997	136	de(16), gr(12), es(18), fr(21), it(20), nl(12), at(9), pt(7), fi(4), se(6), uk(11)
1998	144	de(16), gr(12), es(18), fr(21), ie(2), it(20), nl(12), at(9), pt(7), fi(6), se(8), uk(12)
1999	131	de(16), gr(12), es(18), fr(21), ie(2), it(20), nl(12), at(9), pt(7), fi(5), se(8)
2000	96	de(16), gr(13), fr(21), ie(2), it(20), at(9), pt(7), se(8)
	1,465	

4

Gary A. Dymski and Carolyn B. Aldana

The Racial U-Curve in U.S. Residential Credit Markets in the 1990s

Empirical Evidence from a Post Keynesian World

Introduction

Reflections on Post Keynesian Approaches to Empirical Analysis

Post Keynesian economic theory mainly makes theoretical assertions about certain macroeconomic relationships—in particular, aggregate demand drives aggregate supply, investment precedes saving, and the supply of money is endogenous.

Of course, these macroeconomic assertions are far from the sum of Post Keynesian economics. Keynes himself, as well as Shackle (1974), Davidson (1994), and Minsky (1975), emphasized the prevalence of fundamental uncertainty in economic decision making. Several Post Keynesian authors have introduced the idea that power relations are fundamental elements of the contemporary economy. John Kenneth Galbraith (1956) introduced the idea of countervailing power, while Eichner (1976) wrote about the activities and impact of "megacorps." Both authors described the drive for oligopolistic profits, and the need for constraints on the social influence of large organizations. Galbraith, like Eichner, discussed the microfoundations of behavior, and was interested in the interaction between the macro and micro levels.[1] Other Post Keynesians have developed complementary microanalyses building on some of the core ideas formulated initially at a macroeconomic level. Dunn (2001), for example, argues that firm strategies aim to reduce uncertainty.

The explicit recognition of power, and of micro-macro linkages, vastly extends the range and social implications of the Post Keynesian approach. It links Keynesian ideas to American institutionalism and to contemporary neo-Marxian theory, both of which emphasize the impact of asymmetric power on economic outcomes. These linkages, and the large number of contemporary thinkers that draw on these multiple frameworks, suggest the possibility of constructing a contiguous body of heterodox economics.[2]

This expansion also suggests a need for understanding social relations—a broader agenda than may have been anticipated by the Post Keynesian "founding fathers." Post Keynesian economists have worked explicitly on some aspects of social inequality, but have paid little attention to others. Among the topics given too little consideration by Post Keynesians are racism and sexism (Danby 2004).

There is no reason, however, to restrict the social purview of Post Keynesian theory to some aspects of social inequality but not others. Post Keynesian insights about uncertainty, aggregate demand, and asymmetric power in the economy are peculiarly powerful, and are readily transported from one context to another. And, in addition to asking what Post Keynesian theory says to those concerned with racial and gender inequality, we can ask about the implications of social inequality for Post Keynesian theory.

Anyone who has read *The General Theory* will readily recognize that Keynes pays attention to the fact that social forces and economic forces are intertwined. In the last chapter of that volume, Keynes reflects soberly on the implications of pursuing economic policies that ignore uncertainty and aggregate demand: a terrain of social need emerges, shaped by struggles over insufficient income, capital, and jobs. One of his main points was that it need not be like this; well-designed policies can generate jobs and income flows sufficient to provide the good life for the vast majority of people.

It is sometimes argued that the systematic application of Keynesian policies in the middle years of the past century created a Golden Age, at least in upper-income countries (Marglin and Schor 1990). This illustrated the advantages of policy interventions bold enough and big enough in scale to shrink income inequality, and to make wealth accumulation accessible to more than the elite few. But this age did not last, and its did not raise the water high enough to raise all boats; minorities and women, who began the Golden Age with fewer economic resources and opportunities than white men, did not catch up in this period.

The stalling of the New Deal and the "war on poverty" policy, promising as they did to combine proactive Keynesian interventionism with sensitivity to social inequality, has led some economists to reconsider the interdependence between social forces and economic outcomes that Keynes pointed out. For example, Brown (2004) shows that an increasingly unequal distribution of income adversely affects aggregate demand and the responsiveness of aggregate demand to policy interventions. Amplifying this trend is the increasing importance of racial minorities and of women among the unemployed, and the concentration of the unemployed in spatial areas that are increasingly falling behind in income and wealth levels. Dymski (1996) has pointed out that in the U.S., which has severe race/gender divides, demand-management policies are increasingly ineffective because they do not take into account these inequalities in the structure of market opportunities.

In any event, the idea of using government intervention to maintain adequate investment and jobs is now a distant memory. If the Golden Age was a Keynesian period, we are certainly in a Post Keynesian period now. And in this Post Keynesian world—with inadequate flows of credit, capital, and jobs—social divides play a key role in determining the location, terms, and conditions of investment and employment. Because social and political struggles in a Post Keynesian world will play out along some of these divides, understanding the linkages between core Keynesian ideas and these divides is of fundamental importance.

This chapter explores the empirical impact of racial inequality on credit flows for home loans. This topic has not been addressed to date by Post Keynesian authors. We have noted that Post Keynesian studies sometimes emphasize macro-linkages, sometimes micro-behaviors, and sometimes micro-macro linkages. In the spirit of a concern with society as a whole, this chapter attempts a study of this phenomenon for a large sample of U.S. urban areas. This gives a "macroscopic" overview of the operations of the residential credit market through the nation's (micro) localities. The focus of this study is the extent to which the race of a borrower facilitates or blocks access to credit.

We do not explicitly model the behavior of the financial firms that decide to whom, and under what terms, to give credit. Dunn's (2001) insight about the link between uncertainty and firm strategy readily suggests why firms might deny loans to minority or female loan applicants at higher rates than other applicants. If most firms are headed by whites (a stylized fact borne out by national statistics), and if whites have higher levels of trust with other whites, and less uncertainty about whites' prospects than about minorities' prospects, then uncertainty reduction will lead the firm to discriminate (on the basis of race or gender).[3] And "discriminate" here means to deny loans more frequently, all else being equal, to some category of creditworthy applicants.

This is not a rejection of the Post Keynesian assertion that money is endogenous in advanced capitalist economies. Rather, this study asks whether and to what extent banks, and other lenders who control the greater volume of credit, restrict access to some borrowers because of their race. It also asks whether any societal patterns emerge with respect to this race-sensitive behavior. It turns out that a pattern does emerge—one suggesting that lenders respond (at least in part) to the presence or absence of countervailing power on the part of racial minorities in the credit market. This pattern constitutes a bridge between a core concept of John Kenneth Galbraith and empirical work on racial inequality in the credit market. The implications of this bridge for Post Keynesian economics, and for the economic analysis of racial inequality, are discussed briefly in our conclusion.

Empirical Work on Racial Discrimination in Credit Markets: The Context

Since the mid-1970s, academic researchers and activists have examined whether redlining and racial discrimination exist in U.S. residential credit markets. Redlining refers to situations in which fewer loans are made, or more loans on disadvantageous terms, in inner-city areas with many minority residents. Racial discrimination refers to situations in which minority applicants are disadvantaged in credit markets relative to other loan applicants. Data on residential credit markets, available since the late 1970s under the Home Mortgage Disclosure Act (HMDA), has provided the figures for investigating these phenomena.

Regional differences in credit-market outcomes may significantly affect the conclusions drawn. Discrimination may differ in magnitude and in character from place to place; and studies of different places may reach different conclusions about an implicitly universal phenomenon (discrimination) that operates in very different ways from one place to another. This is especially true if discrimination is examined in terms of residential segregation.

Two other overlooked factors that may significantly affect empirical results are also emerging. One is the increased number of years for which data is available. Data on residential credit market applications is now available for consistently defined census tracts for the period 1992–98. This period is long enough to allow some temporal drift. Just as studies of Boston and Atlanta may reach different conclusions, since race is constituted and perceived differently in these two cities, so too studies done in 1992 and in 1998 may reach different conclusions because structural economic conditions change over the period.

Another emerging element is the increasing importance of multiethnic (instead of exclusively black-white) differences in U.S. society. The "new immigration" of the past two decades vastly increased the number of Latino/Chicano and Asian American residents in many cities, so a simple bi-polar analysis is no longer adequate. It cannot be assumed that results showing lower racial barriers for members of one ethnic group imply lower barriers for members of other ethnic groups. Nor can it be assumed that the position of ethnic groups remains fixed relative to white applicants.

The empirical investigation undertaken here attempts to gain some perspective on the significance of geographic heterogeneity, of temporal drift, and of multiple ethnicities in residential credit markets. We examine HMDA loans for eighty-four metropolitan areas, and probe the intertwined patterns of ethnic, regional, and temporal difference based on the varying racial compositions. The results are compared with changes in the residential segregation of households between 1990 and 2000. The results provide some evidence of a racial U-curve in lending markets, where white advantage and minority disadvantage is smaller when cities have many or few minority residents. There is also evidence that some socio-economic aspects of cities (crime rates and unemployment) affect white and African American home-loan applicants very differently. This suggests that the presence or absence of countervailing power on the part of minority applicants is a key determinant of outcomes in credit markets.

Descriptive Statistics of the Eighty-four Metropolitan Areas

The eighty-four cities examined here differ substantially in their racial/ethnic, income, and regional characteristics, among others. Appendix 4.1 lists these metro-

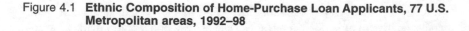

Figure 4.1 **Ethnic Composition of Home-Purchase Loan Applicants, 77 U.S. Metropolitan areas, 1992–98**

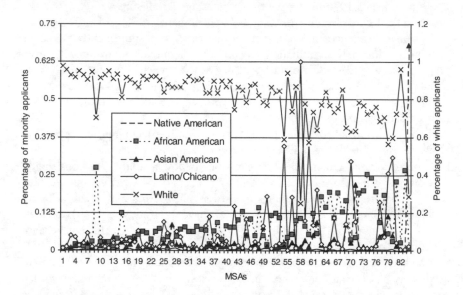

politan statistical areas (MSAs, as defined by the U.S. Census Bureau), the number of residents in 1990, and the 1992, 1994, 1996, and 1998 home-loan applicants. It also shows this data by percentages by ethnicity.[4] The extensive nature of this investigation is evident in the totals shown at the bottom of Appendix 4.1: the MSAs included contain a 1990 population of 132.7 million residents and a 2000 population of 153.1 million residents.

Because our focus is on racial inequality, Figure 4.1 sorts the data by the proportion of whites in the area, and then examines patterns in home-loan applications (for 1992, 1994, 1996, and 1998). At one extreme is Scranton (97.6 percent white); at the other is Miami (24.9 percent white). Figure 4.2 suggests a correlation between the racial proportion of home-loan applicants and the cities' racial composition. The drop-off for white applicants is very slight, however; whites comprise more than half the home-loan applicants even in cities at the far right side of Figure 4.1. Among minorities, African Americans most often have the largest proportion of applicants. The Latino proportion of the applicant pool is "spiky" and varies substantially from city to city.[5]

Regional variation is very important in residential credit markets (Dymski 1999). Figure 4.2 indicates that regional differences matter in terms of the ethnic composition of loan markets. At one extreme are the northeastern and mid-Atlantic cities, where whites comprise almost 90 percent of home-loan applicants on average and African Americans are the largest minority group at about 7 percent. In southeast-

Figure 4.2 **Ethnic Composition of Home-Purchase Loan Applicants, by Region, 77 U.S. Metropolitan Areas, 1992–98**

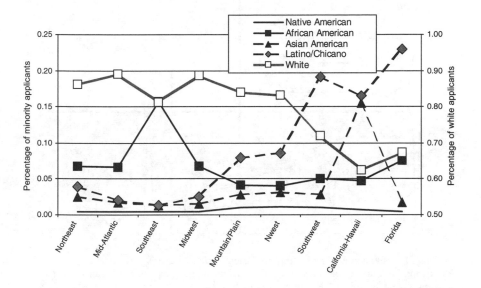

ern states, white applicants dip to an average of 81 percent, while the African American percentage climbs above 16 percent. The proportion of Latino applicants becomes larger than African American applicants in mid-western, mountain/ plains, and northwestern cities; but whites still comprise more than 80 percent of applicants. In southwestern cities, in California, and in Florida, the white applicant percentage falls substantially, and the average for Latinos exceeds 15 percent, well above the African American average. The Asian American applicant percentage is greater in western areas than in the east, and highest (over 15 percent on average) in California and Hawaii.

Figures 4.3 through 4.6 provide images of the home-loan applicant and population pools. In Figure 4.3, the eighty-four MSAs are rank ordered by the proportion of African Americans in the population. The curve depicting population proportion is approximately linear, with break points at the 30 percent and 20 percent population levels. A lighter curve depicts the proportion of African Americans in the loan pool for 1992–98. This curve is spikier, but still relatively smooth; it shows that African Americans consistently have proportions in the loan market equal to about two-thirds of their population percentage. Only five cities constitute exceptions to this rule (Knoxville, TN, Pittsburgh, PA, San Diego, CA, Scranton, PA, and Stockton, CA).

Overlaid on this figure is a broken horizontal line depicting the African Ameri-

Figure 4.3   **African American Share of Population and Home-Purchase Loan Applications, 1992–98**

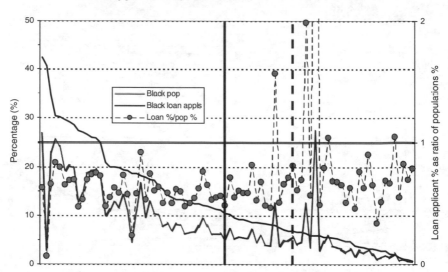

Note: In 1990 some 80 percent of all African Americans resided in metro areas to the left of the broken vertical line; the solid vertical line represents the break point for 80 percent of African American loan market applicants.

can percentage in the loan pool relative to their percentage in the population. This ratio is consistently below 1, with no evident trend as the proportion of African Americans in the population increases. A broken vertical line is inserted at the point where 80 percent of all African American residents in these eighty-four cities have been accounted for; and a solid line is inserted at the point at where 80 percent of all African American home-loan applicants have been accounted. The solid line is to the left of the broken line, indicating that African American loan applicants are concentrated in cities with a high percentage of African Americans.

Figure 4.4 depicts the same information for the Latino/Chicano population. Note that the curves depicting proportional representation in the population, and in the loan pool, are both convex with respect to the origin, indicating that this population is far more concentrated spatially than is the African American population. This figure also suggests that home-loan applications for Latinos/Chicanos are highly concentrated in cities with large proportions of Latino residents. The loan-applicants/population ratio is below 1 on average. It is systematically below 1 in cities with the highest proportion of Latino/Chicano residents, but often above 1 in other cities.

Figure 4.5 finds similar patterns for Asian Americans, where the convexity of the population and applicant curves is even more pronounced. However, in con-

Figure 4.4   **Latino/Chicano Share of Population and Home-Purchase Loan Applications, 1992–98**

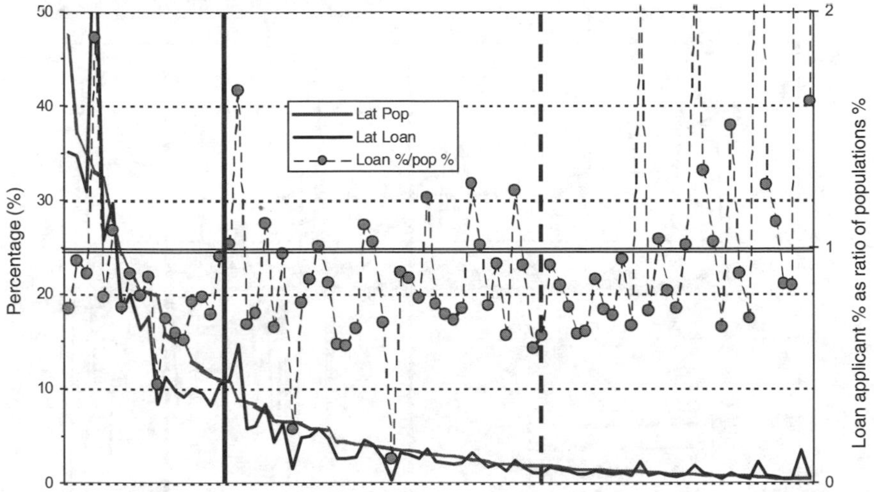

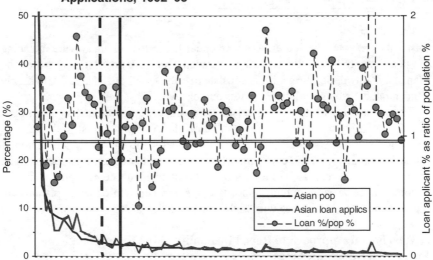

In 1990, 80 percent of all Latino/Chicanos resided in metro areas to the left of the broken vertical line; the solid vertical line represents the break point for 80 percent of Latino/Chicano loan market applicants.

Figure 4.5   **Asian American Share of Population and Home-Purchase Loan Applications, 1992–98**

In 1990, 80 percent of all Asian Americans resided in metro areas to the left of the broken vertical line; the solid vertical line represents the break point for 80 percent of Asian American loan market applicants.

Figure 4.6   **White Share of Population and Home-Purchase Loan Applications, 1992–98**

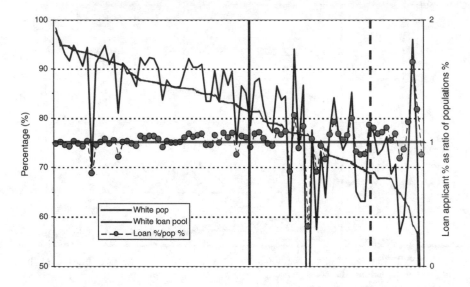

In 1990 80 percent of the white population resided in metro areas to the left of the broken vertical line; the solid vertical line represents the break point for 80 percent of white loan market applicants.

trast to the previous two figures, Asian American home-loan applicants are spreading out to areas with lower concentrations of Asian American population. Further, the loan applicants/population ratio is consistently above 1, both in areas with highly concentrated Asian population clusters and elsewhere.[6]

The patterns for whites, presented in Figure 4.6, are quite interesting. The population curve is concave with respect to the origin. And in contrast to the relative smoothness of the African American and Latino/Chicano curves for proportion of home-loan applicants, the curve for whites is extremely spiky. Not surprisingly, the ratio for the percentages of loan applicants and residents centers on 1; this ratio becomes more variable in high-minority cities. Further, white loan applicants are highly concentrated in cities with high proportions of white residents.

A Total Factor Approach to Racial Inequality in the Eighty-four Largest Metropolitan Areas

The definitions of racial redlining and of racial discrimination offered earlier in this chapter are intentionally nonspecific concerning the motives of those supplying credit and the circumstances of those seeking credit. These are points of controversy regarding the line between just and unjust outcomes.

There are many points of views concerning what is occurring. In what might be termed the "market-power" view, redlining and racial discrimination arise because lenders can impose worse terms on minority borrowers than on other borrowers, or favor white persons over minorities (Ondrich, Stricker, and Yinger 1998). In the "taste-based" view, redlining and racial discrimination arise only if lenders purposely avoid minority applicants or areas, and are willing to pay for this aversion by making profitable loans to minorities. Lender aversion results in "personal" discrimination, which is motivated by the racial animus of those who control scarce resources for which minorities compete (such as credit).[7] In the first view, it is irrelevant whether lenders have an aversion toward minorities; their behavior is rational in that they use their market power to extract rents from those who lack exit options. The second view assumes that lenders must pay a price for deviating from purely profit-driven behavior. A third view, which can be termed the "rational-discrimination" approach, asserts that redlining and racial discrimination arise because minority households, minority businesses, and minority areas are afflicted by a large number of factors rendering them less creditworthy than whites and residents of white areas. It may be difficult for lenders to identify all these factors, and to distinguish precisely the creditworthiness of each minority applicant. Lenders may thus use borrower race, or the racial complexion of the borrower's area, as one component in their decision-making (or term-setting) algorithms. Whether or not they do so is controversial; even more controversial is whether they are justified in making such distinctions. If it is "rational" to take applicant or area race into account, then lenders are not to blame for discriminating on this basis—especially if the potential gains from identifying additional factors correlated with race are less than the cost of obtaining this additional information. This behavior may be rooted in long-standing practices, sanctioned by the Federal Housing Administration in its early years of existence by printing up material that read "if a neighborhood is to retain stability, it is necessary that properties shall continue to be occupied by the same social and racial groups" (Schiller 1995). Although these practices ended with the equal-opportunity dictates of the early 1960s, the appreciation of homogeneous neighborhoods had already been established.

A fourth view is that unfair outcomes exist when significant disadvantages exist in credit-market outcomes for minority applicants—even if these are partially or fully justified by differences in factors correlated with race. According to this "structural" approach to discrimination, the legacy of racial inequality deepens over time due to embedded sources of racial difference. The only way to overturn this historical trajectory of inequality is to define the entire racial gap as unjust.

Differing viewpoints about defining "discrimination" and "redlining" mean that researchers and analysts often use the same word to talk about different things. These definitional differences spill over into differences in empirical procedures, tests, and inferences. The "structural" approach simply looks for evidence of racial differences in loan-market outcomes, such as loan-approval/denial rates and loan terms and conditions. To the extent that minority applicants and areas are at a disadvantage, the magnitude of structural discrimination can be specified. In the market-power approach, behavioral variables that summarize elements of borrower creditworthiness should be accounted for in any measure of the magnitude of unjust racial inequality in credit markets. The idea is to construct an empirical model that captures the basic elements of applicant creditworthiness, and then to determine what racial residuals remain in approval/denial rates. Such differences can be attributed to lender market power. The problem is that the statistical-discrimination approach will attribute any racial residuals to one of two factors: either the absence of borrower characteristics that lenders really use, or the size of the racial "signal" itself. The statistical model of discrimination cannot decide between these two interpretations unless we have an exact rendering of what lenders do measure concerning applicants.

This two-sided interpretation of regression coefficients bedevils efforts to understand the scope and importance of discrimination by "letting the numbers speak."[8] Showing that market power (unfairly high denial rates and unfairly adverse terms) is not being exerted by lenders requires that more and more characteristics of borrowers be brought into the explanatory equation. In principle, only if racial disadvantage remains after all such factors have been incorporated can it be said that market power was unfairly exerted. But this effort to counter the hypothesis that racial inequality reflects unjust exercise of market power undercuts any ability to determine whether and how rational discrimination is used. If one builds in an equation that incorporates as many variables as possible that are correlated with race, one has a model that lenders might have used; but one loses track of whether lenders used a simpler equation and simply factored in applicant or area race to proxy for a wide range of excluded variables that may be costly to obtain.

This discussion has important implications. First, there is no way to formulate econometric tests that distinguish clearly among the different theories concerning what discrimination is or how agents take race into account in credit markets. Second, different definitions, and different degrees of disbelief regarding the plausibility of race effects, will have researchers talking past one another. Third, the history of racial inequality will undercut all but laboratory efforts to isolate purely personal discrimination from structural or statistical discrimination. Fourth, statistical discrimination can never be conclusively proven or disproved, because the assertion that a given firm or individual is discriminating on this basis turns on an unverifiable event.

Where does this leave us? Theorists will and should continue to debate the importance of race effects in an abstract sense. Empirical researchers have done and will continue to do important work concerning race effects in credit markets. It is useful to know, for example, whether a typical African American loan applicant in a Midwestern city has a 10 percent lower chance or a 60 percent lower chance of obtaining a loan than a typical white applicant, controlling for a specified list of factors. But investigators must accept that they are not identifying truths about discrimination; rather they are making race effects clearer. Different theoretical and empirical results should be compared; at the same time, it must be understood that the incompatibility of one study with another does not invalidate it. Further, amplifying a theme presented in our introduction, the relative and incomplete character of empirical results about racial inequality in credit markets makes it crucial to relate these empirical results to the underlying theoretical frameworks that motivated the empirical studies in the first place. This will permit a coherent interpretation of the results, and crucial empirical feedback that might permit those operating in particular theoretical frameworks to make appropriate modifications to the parameters that explicitly or implicitly underlie their models.

As the introduction also suggests, different kinds of discrimination have different effects, and some studies of discrimination (such as Han 2000) attempt to isolate the specific empirical effects of different categories of discrimination. Our study takes the opposite approach; its empirical method embodies a "total factors" approach to racial inequality.

Our empirical model asks two questions: What advantages accrue to white status for home-loan applicants, and what disadvantages accrue to minority status for home-loan applicants? These questions are put into operation via a model that seeks to capture the combined effects of taste-based and market-power discrimination, and structural discrimination.[9] All these factors operate in any given locality at any point in time. And while it is important to understand these different types of discrimination, all are in operation, all affect credit-market outcomes, and all contribute to racial inequality. As discussed in Dymski (2000), the total factors approach embodies a holistic perspective at odds in two ways with the choice-theoretic framework of neoclassical economic theory. First, an explanation is complete in neoclassical theory only when it traces an effect to preferences or market structures or endowments—in this case, to one of these forms of discrimination to the exclusion of the others. Second, for neoclassical theory only the taste-based and market-power notions of discrimination are acceptable. Neoclassical economic theory aims at being ahistorical; hence, it seeks to control for the historical gaps associated with structural discrimination, not to incorporate them.

Apart from the conceptual ambiguity concerning discrimination, there are special challenges in implementing our econometric tests for structural discrimination. Virtually all econometric tests of credit-market discrimination to date have involved one year of data and one city or region. However, we require consistent measures over time; further, we must sample empirical experience in different regions, lest we inappropriately generalize from a special case. But a multiregional approach means dealing with the multiracial character of exclusion in credit markets; a black-white framework will not suffice, nor a brown-white contrast. Instead, our model must allow for race effects involving all categories of minority applicants, since the proportion of minority residents, and their wealth and income levels, vary from place to place.[10]

We deal with these challenges by running a logistical regression model on HMDA data for the eighty-four largest U.S. metropolitan areas. HMDA data encompasses a range of residential loans—home purchase, refinancing, and rehabilitation; single family and multifamily; owner occupied and absentee owned. The determinants of loan decisions for these different loan types may be quite different. To insure uniformity, our sample is restricted to single-family home loans. We control for regional differences in racial/ethnic composition by including four categories of minority applicant (African American, Asian American, Latino/Chicano, and Native American) and by using a uniform method to identify high minority areas.[11] We estimated the following model for any city.

> Probability of loan approval in the period 1992–98 = Intercept term,
> Year 1992 dummy variable,   *[controls for year effects]*
> Year 1994 dummy variable,
> Year 1996 dummy variable,
> Applicant's loan/income ratio, *[applicant characteristics]*
> Log of applicant's annual income,
> Dummy variable for female applicants,
> Dummy variable for Native American applicants for 1992, 1994, 1996, and 1998,
> Dummy variable for Asian American applicants for 1992, 1994, 1996, and 1998,
> Dummy variable for African American applicants for 1992, 1994, 1996, and 1998,
> Dummy variable for Chicano/Latino applicants for 1992, 1994, 1996, and 1998,
> [or, in lieu of the above-four minority dummy variables:
> Dummy variable for white applicants for 1992, 1994, 1996, and 1998],
> [Census tract] Median 1990 income,   *[census tract characteristics]*
> Median 1990 income squared,
> Residential density (average population per residential unit),
> Proportion of owner-occupied residential units,
> Dummy variables for high-minority areas (those 25 percent of each city's census tracts with the highest proportion of minority residents) for 1992, 1994, 1996, and 1998.

Equations using the dummy-variable method measure race effects relative to the level of the intercept term. Then two independent equations measuring race effects will generally have different intercept-term coefficients as well as race-effect coefficients. When these equations are structural measures for two different places, intercept-coefficient differences can be interpreted as accounting for unmeasured differences in local economic conditions. This interpretation can be problematic when interpreting race-effect variables for a given place. If a given equation is run on independently determined data for two different years (say), then the estimated intercept coefficients can be interpreted as representing changes in unmeasured structural conditions between the two years. Equations using U.S. census data as a cross-sectional measure of structural difference, however, normally violate this condition: the same data (say, 1990 census data) is used to depict local structural conditions. When two equations measuring race effects for two different years in one area have different intercept terms, interpretive ambiguity arises: each intercept coefficient depicts the effects of both unvarying unmeasured structural variables and conditions particular to each year. The equation estimated here avoids this ambiguity by specifying separately an intercept term and year dummies. This insures that within each city trends in race variables are measured consistently over time.[12]

The multiyear and multicity character of our investigation requires sacrificing empirical depth for empirical range. This is an unfortunate trade-off, but one that makes this experiment possible in the first place. Our dummy coefficients for race encompass structural, market-power, and personal discrimination. The idea is not to distinguish between structural and personal aspects of discrimination, but to generate meaningful information about racial trends in mortgage credit markets.

Raw Logit Results: A First Pass

The logit equation specified above was run for each of the eighty-four cities. Since dummy variables are used, a positive coefficient indicates a positive effect of that dummy on loan approval. For African Americans, 1992 was the worst year; but coefficients are consistently negative for all four years (Albany, NY, Las Vegas, NV, Miami, FL, Nashville, LA, Omaha, NE, and Washington, DC, being the few exceptions). Improvement after 1992 is less notable for Latino/Chicano applicants, although 1998 coefficients are generally higher than those for 1992. Most values are in the negative range, but twenty cities have coefficient values in the positive range.

A positive trend is evident for Asian Americans. Most coefficients for 1992 and 1994 fall into the negative range, while those for 1996 and 1998 are primarily in the positive range. A pattern of extreme variability is also evident.

A reverse trend is found for white applicants: the 1992 coefficients are often higher than those for later years. Negative values are evident for 1998 for nine cities: Allentown, PA, Bakersfield, CA, Jacksonville, FL, Las Vegas, NV, Little Rock, AR, Miami, FL, Nashville, TN, Omaha, NE, and Rochester, NY. Several of these cities have positive coefficient values for Latinos or African Americans.

Comparison of Logit Results with Changes to Racial Separation Indexes, 1990–2000

One immediate consequence of discrimination in housing markets is greater racial segregation. Turner and Weink (1991) show that U.S. residential segregation is higher than affordability considerations or individual preferences alone would predict, and they suggest this extra segregation is due to discrimination in lending.

The sort of discrimination at work is difficult to establish. For one thing, behavioral and structural factors overlap. The disparate treatment of minorities reduces minority demand for housing in white areas, and decreases the minority-owned housing supply offered to whites. Discrimination by real-estate agents and residents increases white demand in white areas, and reduces it in mixed areas. At the same time, structural discrimination means fewer minorities can afford homes. The correlation of minority status with lower incomes, and of minority neighborhoods with lower levels of public investment (what Galster and Keeney [1988] call the "nexus of urban racial phenomena"), encourages bias against minority areas in the housing market.

Leigh (1992) documents the persistence and growth of racial segregation and isolation: despite black gains in suburbanization, the elimination of racial covenants, and the presence of fair-housing laws, racial segregation and isolation have remained stable or have even deepened over time.[13] Massey and Denton (1993) argue that racial segregation, in turn, deepens structural discrimination, independent of other economic dynamics:

> With or without class segregation, residential segregation between blacks and whites builds concentrated poverty into the residential structure of the black community and guarantees that poor blacks experience a markedly less advantaged social environment than do poor whites. (ibid., 125)

An interesting question is how the raw logit results compare with the overall changes to residential segregation between 1990 and 2000 for our eighty-four MSAs. To answer this question we rely on the dissimilarity index (White 1983, Ransom 2000). This index, also called "the segregation index," measures the uneven distribution of households by race across physical space. Its value varies directly with the extent of residential segregation, so the index is a relatively reliable measure of residential segregation. It is defined as follows:

$$D = \tfrac{1}{2} \Sigma \left| \frac{N_{1i}}{N_1} - \frac{N_{2i}}{N_2} \right| , \qquad (1)$$

where N_{1i} = population of group 1 in the ith tract, N_{2i} = population of group 2 in the ith tract, N_1 = total population of group 1 in the MSA, and N_2 = total population of group 2 in the MSA. The value of D equals the proportion of the N_1 population that would have to relocate to another tract if each tract were to have the same proportions of the two racial groups as the MSA as a whole. In this study, N_2 represents the white population, while N_1 represents non-white populations (African Americans, Latinos, or Asian Americans). Using racial household and homeownership census data, indexes are constructed for each MSA for 1990 and 2000. Indexes for

2000 were calculated using one-race-only figures. Iceland, Weinberg, and Steinmetz (2002) and Li ct al. (2002) find these variables differ only slightly from indexes using "alone or in combination" figures.

Dissimilarity indexes have two attractive features. First, they involve minimal data retrieval. We only need census tract data on households and homeowners by racial groups. Second, index values have a clear and intuitive interpretation. They vary between 0 and 1. A value of 0 signifies that all tracts within the MSA have the same racial composition, implying that there is no segregation. A value of 1 means that there is complete segregation within the MSA. These two advantages are offset by one disadvantage—our dissimilarity index provides only a rough measure of inter-group spatial segregation; it does not identify group clusters within the area under examination. Nonetheless, as a benchmark of racial separation, the index is very useful.

Appendix 4.3 contains dissimilarity indexes for households and for homeowners based on the 1990 and 2000 censuses. It also contains the changes to these indexes between 1990 and 2000. Appendix 4.4 contains selected highlights related to these indexes. For example, how well do the positive coefficients for African Americans correlate with decreases in residential segregation for households and homeowners between 1990 and 2000? Appendix 4.4 shows that of the six MSAs containing positive coefficients throughout the 1990s, in Washington, DC, residential segregation for both households and homeowners decreases the most. Las Vegas is among the ten MSAs showing decreased segregation for African American homeowners. Albany was among the top-ten MSAs with the greatest increases to residential segregation for African American households, while Miami was among the top ten showing greatest increases for African American homeowners; the increase was small, however. There were only two MSAs showing increased segregation for African American homeowners, signifying that segregation decreased for eighty-two MSAs between 1990 and 2000. For Latinos, of the twenty MSAs with coefficients in the positive range for the loan periods examined, three (Knoxville, Pittsburgh, and Scranton) were among the ten MSAs showing the greatest decreases in residential segregation among Latino households. Toledo, OH, showed the greatest decrease in residential segregation for Latino homeowners, while Kansas City, MO, and Tulsa, OK, appeared among the top-ten MSAs with increases in residential segregation for Latino households.

Our logit results for Asians demonstrated the most volatility; they also showed the greatest decreases in residential segregation. Only Sacramento, CA, showed increased segregation for Asian homeowners. As for whites, of the nine MSAs containing negative coefficients throughout the 1990s, only Las Vegas was among the top-ten MSAs with decreases to residential segregation for African American homeowners, with Omaha appearing on the top-ten list for decreased segregation for Asian homeowners. Las Vegas, however, appears on the top-ten lists of Asian and Latino households for increases in residential segregation for households. Rochester and Miami show a slight increase in segregation for African American households.

Conclusion

Is There a Racial U-Curve in Residential Credit Markets?

These results provide evidence of the persistence and stability of African American disadvantage in residential credit markets across the U.S. With few exceptions, they show that African Americans are at a disadvantage in home-loan markets due to a combination of structural inequality, lender racial animus, and market power. On a positive note, residential segregation appears to be decreasing in most MSAs.

Our results suggest the presence of something like a racial U-curve in lending markets. This idea is based on the notions of racial competition and group power advanced by Darity (1989) and Williams (1991). Their view is that discrimination may reflect the outcome of a process of racial competition for scarce resources. If not everyone can have enough credit, the economic game may be rigged through coalition building, influence, and other means, so that African Americans (in particular) are left out in the hunt for stable jobs and for capital.

If this notion is right, then the proportion of minorities in a given city may affect how this racial competition plays out. If there are a large number of white persons, and relatively few persons of color, the latter pose little threat, since they will draw few resources away from white competitors. However, as the fraction of minorities in an area grows, they become a threat and white competitive reactions may be activated. The process could well be subtle, and play out through indirect means—for example, by shunting minority residents into particular parts of town, by white home-buying preferences, or by real estate agent impressions of property desirability in different locations. However, as the fraction of minorities in a city increases further, it may be less feasible to play this game because of the cost to some players. For example, if a large share of the home-buying or small-business market consists of minorities, then screening out minorities will be costly for suppliers of credit and housing. At this point, ironically, we may get a Beckerian outcome, in which racial discrimination lessens because its perpetrators lose income if they engage in such behavior. But in cities with a moderate proportion of minorities, profit-seeking and racial competition may be consistent.

If this logic has any merit, then a racial U-curve may be at work, with greater racial competition and minority disadvantage in cities with a moderate proportion of minority residents and businesses. This suggests a Goldilocks effect; if there are too many or too few minorities, racial competition fades because it is either unprofitable or irrelevant.

Further evidence of a racial U-curve comes from our logit results. We again use odds ratios and not coefficients. Figures 4.7 to 4.10 provide average odds ratios for each year and for each city cluster. If the U-curve has merit, then cities with low fractions of minorities (white cities) and with high fractions of minorities (minority cities) should have the highest average odds for minority applicants (and the

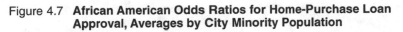

Figure 4.7 **African American Odds Ratios for Home-Purchase Loan Approval, Averages by City Minority Population**

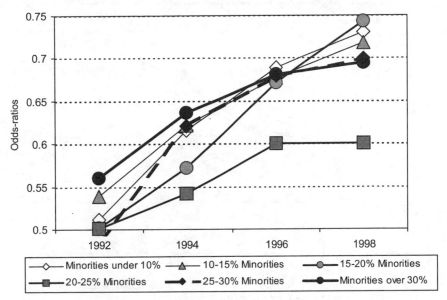

Figure 4.8 **Latino/Chicano Odds Ratios for Home-Purchase Loan Approval, Averages by City Minority Population**

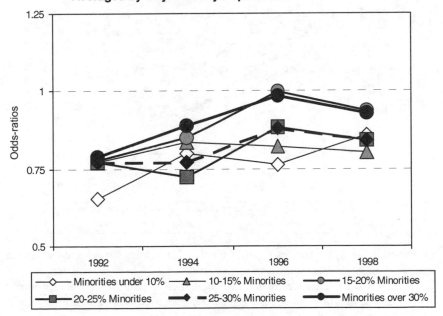

Figure 4.9 **Asian-American Odds Ratios for Home-Purchase Loan Approval, Averages by City Minority Population**

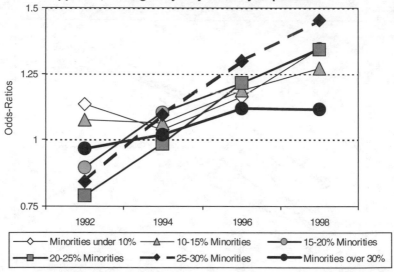

Figure 4.10 **White Odds Ratios for Home-Purchase Loan Approval, Averages by City Minority Population**

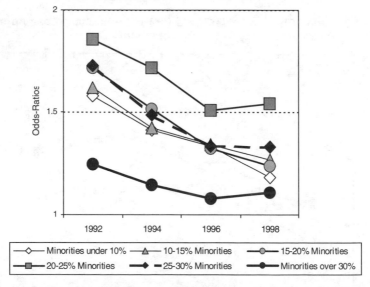

lowest odds for white applicants). In Figure 4.7, the odds for African American applicants in white and minority cities are among the highest, but not uniquely so. In Figure 4.8, the U-curve result obtains for Latino/Chicano applicants in minority cities, but not in white cities. And Figure 4.9 provides no evidence of an Asian

American U-curve. As predicted, Figure 4.10 finds that white applicants have the lowest odds in minority cities, and the next lowest in white cities.

These figures provide some support to the notion of a racial U-curve in credit markets due to the variability of racial competition across cities with different proportions of minorities. More conceptual and empirical work remains to be done both to test the theory and to explore the ways that racial inequality and racial competition play out in American cities of different types. The minority-percentage classification used here is just one possibility; regional difference, proportion of new immigrants, and other criteria can be explored in future research.

Postscript: Some Implications for Post Keynesian Empirical Work

This chapter began by reflecting on the idea that empirical work by Post Keynesian economists might be aimed at proving or disproving core theoretical propositions of stylized Post Keynesian and neoclassical macroeconomic models. This might be termed the first Post Keynesian empirical agenda.

There has been no such test here; nor has an effort been made to determine the viability of this agenda.[14] Instead, this chapter has followed the line of argument presented in the introduction. Microeconomic relations matter, and they matter at the aggregate level (across the entire economy). Power matters in economic relations, and this power is commonly asserted in microeconomic markets that are usually left out of aggregate models. We went on to argue that in a Post Keynesian world, where flows of jobs, capital, and credit are insufficient to permit broad-based prosperity, social divides (such as racial inequality) might govern access to scarce economic resources. This implies a second Post Keynesian empirical agenda: to explore the links between social divides that matter for economic outcomes, on the one hand, and key Post Keynesian concepts such as uncertainty, sufficiency of aggregate demand, endogenous money, and power. This second agenda will provide key bridges between researchers and activists focused on particular social problems, and Post Keynesian scholars. It is important to find ways to use core Keynesian concepts to render visible aspects of social problems that many investigators (few of whom may be initially familiar with Post Keynesian theory) are exploring.

The study undertaken here has incorporated three Post Keynesian concepts into a study of racial inequality in U.S. residential credit markets. First, it has explored the operation of lending decisions in real economic settings. Given that banks control the volume of money, and given that they do so by determining the volume of credit money, how does this control work? Moore (1988), in a volume that pays little attention to micro-foundational behavior, asserts that banks never say no. Goodhart (1991), among others, has asserted that Moore goes too far because cyclical changes in lender confidence will affect banks' willingness to make loans. This is not the only reason lenders might not always be willing to make loans. Structural or perceived differences among borrowers (who has collateral and who doesn't, who is perceived as reliable and who is not) may also come into play, as well as racial difference per se, too. The evidence presented here suggests that radical differences are important.

A second Post Keynesian idea explored here is the idea of power as a determinant of economic outcomes. This interacts with social antipathy toward non-whites at a personal or institutional level in a wide range of economic and social settings. So, the degree to which racial minorities face special barriers in applying for residential credit may be systematically related to the share of the market that these minorities comprise, and to the extent of residential segregation in the geographic areas over which this lending takes place. When the share of minority borrowers in a given locale surpasses a certain level (that is, when borrowers have countervailing power in the marketplace), the disadvantage facing minority loan applicants in residential credit markets lessens. Below this threshold is another zone, where minority loan applicants are a social threat and not a significant numerical component of the credit market. In this zone, no countervailing power is available to offset the sense of social threat, and minority applicants face greater disadvantages in applying for credit. Below some level, there are too few minority applicants to constitute a social threat, and the degree of minority disadvantage in credit-market applications lessens.

The third Post Keynesian aspect of our study consists of approaching economic phenomena from an aggregate viewpoint. We do this by obtaining micro-market empirical results for enough markets to generate a broad sense of the outcomes in residential credit markets taken as a whole.

Notes

1. Dunn and Pressman (2005), in a comprehensive summary of John Kenneth Galbraith's contributions to economic theory and policy, highlight his work on the concentration of power in the large corporation.

2. Many contemporary economists have combined insights of Marx and Keynes—for example, Harry Magdoff and Paul Sweezy (1977). The core concepts of American institutionalism reflect this mix; they include: theoretical recognition of the historically embedded character of experience; emphasis on the construction by economic agents of stable, routine practices to organize human experience; the mutual determination or co-determination of economic outcomes by multiple forces, both inside and outside the framework of market-based activity per se; the centrality of power and exploitation to human interaction; and the importance of real time and uncertainty.

3. How much the overall loan-approval rates for white persons and for other borrowers vary may, in turn, depend on the broader macro environment; however, this sort of variability is not tested here.

4. Note that several metropolitan areas contain cities whose data is grouped separately in HMDA reports. These are: Cleveland, OH, which encompasses both Cleveland and Akron, OH, in HMDA reports; Chicago, IL, which includes Chicago and Gary, IN, in HMDA reports; San Francisco, CA, which includes San Francisco, Oakland–East Bay, CA, and San Jose; New York, NY, which includes New York City, Newark, NJ, and several smaller suburban counties not encompassed here; and Los Angeles, which includes the southern

California counties of Los Angeles, Riverside–San Bernardino, Orange, and Ventura (not included here).

5. Due to the small number of Native Americans in the applicant pools studied here, this population is excluded in most of the analyses herein.

6. In ongoing work on ethnic banking in southern California conducted with several other scholars, we attribute the large proportion of Asian American loan applicants (and their success in residential and commercial development) to the robust Asian American banking sector. See Dymski and Mohanty (1999) and Li et al. (2002).

7. None of the other approaches to discrimination introduced here requires the personal animus of suppliers of credit; the race effects that arise are purely a matter of market power, of cost minimization, or of historical difference.

8. This empirical dilemma about modeling and interpreting the right-hand side of the equation determining creditworthiness is less important for the taste-based approach to racial inequality in credit markets. When empirically implemented, this approach must try to empirically test its fundamental premise—that is, that some lenders may forgo good loans to minority borrowers because of their distaste for conducting transactions with people of color. The taste-based view assumes that the lender expresses its racial distaste by its refusal to offer a contract, not by its agreeing to offer a contract only at inferior terms. This view proceeds from the view that racial minorities have exit options and can find competitive credit contracts elsewhere. Minority applicants would deal with bigoted banks only because of these banks' willingness to forgo profits by offering terms that are "better" than they would otherwise be.

9. Dymski (2001) argues that statistical discrimination is difficult or impossible to distinguish in empirical tests from structural discrimination.

10. Another challenge in evaluating shifts over time is variability over the economic cycle. During the 1992–98 period, the economy was in recession in 1992 and then in an expansionary phase thereafter. The impact of recession on the 1992 results is examined below.

11. High-minority areas are defined as the 25 percent of census tracts in each MSA with the highest proportion of minority residents.

12. The years 1993, 1995, and 1997 are excluded for analytical economy. To check whether this introduces bias, an equation was run for Los Angeles using all seven years' application data. No anomalies were found in the excluded years' coefficients, and the coefficients for 1992, 1994, 1996, and 1998 differed only incidentally from those obtained in the equation reported here.

13. The shift of some minorities to suburbs has often led to segregated suburbs, not to integrated ones; indeed, by numerous measures, minorities' geographical isolation has increased (Abramson, Tobin, and VanderGoot 1995).

14. The indeterminacy of empirical results in the relatively well-developed literature on race effects in credit markets suggests caution about whether any set of empirical results based on any set of variables can settle any debate rooted in theoretical difference.

References

Abramson, A., M. Tobin, and M. VanderGoot. 1995. "The Changing Geography of Metropolitan Opportunity: The Segregation of the Poor in US Metropolitan Areas." *Housing Policy Debate* 6(1): 45–72.

Brown, C. 2004. "Does Income Distribution Matter for Effective Demand: Evidence from the United States." *Review of Political Economy* 16(3): 291–307.

Danby, C. 2004. "Toward a Gendered Post Keynesianism: Subjectivity and Time in a Nonmodernist Framework." *Feminist Economics* 10(3): 55–75.

Darity, W. 1989. "What's Left of the Economic Theory of Discrimination?" In *The Ques-*

tion of Discrimination: Racial Inequality in the US Labor Market, eds. S. Shulman and W. Darity, Jr. Middletown, CT: Wesleyan University Press.

Davidson, P. 1994. *Post Keynesian Macroeconomic Theory*. Aldershot, UK: Edward Elgar.

Dunn, S. 2001. "Uncertainty, Strategic Decision-making, and the Essence of the Modern Corporation: Extending Cowling and Sugden." *The Manchester School* 69(1): 31–41.

Dunn, S., and S. Pressman. 2005. "The Economic Contributions of John Kenneth Galbraith." *Review of Political Economy* 17(2): 161–209.

Dymski, G. 1996. "Economic Polarization and U.S. Policy Activism." *International Review of Applied Economics* 10(1): 65–84.

———. 1999. *The Bank Merger Wave: The Economic Causes and Social Consequences of Financial Consolidation*. Armonk, NY: M.E. Sharpe.

———. 2000. "Racial and Gender Disadvantage in the Credit Market: Social Injustice and Outcome Equality." In *Capitalism, Socialism and Radical Political Economy: Essays in Honor of Howard J. Sherman*, ed. R. Pollin. Cheltenham, UK, and Northampton, MA: Edward Elgar.

———. 2001. "Is Discrimination Disappearing? Racial Differentials in Access to Credit, 1992–98." *International Journal of Social Economics* 28(10/11/12): 1025–45.

Dymski, G., and L. Mohanty. 1999. "Credit and Banking Structure: Insights from Asian and African American Experience in Los Angeles." *American Economic Review* 89(2): 362–66.

Eichner, A. 1976. *The Megacorp and Oligopoly: Micro Foundations of Macro Dynamics*. New York: Cambridge University Press.

Galbraith, John K. 1956. *American Capitalism: The Concept of Countervailing Power*. Boston: Houghton Mifflin.

Galster, G., and M. Keeney. 1988. "Race, Residence, Discrimination and Economic Opportunity." *Urban Affairs Quarterly* 24: 87–117.

Goodhart, C.A. 1991. "Has Moore Become Too Horizontal?" *Journal of Post Keynesian Economics* 12(1): 29–34.

Han, S. 2000. "The Economics of Taste-Based Discrimination in Credit Markets." School of Business Administration, University of Mississippi, Mimeograph.

Iceland, J., D. Weinberg, and E. Steinmetz. 2002. *Racial and Ethnic Residential Segregation in the United States: 1980–2000*. U.S Department of Commerce, U.S. Census Bureau.

Leigh, W. 1992. "Civil Rights Legislation and the Housing Status of Black Americans: An Overview." In *The Housing Status of Black Americans*, eds. W. Leigh and J. Stewart. New Brunswick, NJ: Transaction Publishers.

Li, W., G. Dymski, Y. Zhou, M. Chee, and C. Aldana. 2002. "Chinese American Banking and Community Development in Los Angeles County." *Annals of Association of American Geographers* 92(4): 777–96.

Magdoff, H., and P. Sweezy. 1977. *The End of Prosperity: The American Economy in the 1970s*. New York: Monthly Review Press.

Marglin, S., and J. Schor. 1990. *The Golden Age of Capitalism*. Oxford: Oxford University Press.

Massey, D., and N. Denton. 1993. *American Apartheid: Segregation and the Making of the Underclass*. Cambridge, MA: Harvard University Press.

Minsky, H. 1975. *John Maynard Keynes*. New York: Columbia University Press.

Moore, B. 1988. *Horizontalists and Verticalists: The Macroeconomics of Credit Money*. New York: Cambridge University Press.

Ondrich, J., A. Stricker, and J. Yinger. 1998. "Do Real Estate Brokers Choose to Discriminate? Evidence from the 1989 Housing Discrimination Study." *Southern Economic Journal* 64(4): 880–901.

Ransom, M. 2000. "Sampling Distributions of Segregation Indexes." *Sociological Methods & Research* 28(4): 454–75.

Schiller, B. 1995. *The Economics of Poverty and Discrimination*, 6th ed. Englewood Cliffs, NJ: Prentice-Hall.

Shackle, G. 1974. *Keynesian Kaleidics: The Evolution of a General Political Economy.* Edinburgh: Edinburgh University Press.

Turner, M., and R. Weink. 1991. "The Persistence of Segregation: Contributing Causes." Washington, DC: Urban Institute, Mimeograph.

White, M. 1983. "The Measurement of Spatial Segregation." *American Journal of Sociology* 88(5): 1008–18.

Williams, R. 1991. *If You're Black, Get Back; If You're Brown, Stick Around; If You're White, Hang Tight: A Primer on Race, Gender, and Work in the Global Economy.* Department of Afro-American Studies, University of Maryland, College Park. Mimeographed.

Appendix 4.1

Number and Ethnicity of Residents and Home-Purchase Loan Applicants in the 84 Metropolitan Areas Included in This Study

Metropolitan statistical areas	Number of applicants in 92–94 to 96–98	Percent of all loan applicants who were:				Number of all loan applicants who were:			
		Black	Asian American	Latino/ Chicano	White	Black	Asian American	Latino/ Chicano	White
Albany	48,277	3.0	1.1	1.1	94.4	1,435	538	545	45,564
Albuquerque	74,707	1.9	1.5	34.7	59.1	1,410	1,088	25,918	44,147
Allentown	35,449	2.1	1.4	4.5	91.7	728	501	1,607	32,499
Atlanta	374,880	19.1	2.7	2.4	75.4	71,753	10,138	8,921	232,709
Austin	130,619	5.4	2.8	17.6	73.7	7,064	3,621	23,042	96,257
Bakersfield	40,002	3.7	2.7	29.7	63.1	1,494	1,098	11,877	25,243
Baltimore	179,412	19.4	2.2	1.1	77.0	34,759	3,872	2,036	138,061
Baton Rouge	51,244	19.3	1.0	0.9	78.6	9,867	490	454	40,282
Birmingham	81,420	14.4	0.5	0.7	84.1	11,712	444	537	68,483
Boston	190,061	4.5	4.0	2.6	88.6	8,499	7,639	5,004	168,348
Buffalo	54,210	7.3	0.9	1.2	90.0	3,959	469	673	48,801
Charleston	61,911	24.2	0.8	0.9	73.6	14,964	500	551	45,575
Charlotte	150,968	12.5	1.5	1.8	83.7	18,904	2,277	2,671	126,286
Chicago-Gary	591,623	11.0	4.0	11.0	73.5	65,143	23,651	64,932	434,833
Cincinnati	139,153	6.2	1.0	0.4	92.1	8,616	1,329	603	128,202
Cleveland-Akron	191,951	10.1	1.2	1.7	86.6	19,446	2,318	3,342	166,182
Colorado Springs	59,729	4.7	2.0	6.1	86.3	2,803	1,189	3,653	51,545
Columbia SC	53,719	25.3	0.7	0.9	72.7	13,594	389	485	39,028
Columbus	130,182	7.8	1.7	0.7	89.5	10,193	2,230	847	116,482
Dallas	296,059	8.3	3.5	10.0	77.6	24,689	10,261	29,649	229,717
Dayton	71,522	8.0	1.1	0.5	90.2	5,696	761	348	64,533

(continued)

Appendix 4.1 (continued)

Metropolitan statistical areas	Number of applicants in 92–94 to 96–98	Percent of all loan applicants who were:				Number of all loan applicants who were:			
		Black	Asian American	Latino/ Chicano	White	Black	Asian American	Latino/ Chicano	White
Denver	236,085	3.5	2.4	9.5	83.8	8,337	5,731	22,521	197,730
Des Moines	39,507	1.7	1.6	1.6	94.7	674	641	640	37,428
Detroit	362,855	10.0	1.8	1.0	86.7	36,298	6,583	3,769	314,694
Fort Collins	26,453	0.4	1.1	4.9	93.0	118	288	1,306	24,604
Fresno	43,537	3.2	5.3	30.8	60.0	1,398	2,299	13,425	26,116
Grand Rapids	87,823	3.4	1.3	3.7	91.2	2,953	1,185	3,265	80,069
Greensboro NC	119,251	14.1	1.0	2.2	82.3	16,867	1,141	2,663	98,113
Greenville NC	92,816	12.9	0.8	1.0	85.0	11,978	746	958	78,876
Harrisburg	39,054	4.1	1.3	1.2	93.2	1,591	509	463	36,392
Hartford	62,070	7.1	1.7	4.5	86.4	4,384	1,059	2,765	53,631
Honolulu	34,681	1.0	68.1	1.5	28.7	361	23,629	527	9,957
Houston	312,252	9.6	4.8	16.3	68.8	29,866	14,911	50,945	214,683
Indianapolis	137,960	6.9	1.0	0.9	90.8	9,552	1,418	1,237	125,313
Jackson	35,950	26.8	0.6	0.4	72.1	9,621	200	157	25,915
Jacksonville	103,491	11.0	1.5	2.5	84.5	11,418	1,585	2,562	87,440
Kansas City	138,206	6.4	1.4	2.0	89.7	8,884	1,921	2,749	123,945
Knoxville	90,293	27.4	1.1	0.7	70.2	24,710	998	649	63,382
LA-OC-Riv-SB	945,988	5.7	11.4	25.7	56.6	54,154	107,972	243,260	535,582
Las Vegas	160,100	5.2	5.3	10.4	78.4	8,328	8,450	16,709	125,470
Little Rock	54,168	11.6	0.6	0.8	86.6	6,309	341	408	46,888
Louisville	87,773	6.3	0.8	0.6	92.1	5,488	662	508	80,861
Memphis	63,345	2.7	0.5	0.5	95.9	1,708	330	314	60,763
Miami	148,774	10.8	1.4	62.5	24.9	16,055	2,018	93,056	37,101
Milwaukee	94,312	8.2	1.6	3.2	86.7	7,723	1,526	2,973	81,784
Minneapolis	248,625	2.8	2.7	1.2	93.0	6,838	6,697	2,941	231,124
Mobile AL	50,071	12.9	0.7	0.7	85.2	6,465	354	338	42,639

(continued)

Appendix 4.1 (continued)

Metropolitan statistical areas:	Number of applicants in '92–'94- to 96–'98	Percent of all loan applicants who were:				Number of all loan applicants who were:			
		Black	Asian American	Latino/ Chicano	White	Black	Asian American	Latino/ Chicano	White
Nashville	116,665	7.7	1.2	1.1	89.6	9,001	1,444	1,300	104,523
New Haven	29,024	9.2	2.0	5.0	83.5	2,677	570	1,445	24,236
New Orleans	78,072	22.8	1.6	2.7	72.5	17,811	1,269	2,126	56,578
Norfolk–VA Beach	114,546	19.8	2.0	1.7	76.2	22,634	2,255	1,931	87,249
NYC-Newark	333,340	16.7	8.8	9.1	65.1	55,616	29,176	30,192	216,912
Oklahoma City	85,809	5.0	2.1	3.0	88.1	4,333	1,818	2,547	75,587
Omaha	52,553	4.0	2.1	3.1	90.1	2,085	1,100	1,651	47,372
Orlando	144,345	7.7	2.5	14.7	74.7	11,076	3,593	21,206	107,870
Philadelphia	118,988	4.4	0.9	0.4	94.1	5,289	1,027	444	111,921
Phoenix	337,202	2.2	2.0	11.2	83.4	7,397	6,643	37,884	281,379
Pittsburgh	219,352	12.5	2.7	3.5	81.0	27,354	5,903	7,742	177,600
Portland	169,933	1.4	4.5	2.6	90.8	2,423	7,724	4,376	154,367
Providence	52,360	2.9	1.5	4.1	91.1	1,499	797	2,156	47,717
Raleigh-Durham	124,574	18.0	2.1	2.3	77.2	22,412	2,613	2,890	96,114
Richmond	75,842	20.1	1.5	1.0	76.9	15,210	1,167	794	58,349
Rochester	59,224	5.6	1.2	2.1	90.7	3,336	719	1,238	53,713
Sacramento	115,191	4.9	7.7	8.2	78.5	5,611	8,918	9,417	90,431
Salt Lake City	118,213	0.7	2.5	5.7	90.6	770	2,991	6,789	107,143
San Antonio	124,436	5.5	1.4	35.1	57.4	6,885	1,718	43,698	71,479
San Diego	249,941	12.5	5.3	8.4	73.3	31,359	13,237	21,020	183,105
Scranton	29,046	0.8	0.5	0.8	97.6	244	155	226	28,348
Seattle	210,840	2.4	8.4	2.1	86.4	5,115	17,752	4,340	182,212
SF-Oak-SJ	387,988	4.5	22.0	9.7	63.2	17,453	85,342	37,578	245,384
Spokane	33,773	0.8	1.4	1.4	95.7	261	471	458	32,309

(continued)

Appendix 4.1 (continued)

Metropolitan statistical areas	Number of applicants in 92–94 to 96–98	Percent of all loan applicants who were:				Number of all loan applicants who were:			
		Black	Asian American	Latino/ Chicano	White	Black	Asian American	Latino/ Chicano	White
Springfield MA	27,286	4.6	1.6	5.8	87.7	1,257	439	1,590	23,929
St. Louis	217,180	10.4	1.1	0.8	87.3	22,650	2,486	1,629	189,503
Stockton CA	31,047	5.8	9.4	20.1	63.9	1,805	2,923	6,235	19,854
Syracuse	41,920	2.9	1.0	0.8	94.8	1,197	435	330	39,725
Tampa	207,924	5.2	1.6	6.4	86.4	10,847	3,233	13,320	179,653
Toledo	44,524	6.2	0.9	2.3	90.2	2,769	406	1,025	40,176
Tucson	76,231	2.0	1.6	18.1	77.1	1,554	1,225	13,760	58,766
Tulsa	65,097	3.8	1.2	1.9	89.8	2,462	763	1,239	58,489
Washington DC	331,205	18.5	5.6	4.7	70.7	61,383	18,645	15,636	234,062
Wichita	46,445	3.8	1.1	2.6	92.2	1,783	496	1,199	42,813
Worcester	27,554	1.4	2.6	2.6	92.9	395	728	716	25,587
W. Palm Beach FL	107,538	6.7	1.3	8.3	83.3	7,223	1,416	8,928	89,589
Youngstown	35,231	6.2	0.4	1.0	92.2	2,187	132	355	32,484
TOTALS	11,462,977					1,024,169	499,726	968,213	8,909,805

Source: Home Mortgage Disclosure Act from the Federal Financial Institutions Examination Council for 1992, 1994, 1996, and 1998.

Appendix 4.2

Ethnicity of Residents in the 84 Metropolitan Areas Included in This Study

Metropolitan statistical areas	Population (1990 census)	Percent of 1990 residents who were:				Population (2000 census)	Percent of 2000 residents who were:			
		Black	Asian American	Latino/ Chicano	White		Black	Asian American	Latino/ Chicano	White
Albany	861,424	4.7	1.3	1.8	93.2	875,583	6.4	2.2	2.7	88.1
Albuquerque	585,576	2.7	1.5	36.9	77.1	712,738	2.6	2.3	41.6	47.7
Allentown	595,081	2.0	1.1	4.1	94.6	637,958	3.0	1.9	7.9	86.6
Atlanta	2,959,950	26.0	1.8	1.9	71.3	4,112,198	29.2	3.8	6.5	59.8
Austin	846,227	9.2	2.3	20.2	76.9	1,249,763	8.1	3.4	26.2	60.7
Bakersfield	543,477	5.5	3.0	27.7	69.8	661,645	6.1	42.3	38.4	49.5
Baltimore	2,382,177	25.8	1.8	1.2	71.8	2,552,994	27.8	3.2	2.0	66.5
Baton Rouge	528,264	29.6	1.0	1.4	68.9	602,894	32.1	1.7	1.8	63.9
Birmingham	840,140	27.0	0.5	0.4	72.2	921,106	30.2	1.0	1.8	66.4
Boston	3,226,935	5.7	2.9	4.5	89.0	3,406,829	7.2	5.5	5.9	80.0
Buffalo	1,189,288	10.2	0.9	2.0	87.2	1,170,111	12.0	1.5	2.9	82.5
Charleston	506,875	30.2	1.2	1.4	67.9	549,033	31.0	1.7	2.4	64.0
Charlotte	1,499,293	19.9	0.9	0.8	78.5	1,162,093	20.7	2.2	5.1	71.2
Chicago-Gary	7,410,858	19.1	3.2	10.8	71.6	8,272,768	19.0	52.0	17.1	58.0
Cincinnati	1,526,092	11.6	0.8	0.5	87.3	1,646,395	13.3	1.4	1.1	83.5
Cleveland-Akron	2,202,069	16.0	1.0	1.9	82.0	2,250,871	18.9	1.7	3.3	75.4
Colorado Springs	397,014	7.1	2.4	8.4	86.2	536,929	7.1	3.7	11.3	76.2
Columbia SC	453,163	30.4	1.0	1.3	67.9	536,691	32.2	1.8	2.4	62.9
Columbus	1,345,454	11.9	1.5	0.7	86.0	1,540,157	14.1	2.8	1.8	80.4
Dallas	2,676,248	14.3	2.5	13.0	75.3	3,519,176	15.2	4.6	23.0	56.2
Dayton	951,266	13.3	0.9	0.7	85.3	950,558	14.8	1.6	1.2	81.6
Denver	1,622,980	5.2	2.3	12.1	86.7	2,109,282	5.8	3.7	18.8	70.4

(continued)

Appendix 4.2 *(continued)*

Metropolitan statistical areas	Population (1990 census)	Percent of 1990 residents who were:				Population (2000 census)	Percent of 2000 residents who were:			
		Black	Asian American	Latino/ Chicano	White		Black	Asian American	Latino/ Chicano	White
Des Moines	392,928	3.7	1.5	1.8	93.9	456,022	4.4	2.7	4.2	88.0
Detroit	4,266,654	20.9	1.5	1.8	76.5	4,441,551	23.3	2.8	2.9	69.7
Fort Collins	186,136	0.6	1.5	6.4	94.7	251,494	0.8	2.1	8.3	87.5
Fresno	755,580	4.9	8.6	34.7	63.5	922,516	5.2	8.4	44.0	40.6
Grand Rapids	937,891	5.9	1.1	3.1	90.8	1,088,514	7.7	1.9	6.3	83.0
Greensboro NC	1,050,304	19.3	0.7	0.6	79.5	1,251,509	20.3	1.6	5.0	72.3
Greenville NC	830,563	17.4	0.7	0.8	81.6	962,441	17.7	1.4	2.7	77.7
Harrisburg	587,986	6.7	1.0	1.6	91.4	629,401	8.2	1.8	3.1	86.4
Hartford	1,156,841	8.7	1.4	6.7	86.1	1,183,110	9.6	2.7	9.6	77.4
Honolulu	836,231	3.1	63.1	6.5	31.7	876,156	2.7	70.7	6.7	20.0
Houston	3,322,025	17.9	3.5	20.5	67.6	4,177,646	17.5	5.9	29.9	46.1
Indianapolis	1,380,491	13.7	0.8	0.9	85.0	1,607,486	14.3	1.5	2.7	80.8
Jackson	395,396	42.5	0.5	0.5	56.9	440,801	45.7	0.9	1.0	52.2
Jacksonville	906,727	20.0	1.6	2.4	77.4	1,100,491	21.8	2.9	3.8	70.4
Kansas City	1,582,841	12.8	1.0	2.9	84.4	1,776,062	13.2	2.0	5.2	78.3
Knoxville	585,960	5.9	0.7	0.6	92.9	687,249	6.0	1.2	1.3	76.1
LA-OC-Riv-SB	8,854,200	8.4	9.2	32.4	64.7	9,519,338	9.9	13.5	44.6	31.1
Las Vegas	851,721	9.5	3.5	10.9	81.3	1,563,282	8.4	6.2	20.6	63.1
Little Rock	513,117	19.9	0.6	0.9	78.9	583,845	22.1	1.3	2.1	73.5
Louisville	948,829	13.1	0.6	0.5	85.9	1,025,598	14.3	1.3	1.5	82.0
Memphis	1,007,306	40.7	0.8	0.7	58.1	1,135,614	43.5	1.7	2.4	51.8
Miami	1,937,094	18.5	1.3	33.1	76.5	2,253,362	19.8	1.9	57.3	20.7
Milwaukee	1,432,149	13.3	1.2	3.5	83.2	1,500,741	16.0	2.5	6.3	7.7
Minneapolis	2,538,089	3.6	2.6	1.4	92.2	2,968,806	6.0	4.8	3.3	84.7
Mobile AL	476,923	27.3	0.7	0.9	71.1	540,258	27.5	1.4	1.4	68.6
Nashville	985,026	12.1	1.5	5.8	83.4	1,231,131	15.9	2.0	3.3	78.0

(continued)

Appendix 4.2 (continued)

Metropolitan statistical areas	Population (1990 census)	Percent of 1990 residents who were:				Population (2000 census)	Percent of 2000 residents who were:			
		Black	Asian American	Latino/ Chicano	White		Black	Asian American	Latino/ Chicano	White
New Haven	530,188	34.8	1.7	4.2	62.2	542,149	13.3	3.1	9.8	73.0
New Orleans	1,285,270	28.5	2.5	2.2	67.9	1,337,726	37.6	2.5	4.4	54.7
Norfolk–VA Beach	1,443,244	18.2	4.8	15.0	70.3	1,569,541	31.3	3.5	3.1	61.1
NYC-Newark	10,456,611	10.5	1.8	3.4	81.3	11,347,224	23.4	9.2	23.0	43.0
Oklahoma City	958,839	8.3	1.1	2.5	89.1	1,083,346	1.1	3.1	6.7	72.9
Omaha	639,580	12.4	1.9	8.8	82.8	716,998	8.8	19.6	5.5	82.8
Orlando	1,224,852	18.6	2.1	3.6	77.0	1,644,561	14.0	3.4	16.5	62.1
Philadelphia	4,917,570	3.5	1.7	16.0	84.9	5,100,931	20.3	3.8	5.1	70.2
Phoenix	2,238,480	8.0	0.7	0.5	91.1	3,251,876	3.9	2.7	25.1	65.8
Pittsburgh	2,394,811	2.8	3.4	3.3	91.5	2,358,695	8.5	1.3	0.7	89.1
Portland	1,515,452	3.2	1.7	4.0	92.6	1,918,009	3.1	5.8	7.4	81.6
Providence	1,134,350	24.9	1.9	1.1	72.5	1,188,613	4.3	2.7	7.9	83.4
Raleigh-Durham	855,545	29.2	1.4	1.0	68.8	1,187,941	23.0	3.3	6.1	66.8
Richmond	865,640	9.3	1.3	2.9	87.6	996,512	30.4	2.4	2.3	64.0
Rochester	1,062,470	6.8	7.8	11.4	79.1	1,098,201	10.5	2.2	4.3	82.2
Sacramento	1,340,010	0.9	2.4	5.7	93.4	1,628,197	8.2	11.0	14.4	64.3
Salt Lake City	1,072,227	6.8	1.2	47.4	75.2	1,333,914	1.3	2.9	10.8	82.8
San Antonio	1,324,749	6.3	8.0	20.0	75.1	1,592,383	0.7	2.1	51.2	39.4
San Diego	2,498,016	1.0	0.5	0.8	98.2	2,813,833	6.0	10.8	26.7	55.0
Scranton	638,466	4.8	6.4	2.8	86.5	624,776	1.6	0.8	1.2	96.2
Seattle	2,033,156	8.6	14.8	15.1	69.4	2,414,616	5.0	11.3	5.2	76.3
SF-Oak-SJ	3,686,592	1.4	1.8	1.6	94.8	4,123,740	10.0	21.7	17.8	49.1
Spokane	361,364	6.6	1.0	8.7	86.6	417,939	2.1	2.7	2.8	89.8
Springfield MA	264,346	17.3	0.9	1.0	81.3	325,721	2.1	1.2	1.7	93.5
St. Louis	2,492,525	5.6	12.4	22.7	73.5	2,603,607	18.7	1.8	1.5	77.4
Stockton CA	480,628	5.9	1.1	1.2	91.9	563,598	6.9	14.0	30.5	47.4

(continued)

Appendix 4.2 (continued)

Metropolitan statistical areas	Population (1990 census)	Percent of 1990 residents who were:				Population (2000 census)	Percent of 2000 residents who were:			
		Black	Asian American	Latino/ Chicano	White		Black	Asian American	Latino/ Chicano	White
Syracuse	742,177	8.9	1.1	6.6	88.4	732,117	6.9	1.8	2.1	88.0
Tampa	2,067,959	11.3	1.0	3.0	85.9	2,395,997	10.3	2.3	10.4	76.0
Toledo	614,128	3.1	1.8	24.2	78.9	618,203	13.3	1.4	4.4	80.1
Tucson	666,880	8.1	0.9	2.0	83.4	843,746	3.2	2.7	29.3	61.5
Tulsa	708,954	26.6	5.1	5.6	65.8	803,235	9.4	1.6	4.8	73.9
Washington DC	4,223,404	7.5	1.8	3.8	87.5	4,923,153	26.5	7.7	8.8	56.1
Wichita	485,270	2.2	1.7	4.4	93.5	545,220	8.4	3.4	7.4	79.0
Worcester	482,951	12.4	1.1	7.5	84.9	511,389	3.1	3.3	7.1	85.5
W. Palm Beach FL	863,518	11.1	0.4	1.4	87.7	1,131,184	14.4	1.9	1.2	70.6
Youngstown	600,895	12.4	1.1	7.5	84.9	594,746	10.6	0.6	1.8	86.4
TOTALS	132,702,776					151,015,833				

Source: U.S. Census Bureau, 1990 and 2000.

Appendix 4.3

Selected Highlights Based on Dissimilarity Index Calculations for 1990 and 2000

	Top 10				Top 10			
	Greatest Segregation - 1990				Greatest Segregation - 2000			
	Households		Homeowners		Households		Homeowners	
MSA	MSA	White-Asian	MSA	White-Asian	MSA	White-Asian	MSA	White-Asian
	Detroit	0.850	Syracuse	1	Detroit	0.826	Detroit	0.858
	Chicago-Gary	0.830	Birmingham	1	Milwaukee	0.802	Milwaukee	0.825
	Milwaukee	0.809	Memphis	1	Chicago-Gary	0.800	Chicago-Gary	0.824
	Buffalo	0.800	Des Moines	1	NYC-Newark	0.783	Buffalo	0.807
	Cleveland-Akron	0.800	Knoxville	1	Buffalo	0.781	Cleveland-Akron	0.792
	NYC-Newark	0.797	Springfield MA	1	Cleveland-Akron	0.757	Toledo	0.775
	W. Palm Beach FL	0.775	Greenville SC	1	Cincinnati	0.732	Dayton	0.775
	St. Louis	0.764	Pittsburgh	0.996	St. Louis	0.728	St. Louis	0.772
	Syracuse	0.761	Portland	0.993	Youngstown	0.722	NYC-Newark	0.761
	Harrisburg	0.760	Little Rock	0.991	Harrisburg	0.715	Youngstown	0.755
MSA	MSA	White-Asian	MSA	White-Asian	MSA	White-Asian	MSA	White-Asian
	Birmingham	0.640	Mobile AL	1	Pittsburgh	0.556	Hartford	0.643
	Mobile AL	0.639	Knoxville	1	Syracuse	0.541	New Haven	0.555
	Scranton	0.634	Greenville SC	1	Detroit	0.525	Buffalo	0.521
	Pittsburgh	0.624	Buffalo	1	Buffalo	0.520	Houston	0.512

(continued)

Appendix 4.3 *(continued)*

Top 10 Greatest Segregation - 1990

Households	White-Latino	Homeowners	White-Latino
Baton Rouge	0.610	Syracuse	1
Knoxville	0.602	Columbus	1
Youngstown	0.591	Des Moines	1
Greenville SC	0.580	Springfield MA	1
Buffalo	0.580	Columbia SC	1
Syracuse	0.553	Raleigh-Durham	1

MSA	White-Latino	MSA	White-Latino
NYC-Newark	0.646	Toledo	1
Hartford	0.640	Harrisburg	0.660
Miami	0.635	Birmingham	0.640
Philadelphia	0.603	Cleveland-Akron	0.610
Chicago-Gary	0.590	Chicago-Gary	0.600
Cleveland-Akron	0.580	Cincinnati	0.600
Allentown	0.570	Buffalo	0.580
Buffalo	0.570	Columbus	0.560
Rochester	0.566	Greensboro NC	0.560
New Haven	0.564	Dayton	0.550

Top 10 Greatest Segregation - 2000

Households	White-Latino	Homeowners	White-Latino
Mobile AL	0.514	Nashville	0.504
Baton Rouge	0.511	New Orleans	0.504
NYC-Newark	0.494	Baton Rouge	0.501
Birmingham	0.493	Youngstown	0.500
New Orleans	0.490	Detroit	0.499
Houston	0.488	Sacramento	0.487

MSA	White-Latino	MSA	White-Latino
Providence	0.683	Providence	0.592
Hartford	0.645	Philadelphia	0.556
NYC-Newark	0.638	Springfield MA	0.545
Springfield MA	0.633	Cleveland-Akron	0.526
New Haven	0.627	Allentown	0.507
Allentown	0.620	Chicago-Gary	0.501
Worcester	0.601	NYC-Newark	0.479
Boston	0.601	Milwaukee	0.473
Miami	0.598	Boston	0.470
Philadelphia	0.581	Worcester	0.462

(continued)

Appendix 4.3 *(continued)*

Bottom 10 — Least Segregation - 1990

White-Black

Households		Homeowners	
MSA	White-Black	MSA	White-Black
Albuquerque	0.440	San Diego	0.304
Colorado Springs	0.440	Miami	0.659
Tucson	0.447	Orlando	0.666
Spokane	0.458	NYC–Newark	0.762
Las Vegas	0.467	Albuquerque	0.770
Raleigh-Durham	0.475	Tampa	0.781
Charleston	0.480	Scranton	0.797
Honolulu	0.482	W. Palm Beach FL	0.818
Phoenix	0.487	Norfolk–VA Beach	0.824
Greenville SC	0.490	Charleston	0.830

White-Asian

Households		Homeowners	
MSA	White-Asian	MSA	White-Asian
Las Vegas	0.262	Sacramento	0.307
Orlando	0.310	Honolulu	0.494
Albuquerque	0.320	Stockton CA	0.648
Washington DC	0.329	SF–Oak–SJ	0.655
Denver	0.330	San Diego	0.682
Salt Lake City	0.338	LA–OC–Riv–SB	0.733
Colorado Springs	0.340	Norfolk–VA Beach	0.746
Tucson	0.342	Bakersfield	0.780
Spokane	0.351	Fresno	0.790
Portland	0.352	Jacksonville	0.791

Bottom 10 — Least Segregation - 2000

White-Black

Households		Homeowners	
MSA	White-Black	MSA	White-Black
Washington DC	0.299	Washington DC	0.299
Fort Collins	0.308	Fort Collins	0.308
Albuquerque	0.316	Albuquerque	0.316
Spokane	0.343	Spokane	0.343
Salt Lake City	0.382	Salt Lake City	0.382
Tucson	0.422	Las Vegas	0.409
Colorado Springs	0.414	Phoenix	0.411
Las Vegas	0.409	Colorado Springs	0.414
Honolulu	0.452	Tucson	0.422
Phoenix	0.411	Charleston	0.433

White-Asian

Households		Homeowners	
MSA	White-Asian	MSA	White-Asian
Spokane	0.238	Spokane	0.234
Washington DC	0.257	Tucson	0.264
Colorado Springs	0.264	Washington DC	0.268
Albuquerque	0.278	Fresno	0.271
Tucson	0.285	Salt Lake City	0.273
Salt Lake City	0.286	Colorado Springs	0.284
Las Vegas	0.305	Albuquerque	0.300
Denver	0.309	Denver	0.301
W. Palm Beach FL	0.311	Fort Collins	0.310
Phoenix	0.315	Phoenix	0.313

(continued)

Appendix 4.3 *(continued)*

Bottom 10 — Least Segregation - 1990

Households		Homeowners	
MSA	White-Latino	MSA	White-Latino
Las Vegas	0.241	Miami	0.069
Fort Collins	0.250	San Antonio	0.074
Kansas City	0.260	Orlando	0.113
Jacksonville	0.260	Tampa	0.118
Seattle	0.267	Stockton CA	0.130
Orlando	0.270	W. Palm Beach FL	0.146
Portland	0.280	Houston	0.154
Colorado Springs	0.290	LA-OC-Riv-SB	0.175
New Orleans	0.307	Tucson	0.182
Spokane	0.319	New Orleans	0.185

Bottom 10 — Least Segregation - 2000

Households		Homeowners	
MSA	White-Latino	MSA	White-Latino
Spokane	0.182	Spokane	0.143
Fort Collins	0.207	Knoxville	0.188
Knoxville	0.247	Seattle	0.190
Mobile AL	0.249	Raleigh-Durham	0.217
Jacksonville	0.264	St. Louis	0.223
Dayton	0.264	Charleston	0.227
St. Louis	0.270	Fort Collins	0.230
Seattle	0.271	Little Rock	0.230
Washington DC	0.289	Washington DC	0.232
Cincinnati	0.290	Louisville	0.243

Appendix 4.4

Changes to Dissimilarity Indexes, 1990–2000

Top 10 Greatest Increase in Segregation - 1990–2000

Households		Homeowners	
MSA	White-Black	MSA	White-Black
Kansas City	0.103	San Diego	0.272
Springfield MA	0.072	Miami	0.016
Providence	0.035	NYC-Newark	-0.001
New Haven	0.028	Chicago-Gary	-0.106
Worcester	0.019	Philadelphia	-0.110
Baton Rouge	0.009	Cleveland-Akron	-0.118
Albany	0.006	Orlando	-0.121
Rochester	0.003	Tampa	-0.121
Sacramento	0.002	Detroit	-0.132
New Orleans	0	Milwaukee	-0.139
MSA	White-Asian	MSA	White-Asian
Worcester	0.062	Sacramento	0.180
Orlando	0.050	Honolulu	-0.143
Las Vegas	0.043	SF-Oak-SJ	-0.191
LA-OC-Riv-SB	0.029	San Diego	-0.217
Grand Rapids	0.029	Stockton CA	-0.240

Top 10 Greatest Decrease in Segregation - 1990–2000

Households		Homeowners	
MSA	White-Black	MSA	White-Black
Washington DC	-0.368	Fort Collins	-0.662
Fort Collins	-0.224	Washington DC	-0.578
Portland	-0.132	Salt Lake City	-0.576
Albuquerque	-0.131	Raleigh-Durham	-0.535
Salt Lake City	-0.123	Greensboro NC	-0.524
W. Palm Beach FL	-0.118	Phoenix	-0.522
Spokane	-0.113	Las Vegas	-0.514
Scranton	-0.112	Colorado Springs	-0.506
Des Moines	-0.093	Tucson	-0.495
Stockton CA	-0.079	Worcester	-0.483
MSA	White-Asian	MSA	White-Asian
Scranton	-0.209	Spokane	-0.766
Birmingham	-0.147	Salt Lake City	-0.700
New Haven	-0.140	Springfield MA	-0.654
W. Palm Beach FL	-0.132	Omaha	-0.643
Mobile AL	-0.125	Washington DC	-0.642

(continued)

Appendix 4.4 *(continued)*

	Top 10 — Greatest Increase in Segregation - 1990–2000			Top 10 — Greatest Decrease in Segregation - 1990–2000		
	Households	Homeowners		Households	Homeowners	
Raleigh-Durham	0.028	LA-OC-Riv-SB	−0.287	Knoxville	−0.123	Phoenix	−0.640

Restructured:

Top 10 — Greatest Increase in Segregation - 1990–2000

Households		Homeowners	White-Latino
Raleigh-Durham	0.028	LA-OC-Riv-SB	−0.287
SF-Oak-SJ	0.022	Norfolk–VA Beach	−0.336
Austin	0.012	Bakersfield	−0.343
Sacramento	0.011	Hartford	−0.347
Atlanta	0.010	New Orleans	−0.373

MSA	White-Latino	MSA	White-Latino
Springfield MA	0.272	Tampa	0.310
Kansas City	0.170	Miami	0.308
Las Vegas	0.140	Providence	0.296
Providence	0.134	Springfield MA	0.280
Orlando	0.120	Orlando	0.266
Atlanta	0.098	Houston	0.255
New Haven	0.063	San Antonio	0.254
Houston	0.058	Tucson	0.250
Tulsa	0.058	LA-OC-Riv-SB	0.247
Portland	0.057	Phoenix	0.236

Top 10 — Greatest Decrease in Segregation - 1990–2000

Households	White-Latino	Homeowners	White-Latino
Knoxville	−0.123	Phoenix	−0.640
Youngstown	−0.122	Colorado Springs	−0.626
Des Moines	−0.119	Des Moines	−0.617
Spokane	−0.113	Columbia SC	−0.617
Jackson	−0.106	Memphis	−0.617

MSA	White-Latino	MSA	White-Latino
Knoxville	−0.227	Toledo	−0.675
Pittsburgh	−0.206	Cincinnati	−0.354
Dayton	−0.186	Birmingham	−0.343
Cincinnati	−0.170	Greensboro NC	−0.313
Scranton	−0.142	Columbus	−0.300
Spokane	−0.137	Dayton	−0.288
Mobile AL	−0.108	Harrisburg	−0.228
Columbia SC	−0.106	Albany	−0.199
Washington DC	−0.096	Charlotte	−0.186
Louisville	−0.096	Greenville SC	−0.184

(continued)

Appendix 4.4 *(continued)*

Bottom 10

Least Segregation - 1990

Households		Homeowners	
MSA	White-Black	MSA	White-Black
Albuquerque	0.440	San Diego	0.304
Colorado Springs	0.440	Miami	0.659
Tucson	0.447	Orlando	0.666
Spokane	0.458	NYC-Newark	0.762
Las Vegas	0.467	Albuquerque	0.770
Raleigh-Durham	0.475	Tampa	0.781
Charleston	0.480	Scranton	0.797
Honolulu	0.482	W. Palm Beach FL	0.818
Phoenix	0.487	Norfolk–VA Beach	0.824
Greenville SC	0.490	Charleston	0.830

Households		Homeowners	
MSA	White-Asian	MSA	White-Asian
Las Vegas	0.262	Sacramento	0.307
Orlando	0.310	Honolulu	0.494
Albuquerque	0.320	Stockton CA	0.648
Washington DC	0.329	SF-Oak-SJ	0.655
Denver	0.330	San Diego	0.682
Salt Lake City	0.338	LA-OC-Riv-SB	0.733

Bottom 10

Least Segregation - 2000

Households		Homeowners	
MSA	White-Black	MSA	White-Black
Washington DC	0.299	Washington DC	0.299
Fort Collins	0.308	Fort Collins	0.308
Albuquerque	0.316	Albuquerque	0.316
Spokane	0.343	Spokane	0.343
Salt Lake City	0.382	Salt Lake City	0.382
Tucson	0.422	Las Vegas	0.409
Colorado Springs	0.414	Phoenix	0.411
Las Vegas	0.409	Colorado Springs	0.414
Honolulu	0.452	Tucson	0.422
Phoenix	0.411	Charleston	0.433

Households		Homeowners	
MSA	White-Asian	MSA	White-Asian
Spokane	0.238	Spokane	0.234
Washington DC	0.257	Tucson	0.264
Colorado Springs	0.264	Washington DC	0.268
Albuquerque	0.278	Fresno	0.271
Tucson	0.285	Salt Lake City	0.273
Salt Lake City	0.286	Colorado Springs	0.284

(continued)

Appendix 4.4 (continued)

Bottom 10

Least Segregation - 1990

Households	White-Latino	Homeowners	White-Latino
Colorado Springs	0.340	Norfolk–VA Beach	0.746
Tucson	0.342	Bakersfield	0.780
Spokane	0.351	Fresno	0.790
Portland	0.352	Jacksonville	0.791

MSA	White-Latino	MSA	White-Latino
Las Vegas	0.241	Miami	0.069
Fort Collins	0.250	San Antonio	0.074
Kansas City	0.260	Orlando	0.113
Jacksonville	0.260	Tampa	0.118
Seattle	0.267	Stockton CA	0.130
Orlando	0.270	W. Palm Beach FL	0.146
Portland	0.280	Houston	0.154
Colorado Springs	0.290	LA-OC-Riv-SB	0.175
New Orleans	0.307	Tucson	0.182
Spokane	0.319	New Orleans	0.185

Bottom 10

Least Segregation - 2000

Households	White-Latino	Homeowners	White-Latino
Las Vegas	0.305	Albuquerque	0.300
Denver	0.309	Denver	0.301
W. Palm Beach FL	0.311	Fort Collins	0.310
Phoenix	0.315	Phoenix	0.313

MSA	White-Latino	MSA	White-Latino
Spokane	0.182	Spokane	0.143
Fort Collins	0.207	Knoxville	0.188
Knoxville	0.247	Seattle	0.190
Mobile AL	0.249	Raleigh-Durham	0.217
Jacksonville	0.264	St. Louis	0.223
Dayton	0.264	Charleston	0.227
St. Louis	0.270	Fort Collins	0.230
Seattle	0.271	Little Rock	0.230
Washington DC	0.289	Washington DC	0.232
Cincinnati	0.290	Louisville	0.243

5

Robert H. Scott, III

An Analysis of
Credit Card Debt Default

Introduction

It is becoming a common belief among some heterodox economists that empirical quantitative analysis is not valid or useful (Lawson 2003, Goertzel 2002). In addition, many heterodox economists believe that trying to quantify a complex dynamic system is impossible. However, other heterodox economists see econometrics as a tool that is used at the discretion of researchers; for these individuals it is the interpretation, not the method, that matters most (Downward and Mearman 2000). Good assumptions and a good theory lead to useful results; bad assumptions, on the other hand, lead to worthless results.

Bad assumptions made by econometricians revolve around the belief that we live in a closed system—the equilibrium assumption—meaning we can analyze the economy the same way a chemist studies reactions in a laboratory. When economists accept the idea that we live in a world that is nonergodic, complex, and open, many of the arguments against using econometrics as an interpretive tool will disappear.

Regardless of how beautiful a mathematician's techniques, if they are handicapped by bad data and/or poor theory the results are never good. It is important for researchers to step away from the mathematics involved in econometrics and evaluate an econometric result by looking at three important elements: (1) how good is the data and where did the data come from (the best data is obtained when a researcher independently gathers the data), (2) what is the object of study and can econometrics produce insight (sometimes econometrics is useful, and sometimes it detracts from the research objective), and (3) is the interpretation meaningful and accurate. The ideal research project will involve a mixture of both quantitative and qualitative techniques, but if the quantitative elements were removed, the qualitative parts are still grounded. Too much empirical research relies on *a priori* and ad hoc assumptions. Furthermore, if the quantitative elements were removed from many mainstream economics articles, there would be little, if anything, left.

The following research develops an empirical model of credit card-debt default using unconventional econometric methods. The research techniques used may prove useful to other researchers wanting to perform quantitative analysis but still remain pluralistic/heterodox without appearing blindly positivistic. We begin the processes of developing a Post Keynesian theory of credit card-debt default. This research utilizes the techniques of exploratory data analysis (data mining) and cross-validation to develop a model of credit card debt default and uses a new and unique data set, the Buckeye State Poll (BSP). This data set was used to test various assumptions about credit card debt default. This paper finds that Hyman Minsky's financial-instability hypothesis (FIH) is better than mainstream economic theory at explaining credit card default, the volatility of the credit card industry, and why we should be concerned about rising consumer debt.

Credit card default is a relatively new research topic. Credit cards began to cause problems for consumers once the credit card industry became deregulated in the early 1980s. This deregulation allowed credit card companies to charge arbitrarily high rates of interest on their credit card loans. Because credit card companies were able to generate substantially higher revenue, due in part to increased interest charges, they began issuing credit cards to more people. As the number of people with credit cards increased, so did the number of risky borrowers. The credit card industry's loose underwriting practices have brought about many of the problems experienced by consumers regarding their credit cards (Ausubel 1991, 52).

The business practices of credit card companies are noted as the most significant reason for the increase in credit card default. First, companies began to mass mail credit cards to millions of households that did not need, want, or deserve one; however, many people have gotten into credit card trouble simply because they received preapproved credit cards in the mail and as credit became too available. According to some authors (Manning 2001, Brito and Hartley 1995), the more indebted the borrower became, the more credit cards they would receive in the mail. Second, companies began charging various fees—late fees, and over-limit fees—that resulted in increased corporate profits. Third, underwriting practices eventually became less strict. Fourth, many companies lowered the minimum payments required on outstanding balances, which made it increasingly difficult to pay back a loan by paying only the minimum payment. As consumers increased their dependence on credit cards, and had more credit cards and higher credit limits, many credit card borrowers began to default on their credit card debt (Stavins 2000).

Credit card default affects consumers in a number of ways. Specifically, consumers' credit reports are used for the following: (1) to determine insurance rates (and even insurability), (2) to determine levels of risk associated with most loans (home, car, etc.), and (3) by employers as a hiring criterion. Default alone has a number of negative effects on consumer psychology and general physical health (Kellison et al. 2003, Manning 2001). There is also an ongoing debate as to whether the proliferation of credit cards has led to an increase in personal bankruptcy filings. Much of the literature on this subject supports the claim that credit cards indeed have (Stavins 2000, 24–30).

Theoretical Considerations

This section outlines the methods and practices used to develop an econometric model using exploratory data analysis (EDA) and cross-validation techniques that help us to determine the significant variables associated with credit card-debt default among residents in the U.S. state of Ohio. Beginning with a set of *a priori* assumptions about the significance of particular explanatory variables, a negative binomial specification of EDA was used to create a final equation.

The model of default developed below serves as a proxy for the FIH. The FIH theory states that there are "three distinct income-debt relations for economic units, which are labeled as hedge, speculative, and Ponzi finance" (Minsky 1992, 6). A hedge financing unit is able to pay off accrued debt with its income (or wealth). A speculative financing unit is only able to pay off the interest accumulated on the debt, thus rolling over the principal to the next payment cycle. A Ponzi finance unit is one that cannot even pay off interest payments, but rather must take on new debt in order to roll over old debt. The FIH is modeled in terms of the macroeconomy, and Minsky refers to debtors as businesses. However, debtors can also be people. Following Minsky's logic, as people move from a stable scheme, such as that associated with a hedge scheme, to unstable schemes, such as speculative and Ponzi finance, the system becomes erratic and unbalanced. In Minsky's system, the correction to this disequilibrium may best be made by government. However, in a situation such as individual credit card debt, which is widely dispersed, it will require strong policy guidelines to tame the consumer credit card market (Minsky 1982, 1986, 1992).[1]

Post Keynesian theorists assert, contrary to neoclassical theorists, that consumers are not entirely rational. Rather, people tend to work from a framework of habits and instincts. Therefore, human behavior (consumption behavior especially) is mostly the product of society's influence; that is, people are imitative. Thus, issuing large amounts of credit to people who are incapable of handling the possible debt burden and who live in a consumer-driven society produces a situation in which households are likely to move quickly to Ponzi finance. In addition, consumers are not knowledgeable enough about how credit scores, banking, and such work. Therefore, it is hard for them to make informed decisions regarding the amount of credit they can handle. Unfortunately, this decision is left entirely up to the credit card companies, with no regulatory control.

Minsky mainly hypothesized about businesses' influence on the instability of the economy. But we can extend Minsky's analysis to the consumer. Debt can finance consumption, but at some point, the debt becomes a destabilizing factor in the economy. When this happens, consumers cannot meet their minimum payments and must cut back on consumption, which translates into a decrease in economic growth. Credit cards involve two entities, however, consumers and businesses. The businesses (credit card companies) produce the catalyst by which the potential for instability is created, and then consumers (by their instinctual nature) spend the over-issuance of credit that companies give them, thus completing the circuit that leads to greater economic instability. According to Dunn and Pressman (2005), John Kenneth Galbraith argued that if the technostructure of the modern economy is to be upheld, a rampant amount of consumer spending must occur. This means that consumers must keep taking on more debt and saving less (if anything at all) for the economy to continue growing. According to Dunn and Pressman, what Galbraith predicted in the 1950s is happening in the economy today, and it contributes to economic instability.

The permanent income hypothesis (PIH) developed by Milton Friedman argues that consumers want to smooth their consumption over time. Consumers maintain stable consumption by assuming a normal income; that is, they do not always believe that an increase in income will be permanent. Furthermore, people strive to maintain a stable consumption pattern so as not to create instability in their standards of living. Therefore, changes in income will not drastically change consumers' spending habits because they presuppose their incomes will fluctuate over time. The life-cycle hypothesis (LCH) developed by Franco Modigliani argues that people consume based upon how long they expect to live. Thus, consumers anticipate how long they will live and plan their consumption accordingly. In neither the PIH nor LCH is the discussion of consumer debt mentioned. A main reason for this oversight is that you cannot, on the one hand, assume that people are rational, and, on the other, state that individuals regularly take on unmanageable amounts of debt, which accrue high rates of interest (Dornbusch, Fischer, and Startz 1998, 302–5).

It is reasonable to posit that credit cards, which make up more than 10 percent of consumer debt (including mortgages), are a source of economic instability. Credit cards are not the only cause of instability in the system; however, they can serve as a signal that something is amiss in the banking sector of an economy. And as this instability worsens (i.e., as more people move from a hedge to a speculative to a Ponzi finance scheme), then the greater the imbalance in the economy. Furthermore, if the underwriting practices of credit card companies in the United States are not controlled soon, then a federal bail-out of the credit card industry may be necessary (Godley 2000; Minsky 1986, 1982, 99).

Converse to Minsky's theory, the mainstream economic literature tends to view credit card debt and default from an atomistic perspective. Mainstream theorists believe the answer to understanding the exigencies of credit card debt problems relies on focusing upon the behavior of the individual (Haliassos and Reiter 2003). For example, Gross and Souleles (2002) developed a model known as the "accountant-shopper" model in which the individual is both consumer (shopper) and bill payer (accountant), and in between the two extremes exists a rational individual. According to mainstream economists, revolving credit card debt helps tame consumers whose spending habits are out of control. Unfortunately, mainstream theory completely overlooks the influence of deregulation and the loose underwriting practices of credit card companies as the cause of consumer credit card-debt default. It seeks to resolve an institutional system failure by changing individual behavior. No policy exists that can cure excessive consumer consumption, but policies are available that could address systematic afflictions such as loose credit underwriting practices, which would mitigate consumer credit card debt.

Exploratory Data Analysis

Exploratory data analysis (EDA) and cross-validation permit the testing of numerous equations using the same data set that contain variables chosen *a priori* (through a thorough review of the literature and empirical observation). Cross-validation involves first taking a data set, selecting a random portion thereof, and using inferential statistical techniques (regression tests) to observe which variables are statistically significant. Then, using the withheld data set, one formally tests the model that was constructed using the initial data set. No behavioral theory was directly used in the construction of Equations (1) and (2), tested further below, which is a primary reason one performs EDA and cross-validation.[2] Typically when testing an econometric model, a researcher must assume an underlying behavioral theory. Most behavioral theories available to economists are neoclassical theories, which are usually undesirable. Post Keynesians hold that people are not wholly rational—rather, behavior is driven by habits and imitation. EDA allows Post Keynesians to analyze how best to control for the habitual nature of people; that is, not assuming that all people are the same.[3] Researchers thus have certain freedom, allowing their data and literature reviews to guide their choice of variables to include in their models, which is precisely the approach this research takes. Another compelling reason for using EDA and cross-validation techniques is that there are only limited theories and models available on credit card-debt default. EDA and cross-validation allow for new insight into which particular variables affect credit card-debt default. In addition, while one may admire a model or behavioral theory that another researcher has constructed, obtaining good statistics with all the necessary variables needed to test the same model/theory is often difficult. EDA and one-step backward regression almost guarantees the development of a unique model, which is important if one seeks to draw new inferences about a phenomenon.

As mentioned, the data used in this analysis is taken from the BSP data set, which, in its original form, consisted of 39,313 observations. In essence, two random data sets are constructed from one data set. A random number generator was used to scramble the BSP data set.[4] It was then necessary to split the data set in half, save each half in a separate spreadsheet, and reorganize them into their original ascending order. The data set encompassing the first half of the observations (19,656) was labeled BSPEDA, and was used to run preliminary regressions and

EDA tests, which led to Equation (2) tested with the second data set (the withheld data set). The second data set encompasses the remaining 19,657 observations, labeled BSPREG; this data set was tested using Equation (2) created through the EDA processes. The second data set was tested only once and was not studied or utilized except in the stage of testing Equation (2).[5] Cross-validation is useful because it gives the researcher a lot of liberty to try new statistical techniques without fear of engaging in unethical behavior. In other words, a researcher can use the same data set to test all the variables desired (the number of variables available is only limited by the researcher's imagination: dummy variables, interaction variables, time-dependent variables, etc.). A researcher should thoroughly test different models using all manner of variables. Eventually, through this trial-and-error process, a clear model is formed, though it is up to the researcher to decide when this process is complete. The researcher, having exhaustively analyzed the topic at hand using all available tools, can be confident that the model developed is indeed the best possible. This technique is far more powerful than the alternative; that is, taking a data set and arbitrarily hypothesizing (read: guessing) about which variables are significant, and then reporting the results—good or bad—as conclusive.

In the process of developing a model, it was necessary to select all possible variables thought to affect credit card-debt default. Finding the relevant variables involved performing an exhaustive review of the literature. Once the review of literature was complete, a list of variables thought to influence debt default was organized into a basic model. It is also important to use good sense to determine whether there are other interesting variables that should be in the first model. One-step backward regression involves taking all possibly relevant variables and putting them into a model; then, instead of the researcher having to decide beforehand which variables ought to be kept and which discarded, the researcher allows the results of the first regression test to set the benchmark about which variables to eliminate. Before the regression is run, the researcher must choose some arbitrary measure with which to determine whether a variable should be kept in the model or eliminated. In the following analysis, the p-value was used as the most appropriate measure of significance. Before the first regression test was run it was predetermined that any "stand-alone" variable with a p-value equal to or greater than 0.30 would be eliminated. A stand-alone variable is any variable not within a vector of variables. For example, GENDER, which measures whether the respondent is male or female, is a stand-alone variable; it is not dependent upon any other variable. In contrast, the vector of education variables has eight dummy variables; if one of those variables has a p-value equal to or greater than 0.30, it cannot be discarded because it depends upon all the other variables in the vector. A likelihood-ratio test is the preferred choice in testing the significance of vectors of variables.[6, 7]

There were a number of missing values associated with particular variables, mostly because these variables were not included in the original questionnaire (they were added later). Therefore, once the data was filtered (eliminating the missing values) it covered a shorter period due to the inclusion of several time-constrained variables.

The most constrained of these variables (*TOTCARD*, see below) was not included until September 1999, thus constraining the BSPEDA data set to only 3,535 observations. However, the variable *TOTCARD* was eliminated during the backward regression test and was not included in the final econometric equation, Equation (2). It was then necessary to go back to the original data set and get the legitimate variables that were eliminated due to having included *TOTCARD*. After the data set was recoded to obtain all legitimate variables, the BSPEDA data set had 5,820 observations; the final model was run again using this data set.

The EDA process includes the production and analysis of descriptive statistics. Using the BSPEDA data set, a number of descriptive statistic tests were used to construct a robust model of default. Some of these statistics are presented in a later section.

Buckeye State Poll

The Buckeye State Poll was conducted by the Survey Research Center at the Ohio State University. It covers the period beginning November 1996 and ending April 2002 (sixty-six months), and comes from a monthly random telephone survey.[8] The data set is pooled cross-section and time series data.[9] The data is respondent level, not household level (except for income) (L. Dunn, personal communication, March 12, 2004).[10] Each month of the sample consists of no fewer than ninety respondents, and for most months more than 100 respondents. The BSP only covers the state of Ohio. The project was funded by the Federal Reserve Bank of Cleveland, Ohio State University's College of Social and Behavioral Sciences, the *Columbus Dispatch*, and WBNS-TV. The estimated cost of the project was roughly $1 million.

This data set is important for a number of reasons. First, there are no other data sets available that include many of the important variables covered by the BSP, and that are necessary to develop a model for studying credit card-debt default. These variables are available in the BSP data set, but not in any other data set on consumer finances and debt. Kim (2000), in one of the most extensive studies of credit card default to date, found three variables to be important determinants of default: (1) total minimum required payment, (2) total credit card balances, and (3) number of credit cards on which the user is charged to the maximum limit. Second, the majority of research to date has relied almost entirely upon the U.S. Federal Reserve Board's Survey of Consumer Finances (SCF), a triennial survey of the balance sheet, pension, income, and other demographic characteristics of U.S. families. However, the SCF has been thoroughly mined, leaving little analysis left unperformed.

First Econometric Model

The first econometric model includes all of the variables available that are thought to determine the respondent's likelihood of defaulting on his/her credit card debt.[11] These variables were chosen because they were noted in research as potential determinants of default. Also, many of these variables were included in previous empirical studies by Stavins (2000) and Kim (2000). This model is referred to as the full model.

$$DEFAULT_i = \alpha_0 + \beta_1 TOTCARD_i + \beta_2 MAXCARDS_i + \beta_3 IR1_i + \beta_4 IR2_i + \beta_5 IRX_i$$
$$+ \beta_6 OWNRENT_i + \beta_7 KIDSNUM_i + \beta_8 INCOME_i + \beta_9 MINPAY_i$$

$$+ \beta_{10} AMNTOWD_i + \beta_{11} GENDER_i + \beta_{12} DREC_i + \beta_m \sum_{m=1}^{2} AGE_{mi} \qquad (1)$$

$$+ \beta_r \sum_{r=1}^{2} DURBCTY_{ri} + \beta_g \sum_{g=1}^{3} MARITAL_{gi} + \beta_v \sum_{v=1}^{3} DMAG_{vi}$$

$$+ \beta_f \sum_{f=1}^{6} EDUCAT_{fi} + \beta_k \sum_{k=1}^{6} WORKSELF_{ki} + \beta_w \sum_{w=1}^{11} MONTH_{wi} + \varepsilon_i.$$

Dependent Variable Specification

The dependent variable used in Equation (1) is *DEFAULT*; resulting from the follow-ing BSP survey question: "In the last 6 months, how many times did you not at least pay off the minimum amount due on any of your credit cards?" *DEFAULT* measures in the BSPEDA anywhere between 0 and 8; in other words, *DEFAULT* is a count (discrete) variable and was therefore tested using a negative binomial regression.[12] In the BSP, credit cards are defined as any type of credit card. Therefore, store credit cards, bank credit cards, gasoline credit cards, and so forth, are all considered credit cards. This distinction is important because some data sets only consider bank credit cards. Debit cards were not included because they work like a check; that is, they withdraw money from a checking account automatically; they operate like credit cards, but their internal machinations are wholly different since they do not work on credit.

Explanatory Variables Specifications

Equation (1) has twelve stand-alone variables and seven vector variables, containing a total of thirty-four variables: *TOTCARDS* is the total number of active cards the respondent has; *MAXCARDS* measures how many times the respondent has defaulted on their credit card debt in the past six months; *IR1* measures the interest rate of the respondent's primary credit card; *IR2* accounts for whether *IR1* is an introductory interest rate or not—coded as a 1 if an introductory rate, and 0 otherwise; *IRX* is an interaction variable that is the result of multiplying *IR1* and *IR2*;[13] *OWNRENT* is a dummy variable taking a value of 1 if the respondent owns a residence, and 0 other-wise; *KIDSNUM* is the number of kids under the age of eighteen the respondent has; *INCOME* is household income; *MINPAY* measures the total minimum payments that a person was required to make on all of his/her credit cards combined last month, measured in thousands of U.S. dollars; *AMNTOWD* is the amount still owed on all credit card accounts just after the respondent had paid the most recent credit card bill, measured in thousands of dollars; *GENDER* is a dummy variable, coded as 1 if the respondent is male, and 0 if female; *DREC* is a dummy variable designed to control for the possible influence that the employment recession (two or more consecutive quarters of significant job loss) had on Ohioans' default rate—measuring 1 if the month occurred during the recession (February 2001 to the end of the data set period), and 0 otherwise;[14] *AGE* is a vector containing a variable that measures *AGE* and one that takes the square of age *AGESQRD*;[15] *DURBCTY* is a vector of three dummy variables, each dummy variable accounting for different levels of population density (very urban, urban, rural);[16] the dummy variable that accounts for urban counties was eliminated as the base; *MARITAL* is a vector of four dummy variables accounting for the respondent's marital status, *MARRIED* was eliminated as the base;[17] *DMAG* is a vector of four interaction variables that multiplies all of the variables in the *MARITAL* vector with *GENDER, AGE,* and *AGESQD*; the interaction variable (*DMAG1*) that contains the *MARRIED* dummy variable was eliminated as the base; *EDUCAT* is a vector of eight dummy variables that measure the respondent's level of education, of which a high school diploma was chosen as the base;[18] *WORKSELF* is a vector of eight dummy variables each measuring the respondent's employment status,[19] on which *FTEMP* (full-time employment) and *JOBVAC* (employed but on vacation) were eliminated as the base;[20] *MONTH* is a vector of twelve dummy variables accounting for each month in the year, these variables are setup to account for seasonal fluctuations in default, and *DFEB* was eliminated as the base; and e_i is the error term.

A variable widely used by researchers (e.g., Kim 2000, Stavins 2000) studying default is the debt-to-income ratio. This is calculated by taking the aggregate of household debt divided by household income. It should be clear to many that the debt/income ratio is not the optimal way to measure a household's probability of default because it takes into account all household debt, not specifically credit card debt. According to Kim (2000), "the debt/income ratio has long-run significance as an indicator [of] a consumer's [overall] debt condition" (ibid., 4). Many researchers that study credit card default include the debt/income ratio because, to date, there has been no better measure available, mainly because the empirical data has been limited. In Equation (2) below, however, the ratio of required-credit card payment to income is more relevant than the debt/income ratio because it defines the problem more specifically; that is, targeting credit card debt rather than overall debt. Since the goal of this study is to analyze the causes of credit card default, it is preferable not to use all forms of debt as a proxy for credit card debt in general. In addition, there were too few observations available in the BSP that measure an Ohio respondent's debt level. Therefore, we do not include the debt/income variable in the model below.

Descriptive Statistics

The following descriptive statistics give an overall look at the composition of the BSPEDA data set. Because the withheld data set BSPREG was to remain untouched until the final regression test, the descriptive statistics used for the EDA had to come from the BSPEDA.

Table 5.1

Sample Breakdown of EDA Data Set

Variable	N	Percent of sample
Total sample	5,820	100
Nondefaulters	5,149	88.47
Defaulters	671	11.53

Default occurs when the respondent has missed making the minimum payment on at least one of his/her credit cards in the last six months. Looking at Table 5.1, 11.53 percent of the sample missed paying their minimum balances in the last six months, while 88.47 percent paid at least the minimum balance every month. According to Minsky's theory of market instability, almost 12 percent of this sample is comprised of individuals in a Ponzi finance scheme, meaning they are unable to pay off any of the principal on their debt and cannot make even the minimum payment. As more people move from speculative to Ponzi schemes the greater the instability of the credit card market. Considering the fact that credit card-debt default continues to steadily rise in the United States, it is reasonable to posit that the credit card market is becoming quite unstable.

The following table presents statistics on credit card users in the BSP, broken into three categories: (1) all sample, (2) nondefaulters, and (3) defaulters. In Table 5.2, several differences between credit card defaulters and nondefaulters are obvious. The difference in interest rates (*IRI*) between defaulters (15.90 percent) and nondefaulters (14.28 percent) is minimal, less than 2 percent, which goes against the mainstream theory that interest rates are to blame for high default rates. There does exist however, a gender influence—35.8 percent of defaulters were men, but 45 percent of nondefaulters were men. The difference in age between defaulters and nondefaulters is over five years (40.8 and 46.2, respectively). The average household income of nondefaulters ($59,509) is almost $7,000 higher than that of defaulters ($52,551). Looking at the employment statistics, the one variable that stands out is *RETIRED:* the average number of nondefault respondents who are retired equals 15.5 percent, but only 5.7 percent of defaulters are retired.

One-Step Backward Regression

One-Step Backward Regression (or, retrocession) is performed by taking all variables thought to have an influence on the dependent variable and putting them into one model. It is also important to choose a benchmark value; in other words, we need to set a *p*-value such that if a variable has a *p*-value equal to or greater than the predetermined benchmark value, then that variable is removed from the model. There is no general rule for what the critical *p*-value should be; however, choosing a low *p*-value will generate a smaller model, which is typically desirable. The model is then

Table 5.2

Statistics of Credit Card Users

Variable[1]	All Sample		Nondefault		Default	
	Mean	Standard deviation	Mean	Standard deviation	Mean	Standard deviation
Default	0.268	0.918	0.0	0.0	2.3279	1.5853
Maxcards	0.210	0.793	0.150	0.631	0.671	1.470
Ir1	14.463	5.491	14.276	5.446	15.897	5.627
Ownrent	0.818	0.386	0.829	0.376	0.735	0.442
Gender	0.441	0.497	0.452	0.498	0.358	0.480
Age	45.607	14.332	46.228	14.433	40.845	12.562
Income	58.707	70.413	59.509	73.531	52.551	38.395
Married	0.637	0.481	0.644	0.479	0.583	0.493
Divorced	0.112	0.315	0.110	0.313	0.125	0.331
Single	0.193	0.394	0.185	0.388	0.253	0.435
Widow	0.058	0.234	0.060	0.238	0.039	0.193
Ftemp	0.608	0.488	0.600	0.490	0.668	0.471
Ptemp	0.086	0.280	0.084	0.277	0.098	0.298
Unemployed	0.017	0.129	0.017	0.127	0.019	0.138
Retired	0.144	0.351	0.155	0.362	0.057	0.231
In school	0.016	0.124	0.016	0.125	0.013	0.115
Keep house	0.074	0.262	0.075	0.264	0.069	0.253
Wslfothr	0.041	0.199	0.039	0.194	0.055	0.228
D1ubcty	0.282	0.450	0.284	0.451	0.265	0.442
D2ubcty	0.240	0.427	0.241	0.428	0.235	0.425
D3ubcty	0.475	0.499	0.472	0.499	0.499	0.500

Source: Buckeye State Poll.
[1]See Appendix 5.1.

run using a regression model (any regression model will work: probit, logit, negative binomial). We then eliminate the insignificant stand-alone variables; that is, those nonvector variables with p-values equal to or above the benchmark. Once all insignificant variables are identified and eliminated, one can test if eliminating the insignificant variable(s) was statistically justified by running a likelihood-ratio test (see above) (Kennedy 2003, Green 2000, 880–82). One-step backward regression is known as "one step" because after eliminating all stand-alone variables with p-values equal to or above the benchmark value, the process is over; that is, it is a one-step process.

After performing a one-step backward regression and likelihood-ratio tests, the above model was simplified to the final model.[21] The backward regression method works as a filter that takes a bulky model and pares it down to a more manageable size. It is always best to have a succinct, or small, model because we want to identify essential elements and not simply include every variable available. Unfortunately, the backward regression technique tells us little about why the eliminated variables were insignificant. In some cases, such as with the employment-recession dummy variable (*DREC*) the answer is obvious: It registered a p-value of over 0.99, which indicates it is highly correlated with another explanatory variable in the model—with which one, however, is indeterminable. Therefore, *DREC* was removed.

Our final model is the product of thorough EDA. It is a much tighter model than that originally developed, and allows for an accurate assessment of the causes of credit card-debt default and of which factors most influence default.

Final Econometric Model

$$\text{DEFAULT}_i = \quad \alpha_0 + \beta_1 \text{MAXCARDS}_i + \beta_2 \text{IR1}_i + \beta_3 \text{OWNRENT}_i \tag{2}$$

$$+ \beta_4 \text{INCOME}_i + \beta_5 \text{GENDER}_i + \beta_m \sum_{m=1}^{2} \text{AGE}_{mi} + \beta_r \sum_{r=1}^{2} \text{DURBCTY}_{ri}$$

$$+ \beta_8 \sum_{g=1}^{3} \text{MARITAL}_{gi} + \beta_v \sum_{v=1}^{3} \text{DMAG}_{vi} + \beta_k \sum_{k=1}^{6} \text{WORKSELF}_{ki}$$

$$+ \beta_w \sum_{w=1}^{11} \text{MONTH}_{wi} + \varepsilon_i$$

There are several methods for interpreting the above coefficients (see Long [1997] for the complete mathematical explanation of such various methods); however, the most effective and reader-friendly methods are used below.[22]

The analysis of the parameters begins with the variable *MAXCARDS*. For every additional credit card an Ohioan maxes out, his/her expected number of defaults increases by 0.2199, holding all other variables constant. For the interest rate variable (*IR1*), with every tenth-of-a-percentage-point increase the expected number of defaults rises by 0.0088. For the *OWNRENT* variable, people who own their home decrease their expected number of defaults by a count of 0.0866. Looking at the variable *GENDER*, being a male Ohio resident decreases the expected number of defaults on his credit card debt by a count of 0.1733. If an Ohioan's household income increases by $1,000, the expected number of defaults on his/her credit card debt decreases by 0.0012. Table 5.4 lists the interpretive results for all variables.

Final Econometric Model Test

The final model tested above was again tested using the withheld portion of the BSP data, BSPREG. This data had not been analyzed or handled in any way previous to this test that could compromise the validity of its results. The results of the negative binomial regression analysis using BSPREG are presented in Table 5.5.[23]

Interpretation of BSPREG Regression Results

Included in Table 5.6 are the marginal effects associated with the BSPREG regression (Long 1997).

Table 5.3

Results of Final EDA Negative Binomial Regression

Variable	Estimate	Standard error	p–value
Intercept	−1.1224	0.7609	0.1402
Maxcards***	0.4747	0.1005	0.0000
Ir1**	0.0189	0.0096	0.0476
Ownrent	−0.1870	0.1774	0.2916
Income*	−0.0027	0.0014	0.0578
Gender***	−0.3742	0.1308	0.0042
Age	0.0294	0.0355	0.4074
Agesqd	−0.0006	0.0004	0.1434
D1urbcnty*	−0.2480	0.1381	0.0730
D2urbcnty	−0.0542	0.1301	0.6768
Divorcd	−0.0889	0.2168	0.6817
Single	0.0851	0.1909	0.6558
Widow	0.4209	0.3063	0.1694
Dmag2	0.0000	0.0000	0.7083
Dmag3	−0.0000	0.0000	0.6890
Dmag4	−0.0000	0.0000	0.4185
Ptemp	−0.0738	0.2049	0.7187
Unemp	−0.2706	0.4046	0.5036
Retired	−0.5137	0.3179	0.1061
Inschl	−0.5410	0.4351	0.2137
Keephse*	−0.3528	0.2002	0.0780
Wslfothr	0.0938	0.2675	0.7259
Dnov	−0.1114	0.2512	0.6575
Ddec**	−0.5158	0.2546	0.0428
Djan	−0.2854	0.2468	0.2476
Dmar	−0.3563	0.2379	0.1343
Dapr	−0.1030	0.2449	0.6740
Dmay	0.0330	0.2393	0.8902
Djun	−0.2227	0.2495	0.3723
Djul	−0.2948	0.2636	0.2634
Daug	−0.0146	0.2591	0.9552
Dsep	−0.0504	0.2649	0.8492
Doct*	−0.5150	0.2691	0.0556

Source: Buckeye State Poll.
*Indicates statistical significance at the 10 percent level.
**Indicates statistical significance at the 5 percent level.
***Indicates statistical significance at the 1 percent level.

Looking at the percent change of the *MAXCARDS* variable, there is a significant increase in an Ohioan's expected number (0.1781) of defaults on their credit card debt for each additional credit card charged to the maximum limit.

The variable *INCOME* shows that with every $1,000 increase in income, the respondent's expected number of defaults decreases by 0.0016. The variables AGE and *AGESQD* were significant; they show that for each additional one-year in-

Table 5.4

Interpretation of Results from EDA Negative Binomial Regression

Variable	Marginal effect
Intercept	−0.5199
Maxcards***	0.2199
Ir1**	0.0088
Ownrent	−0.0866
Income*	−0.0012
Gender***	−0.1733
Age	0.0136
Agesqd	−0.0003
D1urbcnty*	−0.1149
D2urbcnty	−0.0251
Divorcd	−0.0411
Single	0.0394
Widow	0.1949
Dmag2	0.0000
Dmag3	−0.0000
Dmag4	−0.0000
Ptemp	−0.0342
Unemp	−0.1253
Retired	−0.2379
Inschl	−0.2505
Keephse*	−0.1634
Wslfothr	0.0434
Dnov	−0.0516
Ddec**	−0.2389
Djan	−0.1322
Dmar	−0.1650
Dapr	−0.0477
Dmay	0.0153
Djun	−0.1031
Djul	−0.1365
Daug	0.0067
Dsep	−0.2333
Doct*	−0.2385

*Indicates statistical significance at the 10 percent level.
**Indicates statistical significance at the 5 percent level.
***Indicates statistical significance at the 1 percent level.

crease in the respondent's age up to some maximum, his/her expected number of defaults increases by 0.0242, but then, after reaching that maximum age level, the expected number of defaults decreases by 0.0004 each year.

In an attempt to make comparing the regression results above to those presented earlier (Table 5.3) easier, Table 5.7 was constructed. It presents the regression results from the EDA next to those from the final regression BSPREG, and a brief conclusion about whether the variable is significant.

Table 5.5

Results of the Final Econometric Model using BSPREG

Variable	Estimate	Standard error	P–value
Intercept***	−2.3636	0.6837	0.0005
Maxcards***	0.5109	0.1101	0.0000
Ir1	0.0006	0.0097	0.9514
Ownrent	0.1172	0.1725	0.4968
Income***	−0.0047	0.0017	0.0062
Gender	0.0276	0.1296	0.8312
Age**	0.0693	0.0287	0.0157
Agesqd***	−0.0010	0.0003	0.0009
D1urbcnty*	0.2125	0.1286	0.0984
D2urbcnty	−0.0076	0.1348	0.9550
Divorcd	0.2054	0.2010	0.3068
Single	−0.2064	0.1872	0.2701
Widow	0.0359	0.2999	0.9046
Dmag2	−0.0000	0.0000	0.1091
Dmag3	0.0000	0.0000	0.5620
Dmag4	−0.0000	0.0000	0.4899
Ptemp	0.0456	0.2140	0.8312
Unemp	0.1348	0.4183	0.7472
Retired	−0.03056	0.2444	0.9005
Inschl	−0.2214	0.4992	0.6574
Keephse	−0.3770	0.2172	0.8622
Wslfothr	−0.1438	0.2759	0.6021
Dnov	0.3546	0.2448	0.1475
Ddec	0.1165	0.2400	0.6274
Djan	−0.1907	0.2318	0.4106
Dmar	0.5498	0.2370	0.8165
Dapr	−0.0131	0.2400	0.9564
Dmay	0.2318	0.2638	0.3796
Djun	−0.0049	0.2536	0.9846
Djul	−0.2293	0.2668	0.3901
Daug	0.0157	0.2504	0.9499
Dsep	0.0247	0.2580	0.9238
Doct	0.1832	0.2544	0.4713

*Indicates statistical significance at the 10 percent level.
**Indicates statistical significance at the 5 percent level.
***Indicates statistical significance at the 1 percent level.

In reviewing Table 5.7, it quickly becomes evident that only two variables are significant in both regressions: (1) *MAXCARDS* and (2) *INCOME*. Therefore, these variables will receive the most attention below.

MAXCARDS is a variable which no other data set (to my knowledge) contains. The primary idea behind this variable is that the more cards an Ohioan has maxed out, the greater is his/her expected number of defaults. A secondary idea behind the *MAXCARDS* variable is that borrowers may have a different attitude toward

Table 5.6

Interpretation of Results from BSPREG Regression

Variable	Marginal effects
Intercept***	−0.8240
Maxcards***	0.1781
Ir1	0.0002
Ownrent	0.0409
Income***	−0.0016
Gender	0.0096
Age**	0.0242
Agesqd***	−0.0004
D1urbcnty*	0.0741
D2urbcnty	−0.0027
Divorcd	0.0716
Single	−0.0720
Widow	0.0125
Dmag2	−0.0000
Dmag3	0.0000
Dmag4	0.0000
Ptemp	0.0159
Unemp	0.0470
Retired	−0.0107
Inschl	−0.0772
Keephse	−0.0131
Wslfothr	−0.0501
Dnov	0.1236
Ddec	0.0406
Djan	−0.0665
Dmar	0.0192
Dapr	−0.0046
Dmay	0.0808
Djun	−0.0017
Djul	−0.0799
Daug	0.0055
Dsep	0.0086
Doct	0.0639

*Indicates statistical significance at the 10 percent level.
**Indicates statistical significance at the 5 percent level.
***Indicates statistical significance at the 1 percent level.

their spending needs and/or ability to repay debts compared to what the credit card company thinks they need and/or are capable of repaying. Therefore, this variable allows us to test the significance of individuals' opinions of their debt capabilities in relation to their actual payment behavior (Kim 2000, 6–7).

The *INCOME* variable results support the claims made by other researchers (Bertaut and Haliassos 2001, Kim 2000, Stavins 2000, Yoo 1997) that income is

Table 5.7

BSPEDA Regression and BSPREG Regression Results

Variable	Estimate BSPEDA	Estimate BSPREG	Conclusion
INTERCEPT	−1.1224 (0.1402)	−2.3636 (0.0005)	N/A
MAXCARDS	0.4747 (0.0000)	0.5109 (0.0000)	Significant
IR1	0.0189 (0.0476)	0.0006 (0.9514)	Not significant (bspreg p-value is too high)
OWNRENT	−0.1870 (0.2916)	0.1172 (0.4968)	Not significant (opposing signs, and p-values are too high)
INCOME	−0.0027 (0.0578)	−0.0047 (0.0062)	Significant
GENDER	−0.3742 (0.0042)	0.0276 (0.8312)	Not significant (opposing signs, and bspreg p- value is too high)
AGE	0.0294 (0.4074)	0.0693 (0.0157)	Not significant (bspeda p-value is too high)
AGESQD	−0.0006 (0.1434)	−0.0010 (0.0009)	Not significant (bspeda p-value is too high)
D1URBCNTY	−0.2480 (0.0730)	0.2125 (0.0984)	Not significant (opposing signs)
D2URBCNTY	−0.0542 (0.6768)	−0.0076 (0.9550)	Not significant (p-values are too high)
DIVORCD	−0.0889 (0.6817)	0.2054 (0.3068)	Not significant (opposing signs, and p-values are too high)
SINGLE	0.0851 (0.6558)	−0.2064 (0.2701)	Not significant (opposing signs, and p-values are too high)
WIDOW	0.4209 (0.1694)	0.0359 (0.9046)	Not significant (p-values are too high)
DMAG2	0.0000 (0.7083)	−0.0000 (0.1091)	Not significant (opposing signs, and p-values are too high)
DMAG3	−0.0000 (0.6890)	0.0000 (0.5620)	Not significant (opposing signs, and p-values are too high)
DMAG4	−0.0000 (0.4185)	−0.0000 (0.4899)	Not significant (p-values are too high)
PTEMP	−0.0738 (0.7187)	0.0456 (0.8312)	Not significant (opposing signs)
UNEMP	−0.2706 (0.5036)	0.1348 (0.7472)	Not significant (opposing signs, and p-values are too high)

Table 5.7 *(continued)*

Estimate Variable	Estimate BSPEDA	BSPREG	Conclusion
RETIRED	−0.5137 (0.1061)	−0.03056 (0.9005)	Not significant (*p*-values are too high)
INSCHL	−0.5410 (0.2137)	−0.2214 (0.6574)	Not significant (*p*-values are too high)
KEEPHSE	−0.3528 (0.0780)	−0.3770 (0.8622)	Not significant (bspreg *p*-value is too high)
WSLFOTHR	0.0938 (0.7259)	−0.1438 (0.6021)	Not significant (opposing signs, and *p*-values are too high)
DNOV	−0.1114 (0.6575)	0.3546 (0.1475)	Not significant (opposing signs, and *p*-values are too high)
DDEC	−0.5158 (0.0428)	0.1165 (0.6274)	Not significant (opposing signs, and bspreg *p*-value is too high)
DJAN	−0.2854 (0.2476)	−0.1907 (0.4106)	Not significant (*p*-values are too high)
DMAR	−0.3563 (0.1343)	0.5498 (0.8165)	Not significant (opposing signs, and *p*-values are too high)
DAPR	−0.1030 (0.6740)	−0.0131 (0.9564)	Not significant (*p*-values are too high)
DMAY	0.0330 (0.8902)	0.2318 (0.3796)	Not significant (*p*-values are too high)
DJUN	−0.2227 (0.3723)	−0.0049 (0.9846)	Not significant (*p*-values are too high)
DJUL	−0.2948 (0.2634)	−0.2293 (0.3901)	Not significant (*p*-values are too high)
DAUG	−0.0146 (0.9552)	0.0157 (0.9499)	Not significant (opposing signs, and *p*-values are too high)
DSEP	−0.0504 (0.8492)	0.0247 (0.9238)	Not significant (opposing signs, and *p*-values are too high)
DOCT	−0.5150 (0.0556)	0.1832 (0.4713)	Not significant (opposing signs, and bspreg *p*-value is too high)

Note: p-values are in parentheses.

inversely related to credit card debt default. This result is an obvious one, but it allows us to highlight the evidence that a lack of sufficient income is a determinant of default. Thus credit card companies should be encouraged to place a greater importance on borrowers' income levels when making lending decisions.

The *AGE* and *AGESQRD* variables returned the expected signs using both data sets, and *AGESQRD* was nearly significant at the 10 percent level in the BSPEDA regression, and was significant at the 1 percent level using the BSPREG data set. The results suggest that as the cardholders' age rises, their expected number of defaults increases to some maximum point, then the expected number of defaults decreases as age increases.

Post Keynesian Econometrics

> [Keynes] argued that in a subject like economics there is a spectrum of appropri-
> ate languages, running from intuition and poetry through lawyer-like arguments
> to formal logic and mathematics. All have a role depending on the issue . . . being
> discussed. Mathematics is a good servant, but a bad master. (Harcourt 2003, 70)

The above techniques, as Keynes and Harcourt argue, allow us to use econometrics as a servant rather than a master. They let us analyze the data without making
a priori assumptions. Furthermore, we can research the literature on a subject then
thoroughly analyze the available data and construct a model knowing that we have
systematically studied all the relevant information on the topic. This removes all
supercilious assumptions (such as ergodicity) that are required when one skips
crucial empirical steps.

The following steps describe the analytical process used above to empirically
analyze credit card-debt default:

1. Choose a problem or issue to analyze (the more specific the better).
2. Review the literature about the chosen topic, exhaustively (keep diligent
    notes on articles and books on the subject; keep a running bibliography).
3. Collect the data (ideally by oneself, but, if necessary, find a good alterna-
    tive data source).
4. Mix up the data using a random number generator, then split the data (50 :
    50 if you have enough observations, or take a smaller percentage of the
    data set so as to explore).
5. Analyze one of the data sets thoroughly, using every descriptive tool
    necessary.
6. Define the dependent variable and decide which types of econometric
    techniques are available for analysis (for example, is the dependent vari-
    able a count, binary, or limited).
7. Assemble a full model including all variables thought to have an influ-
    ence (include explanatory variables based on the literature review and
    intuition).
8. Run a one-step backward regression (set the *p*-value elimination level
    low enough to eliminate the insignificant stand-alone explanatory vari-
    ables; and, if necessary, run other tests, such as likelihood-ratio tests, to
    test the significance of vectors of variables).

9. Test the final model using the withheld portion of the data.
10. Compare the results of the analyses from the two data sets.

Through the use of descriptive analysis, with cross-validation and with one-step backward regression, a researcher can avoid the constrictions of traditional neoclassical econometric models. When looking for models to test theories, most of them are neoclassical in design; that is, neoclassical assumptions are imbedded in the model. One of the ways to escape this "constraint" is to encourage Post Keynesians to develop and test their own theories using econometrics. Even if the process is as simple as collecting a basic data set and running descriptive statistics, this is still a valuable contribution to the field, and gives theories more validity (Downward and Mearman 2000, Harcourt 2003, Leamer 1983).

A researcher generally begins a project with the idea that a problem exists, then reviews the literature on the topic exhaustively. Once a researcher has an idea of the issues involved, he/she can proceed to obtain data, either by collecting it him/herself (the best method) or by finding and ancillary source (making sure that the source and data are legitimate). Post Keynesians are likely to include unique variables not used by neoclassical economists, some of which may include variables concerned with individual behaviors of respondents (i.e., getting at the psychological makeup of respondents); or including variables that attempt to quantify expectations, habits, causal mechanisms, and such. Now the researcher can start to analyze the data. It is argued here that the best way to analyze data is by first getting to know the data. However, if a researcher wants to test a theory formally, he/she cannot mine the data beforehand. But a researcher can use the techniques presented above to get around this problem. Most times, a good model (or any model, for that matter) on a topic is unavailable; therefore, a researcher has to develop one. Using descriptive statistical analysis and a one-step backward regression, the researcher can develop a new model on the respective topic without succumbing to the traditional neoclassical behavioral models.

Furthermore, using the techniques above as a guideline allows Post Keynesians to welcome the use of econometrics. There are many theories posited by institutionalists (instrumental valuation) and Post Keynesians (the monetary circuit, incomes approach to inflation, etc.); it is about time that these theories be developed into testable models (even if only part of the theory can be modeled, it is a start).[24] By following the preceding processes, a researcher can let the data and the problem statement guide the econometrics, instead of the other way around; that is, as Harcourt (2003) states, let the econometrics be your servant rather than your master.

Policy Implications

The subject of credit card default has been only casually studied by a small number of researchers. However, with the increases in credit card debt, credit card loans, and credit card lending/borrowing restrictions, there is little doubt that default is a significant topic for economic-policy analysts with which to be concerned. According to many authors (Dunn and Pressman 2005; Godley 2000; Minsky 1982, 1986; Scott 2005), increases in consumer debt creates macroeconomic instability, and credit card-debt default is an indicator that credit card debt has reached an unsustainable level. There are many issues raised in this chapter that should be included in any policy analysis concerning credit card default. The principal conclusions of the empirical analysis show two things: First, if a respondent charges a credit cards to its maximum limit, his/her expected number of credit card-debt defaults increases dramatically; and second, the higher a person's income, the lower are his/her expected number of defaults. Therefore, if a policy were initiated to help decrease the number of consumer credit card-debt defaults, it is logical to start by putting limitations on people's access to credit if they have charged even one credit card to its limit. This policy is the exact opposite of that used today (Manning 2001). Presently, if a person charges their credit card to the maximum limit he or she is rewarded with more credit cards and an increased spending limit.

In addition, credit card companies should attempt to keep closer watch over the incomes of their borrowers. A student who lives on a fixed income should not be given a credit card with a $10,000 spending limit (Manning 2001). Credit card companies do not caution against charging their credit cards to the limit. It is they, in fact, who determine the consumers' limits. Credit card companies are well aware of the behaviors of their borrowers; they know that by raising credit limits they lead consumers into a perpetual debt cycle. Further, many people in the United States today are not, in general, financially responsible; credit card companies take advantage of this, and, in many cases, push people into a Ponzi finance situation. The standards used for giving commercial or home loans are very different from those used for credit card loans. It seems reasonable that companies begin to take a more rigid approach to credit card lending based on some key factors, such as those outlined above.

Going back to Minsky's FIH, it is now clear that almost 12 percent of the respondents in the BSPEDA sample are working within a Ponzi environment. Furthermore, we know that this situation creates discontent for consumers. The implications of the lending market pushing consumers into a speculative/Ponzi environment have suddenly become more important. Credit-card companies recently helped pass the Bankruptcy Abuse Prevention and Consumer Protection Act of 2005, which makes filing Chapter 7 bankruptcy more difficult.[25] Instead, most people in credit card debt now have to file for Chapter 13 bankruptcy, which means they will have a payment plan structured by the courts, and, if they do not pay, then they run the risk of incarceration or fines. This new bankruptcy legislation change will have macroeconomic consequences. There is a connection between this policy and macroeconomic instability. Taking away Chapter 7 bankruptcy as an option for credit card debtors will force consumers with debt to lower their consumption, which can in turn exacerbate fluctuations between consumption and income.

Most credit card companies, even with their charge-off losses, make a substantial profit. Credit card companies, by instigating loose-lending practices and pushing people into a Ponzi situation, have put themselves and credit markets in general financial risk; consequently, it is their risk to bear without unduly shifting this responsibility to consumers.

Another policy issue must also be analyzed in future research. According to James K. Galbraith (1998) and Edward Wolff (2002), since the 1970s, the bottom 80 percent of U.S. citizens' incomes have been declining in real terms. Therefore, some people have probably used their easy access to credit cards as a way to make up for the income gap that has been widening for almost thirty years. It is reasonable to posit that a decrease in income inequality would make it easier for consumers to pay their credit card bills on time, or at least minimize the expected number of defaults. Therefore, policies concerned with analyzing the effects of income inequality in the United States since the early 1980s should consider the effect inequality has had on the increases in credit card-debt default.

Conclusion

The intention of this chapter was threefold: (1) to develop a model that showed the determinants of credit card-debt default; (2) to explain the various techniques used to develop a new model of default, and how these methods can be used by other researchers; and (3) to use the findings from the empirical analysis to suggest areas of focus for policy makers attempting to alleviate the risks associated with credit card-debt default. The model developed did produce some interesting results, and does warrant further research.

There has been an increasing trend in credit card-debt default in the United States over the past decade. This increase has been met with little resistance from the federal government, credit card companies, or consumers. However, the problem is still a growing and persistent one. The study makes it clear that people are harmed by credit card default in a number of ways, and that there is little by way of policy to help restrain credit card companies from making deleterious decisions with regard to consumer credit card lending. This should shed some much needed light upon this imposing subject and bring further attention to how best the problem can be resolved.

Notes

1. In the United States, federal regulation is the most reasonable solution to these problems. This policy must come from the Office of the Comptroller of the Currency (OCC), an agency attached to the Treasury Department. The OCC has the power to regulate national banks.

2. The statistical software programs used for this study are Limdep Version 7.0, SAS Version 9.0, and Stata Version 8.

3. This idea may likely lead to entirely new ways of modeling and statistically treating human behavior.

4. By using the = RAND() function in Microsoft Excel, then sorting the data in ascending order, the data was randomly mixed. After splitting the data in half, it was then necessary to reorganize the now two separate data sets into their original order, so it is now clear which observations are in the first data set and which are in the second. The data is now sufficiently randomized.

5. The BSP data set had a sufficient amount of data that, once split in half, produced two data sets of significant size. However, it is also possible when given a smaller data set to only take a small portion of the original data set in order to run EDA and test various models.

6. Calculate the likelihood ratio (LR) (LR = −2[Log Likelihood (Restricted Model)− Log Likelihood (Unrestricted Model)]) and compare this value against the critical chi-squared value (found using a chi-squared table) using the number of eliminated variables as the degrees of freedom. If the LR is greater than the critical chi-squared value the null hypothesis is rejected; meaning that the eliminated vector does not add significance to the model and can thus be permanently removed.

7. Also, see Kennedy (2003), Green (2000), and Scott (2005).

8. The BSP is no longer being conducted. Therefore, the data used in this research encompasses the entire data set, with no additional data to be added, according to the director of the Survey Research Center, Gerald Kosicki.

9. It is important to note that, while the BSP was collected over a period of almost six years, the survey was random; thus, it is impossible to measure the change of individual income from one period to another. It is possible to see general changes over time, but not fluctuations at the individual respondent level specifically.

10. Lucia Dunn is a professor of economics at Ohio State University. She was a researcher for the BSP project.

11. See Appendix 5.1 for all variables' definitions.

12. Initially, the model was tested using Poisson regression (Scott 2005).

13. Interaction variables are useful analytical tools. By interacting two or more variables, that is, multiplying them together, a researcher can observe from the regression results what impact the two variables have on one another. These types of variables can add complexity and greater depth to a denuded model.

14. The employment recession period was used instead of the GDP recession period because it is commonly believed that significant declines in employment are a better measure of whether an economy is in recession or not.

15. Taking the square of a variable makes that variable assume a nonlinear path. In other words, just including *AGE* in the regression makes *AGE* a linear variable. However, there is strong empirical evidence to support the claim that as a person's age increases, after some maximum point his/her risk of defaulting decreases. Therefore, the function is not continually increasing, but rather increasing up to some apex, then curving downward. Furthermore, it is possible to take the cube of a variable, such as if it were believed that default is higher when you are younger, then decreases through middle age, and then increases again when the person reaches an even older age, then taking the cube of *AGE* would seemingly be appropriate. A benefit to using EDA and cross-validation is that one can test various theories multiple ways, but remembering to always use common sense and good research as a guide.

16. See Appendix 5.2 for details.

17. When deciding which variable to eliminate as the base, researchers should always remember that the variable eliminated as the base is the variable that the other dummy variables are measured against. Meaning, marriage was eliminated as the base of the *MARITAL* vector, therefore it is reasonable to expect the *DIVORCD* variable to return a negative coefficient because people who are married are probably less likely to default on their credit card debt than someone who is divorced. Additionally, a good rule regarding vector dummy variables is to eliminate the variable with the most observations, which is how all of the base variables were chosen for this analysis.

18. See Appendix 5.2 for details.

19. See Appendix 5.2 for details.

20. Here, two variables were chosen as the base, because if the respondent answers that he or she is "employed but on vacation," it is reasonable to assume such has a full-time job. Therefore, as another rule regarding vector dummy variables, if two or more variables are similar (collinear), it is advisable to eliminate all of them to serve as the base.

21. Backward regression was performed by eliminating all stand-alone (nonvector) variables that had p-values equal to or greater than 0.30. For more details, see Scott (2005).

22. The negative binomial regression model takes a nonlinear form. Marginal effects are typically calculated for interpreting regression results. Long (1997) offers an alternative method for interpreting the results from a negative binomial method, which is easily calculated using the statistical software package Stata version 8. However, marginal effects are used in this analysis for ease of interpretation.

23. There were 5,666 observations used from the BSPREG data set, a difference of only 154 observations compared to the BSPEDA data set.

24. As for the institutionalist view, in John Dewey's words, "valuations exist in fact and are capable of empirical observations, so that propositions about them can be verified" (Dewey 1939, 58).

25. Chapter 7 bankruptcy eliminates a filer's credit card debt.

References

Ausubel, L.M. 1991. "The Failure of Competition in the Credit Card Market." *American Economic Review* 81(1): 50–81.

Bertaut C.C., and M. Haliassos. 2001. "Debt Revolvers for Self Control" (available at www.hermes.ucy.ac.cy/publications/working-papers-2001/01-11%20Bertaut-Haliassos.pdf). Accessed December 2005.

Brito, D.L., and P.R. Hartley. 1995. "Consumer Rationality and Credit Cards." *Journal of Political Economy* 103(1): 400–433.

Dewey, J. 1939. *Theory of Valuation.* Chicago: University of Chicago Press.

Dornbusch, R.; S. Fischer; and R. Startz. 1998. *Macroeconomics,* 7th ed. New York: Irwin/McGraw-Hill.

Downward, P., and A. Mearman. 2000. "Critical Realism and Econometrics: Constructive Dialogue with Post Keynesian Economics." Paper presented at the Cambridge Realist Workshop Conference, University of Cambridge, May 5–7, 2000.

Dunn, S.P., and S. Pressman. 2005. "The Economic Contributions of John Kenneth Galbraith." *Review of Political Economy* 17(2): 161–209.

Galbraith, James K. 1998. *Created Unequal: The Crisis in American Pay.* New York: Free Press.

Godley, W. 2000. "Drowning in Debt." *Policy Note* 6. Annandale, NY: The Levy Economics Institute of Bard College. (Available at www.levy.org/pubs/pn/pn00_6.pdf). Accessed December 2005.

Goertzel, T. 2002. "Econometric Modeling as Junk Science." *The Skeptical Inquire* 26(1): 19–23.

Green, W.H. 2000. *Econometric Analysis,* 4th ed. New York: Prentice Hall.

Gross, D., and N. Souleles. 2002. "Do Liquidity Constraints and Interest Rates Matter for Consumer Behavior? Evidence from Credit Card Data." *Quarterly Journal of Economics* 117(1): 149–85.

Haliassos, M., and M. Reiter. 2003. "Credit Card Debt Puzzles." (Available at www.iue.it/FinConsEU/ResearchActivities/EconomicsOfConsumerCreditMay2003/Papers/Halliassos.pdf.) Accessed November 2005.

Harcourt, G. 2003. "A Good Servant but a Bad Master." In E. Fullbrook, ed., *The Crisis in*

Economics: The Post-Autistic Economics Movement: The First 600 Days. New York: Routledge.

Kellison, B., P. Brocket, S. Shin, and S. Li. 2003. "A Statistical Analysis of the Relationship between Credit History and Insurance Losses." Bureau of Business Research, McCombs School of Business, University of Texas at Austin, 2003 (available at www.utexas.edu/depts/bbr/bbr_creditstudy.pdf). Accessed November 2005.

Kennedy, P. 2003. *A Guide to Econometrics*, 2nd ed. Cambridge: MIT Press.

Kim, T.H. 2000. "Investigation of U.S. Credit Card Market Using Original Survey Data." Ph.D. diss., Ohio State University.

Lawson, T. 2003. *Reorienting Economics.* New York: Routledge.

Leamer, E.E. 1983. "Let's Take the Con out of Econometrics." *American Economic Review* 73(1): 31–43.

Long, S.J. 1997. *Regression Models for Categorical and Limited Dependent Variables.* London: Sage.

Manning, R.D. 2001. "Hearing on 'Consumer Bankruptcy,' before the Committee on Judiciary, House of Representatives." 107th Congress, Washington, DC, February 8 (available at http://judiciary.senate.gov/oldsite/te020801rdm.htm&e=6251). Accessed November 2005.

Minsky, H.P. 1982. *Can "It" Happen Again? Essays on Instability and Finance.* Armonk, NY: M.E. Sharpe.

———. 1986. *Stabilizing an Unstable Economy.* New Haven: Yale University Press.

———. 1992. "The Financial Instability Hypothesis." The Levy Economics Institute of Bard College: Working Paper No. 74.

National Bureau of Economic Research. 2001. "The Business Cycle Peak of March 2001." NBER, Cambridge, MA, 2001 (available at www.nber.org/cycles/november2001). Accessed November 2005.

Scott, R.H., III. 2005. "The Determinants of Default on Credit Card Debt." Ph.D. diss., University of Missouri, Kansas City.

Stavins, J. 2000. "Credit Card Borrowing, Delinquency, and Personal Bankruptcy." *New England Economic Review* (July–August): 15–30.

Wolff, E.N. 2002. *Top Heavy: A Study of the Increasing Inequality of Wealth in America and What Can Be Done About It.* New York: New Press.

Yoo, P.S. 1997. "Charging up a Mountain of Debt: Accounting for the Growth of Credit Card Debt." *Federal Reserve Bank of St. Louis Review* 79 (March): 3–13.

Appendix 5.1

Variable Names and Definitions

Variable name	Definition
NOPAYMIN (default)	This variable is a count, and it accounts for the number of times in the past 6 months that the respondent has failed to make even the minimum payment on their credit card debt
TOTCARD	The total number of active credit cards that a respondent possesses
MAXCARDS	The total number of credit cards that the respondent has charged to the card(s) limit in the last 6 months
IR1	The interest rate on the respondents primary credit card
IR2	This is a binary dummy variable that records whether the interest rate on the respondents primary credit card is an introductory rate that will rise after a certain period of time
IRX	Interaction of IR1 and IR2
OWNRENT	A dummy variable equaling 1 if the respondents owns their home; and 0 otherwise
KIDSNUM	The total number of kids living in the respondents house under the age of 18
GENDER	A binary dummy variable coded as 1 if the respondent is male; and 0 if female
DREC	A binary dummy variable used to control for the employment recession that began in February 2001 and ended after the datasets completion
MARRIED	A binary dummy variable coded as 1 if the respondent is married; and 0 otherwise (this variable was eliminated as the base)
DIVORCD	A binary dummy variable coded as 1 if the respondent is divorced; and 0 otherwise
SEPARATED	A binary dummy variable coded as 1 if the respondent is separated; and 0 otherwise (this variable was conflated with DIVORCD)
SINGLE	A binary dummy variable coded as 1 if the respondent is single; and 0 otherwise
COHABITATING	A binary dummy variable coded as 1 if the respondent is cohabitating; and 0 otherwise (this variable was conflated with MARRIED)
WIDOW	A binary dummy variable coded as 1 if the respondent is a widow; and 0 otherwise
DMAG1	An interaction variable: MARRIED * AGE * AGESQD * GENDER (this variable was eliminated as the base)

Appendix 5.1 *(continued)*

Variable name	Definition
DMAG2	An interaction variable: DIVORCD * AGE * AGESQD * GENDER
DMAG3	An interaction variable: SINGLE * AGE * AGESQD * GENDER
DMAG4	An interaction variable: WIDOW * AGE * AGESQD * GENDER
AGE	The age of the respondent
AGESQRD	The age of the respondent squared
INCOME	The household income of the respondent (measured in thousands of dollars)
AMOUNTOWED	This variable accounts for the amount still owed on all credit card accounts *just after* the respondent had paid their most recent credit card bill (measured in thousands of dollars)
MINPAY	The total minimum payments the respondent owed on all credit cards last month (measured in thousands of dollars)
NOHIDIP	The respondent has no high school diploma
HIDIP	The respondent has a high school diploma (this variable was removed as the base)
SOMECOL	The respondent has some college training
ASSOCIT	The respondent has an Associates Degree
BACHELOR	The respondent has a Baccalaureate Degree
SOMEGRAD	The respondent has some graduate school training
MASTER	The respondent has a Masters Degree
PROFESS	The respondent has a Professional Degree
FTEMP	The respondent is employed full-time (this variable was removed as the base)
PTEMP	The respondent is employed part-time
UNEMP	The respondent is unemployed
RETIRED	The respondent is retired
INSCHL	The respondent is in school
KEEPHSE	The respondent keeps house (housewife/househusband)
WSLFOTHR	The respondent works, but does not fit into any of the above categories; i.e. they work contractually (erratically)
DNOV	Binary dummy variable controlling for November months in the sample
DDEC	Binary dummy variable controlling for December months in the sample
DJAN	Binary dummy variable controlling for January months in the sample

Appendix 5.1 *(continued)*

Variable name	Definition
DFEB	Binary dummy variable controlling for February months in the sample (this variable was removed as the base)
DMAR	Binary dummy variable controlling for March months in the sample
DAPR	Binary dummy variable controlling for April months in the sample
DMAY	Binary dummy variable controlling for May months in the sample
DJUN	Binary dummy variable controlling for June months in the sample
DJUL	Binary dummy variable controlling for July months in the sample
DAUG	Binary dummy variable controlling for August months in the sample
DSEP	Binary dummy variable controlling for September months in the sample
DOCT	Binary dummy variable controlling for October months in the sample

Appendix 5.2: Data Codification

It was necessary to take the EDUCAT variable and develop a vector of variables. Each one of these variables is coded as a 1 if the respondent's answer equals the appropriate education level; and 0 otherwise. EDUCAT comes from the following survey question: "What is the highest grade or year of schooling you have received?": (1) no high school degree: 0–11; (2) high school degree: 12; (3) some college: 13; (4) Associates Certificate/2 year program: 14; (5) Bachelor's degree: 15; (6) some graduate school: 16; (7) Master's degree: 17; and (8) Doctorate/ advanced degree: 18. Eight dummy variables were constructed using the EDUCAT variable responses above, they are the following: (1) NOHISCLDIP; (2) HISCHLDIP; (3) SOMECOL; (4) ASSOCIT; (5) BACHELOR; (6) SOMEGRAD; (7) MASTER; (8) PROFESS. The HISCHLDIP variable was eliminated as the base, because this variable was the one with the highest percentage. In Stavins (2000), education was significant and had a negative coefficient; meaning, the higher the respondent's level of education, the less likely they were to default on their credit card debt.

WORKSELF comes from the following survey question: "Last week were you working full-time, part-time, going to school, keeping house, or what?" The answers to this question are categorized as follows: (1) full-time; (2) part-time; (3) with job vacation; (4) unemployed; (5) retired; (6) in school; (7) keeping house; or (8) other. These answers were used to construct the following dummy variables: (1) FTEMP; (2) PTEMP; (3) JOBVAC; (4) UNEMP; (5) RETIRED; (6) INSCHL; (7) KEEPHSE; and (8) WSLFOTHR.

The Census Bureau 2000 data allows for grouping data into persons per square mile in each county in Ohio. The variables created from the Census data and their specifications follow: (1) D1URBCNTY: this binary variable represents the Ohio counties that are considered the most urban, and was created using the COUNTY variables and the 2000 Census data—coded in the following manner: D1URBCNTY equals one if any of the COUNTY variables are those counties with a person per square mile population density that fall within the range of 1980 to 3040; (2) D2URBCNTY: this binary variable represents the Ohio counties that are considered somewhat urban, and was created using the COUNTY variables and the 2000 Census data—coded in the following manner: D2URBCNTY equals one if any of the COUNTY variables are those with a person per square mile population density that fall within the range of 578 to 1337; and (3) D3URBCNTY: this binary variable encompasses the remainder of counties in Ohio, which are considered the rural counties.

Part II

Empirical Studies of Business Investment

6

JERRY COURVISANOS

The Dynamics of Innovation and Investment, with Application to Australia, 1984–1998

. . . Kalecki's analysis provides for an endogenous rate of growth, albeit one which rests on the stimulating effect of innovation on investment.
(Sawyer 1996, 107)

Introduction

Since the origins of the Industrial Revolution in Britain, innovation and investment have been crucial to capitalism and economic development. This chapter sets up a link between innovation and investment in historical time, without reference to any static equilibrium. In this manner, the relationship between the instability of cycles and growth trends can be identified. Australian data is then used to identify important linkages between these two crucial elements.

Technological innovation is based on research and development expenditure.[1] At the technological level, R&D induces new systems and processes, while at the applied and experimental level, R&D adapts new systems and processes to products.

This R&D expenditure determines innovative behavior.[2] Innovation then affects the economy through new investment. Investment creates the means of production (MOP) that enable companies to sell commodities in the marketplace.

The next section contrasts the Post Keynesian approach to innovation and investment with the neoclassical approach. This is followed by a more detailed exposition of the Kaleckian framework linking innovation and investment. We then set out the structural method of employing evolutionary and panel data and the statistical results from this dual approach using Australian data from 1984 to 1998. This is followed by an explanation of the statistical results, and a section that notes some limitations of the results. Finally, we draw out the policy implications of this analysis.

Post Keynesian and Neoclassical Approaches to Innovation and Investment

Over the past two centuries, the link between innovation and investment developed by early economists has become more tenuous. As a result, research in innovation and investment has tended to be uncoupled.

Innovation research has taken two roads. One looks at broad evolutionary change under capitalism, while the other studies entrepreneurship at the company level. Attempts to incorporate investment into a theoretical analysis of innovation have been limited (Stoneman 1983, 202). Literature reviews emphasize that there is no analysis linking innovation with investment (Dodgson and Rothwell 1994, Freeman and Soete 1997). Two major exceptions to this are Salter (1960), from the neoclassical perspective, and Freeman and Perez (1988), from an evolutionary Keynesian perspective. Both provide "snapshot" studies for distinct points in historical time, showing the plausibility of the theoretical relations they derive relating to innovation and investment.

Salter examines technical change and its implications for MOP in different industry sectors. He recognizes the gap between innovation and its application via investment. He shows how market signals can postpone a more innovative MOP and delay scrapping an old MOP, resulting in the capital stock becoming "fossilised" (Salter 1960, 154).

Freeman and Perez (1988) take a structural view of the economy with respect to innovation, and note the mismatch of current investment to new available technology. Rather than market signals, they identify variations in business confidence regarding the new innovation as the cause of this mismatch. In turn, this leads to greater investment instability.

Investment research has also taken two roads. At the company level, investment depends on expected profits under uncertainty. At the aggregate level, investment contributes to effective demand, which impacts upon business cycles and trend growth. In both cases, innovation (or technical progress) adds to investment, but there is no explanation of the link between innovation and investment. The usual justification for this is that "the issues are quite complex and difficult to model" (Lavoie 1992, 316).

From a neoclassical perspective, investment research generally ignores the role of technological innovation, except as an exogenous force. Since the early 1990s, neoclassical investment theory has made significant progress by examining investment decisions under uncertainty. Led by Avinash Dixit and Robert Pindyck, neoclassical economists developed a decision-making model that incorporates the value of waiting to avoid downside risk in an uncertain future. This involves sacrificing profits by waiting instead of going ahead with an investment project immediately (Dixit 1992, 110; see also Dixit and Pindyck 1994). Using this approach, an optimal balance can be found between the decision to invest and the desire to wait for more information. This balance (or equilibrium) can be altered over logical (ahistorical) time.

The Dixit-Pindyck approach involves the optimal allocation of fundamental uncertainty in ahistorical time. From a Post Keynesian perspective, this approach has two flaws. First, uncertainty cannot be treated like risk. Second, the capital stock in this approach is homogenous, which implies no role for innovation.

At the aggregate level, the endogeneity of technical change in new-growth neoclassical models leaves the relationship between investment and innovation highly tenuous. But alternative investment models with innovation are available. For Schumpeter (1939), investment responds to waves of optimism and pessimism creating clusters of innovation, and thus a bunching of investment. This leads to unstable investment cycles and a trigger mechanism to initiate new innovation systems, a process with long-wave implications. Kalecki (1962) reinforces the cycle-trend effect that innovation has on the investment function.[3] The intensity of innovation affects both the amplitude of investment cycles and also shifts the trend path of investment growth by vicious and virtuous circles. Virtuous circles occur as innovation rises, increasing the upper turning point of the investment cycle and shifting the trend path upward.[4] Vicious circles reduce the lower turning point and shift the trend downward. Steindl (1979, 7) models this by having the pace of innovation as a shift parameter for the Kaleckian investment function.

The cause of innovation clustering and the subsequent bunching of investment ("clust-bun") is a matter of debate (see Freeman 1994, 86–89), but the Kaleckian feature of expanded reproduction has not been recognized by the protagonists in this debate. Clustering requires depressions or technological breakthroughs; both reflect reactions by the private sector (in the former case) or the public sector (in the latter) to problems in the downswing of the previous business cycle. Bunching requires effective demand stimulus by public deficit spending and private profits that provide a surplus for investment. Roadblocks to this "clust-bun" effect exist in the institutional framework of nations, in particular to mature industries using older technologies (Freeman and Perez 1988, 58–65). Increased uncertainty arising from large investment into new technology systems also adds a roadblock through increased macroeconomic volatility, which Toivanen, Stoneman, and Diederen (1999) identify as slowing down the diffusion process.

Kaldor (1961) and Schmookler (1966) reverse the causal sequencing of innovation and investment. For them, the rate of investment determines the rate of innovation. Kalecki also recognizes this sequence, despite having identified the innovation-driven process (see note 3). Kalecki (1954, 158) views this investment-driven process as "part and parcel of 'ordinary' investment" or endogenous innovation. Geroski and Walters (1995, 926) support endogenous innovation, concluding that demand matters "although it is evident that it plays only a relatively modest role in stimulating innovative activity." In a note on this study, Collins and Yao (1998) argue that the data does not support this conclusion, and Geroski and Walters (1995, 925) themselves recognize the possibility that "fundamental [exogenous] innovations have different cyclical patterns from the less substantive [endogenous] innovations, and this may explain these differences in results."[5]

The discussion above points to a circular flow, where one innovative process feeds into another. Kaldor (1966) introduces the principle of cumulative causation, where investment demand leads to innovation, which then stimulates further investment. The distinction between exogenous and endogenous innovation specifies how innovation enters this cumulative causation process. Gomulka (1990, 45–47) sees R&D as central to the endogenous innovation process, with large companies, making considerable profit, having the ability to activate large R&D spending. Patents seem to reflect more the clustering of innovations (Geroski and Walters 1995, 924).

The Model

This section develops a Post Keynesian model of innovation and investment. First, it presents the Kaleckian framework. This sets up the dynamic mechanisms that absolve the model from needing to find stability conditions. Second, a flow-chart shows how the model operates over historical time, generating both cycles and trends. Innovation here is crucial to the investment process. Third, a series of equations and a grid matrix is established that will let us tell a plausible empirical story.

Descriptive Kaleckian Framework of Analysis

Three observable variables are central to Kaleckian investment—profits, increasing risk, and excess capacity. Courvisanos (1996) develops a susceptibility cycle model which measures the tensions when investment decisions are made. The three variables above act as barometers of this tension. During an investment boom, tensions grow to such an extent that investment is susceptible to a collapse. Susceptibility can be identified with falling profit rates, increased finance costs, and falling utilization rates. When high susceptibility is reached, any minor factor can add enough additional tension to suspend or cancel investment orders.

All companies experience high susceptibility at the upper turning point of the susceptibility cycle. This leads to a reduction in investment orders. The investment downturn that follows is timed around the pressures on all companies to contract investment (to some degree). The timing and amplitude of the lower turning point are more problematic. Pressures to expand investment orders depend on the more problematic issue of when a company (or industry) wants to take the plunge. Tightly owned companies with less risk aversion tend to lead investment out of the doldrums, while the state tends to assist companies during this period by reducing production costs through subsidies and deficit spending.

For Kalecki, endogenous innovation is of secondary importance. It comes from slight improvements in, or adaptations to, previous capital equipment; some improvement in quality or design, or the new packaging of old products; and some new "vein" or extension of previous raw-material sources. Innovation is most common and involves new investment spending as a matter of course when business is ongoing. Such innovation is called "endogenous" because it is the cycle itself that induces the innovation and investment.[6]

R&D expenditure is a form of investment that needs to be incorporated in long-term business plans. It enables the company to hold a stock of innovations that are ready to be applied. When a company decides to increase investment at relatively low susceptibility, past R&D means the company is ready to implement these innovations.[7] R&D increases the strategic capacity of the company, enabling it to increase innovative MOP. R&D expenditure may be constant throughout the investment cycle, or it may vary under the same susceptibility pressures as MOP commitments. The actual result depends on how important R&D is for the company and the industry. In an industry where innovation is a regular part of competitive strategy, R&D expenditure would be large and would vary under the same susceptibility pressures as capital expenditure. In an industry where innovation is only occasionally implemented, R&D expenditure would be small and constant over the investment cycle.

At high susceptibility, companies are under pressure to postpone investment, shelve endogenous innovations, and reduce R&D expenditures. The company concentrates on profits from old MOP, which have a proven track record, rather than the higher but more unpredictable returns from a new MOP.[8] Only small increases in capacity, to protect existing MOP, emerge at high levels of susceptibility. Postponing innovation adds pressure to the slowdown and leads to a contraction of investment orders. In the context of trend growth, a long postponement of new innovative capital investment would produce a mismatch of current investment to new available technology in the economy, creating a roadblock to the "clust-bun" effect.

At low susceptibility, companies introduce processes and products under the pressure of competition. The technostructure needs to implement the company's long-term investment strategy with innovation incorporated therein: the need creates increasing competitive pressure during the contraction of the susceptibility cycle when investment orders are declining and little new investment is taking place.[9] The cost of postponing a long-term investment strategy increases over time as other large companies in the industry (or ready to enter the industry) develop the technology to increase their market share and grow. These pressures, along with pressures for state stimuli, lead to some increase in investment containing endogenous innovation.

Endogenous innovations make some MOP obsolete and not part of excess capacity, and oligopolies lobby for governmental assistance in reducing the social costs of production through subsidies, tax concessions, or protection (O'Connor 1973, 27). As a result, the rate of increase in susceptibility is reduced and an investment recovery is encouraged. However, these actions by companies and governments are not guaranteed to occur at any particular time or with any particular force. The institutional framework of a country (or region) will determine the strength and timing of the investment upturn.

R&D spending and its innovation effects are bound to generate some major new discovery or invention. This will arise from small developments in laboratories and informal networks between companies and industries, eventually coming to fruition divorced of any specific competitive behavior. New technological paradigms come out of such developments and are the basis of structural change to a new long-wave boom (Freeman and Perez 1988, 47–58). Changes in technological systems and paradigms arise only after all the minor improvements are squeezed out of the old systems by entrepreneurs who want to protect existing MOPs and delay the new paradigm. There is also a log jam of innovations based on the new paradigm, which compounds the latter's slow initial adoption. This occurs when established entrepreneurs, with old MOP, cannot justify shaking up industries since not enough interrelated clusters have been formed.[10]

Technological paradigm shifts lead to exogenous innovation affecting the susceptibility cycle. Introducing a new paradigm produces a large exogenous boost to industry investment at low susceptibility points. This investment boom relates to paradigm changes in large, important industries that adopt new technology systems (e.g., petrochemical innovations) or in the whole economy (e.g., the steam engine). Either way, the investment boom is strong and resilient over a series of future susceptibility cycles.

Exogenous innovation generally occurs in an industry at the low susceptibility point, where competitive pressure leads entrepreneurs to introduce it. When investment activity is high, and susceptibility is high, companies are not receptive to major new developments; instead, they squeeze profits from the old paradigm. As susceptibility falls with investment downturns, the financial constraints in the industry are eased as debts are paid off, or as receivers are appointed. At low susceptibility, the industry is financially restructured and becomes open to new investment. However, it is not clear if or when the lower turning point of investment orders will be based on the decreasing opportunities from the old paradigm (providing only a modest upturn) or on the uncertainty of the new paradigm. The breakdown of an old technological paradigm occurs in readapting this old paradigm through minor innovations. Uncertainty of future profits reduces investment orders and susceptibility further. At this point, even replacement investment is postponed, sending the susceptibility cycle even lower.

As the institutional framework slowly adapts to the new technological system, entrepreneurs follow the new technological trajectories, and investment rises. This creates a new investment boom and establishes "the conditions for a new phase of steady development" (Vercelli 1989, 135). A paradigm shift occurs when the new technological system pervades the whole economy, beginning a new long wave of growth (Kleinknecht 1987).

The analysis in this section allows us to link the two types of innovation described by Baran and Sweezy (1966): normal (or endogenous) and epoch making (or exogenous). A period of secular decline can now be associated with the limitations of scale production in oligopolistic competition, as the old technology systems are running out of new adaptations. Diffusion of the old

Figure 6.1   **Circular Flow of Innovation and Investment**

National Innovation System

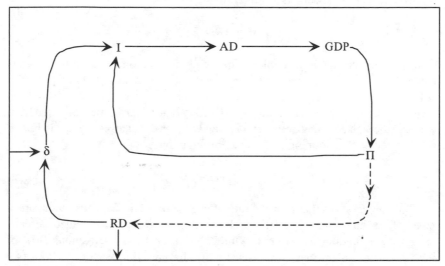

systems slows down and there are fewer imitators. Large powerful corporations attempt to protect existing capital values and ignore the new technological systems being developed on the fringe of the corporate world. This tends to exacerbate the mismatch between new technologies and the powerful institutional framework based around monopoly capital. Steindl recognized this secular decline as the incentive to reduce surplus capacity and invest in established monopoly capital sectors. He stated that he was "ready to admit a possibility which I denied in [the 1952 edition of] my book: that it might be the result of exhaustion of a long technological wave" (Steindl 1976, xv). In this way, the Kaleckian and evolutionary traditions can be integrated.

Flow-chart Macroenvironment and Instability

Figure 6.1 summarizes the cycles and trend dynamics described above. The outside perimeter is the national innovation system (NIS), which carries the institutional framework wherein innovation occurs and investment cycles operate. This framework can also exist at the international level (e.g., vis-à-vis the European Union, the North American Free Trade Agreement, the Association of Southeast Asian Nations) and at the domestic level. The role of the state is not specifically identified in Figure 6.1, with its influence remaining in the NIS perimeter, while the circular flow has no governmental sector and no impact through public expenditures or taxes.

Figure 6.1 is a circular flow through historical time. Explanation of the circular flow can begin at any point. Following Ricottilli (1996), we begin with the innovation decision specified in Equation (1),

$$\delta = f_1 (RD, L),$$ (1)

where δ is the change in technology (or simply innovation). δ depends on R&D expenditure (RD) and the current learning and institutional knowledge capabilities (L) measured in efficiency units. L is determined by the given state of the NIS, including networks of social relations and technological capabilities imported from overseas through licensing, joint ventures, and foreign direct investment.[11] In Figure 6.1, the two arrows pointing to δ represent Equation (1).

$$I = f_2 (\Pi, \delta).$$ (2)

Equation (2) states that I (or the rate of change of MOP) depends on the profit level (Π) and innovation (δ). Profit levels represent the extent that retained earnings are used for funding investment, while δ represents the endogenous flow of innovation into investment, as discussed in the preceding section. These two variables form the crucial decision-making elements connecting susceptibility and the investment process. The Π level in a Kaleckian framework also indicates the ability of companies to obtain external funds through the principle of increasing risk (Kalecki 1937), which explicitly identifies greater profit levels as the increasing ability of companies to attract riskier external funds. A more sophisticated investment model than Equation (2) would also include the change in profits (expectations), increasing risk (gearing ratio) and capacity utilization.[12]

In Figure 6.1, the circular flow from investment (I) follows a Keynesian macroeconomic route, as I feeds into aggregate demand (AD) as its most volatile component. Changes in AD directly affect gross domestic product (GDP). Changes in GDP directly impact the distribution of profits (Π), which consists of a stable level of distributed earnings plus retained earnings (RE) for investment (see Asimakopulos 1975). RE generally account for around 75 percent of business fixed investment in capitalist economies. It represents the direct profit flow of funds back into investment.[13]

In reviewing the innovation literature, Gomulka (1990, 45–47) identifies the influence of profitability on the level of R&D spending (despite larger companies tending to spend less of their profits on R&D than smaller companies). Kalecki (1962) supports this position but notes the long and complex time lag involved for profits to influence "the stream of inventions." Thus the flow from Π to RD in Figure 6.1 is more variable than the Π-I flow and occurs over a longer time horizon. The dotted line indicates that this flow is not in the same time dimension as the other flows.

To close the circular flow, RD has two effects. One is a monetary flow into innovation, via Equation (1). The other is a flow in terms of aggregate expenditure from all companies directly into the NIS.[14] Larger RD has a positive impact on institutional knowledge and learning capabilities. Exogenous innovation flows through the L term back into the circular flow and to the δ variable. At the same time, technical and economic factors push us toward a structural break where a new paradigm emerges, altering the NIS. When the radical break occurs, exogenous innovation becomes the crucial factor through the L term in the paradigm shift, and leads directly to a strong expansion of the investment cycle (as discussed in the preceding section).

Circular-flow dynamics can be exhibited by the virtuous and vicious circles earlier defined. Virtuous circles exist when an increase in RD leads to a rise in δ, which encourages the expansion of I (Nickell and Nicolitsas 1996). This has a positive impact on AD and GDP, and then on Π, which creates an accelerationist effect on I through greater economic activity. Increased innovation intensity, via the dotted line from Π to RD, reinforces this circle. This rise in δ pushes the expansion into a strong boom. The virtuous circle has all the elements of the "Schumpeter Mark II" effect that Malerba and Orsenigo (1993) identify, where more RD leads to "creative accumulation."

As investment orders build up, there is increased susceptibility to an investment downturn through growing excess capacity, rising gearing ratios, and tensions when Π is high (Courvisanos 1996, 161). Figure 6.1 isolates a further tension. As RD continues its endogenous innovation push, there is greater economic uncertainty due to investment in more new products and processes (Driver and Moreton 1992). This is the "Schumpeter Mark I" effect, where new innovations result in the creative destruction of older MOP value controlled by monopolies. This tension will appear as a strong negative force during the innovation-based expansion phase of the cycle.[15] Such negative susceptibility ensures that no investment expansion can ever be permanent, as the level of uncertainty will rise and counter the virtuous circle effect.

A vicious circle appears in the contraction phase of the investment cycle. When there is a decrease in RD, this leads to a decrease in δ, which discourages I. This has a negative impact on AD, GDP, and Π, which then creates a negative "accelerationist" effect on I through lower economic activity. Reinforcing this is the decreased innovation intensity via the dotted flow-line from Π to RD, with the fall in δ pushing the economy further into recession. This vicious circle exhibits weak innovation intensity, deriving from the mature industries of the long-established endogenous innovation effects of a monopoly-controlled, old technological paradigm.

In the susceptibility cycle, investment contractions lead to a trough of indeterminate intensity and length. Susceptibility levels fall to the extent that profits fall and balance sheets are restructured. The length of the trough depends on competitive pressures and the costs of postponing innovation-based investment. Growing inefficiencies of the old MOP weaken the capacity of companies to the point that established MOP capacity is decommissioned and investment builds up again with endogenous innovations. These pressures undermine the vicious circle, and we shift into a virtuous circle. These same pressures are greater under the influence of a new technological paradigm, whereas under the monopoly control of a mature technology paradigm there is less pressure and the vicious circle will tend to continue for a longer period.

The two circular-flow effects result in irregular investment cycles of variable volatility. These cycles have varying degrees of investment fluctuation, expressed as the variance (or standard variation) of I. Although endogenous innovations influence this instability via the amount of I, it is exogenous innovations that distinguish periods of low volatility (with established industries in monopoly control) from periods of higher volatility (when a new technological paradigm is implemented). New systems will generate a strong expansion out of a deep recession, creating the impression of stable growth. This is the expansionary phase of the investment cycle, with growing susceptibility pressures for an eventual strong downturn. Less successful implementation of the new systems will result in aborted efforts to rise out of the deep recession, but they will have only weak, contractionary pressures. These two patterns emerged globally in the 1990s (the former in Southeast Asia and the United States, the latter in Europe and Southern Asia), showing convergence within global regions and divergence across global regions (Hollanders, Soete, and ter Weel 1999).

Equations and Grid Matrix for Industry Sector Analysis

This section examines the flows from RD and Π to I. Equation (3) encapsulates the circular flow described by Equations (1) and (2),

$$I = c \; \Pi^\alpha \, RD^\beta, \tag{3}$$

where P and RD are the two variables that influence I, given the short-term constancy of L. The constant c contains all other influences, including the role of the state. Equation (3) specifies investment as a multiplicative function of profits and R&D, so that raising one of these two inputs also increases the "efficiency" of the other. For estimation purposes it is necessary to turn Equation (3) into log form:

$$ln \; I = ln \; (c) + \alpha \; ln \; (\Pi) + \beta \; ln \; (RD). \tag{4}$$

In Equation (4), the Π-RD link is exogenous, while the link from I to Π is given by the aggregate demand effects of investment, which determine (to a large extent) profits.[16]

Table 6.1 summarizes the above discussion. It lets us identify empirical patterns and analzye contributions to innovation and investment by industry. Table 6.1 differentiates the role of innovation in industries according to their life cycle and

Figure 6.2 **Schematic Representation of Industry Life Cycle R&D and Investment**

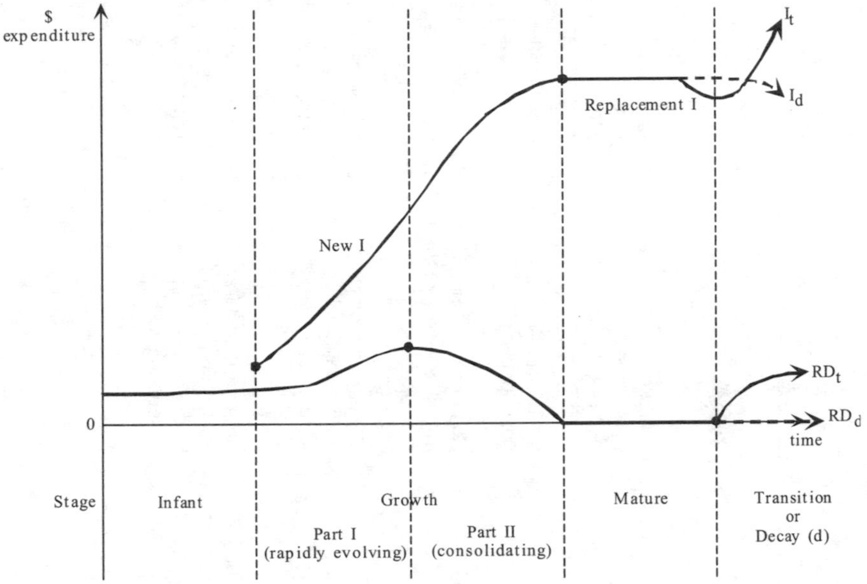

Note: ● Identifies beginning of stage

the type of *RD* they employ. It then relates each industry life-cycle stage to investment decisions and aggregate investment as industries cluster within a life-cycle stage.

Figure 6.2 applies the life-cycle stages in Table 6.1 to the *RD-I* relationship (see Scherer 1984, 4). The length of the stages varies across industries, so Figure 6.2 does not show that each stage is of equal time length. It does draw together *RD* and *I* in an evolutionary approach, and lets us examine each sector's *RD* and *I* data. Figure 6.2 shows endogenous investment takeoff after each industry comes out of the infant stage, when there is relatively little investment and when *RD* is essentially basic (or fundamental) research.

In Part I of the growth stage, the industry is rapidly evolving, with much applied and experimental *RD*, leading to an increasing rate of new investment. Part II of the growth stage has applied and experimental *RD* decreasing. New investment increases, but at a decreasing rate. *RD* falls to virtually zero in the mature stage, as only replacement investment keeps the level of gross investment constant. Human resources devoted to *RD* are the highest in Part II of the growth stage, with large, labor-intensive *RD* activities.

In the final stage, industries have two alternative paths. One is transitional (*t*), which meets the challenges of new technology through the industry reinventing

Table 6.1

Stages of Industry Development—Innovation and Investment

Life-cycle stage	Type of industry	Type of R&D	Role of innovation	Effect on investment decisions	Impact on aggregate investment
Infant	Leading-edge, technologically sophisticated	Highly capital intensive. Basic and applied	Process innovation central	Exogenous stimulation for investment, strong susceptibility	Minimal; insufficient critical mass for aggregate effect
Growth	New-technology based, mass market	Strong labor-expanding. Applied and experimental	Product innovation central	Stimulation to increase market share, subdued susceptibility	Strong expanding cycles with upward trend
Mature	Dominant scale-intensive and information-intensive technologies	Low or zero. Labor based and experimental	Fears of overcapacity; technological frugality	Concentrate on greater utilization, high susceptibility	Sustained capital-stock levels and weak expansion cycles
Transition	Old, dominant-technology based, altering to new technology	Refocus on new-capital based and more applied	Major product innovations; alter processes and diversify	Structural shift in control, joint ventures; leads to severe susceptibility	Exacerbate instability in investment cycles by dominant firms

Source: Adapted from Courvisanos (1996, 201).

Figure 6.3 **Australian Time Series: Investment, Patents, and GDP (1950–98)**
(Index = 1950)

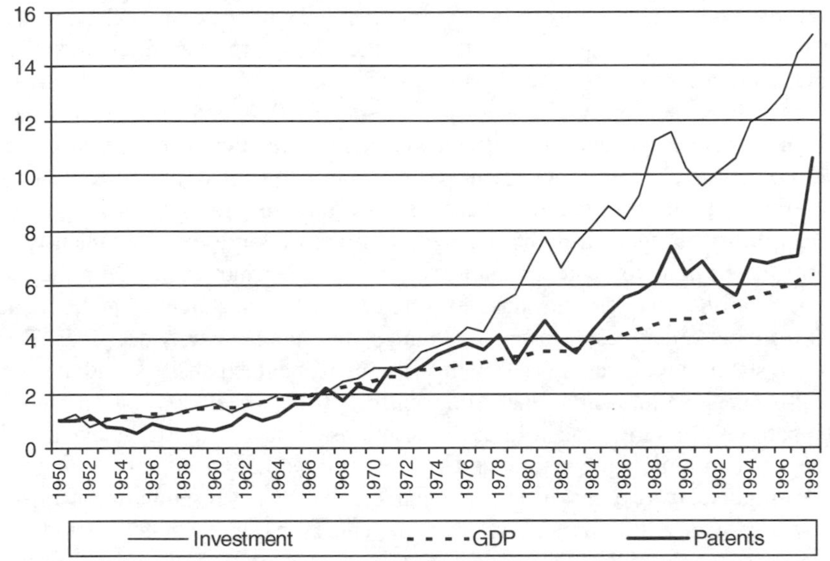

Sources: GDP: Groningen Growth and Development Center, Groningen University, the Netherlands. Investment: Penn World Tables, downloaded from NBER, *OECD Economic Outlook*, June 1999. Patents: US Patent and Trademark Office.

itself, with initially lower investment, but then taking-off into new investment "on the back" of strong *RD* input. The other is a decay stage (*d*), which leads to industry decline, with no *RD* and only replacement investment. This eventually creates such large excess capacity that even replacement investment collapses.

Australian Data and Results

Data on profits, investment, and R&D in the Australian economy was obtained from the Australian Bureau of Statistics (ABS) to test our model. To set the macroenvironment, Figure 6.3 shows levels of investment (*I*), *GDP* (as proxy for *Π*), and Australian patent applications in the United States (proxy for δ) in index number terms, using a base of 1950. The data is from 1950 to 1998.

The investment cycles in Figure 6.3 show subdued cyclical activity, with a modest upward trend through the "Golden Age of investment" in Australia (1950–74), when there was a regulated industrial structure. As the industrial structure became more deregulated and mature, susceptibility increased; fears of overcapacity, technological frugality and market uncertainty in the face of new exogenous innovations in information technology threatened a shift to a completely new industrial paradigm (Freeman and Perez 1988, 52–53). The trend of the investment cycles increased, as did the amplitudes. In Australia, increased volatility and rising trend since the 1979–81 "resources boom" coincided with the first published R&D figures, and help us map the change from the old, energy-based technological paradigm to the new, information-based paradigm.

The increased volatility of investment cycles in the 1980s and 1990s, as observed in Figure 6.3, calls into question the neoclassical interpretation of investment cycles as the outcome of lumpy investment projects and competitive pressures. Lumpy investment in mature, energy-based manufacturing industries magnifies susceptibility in cycle troughs under conditions of large excess capacity, as companies hesitate to make large long-term future commitments.[17] With the rise of information-based service industries, shorter time lags and quicker modification of investment orders result in smaller "lumps" but more capacity decisions. This leads to stabler investment cycles, with sharp investment expansions, and to many small-business failures and much "reinventing of the wheel" by new entrants.[18] Competitive pressures lead to greater variations in susceptibility as expanding industries continually move through technical and market uncertainty.

Patents display a cyclical pattern in Figure 6.3 that closely resembles investment, but with a lower growth trend. With a mature, energy-based technology paradigm, the early post–World War II period has a stable, and even slightly declining, level of patents. From the mid-1960s there is a rising trend in patents, and patent growth increases and becomes more volatile after the recession of 1981–83 as the economy picks up, but with many nascent innovations. There seems to be a strong rise in patents in the late 1990s, especially in software and biotechnology. The pattern of patents provides some support for the innovation-investment link developed above, and justifies examining this relationship more carefully.

GDP in Figure 6.3 has a growth trend with no observable cyclical pattern, despite the cyclical behavior of GDP throughout the period. The scale of the index, and the strong trend, disguises the lower GDP volatility compared to investment and patent indices.[19] Equation (4) forms the basis of our empirical investigation. We develop a panel data set with annual data for I and Π, and RD from 1984–85 to 1997–98. Two-digit industry classifications are used to match investment spending with R&D expenditure and gross profits.

Industry classification until 1991–92 is ASIC (Australian Standard Industrial Classification); it is then replaced by ANZSIC (Australian and New Zealand Standard Industrial Classification). Australian Bureau of Statistics (ABS) guidelines were used to derive a common industry data set. Twelve initial ASIC manufacturing sectors were reduced to eight in this process. The sector Other Manufacturing was removed from the panel data set due to major subgroup shifting within this category between ASIC and ANZSIC. Four service sectors and the mining sector constitute the nonmanufacturing sectors in the panel data. The Communication Services and Scientific Research sectors were not included since no profit figures are available for them. This gives us a panel data set of thirteen industry sectors with 178 observations.[20]

If the variables going into a regression have a unit root there is a danger of everything in the economy growing together and getting a spurious correlation. For panel data, Im, Pesaran, and Shin (2003) suggest running a Dickey-Fuller test for each industry and averaging the t test statistics.[21] The unit-root results show that the residuals in the regression do not have a unit root (what Engle and Granger [1987] call "co-integration"). This means there is a true long-run relationship between the variables and it is likely that no crucial variables have been left out.

The complete data set is put in log form, as per Equation (4), with dummy variables (DV) for the intercept. The Finance and Insurance and Property and Business sectors are removed for log regressions, since both have negative profits. This leaves a data set of eleven industries and 152 observations. Ordinary least squares (OLS) regression is performed on these industries with one-year-lagged RD and Π. The lags on RD and Π allow time for the circular flows from these two variables to affect I, and guarantee exogeneity of the regressors. These lags reduce the observations by one for each industry. We perform six separate regressions by choosing different sample sets from the panel data, following our theoretical framework discussed above. Current Australian dollar values are used to simulate the investment decision-making processes at the time.

Sample 1, using the complete data, is the point of reference for the other regressions. Sample 2 contains manufacturing industries only. To examine volatility, the two expansions of the early 1980s, and the early 1990s recession, are looked at separately in samples 3 and 4. Finally, the evolutionary life-cycle method reveals growth and mature industries, which make up samples 5 and 6 respectively.

Table 6.2 provides OLS results for our sample sets. We performed Im, Pesaran, and Shin (2003) unit-root tests on the residuals. In all cases, we rejected the hypothesis of a unit root, indicating that the results can be interpreted as co-integration equations. Table 6.3 presents these results.

Table 6.2 results can now be examined. All six samples have strong R-squared values and significant f values. The fourth column shows elasticity coefficient for RD as roughly the same, if not higher, than the sixth column Π elasticity coefficient for samples 1, 3, 4, and 5. Sample 2 (manufacturing) reflects a stronger influence from profits than R&D. Sample 6 (mature industries) has a Π coefficient more than double the value of the RD coefficient. These results seem correct as investment decisions in mature industries (mostly manufacturing) tend to be influenced by profits more than R&D.

Unreported in Table 6.2 are the DV coefficients. DV coefficients for all six sample sets range from around 4 to 6. Sample 3 (Expansion A) has many more DV coefficients around 3.1 to 3.8 than in any other sample set. In sample 5 (growth industries), DV coefficients range from 4.9 to 6.3, whereas sample 6 (mature industries) coefficients range from 2.6 to 4.1, indicating that investment decisions in mature industries depend more on profits.

The final three columns in Table 6.2 are partial-determination (PD) coefficients for independent variables RD, Π, and DV (as "one" variable) for each sample set.

Table 6.2

OLS Regression Results in Six Sample Sets

Sample	R square	f-value	RD coefficient	p-value (RD)	π Coefficient	p-value (π)	RD (PD) coefficient	P (π) coefficient	DV (PD) coefficient
1	0.9417	6.8E-72	0.193	3.3E-08	0.233	4.7E-07	0.2128	0.1869	0.8527
2	0.8857	1.5E-39	0.140	0.00067	0.250	2.6E-06	0.1163	0.2103	0.7920
3	0.9642	6.4E-17	0.534	2.8E-05	0.147	0.21532	0.4598	0.0524	0.8992
4	0.9568	5.3E-38	0.217	0.00253	0.208	7.7E-05	0.1337	0.2183	0.9064
5	0.9343	3.9E-25	0.142	0.00296	0.158	0.00481	0.1764	0.1602	0.8786
6	0.9605	8.5E-52	0.220	1.3E-06	0.475	1.9E-09	0.2550	0.3651	0.8673

Table 6.3

Sample Unit-root Tests

Sample	Description	Years in sample	Sample obser-vations	Unit-root average t statistic	Critical value (at significance level)
1	All eleven industries	1984–85 to 1997–98 (fourteen years)	141	−2.74	−2.66 (5%)
2	Manufacturing industries	all fourteen years	104	−2.6	−2.54 (10%)
3	Expansion A years	1984–85 to 1988–89 (five years)	42	No test (too few obser-vations)	N.A.
4	Expansion B years	1991–92 to 1997–98 (seven years)	77	−4.05	−2.88 (1%)
5	Four growth industries	all fourteen years	52	−2.86	−2.88 (1%)
6	Seven mature industries	all fourteen years	89	−2.67	−2.66 (5%)

They are obtained by conducting partial R-square regressions for each of the three variables, while holding the other two variables constant.[22] These regressions give some perspective on the proportion of the variation in I that can be attributed to each of the independent variables. This can be useful in understanding the variance or volatility) when one sample is compared to another in terms of the circular-flow process. As would be expected, in the Equation (4) model (where change in profits, excess capacity, and gearing ratios, are absent), DV has the highest PD coefficient variable for each of the six sample sets.

The evolutionary method is based on industrial life-cycle relations between innovation and investment. The case-study, pattern-matching approach to qualitative data is applied using this method (see Yin 2003). This requires taking the 14 ABS industry sectors as individual case studies and applying the grid matrix of Table 6.1.[23] For each industry, annual R&D data, human resources devoted to R&D, R&D expenditure as a proportion of total expenditure, type of R&D expenditure and activity, and the level and rate of capital expenditure are laid out on a spreadsheet.

There is no need for a complete data set on an annual basis; all available data are included. In most industries, the sporadic R&D data available back to 1976–77 is also included. Each industry has its own pattern. This pattern is classified in terms of percent proportions; high/moderate/low levels; rising/falling/stable over time. Then each industry is matched with the other industries to identify similar patterns. The patterns are then compared to the templates of Table 6.1 and Figure 6.2 so that we can classify the stage of development for each industry.

Table 6.4 summarizes our results. These results were used to identify samples 5 and 6; they can also be examined in their own right. Table 6.4 is arranged with the seven growth industries first, followed by the seven mature industries. Each subgroup is arranged from highest to lowest R&D intensity. There are specific matrices for each of the static, dynamic, and volatility classifications; and there are individual spreadsheets for each industry. A key to the classification code appears at the bottom of Table 6.4.

The second and third columns of Table 6.4 provide a reference point by indicating the pace of innovation across industries in snapshot (column 2) and in early-1990s growth rates (column 3). These indicators are too limited and specific for evaluating the long-run evolutionary processes that influence innovation and investment. A broader picture emerges over the next few columns. Size (static column), change (dynamic column), and variance (volatility column) relate R&D to investment expenditure. Here, the seven growth industries show quite different patterns. Four growth industries exhibited strong investment growth in the 1980s, but relatively weak investment growth in the 1990s. The other three displayed the reverse pattern. There seems to be large investment volatility across this growth group, but with generally rising R&D. The seven mature industries are more consistent, with weak and stable capital expenditures. R&D is also important in the mature industries.

Finally, a simple pattern of R&D can be discerned across all fourteen industries. In the 1970s and early 1980s, labor was the main cost in *all* sectors; this has shifted to "other current costs" in all but three sectors (Property and Business; Finance and Insurance; Printing, Publishing, and Recorded Media). R&D activity is consistently "experimental," around 60–70 percent in all sectors; this reflects the use of overseas technology for Australian conditions. Communications is the only sector where applied research is around 45–50 percent of all research activity. Human-resource effort (in person years) devoted to R&D is relatively low for all sectors, except Machinery and Equipment. Also note some human resource effort increase in the two growth service sectors, Wholesale and Retail and Property and Business.

The Story—An Analysis of Our Results

This section tells a dynamic story that matches the empirical patterns with the theory presented here. A first pattern is derived from the OLS regressions, while a second pattern comes from the evolutionary life-cycle results.

Table 6.4

Evolutionary Life–cycle Results

Industry	R&D Intensity	R&D Growth	Static R&D–I	Dynamic R&D–I	Volatility R&D–I	Recovery from troughs	Panel data classification
Machine and equipment	6.4	13%	High-low	Stab-decl	Nodf-grea L-⇓	Strong-moderate	Growth
Wood and paper	5.0	85%	Low-low	Grth-grth	Grea-grea ⇑	Strong–very strong	Growth
Property and business	1.4	14%	High-moderate	Grth-stab	Grea-grea ⇑	Moderate-moderate	Growth
Finance and insurance	0.3	–11%	Low-low	Decl-decl	Grea-grea ⇒	Moderate-very weak	Growth
Wholesale and retail	0.3	4%	High-high	Grth-decl	Grea-less ⇑⇓-⇓	Moderate-very weak	Growth
Print, publishing, and recorded media	0.3	–13%	Low-low	Grth-grth	Grea-grea ⇑	Weak-strong	Growth
Communications	n.a.	n.a.	Low-low	Decl-decl	Grea-less ⇒	Very strong–very strong	Growth

(continued)

Table 6.4 *(continued)*

Industry	R&D Intensity	R&D Growth	Static R&D–I	Dynamic R&D–I	Volatility R&D–I	Recovery from troughs	Panel data classification
Petrol, coal, and chemicals	4.6	11%	High-low	Decl-decl	Grea-grea ⇒	Strong-none	Mature
Metals	2.9	12%	High-low	Decl-stab	Nodf-great H-⇒	None-moderate	Mature
Nonmetals	2.6	31%	Low-low	Decl-stab	Nodf-less H-⇒	Weak-moderate	Mature
Mining	2.6	46%	High-high	Grth-stab	Grea-less ⇑-⇒	Weak-weak	Mature
Food, beverages, and tobacco	1.9	24%	High-low	Decl-decl	Grea-less ⇓	Weak-weak	Mature
Textile, clothing, footwear, and leather	0.7	19%	Low-low	Stab-decl	Nodf-grea L-⇓	Moderate-weak	Mature
Transport and storage	n.a.	n.a.	Low-mod	Stab-stab	Nodf-nodf L	Moderate-moderate	Mature

(continued)

Table 6.4 (continued)

Industry	R&D Intensity	R&D Growth	Static R&D–I	Dynamic R&D–I	Volatility R&D–I	Recovery from troughs	Panel data classification
KEY	R&D expenditure/total revenue (1955/1996)[1]	Average annual real rate from 1990/1991 to 1995/1996[2]	Average relative size by expenditure and human resource effort[3]	Growth, stable or decline of R&D and I expenditure from 1970s to 1990s[4]	Greater, less no difference vol: ⇑⇓ dir. L/H nodf- low/high[5]	Strong, moderate, or weak early 1980 and 1990s	Classification of industry in relation to both R&D and I across rows troughs[6]

[1]*Source:* Mercer-Melbourne Institute (1998, 2:45, Table 6.2.2).

[2]*Source:* Ibid.

[3]See Appendix 6.3 for details of industry classifications (high, moderate, low) and their size calculations with respect to expenditure relative to proportions spent on R&D and I by the private business sector as a whole. The first classification applies to R&D, the second to Investment (R&D–I). R&D size also incorporates proportion of the human resources devoted.

[4]See Appendix 6.3 for industry classifications and their relative change from the late 1970s to the late 1990s in terms of expenditure in respect to R&D and I. The first classification applies to R&D, the second to Investment (R&D–I).

[5]See Appendix 6.3 for a description of volatility in R&D and I from the late 1970s through to the late 1990s. Arrows indicate general trends in the direction of volatility over this period. H means "high relative volatility in expenditure," while L means "low relative volatility." The code "nodf" means "no difference in volatility" over the period.

[6]See spreadsheets of individual industries, showing the relative expansions of capital expenditure after respective troughs in economic activity. Strong, moderate, and weak indicate the relative strength of capital-expenditure expansions. Spreadsheets are available from the author.

Sample 1 in Table 6.2 indicates that lagged R&D influences investment (0.19) for all industries, and that its influence is only slightly less than lagged profits (0.23). *PD* coefficients show that the variation in investment due to RD_{t-1} (0.21) slightly exceeds Π_{t-1} (0.19). The other sample results from Table 6.2 indicate the relative influence of *RD* on *I* compared to the standard (sample 1) as identified below:

- In Manufacturing, the influence of *RD* is much less than Π (0.13 *cf.* 0.25), and the *RD* variation index is also much lower than for Π (0.12 *c.f.* 0.21). *RD* seems to influence investment in Nonmanufacturing, Mining (old paradigm), and Services (new paradigm).
- Expansion A shows a massive rise in the influence of *RD* (0.53), and the variation index also increases. Π is not significant in this regression. *RD* was important for the expansion out of the 1980s, and the rise of the new, information-based paradigm is evident in this expansion. Wholesale and Retail, Property and Business, Machinery and Equipment all show strong *RD* and *I* expansion.
- Expansion B results are like the standard (sample 1) results regarding the influence of *RD* (0.22) and Π (0.21), and *DV* is the strongest variation index (0.91). Two things are taking place here. First, there is the relatively slow rise out of the early 1990s trough compared to Expansion A, due to greater debt restructuring requirements and higher excess capacity (traditional Kaleckian factors). Second, there is a relatively low *RD* base in several industries with strong *I* expansions (Wood and Paper; Printing, Publishing, and Recorded Media; Transport and Storage). Property and Business and Communications are strong *I* contributors in Expansion B, with rising *RD* influence.
- Growth industries had the most peculiar results. Both *RD* and Π fall and the *DV* coefficients at their largest. The partial coefficients are also low for both *RD* and Π. Statistically there are many complex issues here that remain unexplained, but can be re-examined better using the evolutionary results.
- Mature industries display a more consistent pattern. Both *RD* and Π are important, but Π is more influential. This supports the Kaleckian role of profits in mature industries. *DV* coefficients have their lowest influence here relative to all other samples. This supports the view that profits "fossilize" reinvestment in mature industries, despite the ascent of the information-technology paradigm.

A look at the partial coefficient indices is also instructive. All six samples have *DV* indices around a tight band (0.79 to 0.91) and Π indices with a wider range (0.05 to 0.36), but generally the indices are around 0.21. The *RD* indices are the widest (0.13 to 0.46), reflecting the differential effect on investment variation from this variable compared to Π and *DV*. This is consistent with the role of innovation, particularly in a period of strong structural change, and shows that *RD* variation contributes to the volatility of *I*.

The evolutionary results from Table 6.4 confirm the patterns identified through OLS regression, and also add a degree of qualitative pattern behavior not available from regressions. Table 6.4 contains two sections showing differences between growth and mature industries, and lets us draw the following conclusions.

There is a marked diversity in growth industries. The two strong manufacturing industries (Machinery and Equipment and Wood and Paper) grow from very different bases. The former was a large, R&D-based sector in the 1970s, which transformed itself by adopting the information-technology paradigm. The latter was a small sector in severe decline during the 1970s, but had a strong turnaround in the 1990s. All four growth service industries are also different. Finance and Insurance had impressive 1980s growth, but a poor record in both R&D and *I* during the 1990s. Printing, Publishing, and Recorded Media shows nascent signs of growth. Communications and Property and Business both have a strong base of investment through innovation, but with different mechanisms. Property and Business has seen a significant rise of R&D from 5.6 percent of total expenditure in 1976–77 to 15.3 percent in 1997–98. Communications R&D is poorly reported in the ABS, but it is the only sector with nearly 50 percent in applied research. Also, studies of this industry indicate that innovation comes through large enterprises having different innovation mechanisms than standard R&D spending (Rogers 1998).

There is a marked uniformity in mature industries, based on protecting existing MOP and the tendency for capital stock to become fossilized. The larger mature industries remain strong through substantial reinvestment. Thus, despite weak investment-cycle expansions, they have large absolute investment spending (especially Transport and Storage, and Mining industries). This indicates that the energy-based paradigm still constitutes a power base for capitalism, and will remain so for a while. Only one is a service industry, and it is the most stable of all fourteen industries, but with virtually no R&D (Transport and Storage). The mature manufacturing industries depend on R&D for reinvestment and their relative monopoly control in the economy; however, their R&D tends to be experimental, which is endogenous innovation. Even their adoption of the information-technology paradigm tends to be an "add-on" to their MOP rather than a fundamental change to the nature of their production systems.

Figure 6.2 lets us place Australian two-digit industry sectors in the following stages of industrial development. The four large capital expenditure industries are marked with an asterisk (*).

- *Infant:* Scientific Research.
- *Growth—Part I (rapidly evolving):* Property and Business*; Communications; Machinery and Equipment.
- *Growth—Part II (consolidating):* Wholesale and Retail*; Finance and Insurance.

- *Mature:* Mining*; Transport and Storage*; Petrol, Coal, and Chemical; Metals; Nonmetals; Food, Beverage, and Tobacco; Textile, Clothing, Footwear, and Leather.
- *Transition:* Wood and Paper; Printing, Publishing, and Recorded Media.

The above analysis can be placed within the outlined Post Keynesian model in a way that relates the evolution of industrial development to the circular flow of innovation and investment. Many studies confirm Australia's comparative disadvantage in R&D-intensive manufacturing, and find that Australia has benefited less from international R&D spillovers than other small advanced economies (Engelbrecht 1998, 184). Our results support this, showing a dominance in Australia of experimental research and relatively low human-resources R&D effort.

Tensions exist between mature industry sectors (with "fossilized" MOP and relatively weak RD) and growth industry sectors (with information technology systems backed by rising business RD). Mature industries are "roadblocks" to further innovation and investment. This creates a mismatch between current investment and new technology, and weakens the "clust-bun" effect in growth sectors. The endogenous innovation of mature industries provides weak input for a strong investment recovery. This was exhibited by the longer time it took for investment to recover from the early 1990s trough compared to the early 1980s trough. In addition, once a strong investment boom is under way (as in the late 1990s), these tensions create a susceptibility to downturns. This is reflected in the safety option of profit-based reinvestment in mature industries, or in speculative behavior rather than productive investment in new technology. Supporting this in Australia is the extremely volatile business investment through 1998–99, which produced zero growth over this period (Mercer-Melbourne Institute 1999, 3:24– 25). For Australia, this means a lengthy time for investment to establish a sustainable recovery, and, then, strong GDP growth with growing susceptibility to a sharp and deep investment downturn.[24]

Tension between the two innovation forces also appears in the two circular-flow processes described above. The virtuous circle feeds through both RD and Π, to greater I and stronger GDP, to produce a strong recovery and susceptibility pressures toward the peak of the investment cycle. The vicious circle is evident at two levels. At the national level, the tensions materialize through relatively poor Australian RD flowing into the NIS. This places increasing pressure on the L term to sustain endogenous innovation into investment, which has significant public policy implications. Either dependence must continue to increase on external private-sector L inputs (like licensing, foreign direct investment, joint ventures from abroad, and borrowed technology) or the public sector needs to expand its domestic-based innovation input. If external L is not forthcoming, strong sustainable I levels may not arise and Π-based reproduction in the old technology paradigm dominates. At the regional level, small, isolated areas in Australia have based their production on the old paradigm, and so are in economic decay. The vicious circle operates powerfully in these areas, as reduced Π from traditional energy and resources-based production reinforces low investment levels. Little Π flows into RD, and the L term is sustained with the old-paradigm-based input from external sources. Here there is a strong case for public intervention to end this vicious circle, since systemic failures prevent market forces from providing this structural change.[25]

Technical Details and Limitations

Our research has some limitations stemming from problems in collecting and analyzing data, in applying results, and related to the theoretical tools currently available.

Collecting and Analyzing Data

R&D data has been available only recently in Australia (1984–85).[26] This gives us a limited number of observations (152) for empirical analysis, and even less in the subsamples. Due to public-sector budget cuts, surveys were not conducted in some years (1985–86, 1987–88, 1989–90), and so we had to interpolate from ABS data using the previous year and the year ahead.[27] In addition, there was a shift from ASIC to ANZSIC classifications, different survey techniques were used in different years, and different categories were used in R&D data compared with Π and I data. Also, ABS alters categories within industry sectors to reflect changes in their activities, especially in the services sectors. Such changes require some arbitrary decisions and inconsistencies inevitably arise.

Finally, there are technical problems in the statistical analysis of the data. The unit-root test could not reject the null hypothesis of a unit root in RD and Π in its absolute values. This prevented any panel data regressions on the absolute data. The log form of the data has no unit-root problem, but, as a result, two crucial service industries had to be excluded as they have negative profit figures.

Applying the Results

With R&D costs below 50 percent of total innovation expenditure, there are concerns that "R&D data may give a misleading picture of the extent of innovation" (Mercer-Melbourne Institute 1998, 2:45). The link of R&D to investment and GDP is stronger than other intellectual-property activities such as trademarks and patents.[28] The latter activities often take longer than the one-year regression lag to become incorporated into the investment process.

Rooney and Mandeville (1998, 461) have argued that innovation studies have been "rather narrowly focused on R&D," when the expanding service sector (largely composed of small companies) does not do much R&D as traditionally defined in ABS data. Patent applications are important for small companies (Rogers 1998, 51), but the investment effects are tenuous as many small companies fail and innovation becomes complex before affecting investment. Service industries innovate via learning-by-doing and adapting information technology to produce new processes and products without any R&D data being registered. These issues point to the need to broaden the analysis and incorporate forms of innovative activity besides R&D. But before this can be done, theory must be revised to explain how these other innovation activities affect the investment decision.

Theoretical Limits

The R&D link to investment is one limitation of our theoretical model. There is also the neglect of profit changes, excess capacity and increasing risk, which are all taken as given. Data and statistical problems compound as one attempts to introduce these elements, so our effort can be justified as a first step.

Of greater concern is that the neoclassical obsession with equilibrium (and comparative static equilibrium) of innovation and investment limits efforts to develop a dynamic analysis of innovation and investment. Evolutionary economics provides a long-term perspective, but fails to understand the macroenvironment where tensions of the circular flow develop. On the other hand, the Post Keynesians have only sporadically looked at these questions, and they have generally failed to look at the dynamic elements that the evolutionary school emphasizes.

Summary: Policy Implications and Future Research

The dynamics of innovation and investment involve threading together an evolutionary analysis of industry development with a Kaleckian analysis of investment volatility. Tensions between virtuous and vicious circular flows create uncertainty that induces strategic planning, with resulting patterns of cumulative expansion along with periods of cumulative destruction and insecurity. The resolution of these tensions makes it difficult to predict innovation, which can result in renewed strong investment expansion or extended periods of weak investment cycles. Our panel data results support the circular-flow mechanisms, while our evolutionary data results show the importance of the stages of industry development and their respective contributions to circular-flow dynamics.

From a Post Keynesian perspective, this paper points to the need for a clear policy framework in a dynamic environment. Business strategic planning must move away from static "how-to-do" flow charts and develop a better understanding of dynamic tensions. The introduction of major innovations initially depends on finance for R&D, and the ability to develop a cluster of successful innovations that can create cumulative accumulation. Small companies often lack sufficient retained earnings or a strong equity base. Large companies often are locked into old capital stock to the detriment of innovative activity. This dilemma points to a need for large companies to collaborate with small, innovative companies in order to generate significant innovation. Government may be needed to encourage and monitor such collaborations.

For public policy, the issue is whether the current circular-flow effects are sustainable and in what direction. If regions, sectors, or even nations exhibit vicious circles, shifting to an innovative creative accumulation process can only be done through strategic intervention. On the other hand, booming virtuous circles exhibit fossilized monopoly power positions that are destabilizing. Both effects require public policy to understand the dynamic tensions in the private sector, particularly in relation to uncertainty, and to develop and gain acceptance for a "new direction" that does more than tamper with the static policy tools of depreciation allowances, subsidies, and protection. Systemic perspective planning with voluntary conformity of all sectors of the business community is required. This is the scope for policy research based on Post Keynesian empirical results of the type shown in this chapter.

Notes

This research was produced while the author was a visiting scholar at MERIT, a research institute of the University of Maastricht, July 1999–January 2000. I acknowledge the financial support and teaching relief provided by the Faculty of Commerce and Law, University of Tasmania. Thanks go to all the MERIT staff for academic and physical support, especially when I failed to get on top of the Dutch systems. In particular, I wish to acknowledge the statistical and econometric support by Bart Verspagen (Eindhoven University of Technology). All the statistical testing was completed by my research assistant, Ameeta Jain (Deakin University), who has an extremely quick appreciation of numbers. The employment of Ms. Jain was possible due to two small Australian Research Council (ARC) grants. Harry Bloch (Curtin University) is the intellectual support that enabled the ARC grant to reach this report stage. Thanks also to Paul Blacklow and Ted McDonald (University of Tasmania) for statistical help at various stages in the research. Finally, I appreciate the advice and guidance provided by the editors of this volume on the revised 2003 version of this research. All interpretations and errors remain mine alone.

1. This study ignores nontechnological innovation based on organizational and labor practices and on new marketing angles that do not involve R&D expenditure. Such innovative behavior requires only a minor level of capital expenditure, and as such does not form a significant link between innovation and investment.

2. Innovation behavior is broadly knowledge based and relates to many social and technological capabilities of an economy (see Woolgar 1998). R&D is an identifiable important foundation of this innovation process (Freeman 1995, Jankowski 1998).

3. Kalecki (1991, 455) endorses the Schumpeterian view when he states that "capitalists investing 'today' think to have an advantage over those having invested 'yesterday' because of technical novelties that have reached them." Note, Kalecki often uses the word "invention" instead of "innovation" in many of his discussions of technical progress. See Courvisanos (1996, 107) for resolution of this confusion.

4. Empirical evidence by Toivanen, Stoneman, and Diederen (1999) support the notion of this virtuous circle effect.

5. See Courvisanos (1996, 44–50) for more on the distinction between endogenous and exogenous innovation for Kalecki.

6. Steindl (1976, 133) describes this endogenous innovation very neatly: "Technological innovations accompany the process of investment like a shadow, they do not act on it as a propelling force."

7. The company can also buy out smaller uncompetitive companies during the contractionary stage of the investment cycle, taking advantage of innovations developed by failed companies.

8. See Toivanen, Stoneman, and Diederen (1999) for empirical support.

9. See Galbraith (1974) on the role of technostructure in planning investment strategies and specific technologies for the ongoing survival and growth of the large corporation. For a recent reinterpretation of the technostructure from a Post Keynesian perspective, see Dunn (2000).

10. For example, several different innovations toward a lightweight solar car have been developed, but a strong enough cluster has not been formed to push the steel-framed, petrol-engine automobile into the museum.

11. See Woolgar (1998, 451) on the need for "a process of changing networks of social relations" in the NIS.

12. See Courvisanos (1996, 161–62) for the exposition of this more sophisticated investment function.

13. On the theoretical details of the "double-sided relation between profits and investments," see Asimakopulos (1977).

14. See Jankowski (1998) for evidence on both roles of R&D in the foundations of innovation even as structural changes alter its nature and activity, reflecting the shift to information-technology R&D and its input into the services sector.

15. There is evidence that in the 1990s this innovation-based susceptibility took root more rapidly and strongly in Europe than in the United States and Australia (see Hollanders, Soete, and ter Weel 1999).

16. The Kaleckian I to P link ("capitalists get what they spend") has been confirmed by a series of empirical studies covering the United States (Asimakopulos 1983), United Kingdom (Arestis, Driver, and Rooney 1985–86), and Italy (Del Monte 1981, Sylos Labini 1967).

17. In aggregate terms, this lumpiness tends to be "washed out" by the spread of investment over many years and the bunching of investment by large companies in different industries (Courvisanos 1996, 211–12).

18. Early post–World War II evidence in the United States shows that "there is a much wider fluctuation of capital investment among small than among large organizations" (Boatwright 1954, 109–10).

19. Mercer-Melbourne Institute (various issues) provides a quarterly bulletin on "Reading of the Business Cycle." This bulletin continually updates the Pagan (1996) history of Australian business cycles.

20. See Appendix 6.1 for ABS sources of data, industry-sector classifications, and concordance issues.

21. See Appendix 6.2.

22. The formula used for partial determination coefficient for I on RD (holding P and DV constant) is as follows. The numerator is: (sum of squares of regression [SSR] of all variables) minus (SSR of all variables, except RD). The denominator is: (total SSR model with all variables [TSS]) minus (SSR of all variables, including RD) plus (numerator). For example, in sample 1, for RD: TSS is 112.6797, SSR (all variables) is 106.1153, and SSR (all variables, except RD) is 104.3399. Plugging the values in the formula, the coefficient is calculated to be 0.21288 as an index number for RD as the PD coefficient. Similarly, partial coefficients can be found for I on P, and I on DV for each sample set.

23. All eleven industries in the panel data set are included, plus the three service-sector industries that were dropped from the panel data due to the lack of a statistically complete

set (Communication Services) or due to negative profits in log form (Property and Business, Finance and Insurance).

24. Compared to the European case, where volatility means shorter time to renew investment but shallow investment downturns and lower growth rates.

25. For detailed analyses of this regional policy issue in relation to Australia, with specific application to the small peripheral region of Tasmania, see Courvisanos (1999, 2000, 2001).

26. R&D data became available in the late 1970s in most OECD nations (Mercer-Melbourne Institute 1998, 2:39).

27. For details of formula, see Appendix 6.1.

28. As Mortimer (1997, 14) states, "Innovation is a key driver of growth, and GDP per capita is highly correlated to R&D intensity among developed nations."

References

Arestis, P., C. Driver, and J. Rooney. 1985–86. "The Real Segment of a UK Post Keynesian Model." *Journal of Post Keynesian Economics* 8(2): 163–81.

Asimakopulos, A. 1975. "A Kaleckian Theory of Income Distribution." *Canadian Journal of Economics* 8(3): 313–33.

———. 1977. "Profits and Investment: A Kaleckian Approach." In G.C. Harcourt (ed.), *The Microeconomic Foundations of Macroeconomics*, 328–42. Boulder, CO: Westview Press.

———. 1983. "A Kaleckian Profits Equation and the United States Economy, 1950–82." *Metroeconomica* 35: 1–27.

Baran, P., and P. Sweezy. 1966. *Monopoly Capital.* New York: Monthly Review Press.

Boatwright, J.W. 1954. "Comment." In *Regularization of Business Investment*, 109–12. Princeton, NJ: Princeton University Press.

Collins, A., and S. Yao. 1998. "On Innovative Activity Over the Business Cycle: A Note." *Applied Economics Letters* 5(12): 785–88.

Courvisanos, J. 1996. *Investment Cycles in Capitalist Economies: A Kaleckian Behavioural Contribution.* Cheltenham, UK: Edward Elgar.

———. 1999. "Region in Transition: Schumpeterian Road to Recovery in Tasmania." *Journal of Economic and Social Policy* 4(1): 45–62.

———. 2000. "IT Investment Strategy for Development: An 'Instrumental Analysis' Based on the Tasmanian and New Brunswick Information Technology Strategies." *Prometheus* 18(1): 75–91.

———. 2001. "Regional Economic Decay and Regeneration Under Structural Change." In I. Falk, ed., Learning to Manage Change, 13–22. Melbourne: NCVER.

Del Monte, G. 1981. "Review of MOSYL, 1967 to 1981." *Review of Economic Conditions in Italy* 2 (June): 323–28.

Dixit, A. 1992. "Investment and Hysteresis." *Journal of Economic Perspectives* 6(1): 107–32.

Dixit, A., and R. Pindyck. 1994. *Investment Under Uncertainty.* Princeton, NJ: Princeton University Press.

Dodgson, M., and R. Rothwell, eds. 1994. *The Handbook of Industrial Innovation.* Cheltenham, UK: Edward Elgar.

Driver, C., and D. Moreton. 1992. *Investment, Expectations and Uncertainty.* Oxford, UK: Basil Blackwell.

Dunn, S.P. 2000. "Galbraith, Uncertainty and the Modern Corporation." In M. Keaney, ed., *Economist with a Public Purpose: Essays in Honour of John Kenneth Galbraith.* London: Routledge.

Engelbrecht, H-J. 1998. "Business Sector R&D and Australia's Manufacturing Trade Structure." *Applied Economics* 30(2): 177–87.

Engle, R.F., and C.W.J. Granger. 1987. "Co-integration and Error Correction: Representation, Estimation and Testing." *Econometrica* 55(2): 251–76.

Freeman, C. 1994. "Innovation and Growth." In M. Dodgson and R. Rothwell, eds., *The Handbook of Industrial Innovation*, 78–93. Cheltenham, UK: Edward Elgar.

———. 1995. "The 'National System of Innovation' in Historical Perspective." *Cambridge Journal of Economics* 19(1): 5–24.

Freeman, C., and C. Perez. 1988. "Structural Crises of Adjustment, Business Cycles and Investment Behaviour." In G. Dosi et al., eds., *Technical Change and Economic Theory*, 38–66. London: Pinter.

Freeman, C., and L. Soete. 1997. *The Economics of Industrial Innovation*, 3rd edition. London: Pinter.

Galbraith, John K. 1974 [1967]. *The New Industrial State*, 2nd edition. Harmondsworth, UK: Penguin.

Geroski, P.A., and C.F Walters. 1995. "Innovative Activity Over the Business Cycle." *Economic Journal* 105 (July): 916–28.

Gomulka, S. 1990. *The Theory of Technological Change and Economic Growth*. London: Routledge.

Hollanders, H., L. Soete, and B. ter Weel. 1999. "Trends in Growth Convergence and Divergence and Changes in Technological Access and Capabilities." MERIT Research Memorandum 99–019. Maastricht, NL: Maastricht University.

Im, K.S., M.H. Pesaran, and Y. Shin. 2003. "Testing for Unit Roots in Heterogeneous Panels." *Journal of Econometrics* 115(1): 53–74.

Jankowski, J.E. 1998. "R&D: Foundation for Innovation." *Research Technology Management* 41(2): 14–20.

Kaldor, N. 1961. "Capital Accumulation and Economic Growth." In F.A. Lutz and D.C. Hague, eds., *The Theory of Capital*, 177–228. New York: St. Martin's Press.

———. 1966. *Causes of the Slow Rate of Economic Growth in the United Kingdom*. Cambridge: Cambridge University Press.

Kalecki, M. 1937. "The Principle of Increasing Risk." *Economica* (new series) 4(16): 440–6.

———. 1954. *Theory of Economic Dynamics*. London: Allen and Unwin.

———. 1962. "Observations on the Theory of Growth." *Economic Journal* 72 (March): 134–53.

———. 1991. "The Problem of Effective Demand with Tugan-Baranovsky and Rosa Luxemburg." In J. Osiatynski, ed., *Collected Works of Michal Kalecki*. Volume II: *Capitalism —Economic Dynamics*, 451–58. Oxford: Clarendon Press. (Originally published in Polish in *Ekonomista*, 1967, 2: 241–49.)

Kleinknecht, A. 1987. *Innovation Patterns in Crisis and Prosperity: Schumpeter's Long Cycle Reconsidered*. London: Macmillan.

Lavoie, M. 1992. *Foundations of Post-Keynesian Economic Analysis*. Aldershot, UK: Edward Elgar.

Malerba, F., and L. Orsenigo. 1993. "Technological Regimes and Firm Behaviour." *Industrial Corporate Change* 2(1): 45–71.

Mercer-Melbourne Institute. (various issues: 1998 and 1999). "Reading of the Business Cycle." Quarterly Bulletin of Economic Trends. Parkville: Melbourne Institute of Applied Economic and Social Research, University of Melbourne.

Mortimer, D. 1997. *Going for Growth: Business Programs for Investment, Innovation and Export*. Canberra: Commonwealth of Australia.

Nickell, S., and D. Nicolitsas. 1996. "Does Innovation Encourage Investment in Fixed Capital?" Centre for Economic Performance, London School of Economics and Political Science, Discussion Paper No. 309 (October).

O'Connor, J. 1973. *The Fiscal Crisis of the State.* New York: St. Martin's Press.

Pagan, A. 1996. "The Rise and Fall and Rise . . . of the Business Cycle." Centre for Economic Policy Research Discussion Paper No. 349 (September). Canberra: The Australian National University.

Ricottilli, M. 1996. "Technical Progress and the Process of Economic Development: A Keynesian Macroeconomic Problem in an Evolutionary Context." Paper presented at The Fourth International Post Keynesian Workshop, University of Tennessee, June 27–July 3, 1996. Knoxville: University of Tennessee.

Rogers, M. 1998. "Innovation in Large Australian Enterprises." In Mercer-Melbourne Institute *Quarterly Bulletin of Economic Trends*, No. 2 (June): 50–60.

Rooney, D., and T. Mandeville. 1998. "The Knowing Nation: A Framework for Public Policy in a Post-industrial Knowledge Economy." *Prometheus* 16(4): 453–67.

Salter, W.E.G. 1960. *Productivity and Technical Change.* Cambridge: Cambridge University Press.

Sawyer, M. 1996. "Kalecki on Trade Cycle and Economic Growth." In J.E. King, ed., *An Alternative Macroeconomic Theory: The Kaleckian Model and Post-Keynesian Economics*, 93–114. Boston: Kluwer.

Scherer, F.M. 1984. *Innovation and Growth: Schumpeterian Perspectives.* Cambridge: MIT Press.

Schmookler, J. 1966. *Invention and Economic Growth.* Cambridge: Harvard University Press.

Schumpeter, J.A. 1939. *Business Cycles: A Theoretical, Historical and Statistical Analysis of the Capitalist Process*, 2 vols. New York: McGraw-Hill.

Steindl, J. 1976. *Maturity and Stagnation in American Capitalism.* 2nd edition. New York: Monthly Review Press.

———. 1979. "Stagnation Theory and Stagnation Policy." *Cambridge Journal of Economics* 3(1): 1–14.

Stoneman, P. 1983. *The Economic Analysis of Technological Change.* Oxford: Oxford University Press.

Sylos Labini, P. 1967. "Prices, Distribution and Investment in Italy, 1951–1966: An Interpretation." *Banca Nazionale del Lavoro Quarterly Review* 83 (December): 3–57.

Toivanen, O., P. Stoneman, and P. Diederen. 1999. "Uncertainty, Macroeconomic Volatility and Investment in New Technology." In C. Driver and P. Temple, eds., *Investment, Growth and Employment: Perspectives for Policy.* London: Routledge.

Vercelli, A. 1989. "Uncertainty, Technological Flexibility and Long-Term Fluctuations." In M. Di Matteo et al., eds., *Technological and Social Factors in Long Term Fluctuations*, 130–44. Berlin: Springer-Verlag.

Woolgar, S. 1988. "A New Theory of Innovation." *Prometheus* 16(4): 441–52.

Yin, R.K. 2003. *Case Study Research: Design and Methods*, 3rd edition. Thousand Oaks, CA: Sage Publishers.

Appendix 6.1. Data Sources and Industry-Sector Classifications

Sources for the Panel Data

For *I*: Australian Bureau of Statistics (ABS) (various issues), *Private New Capital Expenditure*, Cat. No. 5625.0, Canberra.

For *RD*: ABS (various issues), *Research and Experimental Development: Business Enterprises, Australia*, Cat. No. 8104.0, Canberra.

For *P*: ABS (various issues), *Company Profits*, Cat. No. 5651.0, Canberra.

The following thirteen industry sectors were set up in the panel data:

INDUSTRY SECTOR CLASSIFICATIONS	ANZSIC
Mining	11–15
Manufacturing	
Food, Beverages, and Tobacco (FBT)	21
Textiles, Clothing, Footwear, and Leather (TCFL)	22
Wood and Paper Products	23
Printing, Publishing, and Recorded Media	24
Petroleum, Coal, Chemical, and Associated Products	25
Nonmetallic Mineral Products	26
Metal Products	27
Machinery and Equipment	28
Services	
Wholesale and Retail Trade	F-G
Finance and Insurance	K
Property and Business Services	77, 782–786
Transport and Storage	I

Classification changes and resulting data requirements:

1. The ASIC classification was replaced by the ANZSIC classification (above) from 1992–93. Concordance guidelines set up by ABS to match the two systems of classification are used in developing a consistent panel data series for the thirteen sectors. Some minor classification problems remain which concordance could not resolve and which do not make the data completely consistent between the ASIC and ANZSIC categories. ABS authorities have assured us that these inconsistencies are minor in terms of the total expenditures for the industry sectors identified below:

    *   Mining under ASIC excludes services to mining, while it includes it under ANZSIC.
    *   Leather-manufacturing subdivision (under "Other Manufacturing" in ASIC, but which cannot be identified as a separate item) has been included with the Textiles, Clothing, and Footwear (ASIC classification) only from 1992–93 to form TCFL.

2. Private New Capital Expenditure figures are in accordance with ANZSIC from 1987–88. Prior to that, the figures are in accordance with ASIC; this is unpublished data that was supplied by the ABS office on request.

3. R&D Expenditure figures are in accordance with ANZSIC from 1992–93. Prior to that, the figures are in accordance with ASIC.
4. Company profit (before income taxes) figures accord with ANZSIC from 1985–86. Prior to that, the figures are in accordance with ASIC. ANZSIC classification is unpublished data that was supplied by the ABS office on request.
5. Two ASIC subdivisions have been combined to form one ANZSIC industry sector and extended back to the beginning of the panel data series. This has been done in two separate cases:

- Basic metal products (ASIC 29) and Fabricated Metal Products (ASIC 31) form Metal Products sector (ANZSIC 27)
- Transport equipment (ASIC 32) and Other Machinery and Equipment (ASIC 33) form Machinery and Equipment (ANZSIC 28).

6. Data for the Transport and Storage category is unpublished and was supplied by ABS upon request. Categories 263 (Paper and Paper Products) and 264 (Printing and Allied Services) have unpublished *RD* and *I* figures, also supplied by ABS upon request.

Data available for all industries from 1984–85 to 1997–98 (i.e., fourteen years), except for:

1. R&D expenditure for years 1985–86, 1987–88, 1989–90 are not available. Only total estimated R&D expenditure figures are available for these specific years. These estimates have been derived by ABS using a stratified random sample of businesses. The method used to calculate values for these years for the respective industry sectors is as outlined below, using FBT for 1985–86 as the example:

- R&D expenditure on FBT in 1985–86 = {(R&D expenditure on FBT in 1984–85 / Total R&D expenditure on all industries in 1984–85) + (R&D expenditure on FBT in 1986–87 / Total R&D expenditure on all industries in 1986–87)} / 2.
- This expression is multiplied by Total R&D stratified sample expenditure in 1985–86. This provides the R&D expenditure for FBT in 1985–86.

2. Transport and Storage and Finance and Insurance have *RD* figures available only from 1986–97 (i.e., twelve years), so the panel data series for these two industries began two years later in both cases. This gives us 178 initial panel data observations instead of 182 (thirteen industries by fourteen years).

Appendix 6.2

Initial Unit–root Test Results on Panel Data, 1984–85 to 1997–98

Based on thirteen industries with 178 observations in non-lagged and non-log form.

Industry	Test statistics for intercept (no trend)			Test statistics for intercept and linear time trend		
	I	RD	Π	I	RD	Π
Mining	2.81	−0.77	−1.87	1.50	−2.40	−2.33
Food, beverage, and tobacco	0.72	−1.40	0.217	−1.15	−3.00	−3.68
Textiles, clothing, footware, and leather	−2.57	−0.21	−2.84	−2.27	−2.57	−2.55
Wood and paper	−1.90	−1.35	−1.16	−1.87	−3.08	−1.87
Print, publishing, and recorded media	−2.29	−0.57	−0.49	−3.07	−2.69	−1.86
Petrol, coal and chemicals	−2.14	−0.85	−2.02	−1.12	−1.87	−2.16
Non-metal products	−2.44	−0.31	−1.93	−3.40	−1.98	−1.76
Metal products	−3.69	−0.93	−2.08	−3.83	−2.49	−2.22
Machinery and equipment	−0.80	−0.42	−1.59	−1.29	−2.28	−2.81
Wholesale and retail	−1.47	−1.13	−2.31	−2.33	−3.41	−2.23
Finance and insurance	−3.68	−2.79	−0.82	−3.65	−2.12	−3.82
Property and bus.	−2.17	2.17	−2.13	−2.07	0.14	−1.94
Transport and storage	−2.01	−2.84	−1.67	−1.87	−2.25	−2.07
Average t-test statistic	−1.67	−0.88	−1.59	−2.03	−2.31	−2.41
Critical value (1%)	−2.24	−2.24	−2.24	−2.88	−2.88	−2.88
Critical value (5%)	−2.02	−2.02	−2.02	−2.66	−2.66	−2.66
Critical value (10%)	−1.90	−1.90	−1.90	−2.54	−2.54	−2.54

Appendix 6.3. Sources for the Evolutionary Method

R&D data on human resources, expenditure, type of R&D, and type of R&D activity are all obtained from: Australian Bureau of Statistics (various issues), *Research and Experimental Development: Business Enterprises, Australia*, Cat. No. 8104.0, Canberra.

Capital expenditure data: Australian Bureau of Statistics (various issues), *Private New Capital Expenditure*, Cat. No. 5625.0, Canberra.

The data for this method covers the period 1976–77 to 1997–98. The early R&D data is sporadic, with figures generally for only years 1976–77, 1978–79, and 1981–82. The complete R&D data series begins from 1984–85, as per the details in Appendix 6.1.

There are fourteen industry sectors that form the basis for this evolutionary method. This consists of the same thirteen industry sectors as in Appendix 6.1, plus Communication Services (ASIC: H; ANZSIC: J). The available data for the communications sector is too sporadic to be used in the panel data series, where continuous annual data is required. The evolutionary method can identify some trends by examining the sporadic data and comparing the trends over time to other sectors with more continuous data series.

Calculations of Code Classifications in Table 6.4.

1. Human resources devoted to R&D (person years)

A scale was formulated for analyzing the person-year effort on R&D per industry. The scale is from zero to the highest number of person years for that particular year per industry sector. Each year is examined across all industries with the following code classification: The industry with the highest number of person years is the standard. "High" classification is where an industry is 50 percent or more of the highest number of person years in the highest industry. If an industry falls within the lower 50 percent value of the highest number of person years, then this subgroup is classified in two categories; as "Low," for the lowest 40 percent within this sub-category and "Moderate" for the remaining 60 percent.

2. R&D industry expenditure as a proportion of total R&D expenditure of all industries for that year:

Static measure based on a scale from zero to the highest expenditure for that particular year. For each year comparison is made on the expenditure across all industries.

High: represents expenditures in the upper one-third of the scale.

Low: represents expenditures in the lower one-third of the scale.

Moderate: the remaining third of the values.

Dynamic measure based on percentage change of R&D expended over the period 1976–77 to 1997–98.

Stable: where the percentages remain roughly the same between the late 1970s and the late 1990s (within +/–2 percent).

Growth: where the percentages show significant increases between the late 1970s and the late 1990s (2 percent or more).

Decline: where the percentages show significant decreases between the late 1970s and the late 1990s (2 percent or more).

Investment expenditure into industry in respect to total gross fixed private capital expenditure for that year.

Static measure based on a scale from zero to the highest expenditure for that particular year. For each year, a comparison is made of expenditures across all industries.

High: represents expenditures in the upper one-third of the scale.

Low: represents expenditures in the lower one-third of the scale.

Moderate: the remaining third of the values.

Dynamic measure based on the rate of expenditure growth for a particular industry from the preceding year.

Stable: where the percentages remain roughly the same between the late 1970s and the late 1990s (i.e., less than 10 percent change on average over twenty-four months).

Growth: where the percentages show significant increases between the late 1970s and the late 1990s (10 percent or more/twenty-four months).

Decline: where the percentages show significant decreases between the late 1970s and the late 1990s (10 percent or more/twenty-four months).

Volatility of R&D expenditure from the late 1970s to the late 1990s:

No difference: refers to essentially no change in the proportions of expenditure in industry compared to total R&D expenditure throughout this period.

High: indicates strong intensity in expenditure proportion changes, reflecting significantly high variance over time (2 percent or more change in proportions). This variance may tend to show upward (⇑) or downward (⇓) volatility.

Low: indicates weak intensity in expenditure proportion changes, reflecting low variance in percentages over time (less than 2 percent). This variance may tend to show upward (⇑) or downward (⇓) volatility.

Volatility of investment from the late 1970s to the late 1990s:

No difference: refers to essentially no change in the percentages of expenditure throughout this period.

High: indicates strong intensity in expenditure changes, reflecting significantly high variance in the rate of growth over time (20 percent or more). This variance may tend to show upward (⇑) or downward (⇓) volatility.

Low: indicates weak intensity in expenditure changes, reflecting low variance in the rate of growth over time (less than 20 percent). This variance may tend to show upward (⇑) or downward (⇓) volatility.

Recovery from the two recessions of 1981–83 and 1989–91:

Strong: immediately following these years, investment in the sector shows strong upward movement (in the range of over 20 percent).

Moderate: immediately following these years, investment in the sector shows some upward movement, but it is between 10 to 20 percent, and may also be delayed by a year or two compared to the "strong" group.

Weak: low (below 10 percent) growth out of the recession.

None: no growth out of the recession (or even a decline in the growth rate) after the recession.

7

Anthony J. Laramie, Douglas Mair, and
Anne G. Miller

Kalecki's Investment Theory:
A Critical Realist Approach

*[T]he determination of investment decision . . . remains, to my mind, the central
pièce de resistance of economics.*

(Kalecki 1971, 165)

Introduction

Professing Post Keynesian economists who practice the black art of econometrics
must be like Caesar's wife. They cannot, on the one hand, adopt a "holier than
thou" attitude to what they consider to be the fallacious practices of mainstream
economists and econometricians while, on the other, using the selfsame procedures to test the empirical validity of their Post Keynesian theorizing. This dilemma has arisen as a consequence of the cathartic process that Post Keynesian
economics has undergone over the past decade. Faced with continuing indifference, or even outright hostility from the mainstream (Walters and Young 1997),
Post Keynesians have sought to define what commitment to the credo of Post
Keynesianism actually means. They have realized that it is no longer sufficient for
them to march shoulder to shoulder under the banner of anti-neoclassicism (Lawson
1994). A number of Post Keynesian scholars (Arestis 1992; Arestis, Dunn and
Sawyer 1999; Dow 1996, 1997, 2001; Lavoie 1992; Lawson, A. 1994, 1997, 1998;
Lawson, T. 1999) have sought to define Post Keynesian economics in terms of its
compatibility with transcendental and critical-realist methodology. While not all
Post Keynesians may yet have accepted all of the implications of sailing under the
flag of transcendental/critical realism, there is an increasing recognition that it
provides a methodological approach that accommodates most Post Keynesians'
perceptions of how socio-economic problems should be studied.

In this chapter, we try to show how a careful use of traditional econometrics can
be reconciled with a critical-realist approach. Our chosen theme takes us to the
interface of economic theory and econometric analysis, namely, what are the determinants of investment, and how should they be estimated? We take Michal

Kalecki's theory of investment as our exemplar because of its centrality to Post Keynesian economics. Beginning with a brief discussion of critical realism and Post Keynesian economics, we go on to argue that it is entirely appropriate to consider Kalecki's theory of investment from a critical-realist perspective. This can be justified from a behavioralist interpretation of Kalecki's theory. On this interpretation, there are important behavioral and institutional elements of Kalecki that Courvisanos (1996) has formulated into an investment susceptibility cycle. This cycle has three objective elements, profits, risk and capacity utilization, that form the core of Kalecki's investment theory. We then proceed to estimate the Kalecki-Courvisanos investment susceptibility cycle with data from the United Kingdom. In so doing we identify certain tensions between Kalecki's theory and econometric theory and practice, and we demonstrate how we have endeavored to resolve them without violating the principles of critical-realist methodology.

Critical Realism and Post Keynesian Economics

In *A New Guide to Post Keynesian Economics*, Holt and Pressman (2001) provide a historical account of the development of Post Keynesian economics, and Dow (2001) sets out its methodological foundations. She identifies something approaching a consensus on Post Keynesian methodology. This consensus recognizes the need to study economics from an open systems approach, involving collections of partial analyses that aim to build up a (fallible) knowledge of different parts of the socio-economic system. Rather than relying on a single formal method, as is the case with neoclassical economics, critical realism draws on a range of methods (formal, institutional, or historical) that in turn draw on different types of data sets (case studies or published data series) to address the problem under investigation. The debate on Post Keynesian methodology is still evolving and a critical aspect of that debate is the proper role for econometrics. Opinion ranges from the near-nihilist stance of Lawson (1997), who argues against the use of econometrics on the grounds that the conditions necessary for its proper application virtually never occur, to the more pragmatic stance of Downward, Finch, and Ramsay (2002), who argue that if event regularities are sufficiently persistent, there may be a legitimate role for econometrics.

Before we proceed to demonstrate how we have attempted to take account of critical-realist caveats on the use of econometrics to study the behavior of investment in a Post Keynesian (Kaleckian) model, there are some important methodological issues that we need to clarify. Our discussion here draws on a number of Post Keynesian authors, including Dow (1999), Downward (2000), and Rotheim (1999). From a critical-realist perspective, the social world is decisively open. By this it is meant that event regularities are not pervasive; rather, underlying mechanisms generate forces, tendencies, and counter-tendencies, so that observed outcomes are the result of a multiplicity of causes. A critical-realist perspective seeks to identify and understand the underlying structures, mechanisms, or tendencies that govern, facilitate, or produce observable surface phenomena. The emerging role that Post Keynesian economists see for themselves is to use the method of critical realism as a set of lenses through which to observe sense data about the relative powers of socio-economic forces and tendencies in order to formulate a theory that sheds light on the sense data that have been observed. Recognizing that the social world is open does not imply that it is necessarily in flux, or that it is random, or that nothing can ever be said about anything that occurs in it. The critical-realist perception of society as an open system means that if Post Keynesians are to build up knowledge of it, then that knowledge should also conform to an open system.

Critical realists argue that mainstream (neoclassical) economics holds a closed-system perception of existence as a justification for its closed-system, deductivist methodology. The deductivist approach entails closed-system modeling and requires two conditions for closure. The intrinsic condition of closure suggests that the structures of the phenomena under study are constant and unchanging, so that for any intrinsic state only one outcome is possible. The extrinsic condition of closure suggests that the phenomena under study are isolated from other potential influences. In the mainstream world, econometrics also requires the presupposition that concepts can be measured, counted, manipulated, and cross-classified, and that, consistent with risk and uncertainty being confined to measurable stochastic errors centered on event regularities, inference can proceed entirely with respect to numerically measurable probability distributions. Thus, given their methodological stance, econometrics is an entirely appropriate approach for mainstream economists to employ. The open-system critical-realist approach, to which Post Keynesians are now tending, argues that even if regularities exist in the social world, there will be a plurality of partial regularities and processes underlying events, which are unlikely to be amenable to the strictures of econometric analysis.

Therefore, Post Keynesians who go down the road of critical realism must take a skeptical view of the relevance of econometrics as a means of illuminating the complex phenomena of the socio-economic world. However, Downward, Finch, and Ramsay (2002) argue that in the complex and confusing world of reality, agents develop and adapt decision-making apparatuses. In conjunction with agents' own mental models, institutions evolve and develop that depend on the tractability of those institutions as decision-making apparatuses. Downward, Finch, and Ramsay (ibid.) describe this process as "quasiclosure" and define it as reflecting the stable conditions upon which agents base their behavior. Critical realism rejects the mainstream assumption of pervasive closure, but recognizes that there may be institutional contexts in which quasiclosure can occur. The role of the researcher is to define and outline these institutional dimensions of behavior so as to identify discernible event regularities. There may then be a role for econometrics to analyze these "demiregularities," but their existence has to be demonstrated not assumed. If agents do manifest persistent, conventional, or institutional decision making, this provides the quasiclosure that justifies the use of quantitative techniques, including econometrics, in an open social system that is otherwise intrinsically nonquantifiable. An important corollary follows from the recognition of quasiclosure, namely, that behavioral and institutional economics have an important role to play in helping to identify the habits and rules that may generate demiregularities.

While acknowledging the criticisms that many Post Keynesians make against both the relevance of econometrics as a whole, and the way that it is applied in practice, we are impressed with the review of the philosophy of econometrics offered by Darnell and Evans in *The Limits of Econometrics* (1990). In their chapter 4, "Traditional Econometric Modelling," they suggest a procedure based on falsification which avoids the worst excesses of modern practice. The procedure is both simple and rigorous, and provides the necessary criteria for judging whether the process has been carried out. They state that a theory provides the researcher with a main hypothesis to be tested and a set of auxiliary hypotheses that provide the context within which the main hypothesis is to be tested, since no hypothesis is an independent statement. There follows a process for developing these hypotheses into a testable form of the theory, which involves initial assumptions (more auxiliary hypotheses) about such things as deciding on the functional form of the equation, the choice of variables, the choice of data for the variables, and the lags for the variables.

Because the theory is to be tested by econometric analysis, a stochastic equation error is added, and a set of assumptions is made about the properties of the error term and its relationship to the other regressors. These assumptions are often referred to as the Gauss Markov (GM) assumptions, and their fulfillment is responsible for yielding the desirable properties (efficiency, linearity, unbiasedness) for the estimators of the classical linear regression model. Darnell and Evans require that these assumptions be tested, and if they are not fulfilled—that is, if the residuals are not consistent with white noise errors—then one cannot with any validity continue to test this particular specification of the main hypothesis. Rather, one must go back to the initial assumptions and adjust these on the assumption that it is these that are causing the GM assumptions to be violated, and repeat the process. We try to adhere to the process recommended by Darnell and Evans (1990) in estimating the Kaleckian investment model and testing its main hypothesis.

Critical Realism and Kalecki

Understanding the forces that drive investment is central to Post Keynesian economics. Indeed, the Post Keynesian economist who has labored longest to understand them is Michal Kalecki, although he ultimately conceded that he had not been as successful as he would have wished in that endeavor (Kalecki 1971). So, had Kalecki been proceeding blindly for most of his academic career, or was it the case that he did have all the pieces of the puzzle but lacked the critical-realist perspective to correctly perceive relationships? At first sight, it may seem inappropriate to view Kalecki's theory of investment from a critical-realist perspective. Kalecki's investment theory, particularly its earlier versions, has been criticized as excessively mechanistic, and Kalecki was never the man to agonize over methodological issues. However, Courvisanos (2003) has identified the strong behavioral strand that permeates Kalecki's work. More specifically, Downward (2000) has observed a clear critical-realist dimension to Kalecki's theory of pricing.

> [I]t is clear that the pricing analyses of Kalecki, Hall and Hitch, Andrews and Means comprise theories that explore the actual determinants, or causal processes, of pricing. These do not constitute (effectively) full-information equilibrium or optimising accounts of pricing and, as such, lack a determinate and deductive emphasis. For this reason, they are consistent with a Post Keynesian commitment to an open-system. (Downward 2000, 214)

On the issue of whether this critical-realist interpretation of Kalecki's theory of pricing can be extended to the broader range of his work, Downward concedes that Kalecki can be interpreted as espousing the presuppositions of a closed system. This arises as a consequence of his emphasis on a mechanical process of combining insights as well as the emphasis he placed on deduction. Moreover, Steedman (1992) has raised doubts over the formal adequacies of Kalecki's process of aggregation. However, Downward argues that these doubts disappear if one accepts that Kalecki was concerned with aggregation in the empirical rather than the functional sense. This can be interpreted as a concern on the part of Kalecki to identify the demiregularities of the capitalist economy, something that is fully in keeping with an open-system approach. Finally, as every Kaleckian scholar is aware, Kalecki's whole emphasis was on understanding the dynamic nature of the capitalist economy, whose long-run path he saw as incrementally determined.

Kalecki's analysis of investment is in historic time. This has led to the conclusion (Meacci 1989, 236) that Kalecki's method for dealing with historical time is what Shackle (1972, 430) calls a "diachronistic mechanism." This is a mechanical (or deterministic) method based on the unstated axiom that history is governed by its own past and that what happens is implicit in what has happened. Thus, the past acts as a guide for the future. However as Courvisanos (1996, 69) points out, the major weakness of this method in relation to investment decisions, based on uncertain expected long-term outcomes, is that, by the time the long term has become the actual historical movement, there will have been novel developments (in society) for which the past cannot be a guide. Therefore, if Kalecki's investment theory is to be interpreted within a critical-realist framework, a more sophisticated approach to its treatment of time and uncertainty is required.

Courvisanos (ibid., 71) argues that this can be achieved by integrating the Keynes-inspired work on uncertainty with the essentially latent treatment of risk and uncertainty in Kalecki's analysis of the business cycle. By so doing, a "behavioral" Kalecki can be identified that replaces the mechanical diachronic mechanism with the altogether more complex kaleidic mechanism that is sensitive to behavioral factors. The thrust of Courvisanos' approach is to uncover the behavioral relations and investment-decision-making patterns of entrepreneurs that provide the motivation implicit in Kalecki's surface elements of investment determination. Thus, Courvisanos is following the critical-realist prescription of seeking to identify the complex underlying forces that explain anomalous surface behavior. He identifies two areas of study that illuminate the search for motivation in Kalecki's investment model. The first (ibid., 71) is the behavioral analysis of the conventions and practices that are sensitive to altered information and related imagination, which are the source of investment instability. Here, Courvisanos is seeking to identify conditions for "demiclosure" that Downward, Finch, and Ramsay (2002) argue are a precondition of the application of econometric analysis, as we saw above. Courvisanos' second area of concern is the evolutionary analysis of technological change that creates technical and market uncertainties in the economy. These exacerbate investment instability due to discontinuities in economic progress that lead to new patterns of behavior. If these two principal sources of uncertainty and change can be accommodated within the framework of Kalecki's investment theory, then it can properly be regarded as open-system Post Keynesian and tested by means of econometric analysis provided the conditions generating demiregularities can be established.

Kalecki and Behavioral Economics

Courvisanos (1996, 72) takes as his starting point Keynes's view of the state of confidence that entrepreneurs have with regard to long-term expectations formed from past knowledge; he argues that Keynes's chief convention is to assume, contrary to all likelihood, that the future will resemble the past. By so doing, entrepreneurs attempt to preserve stability in an uncertain world. They use practices like markup pricing, discounted cash flow, and payback rule as conventions to maintain stability, with different institutional contexts giving rise to different motivations and rules. As O'Donnell (1989, 262) has observed, what Keynes was emphasizing was the susceptibility of long-term expectations to change. The frequency and the extent to which they change are largely empirical matters.

There is a large behavioral economics literature that has developed from the managerial view of the modern corporation. An important feature of that literature is the idea of "cycles of corporate instability" (Earl 1984, 12). These result from mistaken decisions by businessmen and can result in a variety of corporate outcomes, some of which may be catastrophic. There are two essential features of corporate instability that Courvisanos identifies as relevant to developing a "behavioralist" interpretation of Kalecki. The first concerns methodology. Here, the argument is that the extension of the idea of corporate instability into Kalecki's investment model means that companies should be seen, not as deterministic, but as kaleidic mechanisms. The second feature relates to the influence of the corporate instability model in the Kaleckian behavioral investment model. Courvisanos argues (1996, 79) that the surface elements in a deterministic Kaleckian model are better seen as motivating the managerial and financial processes at work in the corporate instability model. Again, this is the methodological approach prescribed by critical realism.

Courvisanos then turns to bounded rationality to explain the corporate investment process. Businessmen cannot know all the alternatives to or consequences of their investment decisions. They base them on a bounded rationality that involves setting targets for satisfactory outcomes and use conventional rule-of-thumb techniques to meet these targets. As Simon (1986, ix) has argued, the task for economists who assume bounded rationality is to understand how information is processed by individuals and organizational procedures in the uncertain, poorly known, and complex world in which decision makers find themselves. Courvisanos uses the inevitable tensions and pressures of the world of bounded rationality as the basic behavioral premise of his Kaleckian investment model.

Kalecki was fully aware of the importance of institutions in determining the dynamic behavior of an economy.

> No "general" theory of economic growth is conducive to understanding economic realities of different social systems; for the institutional framework of a system exerts a profound influence upon its dynamics. (Kalecki 1970, 311)

Kalecki's institutional framework is monopoly capitalism. This structure is dominated by large companies operating in cost-determined markets with constant prime costs up to normal capacity utilization and applying markup pricing. Kalecki's "degree of monopoly" factors are the crucial determinants of the oligopoly structure of an industry. As we have observed above, Downward (2000) has argued that Kalecki's degree of monopoly pricing theory satisfies the requirements of an open-system approach. Mair, Laramie, and Reynolds (2004) have identified such factors as barriers to entry, product differentiation, and degree of exposure to foreign competition as important determinants of the degree of monopoly in the U.K. manufacturing industry.

To develop a "behavioralist" Kalecki, it is necessary to understand the role of the various agents within the company (Courvisanos 1996, 98). Kalecki's original formulation of a "controlling group" has to be modified to recognize the realities of the modern, diversely owned corporation. Two sub-groups are identified: (i) Kalecki's original "entrepreneur-owners," and (ii) "entrepreneur-managers." Thus, there are two groups of capitalists. The first is the industrial capitalists (entrepreneurs) who control the important investment decisions. The second is the financial capitalists, comprising rentiers who are either shareholders or lenders of finance. Both categories of capitalists have strategic interests in the investment decisions of the companies with which they are involved. In Kalecki's terminology, they are "masters of their fate."

The financial behavior of companies is central to developing Kalecki's behav-

ioral theory of investment. Kalecki recognized, but did not stress, the role of financial factors in influencing the behavior of the economy over the cycle. For example, Dymski writes:

> [M]onetary concepts seldom appear in Kalecki's mature writings; when they do
> the author treats them sparingly. For example, in the various permutations of
> Kalecki's dynamic model, financial elements are incorporated only partially and
> the banking system plays a passive role. . . . Kalecki purposely set financial
> factors into the background of the business cycle. (Dymski 1996, 116 and 133)

Dymski (1996) and Sawyer (1999) have recently explored Kalecki's monetary
analysis in some detail. They argue that while Kalecki did have a clear understanding of the operation of the monetary system, he was concerned principally to develop a real rather than a monetary model of the business cycle. Thus, for Kalecki,
the rate of interest was a monetary phenomenon rather than the equilibrating mechanism between savings and investment. But Dymski argues that it is essential to
incorporate a monetary element into Kalecki's analysis.

> Kalecki's framework cannot be encompassed in a real analysis: his theoretical
> building blocks can be consistently combined only in a monetary analysis: this
> implies a monetary analysis irrespective of any conditions imposed on prefer-
> ences and technology. Further, a disequilibrium analysis like Kalecki's is inher-
> ently "monetary" because agents seeking to carry value forward must rely on
> nominal assets whose real value is not predetermined within the system (Dymski
> 1996, 122).

Sawyer (1999, 4–7) concludes that any analysis of the market capitalist economy
which draws on the work of Kalecki should retain the "principle of increasing
risk" as a component. This conclusion is reinforced by Dymski (1996, 123–26).
He poses the question, how important is it to incorporate finance constraints (and
credit relations) explicitly in Kalecki models? The answer depends critically on
the phasing of the investment cycle. In Kalecki's short-period analysis, Dymski
defines three critical phases: (1) the placing of investment orders, (2) the delivery
of investment goods, and (3) the initial production phase of the investment goods.
During the first phase, the short-term finance is required for construction finance
for the supplier of the investment good. The risk factor for the lender is determined
by his/her degree of liquidity in the money market, and there is no risk factor for
the borrower. During the delivery phase, the supplier of the investment good re-
pays the loans provided during the construction phase; the lender's risk is now of
default on the project of the borrower, and the borrower's risk is now an operational one. In the third phase, the short-term finance is the provision of working
capital to the user of the investment good; the risk factors for the lender are liquidity and the interest-rate risk on the lender's liabilities; the borrower's risks are
again operational and associated with market conditions.

The Investment Susceptibility Cycle

Courvisanos (1996, 114–63) brings the various strands of behavioral and institutional economics together into what he calls the investment susceptibility cycle.

> Susceptibility refers to the psychological tension felt by entrepreneurs in relation to their fragile confidence about a particular investment decision, given the level of investment orders already committed. The fragility of this confidence in convention-based investment decisions explains unstable investment behaviour. Increasing fragility arises when tension related to current investment decisions escalates as investment is eroded. This cumulative process renders entrepreneurs' confidence increasingly fragile (or sensitive) as investment order levels rise. When investment order levels are falling, cumulative pressures are being eased on the fragile confidence of entrepreneurs. In this formulation, the level of investment orders is susceptible to change. This susceptibility is a function of the tensions generated by the degree of "fragile confidence" felt by entrepreneurs from exposure to risk and uncertainty. (ibid., 116)

The surface manifestations of fragile confidence in Kalecki's investment theory that Courvisanos brings into play are the three objective elements of profits, increasing risk, and capacity utilization. Companies are motivated by a desire for growth, which is the raison d'être of investment. However, situations will arise when a firm's push for growth and the concomitant investment will result in the emergence of threats to the continuing safety or existence of the firm. At such a level of investment orders, further planned investment becomes increasingly susceptible to postponement or cancellation. The outcome of the relationship between investment decisions and the experience of psychological tension by entrepreneurs is to establish a two-way relationship between susceptibility and investment orders. At a given level of investment orders an increase in investment commitments generates increasing susceptibility, whereas a decrease generates decreasing susceptibility. This reduces the risk and exposure to uncertainty that is the cause of tension. A reduction in susceptibility allows for the possibility of a rise in investment orders driven by the imperative of growth, which again, in turn, will increase the level of susceptibility.

In all cycles, the explanation of turning points is crucial. Courvisanos (ibid., 118) identifies turning points in susceptibility cycles as occurring when entrepreneurs' susceptibility is such that current conventions used for investment decision making are rejected, leading to structural breaks in the pattern of investment behavior, or, in the parlance of critical realism, if demiregularities result in anomalous behavior. If the three observable Kaleckian elements of profits, increasing risk, and capacity utilization can create the objective preconditions for confident investment ordering, this leads to a building up of tension as investment orders are increased. This expansion of investment generates cumulative tension that manifests itself as an inclination to decrease investment commitments and/or postpone investment plans. As tension increases, ultimately some factor (seasonal, secular, or random) or combination of such factors will lead to a postponement or reduction of investment commitments. This will release tension, reduce susceptibility, and the susceptibility cycle will start its contractionary phase, which will be reflected in decreasing investment orders. The process is not symmetrical at the upper and lower turning points of the susceptibility cycle. At the lower turning point, Courvisanos (ibid., 120) argues that it is a situation of increased resilience on the part of more adventurous entrepreneurs that will induce greater risk-taking and lead to higher levels of current and future investment commitments.

The three Kaleckian objective surface elements of entrepreneurial susceptibility identified by Courvisanos are profits, the gearing ratio, and capacity utilization. Their influences on the susceptibility cycle are explained as follows.

Profits

In the 1971 version of his business-cycle theory, Kalecki introduced a complex interaction between (1) the increment in total profits, and (2) the increment in profits from new investment. The latter term can be seen as a better expectations guide to future investment than the former. Thus, Kalecki's (1971) theory is the appropriate version from the point of view of explaining susceptibility as it emphasizes the sensitive nature of incremental profits from new investment. During the upswing of the susceptibility cycle, as a company invests more in new capital equipment, it exposes itself to greater tension as an increasing proportion of its profits will be generated by its new investment, thus leading to greater fragility. This becomes progressively more significant during the upswing of the susceptibility cycle. During the downswing of the susceptibility cycle, the fragility of confidence is reduced as the increments in profits become progressively more attributable to existing capital equipment, whose rates of return are more predictable (Courvisanos 1996, 127–28).

Thus, the profits-related mechanism incorporates systematic contradictory pulls between both the increments in profits from new investment and the total level of profits. This gives rise to conflicting pressures on incremental profits from new investment, which is related to the relative proportions of new equipment to existing equipment. The introduction of the concept of susceptibility into Kalecki's (1971) business-cycle theory brings the advantage of providing an understanding of the contribution of profits to the dynamic nature of investment decision making.

Increasing Risk

The second of the objective Kaleckian factors that Courvisanos introduces into the susceptibility cycle is increasing risk. Kalecki (1937) introduced the principle of increasing risk to argue that the marginal risk of investment increases with the amount invested for two reasons: (i) the greater the amount invested by an entre-preneur the greater the risk to his position of personal wealth in the event of the business being unsuccessful, and (ii) the marginal risk of investment rises with the size of investment because of "illiquidity." The sale of a fixed asset, such as a factory in the event of business failure, will almost always give rise to a loss. Thus, a businessman who has invested his reserves in fixed assets and taken "too much credit" will only be able to borrow at a rate of interest above the market rate. Assuming, as Kalecki did, a horizontal schedule of marginal efficiency of invest-ment, then the operation of the principle of increasing risk will serve to curtail investment to a level lower than would prevail in its absence.

Courvisanos explains the process in the following terms:

> During an upswing of the business cycle, the growth in internally generated funds allows a firm to increase its borrowing and share issue. As outside funds become more easily available during the upswing, the increasing risk involved in com-mitting funds to new investment seems to rise only minimally. Under these cir-cumstances, the firm is well below its gearing ratio limit. Tension builds up only slightly as it relates to small borrowers' risk, when financial [liquid] assets that earn income are converted into illiquid [fixed capital] with a long gestation pe-riod before any income is received. As the boom continues, greater borrowings and share issues bring the principle of increasing risk into operation. (Courvisanos 1996, 130)

This increasing illiquidity leads to increased susceptibility as tension builds. As gearing ratios rise, lenders' risk becomes an increasingly serious short-term issue, shifting investment funding increasingly to equity finance leads to rising share-issue risk, allied with concerns about possible falls in share prices as the increment in profits from new equipment starts to fall relatively. These increas-ing risk factors force entrepreneurs to reduce the rate of new investment com-mitments. Susceptibility continues to rise (even if at a slower rate), threatening the firm's liquidity position. Again, contradictory pulls emerge. In relation to this element, continuing long-term competitive pressure to earn income through investment in illiquid fixed capital eventually creates the need to protect the decreasing short-term liquidity position by doing the exact opposite: reducing investment orders and canceling (or modifying) current investment orders. This lowers the very high tension related to increasing borrower's and lender's risks (and share issue risk) which reduces susceptibility and, with a lag, reduces in-vestment activity (ibid., 131).

In the downswing of a business cycle, increasing risk generates a reverse sus-ceptibility behavior cycle to the one described by Courvisanos in the upswing. Companies' gearing ratios are an important guide to the presence of increasing risk. Their behavior over time can be examined to see how changes alter tension in relation to companies' investment commitments. The element of increasing risk can trace out an unstable cyclical path of investment orders.

Capacity Utilization

The final objective Kaleckian element that Courvisanos identifies as contributing to the susceptibility cycle is capacity utilization. The existence of unplanned excess capacity is an element that is common to all versions of Kalecki's business-cycle theory. Kalecki saw unplanned excess capacity appearing midway through a boom as the means of production rise at an increasing rate, due to investment orders being completed but demand not rising sufficiently quickly to keep pace with the expansion in the means of production. The influence of this excess capacity becomes greater as the increase in demand starts to slow down toward the peak of the business cycle at a time when the increment in companies' profits from new investment is starting to fall. The combination of contradictory pulls between delays in the production of investment goods and changes in effective demand create unplanned excess capacity. Thus, according to Courvisanos (ibid., 134), tension builds up within a self-generating susceptibility cycle. As activity slows down, so inventory investment will rise leading to even higher undesired excess capacity with concomitant increasing tension and fragility of confidence. Thus, investment orders will start to decrease and although companies' productive capacity will continue to expand due to completion of previously committed investment outlays, the decreasing rate at which new capacity comes on stream will start to ease susceptibility.

Courvisanos (ibid., 161) formalizes the susceptibility cycle model in an investment orders function that provides the objective reflection of susceptibility.

$$D_t = f(P_{t-1}, \Delta P_{t-1}, g_{t-1}, c_{t-1}), \tag{1}$$

where D_t is the level of aggregate investment orders in the current period; P_{t-1} = the previous period level of profits; $\Delta P_{t-1} = P_{t-1} - P_{t-2}$, the actual increment in profit levels; g_{t-1} = the previous period gearing ratio; and c_{t-1} = the previous period capacity utilization.

The peak of susceptibility is reached when D_t is at its maximum value. At this point, the contradictory pulls on profits, risk, and capacity utilization create enough susceptibility tension for investment orders to turn down. The peak of susceptibility occurs when:

when P is high and ΔP begins to decrease
when g is greater than the minimum desired proportion of retained earnings
when c rises above a desired degree of utilization.

The trough of susceptibility is reached when D_t is at a minimum value. The trough occurs under the following conditions:

(i) when P is low and ΔP begins to increase
(ii) when the lowest desired limit of g has been reached
(iii) when c falls below a desired degree of utilization.

Estimating the Kalecki-Courvisanos Susceptibility Cycle

Courvisanos' reinterpretation of Kalecki's theory of investment has transformed it from an essentially mechanical closed-system model that shared many of the methodological strictures of neoclassical theories of investment, to an open-system model grounded in an appreciation of the complex factors that impact on the decision-making processes of entrepreneurs. By analyzing the internal decision-making processes of companies, Courvisanos has provided the rationale for demiclosure, a procedure that most critical realists are prepared to recognize, which provides the justification for the use of quantitative methods.

So, is it possible to take the next step and estimate the investment susceptibility cycle? Two important considerations must be borne in mind. The first is that the independent variables in an economic model that purports to measure susceptibility should be interpreted as reflecting rather than defining the factors that impact on the investment decisions of businessmen. The second is to establish the appropriate dependent variable. In every econometric study of which we are aware, the dependent variable has been a measure of investment expenditures or outlays. However, as we argue below, for a study that is seeking to find a quantitative measure of susceptibility, the dependent variable should be investment decisions or orders.

There are important issues to be borne in mind when seeking to estimate Kalecki's investment function. Kalecki (1971) developed version III of his investment theory with investment orders, D, as the dependent variable. Only in the last line of the model did he argue that there would be a time lag, τ, between the placing of an order for new capital equipment and its becoming operational, so that in his final investment-expenditures equation the dependent variable becomes $D_{t+\tau}$. Otherwise, his investment-orders and investment-expenditures equations are identical. In his investment-orders/expenditures equation, Kalecki argued that one of the independent variables should be the lagged dependent variable; in other words, the equation should be autoregressive. This, of course, lays him open to Schumpeter's (1939) jibe that the origins of Kalecki's business-cycle theory are only to be found in the Garden of Eden. More specifically, all that this tells us is that one of the determinants of the current time period's investment orders or expenditures is its value in a previous time period. We did in fact estimate Kalecki's version-III investment-expenditures function and found that the results are overwhelmingly determined by the presence of the lagged dependent variable. None of the other independent variables makes any statistically significant contribution. It is important, therefore, if we are to find out anything meaningful about the factors that underlie investment decisions, to estimate Kalecki's investment function in a form that is not autoregressive.

There is a further reason for selecting Kalecki's investment orders equation as the one to be estimated. This is provided by Krawiec and Szydłowski (1999) in their formulation of a new business cycle model deriving from Kaldor and Kalecki. Their model acknowledges the distinction between investment decisions and their implementation by means of second-order differential-delay equations. Their results show that the dynamics of investment depend crucially on the time-delay parameter, the gestation time period of investment, τ. The mathematics of the Krawiec-Szydłowski model involves the application of the Poincaré-Andronov-Hopf bifurcation theorem, generalized for functional differential equations. Their model demonstrates that even with a linear investment function, the introduction of Kalecki's time delay parameter can create a limit cycle for small values of the parameter. Depending on the length of the time-delay parameter, Kalecki's investment model bifurcates to limit cycle behavior, then to multiple periodic and aperiodic cycles, and eventually tends toward chaotic behavior. The overall conclusion of Krawiec and Szydłowski is that there can be no doubt that time lags in investment and their capacity for generating cycles should be taken into account in the analysis of business cycles. Thus, the appropriate function to be estimated is the investment-orders function. This predates the investment-expenditures function and incorporates the complex factors that comprise the investment-susceptibility cycle.

We now proceed to estimate Equation 1 using the traditional econometric modeling procedure recommended by Darnell and Evans (1990, ch. 4). The purpose is to test our main hypothesis within the context of a set of auxiliary hypotheses. The main hypothesis can only be tested once the initial assumptions about the auxiliary hypotheses have been tested and the GM assumptions about the stochastic equation to be estimated have been examined. Our main hypothesis refers to the role of profits in the investment-orders decision. The auxiliary hypotheses involve the roles of gearing and capacity utilization, the functional form of the equation, the choice of data variables, and the setting up of a testable form of the equation. The dependent variable is investment decisions, D, defined as real new orders received by the manufacturing and construction sectors of the U.K. economy. P represents real net profits after payment of corporation taxes on income and capital.

Being dissatisfied with the available U.K. data on capacity utilization, c, we restate it as: $CU \equiv (Y - Y^*)$, where Y is output and $Y^* = \delta K$, and where Y^* is the output associated with target capacity utilization, which in turn is assumed to be a fixed proportion of capital stock, K. Thus, $CU \equiv (Y - \delta K)$. Adopting this procedure, instead of the more conventional measure of capacity utilization as the ratio of actual output to potential output, has the advantage of providing an estimate for δ, the desired capital/output ratio. $1/\delta$ provides an estimate of the average optimum life for capital stock.

The gearing ratio, g, is usually defined as the ratio of total debt to total equity. Unfortunately, the relevant data is not available for the United Kingdom. Instead, we define the two elements of gearing in the following way: (i) debt, which we define as a new real net borrowing requirement, $RNBR$, from banks by industrial and commercial companies and financial institutions in the current time period; and (ii) real retained earnings, RRE, of industrial and commercial companies and financial institutions minus real net capital issues, $RNCI$, of industrial and commercial companies and financial institutions, in the current time period. This second element we define as real funds *RLFUNDS*. Thus, the conventional measure of the gearing ratio is $g = RNBR/RLFUNDS$. If, however, we were to include g in our specification, then certain of the variables would be expressed in levels and others in ratios. Large differences in magnitude between regressors can lead to estimation problems.

We define an alternative version of gearing in a similar way to capacity utilization above, as $G = (RNBR–RNBR^*)$, where $RNBR^* = \gamma.RLFUNDS$, and where $RNBR^*$ is the borrowing associated with target gearing, which in turn is assumed to be a fixed proportion of company liquidity, *RLFUNDS*. Thus, $G \equiv (RNBR–\gamma.RLFUNDS)$. If the coefficients of G were negative, it would indicate that G was acting as a constraint on investment. Alternatively, if the coefficient is positive, then *RNBR* is acting as cash flow from which to finance the new investment orders. Defining *CU* and G in this way should enable us to identify turning points in the investment-susceptibility cycle. Also, our theory indicates that the equations should be specified without a constant, and indeed one would be difficult to interpret, since it would be the level of new orders that would occur if all of the independent variables were zero.

Inevitably, economic theory gives few clues about the appropriate lags to use and one of the auxiliary hypotheses, or initial assumptions, will include a statement as to a choice of lags that can be adjusted if the GM assumptions about the properties of the equation error are not fulfilled. For the gearing and capacity-utilization variables, we start without lags, but for profits, where some lags are anticipated, we allow for a five-order distributed lag, typical for quarterly data, which allows for the effect of profits to be delayed for up to a year. These initial assumptions lead to the testable form of the Kalecki-Courvisanos susceptibility-cycle equation as follows:

$$D_t = \beta_1.P_t + \beta_2.P_{t-1} + \beta_3.P_{t-2} + \beta_4.P_{t-3} + \beta_5.P_{t-4} + \beta_6.Y_t + \beta_7.K_t \qquad (2)$$
$$+ \beta_8.RNBR_t + \beta_9.RLFUNDS_t + \varepsilon_t$$

where the variables are as defined above, and ε_t is the equation's error term. We expect the coefficients to have the following signs: β_6 and β_9 positive, and β_7 and β_8 negative. The coefficients of the profits variables are likely to be positive, but some may be negative.

We now proceed to estimate Equation 2 using quarterly data for the United Kingdom for the period 1980Q1 to 1996Q4, which allows a maximum of sixty-eight observations. The sources and descriptions of the variables can be found in the Appendix (a table of the data set is available on request from the authors). It should be noted that the "spike" in the new-orders data in 1987Q3 is due to the inclusion of Channel Tunnel new orders. Each datum has been rounded to its nearest integer.

We report in Table 7.1 the results of our ordinary-least-square (OLS) estimation of the specification of the Kalecki-Courvisanos investment-susceptibility model (Equation 2). The table shows estimates of coefficients and their t-values. It should be noted that the R^2, where a constant has been excluded, is based on (1–RSS/OSS), where OSS = original sum of squares, compared with the usual R^2 = (1–RSS/TSS), where TSS = total sum of squares, when a constant is included in the equation. The two formulae for R^2 are not comparable, having different bases. Similarly, the formula for RBAR^2, when a constant is excluded, is RBAR^2 = (1–(RSS * n)/(OSS * (n–k))), where n is the number of observations in the equation and k is the number of regressors.

At first glance, the results of Equation 2 seem very satisfactory, except that the auxiliary hypothesis Ho: $\beta_9 < 0$ is not rejected by a 1-tailed test at the 0.05 level of significance. We follow the Darnell-Evans recommendation that the GM assumptions be tested before testing our main hypothesis, namely, that the set of coefficients of the profits variables is zero, using an F test.

Although our theory suggests that the equation should be specified without a constant, econometric practice recommends that one should be included anyway, in order to act as a catch-all term for the effects of any misspecification of the equation which would violate the Gauss-Markov assumption that $E(\varepsilon_t) = 0$. Thus, the presence of an unexpectedly significant constant could signal some misspecification. Such misspecifications could take the form of the omission of one or more significant regressors, of the incorrect form of an included regressor, or the incorrect lag of an included variable. Sometimes the misspecification results from an incorrect functional form for the equation, such as using a linear approximation for an underlying nonlinear relationship. It is certainly not the case that our equation is a linear approximation for an underlying nonlinear production function, so that possibility is dismissed.

To test the assumption that $E(\varepsilon_t) = 0$, we reestimated Equation 2 with a constant included. If this assumption, that $E(\varepsilon_t) = 0$, is true, then the hypothesis that the coefficient of the constant term is zero should not be rejected. However, the constant term was definitely significantly different from zero, and this had a drastic effect on the other coefficients, reducing their significance. We have to conclude that the model in Equation 2 is misspecified, and that the estimates of the coefficients are biased.

We decided to explore the possibility of incorrectly specified lags in the capacity utilization and gearing variables before examining other possible misspecifications. The capital, K_{t-h}, (h = 0, 1, 2, 3, 4), variable was too highly correlated with its lagged values to be included as a distributed lag. Accordingly, Y_{t-h} and K_{t-h} were inserted contemporaneously one lag at a time. We recognized that the gearing variable could comprise borrowing and equity with different time lags.

In Equation 2, we introduce the lags on the gearing variables as five-order distributed lags on $RNBR_{t-j}$ and $RLFUNDS_{t-j}$, j = 0, 1, 2, 3, 4, and add a constant term. We recast Equation 2 as Equation 2a.

Table 7.1

Equation 2 and Variations

Equation number	(2)	(2a)	(2b)	(2c)	(2d)
	n = 64	n = 64	n = 64	n = 64	n = 64
Variable	k = 9	k = 10	k = 9	k = 8	k = 7
P_t	−0.0441	0.0272	0.0293	0.0293	0.0293
	−0.6100	0.3766	0.4092	0.4165	0.4278
P_{t-1}	−0.0660	**0.1368**	**0.1338**	**0.1338**	**0.1338**
	−0.9419	**2.0283**	**2.0070**	**2.0761**	**2.1504**
P_{t-2}	**0.2862**	**0.2452**	**0.2409**	**0.2409**	**0.2409**
	4.1715	**3.5602**	**3.5550**	**3.7058**	**3.7926**
P_{t-3}	**0.1723**	0.1018	0.1012	0.1012	0.1012
	2.4224	1.3057	1.3074	1.5745	1.6233
P_{t-4}	−0.0024	−0.0420	−0.0606	−0.0606	−0.0606
	−0.0319	−0.5110	−0.8471	−0.8617	−0.8834
Y_t	**0.1577**				
	15.824				
K_t	**−0.0219**				
	−11.458				
Y_{t-3}		**0.1548**	**0.1676**	**0.1676**	
		5.2346	**15.427**	**20.040**	
K_{t-3}		**−0.0248**	**−0.0255**	**−0.0255**	
		−9.4323	**−12.237**	**−15.386**	
CU_{t-3}					**0.1676**
					20.267
$RNBR_t$	**0.0334**				
	2.2225				
$RNBR_{t-2}$		0.0358	**0.0303**		
		1.8440	**1.9813**		
$RLFUNDS_t$	−0.0663	−0.0665	−0.0631		
	−1.5190	−1.4485	−1.4029		
$G_{t-2,t-0}$				**0.0303**	**0.0303**
				3.0197	**3.0875**
Constant		664.186			
		0.4659			
R^2	0.9928	0.7992	0.9930	0.9930	0.9930
$RBAR^2$	0.9916	0.7657	0.9919	0.9920	0.9921
S^2	333187	327618	322955	317187	311610
DW		1.901			

Note: The table shows coefficients and *t*-values. Statistically significant variables shown in bold.

$$D_t = \beta_0 + \beta_1.P_t + \beta_2.P_{t-1} + \beta_3.P_{t-2} + \beta_4.P_{t-3} + \beta_5.P_{t-4} + \beta_6.Y_{t-h} \qquad (2a)$$

$$+ \beta_7.K_{t-h} + \beta_{80}.RNBR_t + \beta_{81}.RNBR_{t-1} + \beta_{82}.RNBR_{t-2}$$

$$+ \beta_{83}.RNBR_{t-3} + \beta_{84}.RNBR_{t-4} + \beta_{90}.RLFUNDS_t$$

$$+ \beta_{91}.RLFUNDS_{t-1} + \beta_{92}.RLFUNDS_{t-2} + \beta_{93}.RLFUNDS_{t-3}$$

$$+ \beta_{94}.RLFUNDS_{t-4} + \varepsilon_t.$$

We estimated Equation 2a for the five different lags of Y and K. The Darnell and Evans procedure requires that each equation estimated in the process be recorded. Unfortunately, space dictates otherwise, and we do not report the results of these five unwieldy estimations. Recognizing that the specification chosen should have unbiased estimates, we adopted the criterion of choosing the variant for which the t-value of the constant term was minimized. This was achieved for Y and K lagged by three quarters, and the constant term was not significantly different from zero at the 0.10 level in a 2-tailed t test. Our next decision was that of choosing a lag for each of $RNBR$ and $RLFUNDS$ out of their distributed lags in which there were no significant t-values. We chose those lags of $RNBR$ and $RLFUNDS$ with the least insignificant t-values. These were $RNBR$ lagged two quarters and $RLFUNDS$ with no lag. We reestimated the equation excluding the other lagged values of $RNBR$ and $RLFUNDS$ and report the results as Equation 2a in Table 7.1, above. We repeated the exercise omitting the constant term and report the results as Equation 2b, in Table 7.2.

Our next step was to create variable $G_{t-2,t-0} = RNBR_{t-2} - \gamma_{t-2,t-0}RLFUNDS_t$, where $\gamma_{t-2,t-0} = (-\beta_9/\beta_8) = -(-0.0631331)/(0.0302897) = 2.084309188$, that is, the ratio of the coefficients of $RNBR_{t-2}$ and $RLFUNDS_t$ from Equation 2b. We reestimated Equation 2b replacing $RNBR_{t-2}$ and $RLFUNDS_t$ by $G_{t-2,t-0}$, and report the results as Equation 2c. Similarly, we replaced Y_{t-3} and K_{t-3} by $CU_{t-3} = Y_{t-3} - \delta_{t-3}K_{t-3}$, also using the relevant coefficients from Equation 2b, $(\delta_{t-3} = -\beta_7/\beta_6 - (-0.0254871)/(0.1675693) = 0.152908863)$, and we report the results as Equation 2d. Equation 2b is our key equation; Equations 2c and 2d (see Table 7.2) are variations, tidying it up. It will be noted that the coefficient of $G_{t-2,t-0}$ is positive and significantly different from zero, indicating that the net borrowing is being used as a cash flow, rather than as a constraint.

Following Darnell and Evans (1990), we examined the GM assumptions for Equation 2b before testing the main hypothesis. Plots of the residuals revealed no signs of heteroscedasticity. The usual diagnostic test for first-order autocorrelation in the error term uses the Durbin-Watson statistic. However, to be valid, the test requires the presence of a constant term in the equation. The DW statistic reported in Equation 2a is DW = 1.901, which lies in the inconclusive range at the 0.05 level of significance. While it could be claimed that new orders of investment equip-

Table 7.2

Economic Interpretation of Equation 2b

$n = 65$ Variable	Mean Value (£million)	Standard Deviation	Coefficient	Average Economic Impact (£million) (mean value* coefficient)	Average Economic Impact (%)
New Orders	6,175.422	1,182.644	1.000	6,175.422	100.00
P_t	8,014.797	2,117.635	0.0293	234.834	3.80
P_{t-1}	7,903.078	2,063.397	0.1338	1,057.432	17.12
P_{t-2}	7,809.203	2,075.707	0.2409	1,881.237	30.46
P_{t-3}	7,734.422	2,034.707	0.1012	782.724	12.67
P_{t-4}	7,665.422	2,020.704	−0.0606	−464.525	−7.52
Y_{t-3}	96,812.70	10,729.88	0.1676	16,225.809	262.75
K_{t-3}	519,569.9	98,927.73	−0.0255	−13,249.032	−214.54
$\delta_{t-3} \cdot K_{t-3}$	79,025.99				
$CU_{t-3} = Y_{t-3}$					
$-\delta_{t-3} \cdot K_{t-3}$	17,786.71		0.1676	2,981.053	48.27
$RNBR_{t-2}$	5,787.000	5,744.344	0.0303	175.286	2.84
$RLFUNDS_t$	7,504.188	2,236.312	−0.0631	−473.763	−7.67
$\gamma. RLFUNDS_t$	15,641.05				
$G = RNBR_{t-2} - \gamma. RLFUNDS_t$	−9,854.05		0.0303	−298.477	−4.83

Notes: $\delta_{t-3} = 0.0254871/0.1675693 = 0.152098863$
$\gamma = 0.0631331/0.0302897 = 2.084309188$

ment contribute to capital stock at a later date, the relationship is not as direct as with actual investment expenditure, for instance, and we assumed that any stochastic errors associated with capital stock were not in relationship with the equation's error term. However, we carried out an h test using the DW statistic and the estimated variance of the coefficient of K_{t-3}. The h value did not reject the null hypothesis of no (first-order) autocorrelation. Finally, there were no obvious effects of collinearity between the regressors, in spite of a correlation of 0.9255 between Y_{t-3} and K_{t-3}, and of correlations from 0.70 to 0.82 between the different profit series, and between profits and Y_{t-3} and K_{t-3}. We carried out a two-tailed F-test to test the null hypothesis that the set of five coefficients of the profits variables from Equation 2b is equal to a zero vector. A value of $F = 8.542$ for (5, 55) degrees of freedom, rejected the null hypothesis at the 0.02 level of significance.

Having adjusted our auxiliary hypotheses (about the lags of the gearing and capacity-utilization variables) in order to obtain unbiased estimates, and having examined the GM assumptions and found them to be not wanting, and having tested the main hypothesis, it is now time to interpret our key Equation 2b.

Table 7.2 contains a list of the dependent and explanatory variables, together with their sample means and standard deviations, and their estimated coefficients from Equation 2b. From the means and coefficients, their economic impact can be gauged in monetary and percentage terms. It will be noted that the largest single influence on new orders is capacity utilization, followed by that of profits lagged by two and one quarters. Both of these profit coefficients are positive, indicating that it is unlikely that ΔP plays a part in influencing new orders. However, profits as a set have a greater impact on new orders than even capacity utilization.

The impact of capacity utilization is large. The estimate of δ_{t-3} is calculated from $\delta_{t-3} = -\beta_7/\beta_6 = -(-0.0254871)/(0.1675693) = 0.152098863$. When Y falls below approximately two-thirteenths of capital stock, then the capacity-utilization composite term, CU, starts to have a negative influence on new orders. The inverse, $1/\delta_{t-3}$, indicates an average optimal life for capital of approximately 6.57 years. δ multiplied by capital stock, K, gives the optimal output associated with the capital stock. In our sample, δ times the mean value of capital stock is £79,026 million, while average actual output for Y_{t-3} is £96,813 million. Thus, δ times the mean value of capital is unexpectedly lower than average actual output and this latter figure as a proportion of the mean of capital stock is 0.1863. An alternative tentative measure of capacity output might be gauged from the maximum value for Y/K in our sample, which was 0.2116. This ratio, based on a single observation, multiplied by the mean value for capital stock, K_{t-3}, gives an average capacity output for our sample of £109,941 million.

The impact of gearing is small. The coefficient of $G_{t-2,t-0}$ is positive, indicating that $RNBR$ is acting as a cash flow rather than as a constraint. In Table 7.2, the value γ is 2.0843, which is larger than expected. This implies that when $RNBR$ drops below 2.0843 times $RLFUNDS$, then the net effect of the composite term, G, becomes negative. The average economic impact of G is negative. Y and profits drive new orders, while K acts as a restraining (negative) tension. The procedure adopted here has identified the most appropriate lags of Y, K, $RNBR$ and $RLFUNDS$, the capacity utilization variables performed well, and profits play a significant role, but not as a first difference.

The Kalecki-Courvisanos model is a behavioral model, where capacity utilization provides the motivation, profits the means, and the equity element of gearing acts as a constraint. In addition, it is interesting to note a "cascade effect." In other words, the effect on new orders of capital stock and the output to which it gives rise is lagged three quarters, while the profits, which derive from the output, are lagged two and one quarters, while the earnings retained out of profits are unlagged.

Conclusion

There is a lacuna in our understanding of investment behavior. The two principal mainstream approaches have been the cost of capital or the q methods. The econometric results produced by both have been disappointing, and mainstream economists recognize that they suffer from serious problems of misspecification (Chirinko 1993, Clark 1979, Dornbusch and Fischer 1984, Sawyer 1982). Numerous attempts at estimating the objective formulation of Keynes's investment theory through the medium of q models have not been successful.

q models have not been noticeably successful in accounting for the time-series variation in aggregate investment. Their explanatory power is low, and serial correlation or dynamic structures using the lagged dependent variable are common. In addition, other variables reflecting liquidity constraints or the state of demand are often significant in the equations although the standard formulation of q does not provide a satisfactory rationale for their inclusion (Blundell et al. 1992, 233).

Post Keynesians claim greater success for Kaleckian-based models of investment. Courvisanos (1996, 13–68) lists a number of such models (Harcourt and Kenyon 1976, Steindl 1952, Sylos Labini 1967, Wood 1975). While these and other models have refined or extended Kalecki's basic theory of investment, it is doubtful whether from a methodological perspective they can be regarded as fundamentally different from mainstream models, and, therefore, subject to the same critical-realist strictures. It seems to us that little is gained from claiming superiority for one category of model over another if all are suffering from the same methodological shortcomings.

Both Keynes and Kalecki recognized the importance of risk and uncertainty in determining investment decisions, although Keynes gave them much greater emphasis. Uncertainty is introduced into Keynesian models indirectly on an ad hoc basis via some measure of the spread of output and prices or of expert forecasts, on the assumption that spread or variance is an appropriate proxy for uncertainty (Baddeley 2001, 11–12). The major contribution of Courvisanos has been to introduce uncertainty into Kalecki's investment theory via the concept of susceptibility. By formulating uncertainty in terms of the objective factors of profits, gearing, and capacity utilization, Courvisanos has taken the analysis of uncertainty a major step beyond a simple assertion of "animal spirits."

In this chapter, we have sought to demonstrate how the objective variables of investment susceptibility can be estimated. For the data set of the U.K. economy that we have used, it would appear that profitability, risk, and capacity utilization all have significant roles to play in influencing businessmen's investment decisions. Our results also suggest that there are other influences at work, which we have not identified. These might include such factors as changes in income distribution or fiscal policy.

Note

This is a revised version of a paper presented initially at the international Kalecki commemorative conference in Warsaw, September 27–28, 1999, and subsequently at the conference of the Eastern Economic Association, New York, February 22–25, 2001.

References

Arestis, P. 1992. *The Post-Keynesian Approach to Economics*. Aldershot, UK: Edward Elgar.

Arestis, P., S. Dunn; and M. Sawyer. 1999. "Post Keynesian Economics and Its Critics." *Journal of Post Keynesian Economics* 21(4): 527–49.

Baddeley, M. 2001. "Bubbles or Whirlpools? An Empirical Analysis of the Effects of Speculation and Uncertainty on Investment." University of Cambridge, Department of Economics. Mimeographed.

Blundell, R., S. Bond, M. Devereux, and F. Schianterelli. 1992. "Investment and Tobin's *q*." *Journal of Econometrics* 51: 233–57.

Chirinko, R. 1993."Business Fixed Investment Spending: Modeling Strategies, Empirical Results and Policy Implications." *Journal of Economic Literature* 31(4): 1875–911.

Clark, P.K 1979. "Investment in the 1970s: Theory, Performance and Prediction." *Brookings Papers on Economic Activity* 1: 73–113.

Courvisanos, J. 1996. *Investment Cycles in Capitalist Economies: A Kaleckian Behavioral Contribution*. Cheltenham, UK: Edward Elgar.

———. 2003. "Michal Kalecki as a Behavioural Economist: Implications for Modern Evolutionary Economic Analysis." In Z. Sadowski, and A Szeworski, eds., *Kalecki's Economics Today,* 27–41. London: Routledge.

Darnell, A.C., and J.L. Evans. 1990. *The Limits of Econometrics*. Aldershot, UK: Edward Elgar.

Dornbusch, R., and S. Fischer. 1984. *Macroeconomics*, 3rd ed. New York: McGraw-Hill.

Dow, S. 1996. *The Methodology of Macroeconomic Thought*. Aldershot, UK: Edward Elgar.

———. 1997. "Mainstream Economic Methodology." *Cambridge Journal of Economics* 21(1): 73–93.

———. 1999. "Post Keynesianism and Critical Realism: What Is the Connection?" *Journal of Post Keynesian Economics* 22(1): 15–33.

———. 2001. "Post Keynesian Methodology." In R.P.F. Holt and S. Pressman, eds., *A New Guide to Post Keynesian Economics*, London: Routledge.

Downward, P. 2000. "A Realist Appraisal of Post-Keynesian Pricing Theory." *Cambridge Journal of Economics* 24(2): 211–24.

Downward, P.; J.H. Finch; and J. Ramsay. 2002. "Critical Realism, Empirical Methods and Inference: A Critical Discussion." *Cambridge Journal of Economics* 26(4): 481–500.

Dymski, G.A. 1996. "Kalecki's Monetary Economics." In J.E. King, ed., *An Alternative Macroeconomics Theory: The Kaleckian Model and Post Keynesian Economics*, Boston: Kluwer.

Earl, P. 1984. *The Corporate Imagination: How Big Companies Make Mistakes*. Brighton, UK: Wheatsheaf.

Harcourt, G.C., and P. Kenyon. 1976. "Pricing and the Investment Decision." *Kyklos* 29(3): 449–77.

Holt, R.P.F., and Pressman, S. 2001. "What is Post Keynesian Economics." In R.P.F. Holt and S. Pressman, eds., *New Guide to Post Keynesian Economics*, London: Routledge.

Kalecki, M. 1937. "A Theory of Commodity, Income and Capital Taxation." *Economic Journal* 47: 444–50.

———. 1970. "Theories of Growth in Different Social Systems." *Scientia* 105(5/6): 311–16.

———. 1971. *Selected Essays on the Dynamics of the Capitalist Economy, 1933–1970.* Cambridge: Cambridge University Press.

Krawiec, A. and M. Szydłowski. 1999. "The Kaldor-Kalecki Business Cycle Model." *Annals of Operations Research* 89(1): 89–100.

Lavoie, M. 1992. *Foundations of Post-Keynesian Economic Analysis*. Aldershot, UK: Edward Elgar.

Lawson, A. 1994. " The Nature of Post Keynesian and its Links to Other Traditions: a Realist Perspective." *Journal of Post Keynesian Economics* 16(4): 503–38.

———. 1997. *Economics and Reality*. London: Routledge.

———. 1998. "Critical Issues in Economics as Realist Social Theory." *Ekonomia* 1(2): 75–117.

Lawson, T. 1999. "Connections and Distinctions: Post Keynesianism and Critical Realism." *Journal of Post Keynesian Economics* 22(1): 3–14.

Mair, D., A.J. Laramie, and P.J. Reynolds. 2004. "Kalecki's Theory of Income Distribution: The Answer to a Maiden's Prayer?" In M. Forstater and R. Wray, eds., *Contemporary Post Keynesian Analysis: A Compendium of Contributions to the Seventh International Post Keynesian Workshop*, Cheltenham, UK: Edward Elgar.

Meacci, F. 1989. "The Principle of Increasing Risk versus the Marginal Efficiency of Capital." In M. Sebastiani, ed., *Kalecki's Relevance Today*. London: Macmillan.

O'Donnell, R. 1989. *M. Keynes: Philosophy, Economics and Politics*. London: Macmillan.

Rotheim, R.J. 1999. "Post Keynesian Economics and Realist Philosophy." *Journal of Post Keynesian Economics* 22(1): 71–103.

Sawyer. C. 1982. *Macroeconomics in Question: The Keynesian-Monetarist Controversies and the Kaleckian Alternative*. Armonk, NY: M.E. Sharpe.

Sawyer, M.C. 1985. *The Economics of Michal Kalecki*. Basingstoke, UK: Macmillan.

———. 1999. "Kalecki on Money and Finance." Leeds University Business School, Discussion Paper E99/03.

Schumpeter, J.A. 1939. *Business Cycles: A Theoretical, Historical, and Statistical Analysis of the Capitalist Process*, 2 vols. New York: McGraw-Hill.

Shackle, G.L.S. 1972. *Epistemics and Economics: A Critique of Economic Doctrines*. Cambridge: Cambridge University Press.

Simon, H.A. 1986. "Foreword." In Bromiley, P., ed., *Corporate Capital Investment: A Behavioural Approach*, Cambridge: Cambridge University Press.

Steedman, I. 1992. "Questions for Kaleckians." *Review of Political Economy* 4(2): 125–51.

Steindl, J. 1952. *Maturity and Stagnation in American Capitalism*. Oxford: Basil Blackwell.

Sylos Labini, P. 1967. "Prices, Distribution and Investment in Italy, 1951–1966: An Interpretation." *Banco Nationale del Lavoro Quarterly Review* 83 (December): 3–57.

Walters, B., and D. Young. 1997. "On the Coherence of Post-Keynesian Economics." *Scottish Journal of Political Economy* 44(3): 329–49.

Wood, A. 1975. *A Theory of Profits*. Cambridge: Cambridge University Press.

Appendix 7.1. Definitions of Variables and Data Sources

The definitions of the variables (all in £ million) and the sources of the data are as follows:

P: Real net profits = gross trading profits of industrial and commercial companies and financial companies and institutions—U.K. taxes on income of industrial and commercial companies and financial companies and institutions (*Economic Trends*. Office of National Statistics, London, Her Majesty's Stationary Office [various editions], Table 1.12) divided by implied GDP deflator (1990 = 100) (*United Kingdom National Income and Accounts*. Office of National Statistics, London, Her Majesty's Stationary Office [various editions], Table 1.1).

D: Real new investment orders = new investment orders from manufacturing and construction sectors (Economic Trends, Table 4.4) divided by implied GDFCF deflator (1990 = 100) (U.K. National Income and Accounts, Table 1.1).

RNBR: Real net borrowing from banks by industrial and commercial companies and financial companies and institutions (Economic Trends, Table 1.16) divided by implied GDP deflator (1990 = 100) (U.K. National Income and Accounts, Table 1.1).

RRE: Retained earnings of industrial and commercial companies and financial companies and institutions (Economic Trends, Table 1.13) divided by implied GDP deflator (1990 = 100) (U.K. National Income and Accounts, Table 1.1).

RNCI: Net capital issues and redemptions of industrial and commercial companies and financial companies and institutions (*Financial Statistics,* Office of National Statistics, London, Her Majesty's Stationary Office [various editions], Table 6.2A) divided by implied GDP deflator (1990 = 100) (U.K. National Income and Accounts, Table 1.1).

K: Capital stock = net capital stock at current replacement cost, all fixed assets of industrial and commercial companies and financial companies and institutions (Economic Trends, Table 14.8) divided by implied GDFCF deflator (1990 = 100) (U.K. National Income and Accounts, Table 1.1).

Y: Output = GDP (Economic Trends, Table 1.12) divided by implied GDP deflator (1990 = 100) (U.K. National Income and Accounts, Table 1.1).

8

Michelle Baddeley

Bubbles or Whirlpools? An Empirical Analysis of the Effects of Speculation and Financial Uncertainty on Investment

Introduction

Investment plays a central role in the determination of employment and growth, but it is sensitive to uncertainty within the macroeconomy. Until the 1980s, orthodox economic analyses of investment neglected the role of uncertainty and the dominant economic paradigms of neoclassical theory were based upon concepts of rational expectations and efficient markets. These allow for quantifiable risk but do not emphasize sufficiently the impacts of fundamental uncertainty on fixed-asset investment. In contrast, during this period of time much of the heterodox Post Keynesian literature, particularly ideas developed within Kaleckian and Minskian traditions, placed great emphasis not only on the role played by uncertainty in the macro-economy, but also by the interactions between uncertainty and financial instability and crisis.

This chapter brings these different ideas together (theoretically and empirically) by looking at the orthodox versus heterodox perspectives on the relationships between investment, financial instability, and uncertainty. In the second and third parts, the role of the stock market and uncertainty within orthodox models of investment is examined. The next section presents an analysis of Keynes's ideas about investment, uncertainty, and the stock market. One of Keynes's most famous insights focuses on the fact that the interactions between financial instability and fixed asset investment create whirlpools of speculative activity and these have the potential to destabilize the economy by destabilizing investment activity. The development of these ideas by Kaleckians and Minskians is explained in the next section, in which the key Post Keynesian insights about the relationships between investment, finance, uncertainty, and cyclical instability are analyzed. In the final section, the theoretical issues are addressed by estimating orthodox and heterodox models of the relationships between investment, uncertainty, and financial instability, using data for the United States and United Kingdom. The explanatory power of these competing models is assessed using non-nested testing techniques. The policy conclusion to emerge from these analyses is that there are clear and significant links between investment, speculation, and financial uncertainty, suggesting that the implementation of financial-market controls can play a crucial role in moderating destabilizing impacts on real activity.

Orthodox Theories of Investment

In early neoclassical theory, factors such as uncertainty, speculation, and stock-market activity were given little consideration. In Jorgenson's (1963, 1971) model, investment is described as a process of adjustment to an optimal capital stock. Gross investment is determined by a scale effect and a relative factor-price effect. The scale effect is captured by output, and the relative factor-price effect is captured by the user (or rental) cost of capital.[1] The size of the effect of changes in the user cost of capital is captured by the elasticity of substitution of capital for labor and the elasticity of capital in response to a change in factor prices. The empirical estimation of standard Jorgensonian/neoclassical models of investment has been a remarkably unsuccessful venture, and these models are invariably characterized by poor predictive power and econometric problems. In addition, the theoretical interpretation of neoclassical investment models has been blurred by the complexity of forces affecting the lag structure of investment.[2] While empirical specifications of accelerator models have performed somewhat better, these models have been criticized because of ad hoc specifications, particularly of lag structures. In addition, as aggregate investment is a component of aggregate expenditure, it is not particularly illuminating or surprising to find that there is a strong correlation between investment and output/expenditure. The orthodox reaction to the empirical difficulties with Jorgensonisan models was the marriage of rational-expectations hypotheses with the Jorgensonian marginalist, maximizing approach. The most predominant of these are the rational-expectations versions of q theories.[3] In essence, by way of the efficient-markets hypothesis and various restrictive assumptions about the specification of the production function, orthodox q theories justify the use of stock-market information as a proxy for expected future profitability of aggregate investment (Abel 1983, 1990).

Empirically, there are problems with the specification and calculation of the key elements of q (Baddeley 1995, 2003; Chirinko 1993). Generally, the empirical results from the estimation of q models have also been disappointing.[4] Despite their sophistication, rational-expectations models of investment, including q models, have been compromised by problems of serial correlation and poor predictive power. One reason for this poor empirical performance is that the rationality assumptions—of optimizing behavior and subjective expectations corresponding, on average, to an objective probability distribution of outcomes—are unrealistic. While unrealistic assumptions are often justified by orthodoxy on positivist grounds, this justification has proved fallible because the actual predictive power of neo-classical and rational-expectations models is poor. Simon (1979) argues that the orthodox description of "substantively rational" goal-oriented, optimizing behavior may be inappropriate to the analysis of many aspects of economic decision making. Alternative approaches to the description of rational decision making that allow "procedurally rational" behavior, or behavior which is the result of "appropriate deliberation" rather than precise mathematical calculation, may be more appropriate to analysis of economic phenomena such as investment activity. This is particularly true in situations characterized by uncertainty, and the next step in the refinement of orthodox theory was the incorporation of uncertainty into the modeling of rational investor behavior.

Uncertainty in Orthodox Investment Theory

The independent role of uncertainty in the determination of investment, always a crucial aspect of Keynes's investment theory (see below) has only recently become the focus of orthodox investment theory.[5] In the 1990s, analyses of uncertainty came to the fore in the more mainstream literature on investment, for example see Viner (1931), Cukierman (1980), Bernanke (1983), and Bertola and Caballero (1994). This led to the evolution of rational-expectations theories of investment under uncertainty, that is, the options theories of irreversible investment of Pindyck (1991, 1993) and Dixit and Pindyck (1994). However, the broad nature of orthodox analyses of investment under uncertainty remains the same and the assumption of the substantively rational, optimizing economic agent is retained in these models. A number of orthodox economists have postulated a positive relationship between investment and uncertainty for perfectly competitive companies facing completely reversible investment decisions (Abel 1983, Hartman 1976, Pindyck 1982, Roberts and Weitzman 1987, Sakellaris 1994). Nickell (1978) argues that a positive relationship between investment and uncertainty emerges because companies will undergo larger increases in capacity in response to uncertain demand if higher profits are expected in the future (ibid., 74). Pindyck (1993) suggests that, under conditions of uncertainty, there is an increased desire for the increased flexibility which larger capital stocks and faster rates of investment allow. A larger capital stock will mean that output can vary more widely in order to take advantage of unanticipated increases in output prices. Similarly, Manne (1961) argues that if companies need capacity to cope with random increases in demand, capacity will be added in larger increments when demand uncertainty increases. However, empirical studies have established a strong negative effect of uncertainty on investment. Whether this negative effect would have been greater if not for the offsetting effects of convexity in the marginal profitability curve is difficult to establish empirically, but certainly, the result of a positive relationship between irreversible investment and uncertainty does not rest easily with intuition.

In contrast to the models described above, many orthodox theorists have recently suggested that the relationship between investment and uncertainty is negative. Viner (1931) argues that, because investment is irreversible, it pays companies to wait until more information that is accurate is available before deciding about what size of plant to build. He argues that this result holds even for risk-neutral companies. Cukierman (1980) argues that risk-averse investors facing irreversible investment decisions and increased uncertainty will require and acquire more information about future demand conditions before they decide to invest. However, while they will delay investment they will not necessarily cancel investment plans altogether, and the length of time devoted to collecting information, the "optimal waiting period," will increase as the variance of expected rates of return increases. Cuikerman relates this result to the precision of information. A decrease in the precision of information about the potential of investments will have ambiguous effects. The overall value of information will decrease, and, therefore, there will be less incentive to wait for information before investing. However, it takes more time to accumulate enough relevant information, thus the optimal waiting period will increase.

Most famously, Pindyck (1982, 1988, 1991, 1993) and Dixit and Pindyck (1994) develop an options approach to investment under uncertainty. They argue that uncertainty has counter-balancing effects on investment: irreversibility will lead to decreased investment under uncertainty, but the convexity of profitability described by Hartman (1976) and others will promote increased investment under uncertainty. The net outcome depends on which effect predominates. Dixit and Pindyck (1994) argue that leeway over the timing of investment has profound effect on the investment process when investment is irreversible and involves sunk costs. Sunk costs arise not only because reinstallation is costly but also because capital goods have a very limited resale value. A large proportion of investment purchases are sunk costs because many investments are industry or company specific. If demand conditions change, other companies within a given industry will be unwilling to buy second-hand capital goods because they face the same demand conditions as the seller of the capital goods. In noncompetitive markets, highly specific capital goods have no resale value because they are of no use to other businesses. Even nonspecific capital goods may be sunk costs if Akerlof's (1970) "lemons principle" applies to the second-hand market for capital goods. The limitations imposed by irreversible investment may also be compounded by institutional and governmental regulations. Arrow (1968) argues that difficulties of resale of capital goods in second-hand markets lead to myopic "optimal" investment policies because companies do not take account of the fact that they can only resell capital goods at much lower prices than they are purchased.

Pindyck (1991) argues that net-present-value (NPV) rules should be modified to advocate investment only when the value of exercising the investment option is greater than the purchase and installation cost plus the value of keeping the option alive. Pindyck and Solimano (1993) argue that uncertainty drives a wedge between the direct cost of an investment and NPV, and thus the critical value beyond which it is optimal to invest is greater than the cost of the investment. For sequential investment, commencing projects may have value in terms of providing information about the future success of projects, and, therefore, should be undertaken even if the NPV of the project overall is negative (see Roberts and Weitzman 1987). Dixit and Pindyck (1994) argue that the use of these NPV investment appraisal techniques without modification will lead to overinvestment. The existence of opportunity costs of investment may explain why real-world companies use hurdle rates of return generally three to four times the cost of capital; even allowing for differences in the risk-adjusted cost of capital, hurdle rates are generally high. McDonald and Siegel (1986), assuming lumpy investment and risk-averse investors, demonstrated that, given irreversible investment under uncertainty, for some it is optimal to defer investment until present value is double the investment cost. Investment-timing decisions are therefore crucial.

But the existing orthodox literature on the effect of uncertainty on investment is largely theoretical because the models constructed are difficult to translate into well-specified empirical models. Uncertainty has been introduced into empirical models, generally on an ad hoc basis, via some measure of the spread of output, prices, or expert forecasts. An increased spread or variance is assumed to reflect increased uncertainty. This approach is not peculiar to orthodox analyses and is consistent with Knightian/Keynesian conceptions of immeasurable uncertainty as long as spread or variance is only assumed to proxy uncertainty.[6] Whatever the theoretical or political perspective, the empirical evidence appears to be unanimous: uncertainty lowers investment.[7]

Theoretical debates about investment involve many areas of disagreement. However, while there is empirical consensus across the different schools, it is difficult to reconcile the different elements of the theories as presented in the rational-expectations literature. While the models of investment described above are consistent with the insights of real business-cycle theory, when it comes to explaining speculative bubbles and irrational forces, the rational-expectations theorists become somewhat unstuck (Baddeley and McCombie 2001). Blanchard and Watson (1982) argue that deviations from fundamental values in asset prices can emerge from rational behavior because the system is characterized by multiple equilibria. However, this justification of speculative bubbles as rational does not rest easily with real business-cycle models describing an unfettered economy as always being in some Pareto optimal state. In contrast, Post Keynesian theories of speculation, investment, and uncertainty are consistent, and, in fact, complement one another. In Keynes, and in the Post Keynesian literature, the destabilizing effects of uncertainty are communicated via financial channels, and thus speculative and financial decisions have key effects on investment. As investment is the leading variable, this volatility and pessimism in investment activity translates into macroeconomic instability.

Keynes on Investment

While the orthodox literature seems only recently to have arrived at the conclusion that uncertainty is a deterrent to investment, this insight was crucial to Keynes's analysis of investment. In chapter 11 of *The General Theory of Employment, Interest and Money,* Keynes focuses on the marginal efficiency of capital (MEK) as a measure of the expected profitability of an investment.[8] The MEK is the major determinant of investment and a critical, dynamic link in Keynes's analysis, and it is through the expectations that form part of the MEK that the future impinges on present activity (Keynes 1936, 145). The influence of expectations and the state of confidence on the MEK means that it is the product of a mixture of subjective as well as objective influences.

In its objective determinants, MEK is a concept similar to the internal rate of return, and, in this sense, Keynes's model of investment has more in common with neoclassical theory than with accelerator theory.[9] However, this association with orthodox theory is all but negated when Keynes introduces expectations into his model. Keynes states that the MEK decreases in the rate of investment for two reasons: firstly, because the prospective yield of a given type of capital will decrease as its supply increases; and, secondly, because increased use of a given type of capital will increase the pressure on production of that type of capital, thus increasing its supply price. The former factor has greater influence the longer the period considered, and the latter has a greater influence in the short term, before capital-goods suppliers have had the opportunity to build up their productive capital. The marginal efficiency of capital in general is the maximum of individual marginal efficiencies, and the aggregate investment-demand schedule is an aggregation of the marginal efficiency of capital schedules for each type of capital.

Abstracting from the complex of interest rates that exist in reality, Keynes argues that investment takes place until the marginal efficiency of capital is equal to the current interest rate. Therefore, investment ceases at the point "where there is no longer any class of capital asset of which the marginal efficiency exceeds the current rate of interest" (ibid., 136). Interest rates will also affect investment via the impact of expectations about future interest rates on the marginal efficiency of capital. If entrepreneurs expect a future decline in interest rates, then the current marginal efficiency of capital will decrease, because the equipment to which these estimates of MEK relate will have to compete with equipment produced in the future, which is "content" with a lower rate of return. However, Keynes argues that expectations of interest rates are captured by the current complex of rates of interest, so should not have a significant additional influence.

In neoclassical style, Keynes argues in chapter 11 that risk, as opposed to uncertainty, affects investment decisions in three ways, via: borrower's risk, lender's risk, and risks of an adverse change in the monetary standard. Borrower's risk is the entrepreneur's doubt about the probability of earning a given prospective yield. Lender's risk reflects both the risk of voluntary default to escape fulfillment of obligations and the risk of involuntary default due to disappointed expectations. Lender's risk is a pure addition to interest costs, but will involve some duplication of borrower's risk. The duplication of the different components of risk means that there are extra costs involved when borrowing-and-lending decisions are separated. This is one of the reasons that interest rates (inclusive of risk premia) will be higher than objective factors indicate. On the other hand, estimates of both lender's and borrower's risk become unusually and "imprudently low" during booms. Lenders will tend to require a wider margin between the pure rate of interest and their charged rate of interest than the entrepreneur/borrower's margin between the expected prospective yield and rate of interest because the borrower is spurred on by spontaneous optimism. Lenders' decisions will not be affected by the spontaneous optimism and animal spirits that determine entrepreneurs' decisions, although they will be affected by the state of confidence. The third source of risk affecting investment is the risk of an adverse change in the monetary standard. Keynes argues that the independent influence of inflationary risk will not be great because expectations of inflation or deflation in the value of money loans will be absorbed within the price of capital assets (ibid., 144).[10]

The quantitative determinism implied by Keynes's construction of an investment-demand schedule contrasts with Keynes's emphasis on limits to quantification and the influence of subjective forces at other stages of his analysis. The emphasis in chapter 12 on mass psychology, conventions, and animal spirits seems to be very much at odds with Keynes's presentation in chapter 11 of a neat, precise, downward-sloping demand curve. Shackle (1967) argues that Keynes's message was lost in the "curiously unsatisfying" chapter 12, which contains only the "scattered bones" of his true message. He argues that Keynes's message about the limits to rational conduct under uncertainty is stated more effectively in his 1937 *Quarterly Journal of Economics* article, "The General Theory of Employment." Shackle observes:

> Chapter 11 shows us the arithmetic of the MEK and its relation with interest rates, a matter for actuaries and slide-rules. Chapter 12 reveals the hollowness of all this. The material for the slide-rules is absent or arbitrary. (Shackle 1967, 130)

Chapters 11 and 12 can be reconciled by assuming that the investment-demand schedule shifts abruptly and rapidly, reflecting the influence of volatile expectations and animal spirits (ibid., 133; Robinson 1962). Expectations are therefore the crucial link that transforms the precision of chapter 11 into the seeming subjectivism of chapter 12.

Keynes treats short- and long-term expectations in very distinct ways. Short-term expectations include expectations of the cost of output, the wage level, and the price of sale proceeds. In practice, short-term expectations are revised gradually and continuously in the light of realized results, and this leads to an overlap in influence of past expectations and past-realized results. Although current decisions depend upon current expectations, past expectations will affect current decisions because they are embodied in the current stock of capital equipment (Keynes 1936, 50). Keynes argues that current expectations are generally based on current performance. The convention of assuming the stability of short-term expectations is established. Generally, short-term expectations may take a while to work themselves out, but they are not volatile. Because of their stability, Keynes assumes that short-term expectations are a given and are not a crucial determinant of economic activity.

Long-term expectations of prospective yields of investments are partly based on existing facts, including capital stock and consumer demand. They are also based on forecasts of future events; for example, future changes in the capital stock, in consumer tastes, changes in wages, and in the strength of effective demand. These forecasts of future events are included in what Keynes calls the state of long-term expectation. The state of long-term expectation has two facets: it is based not only on the most probable forecasts of variables, but also on the state of confidence, or weight, which entrepreneurs place in forecasts.

Objective factors play a limited role because information is scarce.[11] Therefore, in forming their expectations, business decision makers rely on a "practical theory of the future," (Keynes 1937, 214) which incorporates a number of techniques, including:

- *Projection:* Assuming that present conditions are the most reliable guide to the future and projecting them forward, even though past experience has shown that the present is an inadequate guide to the future. This assumption is adopted because of lack of information about the form of future changes, and this technique will persist as long as there is no definite reason to expect change.
- *Convention:* Accepting the existing state of opinion until new information emerges because this state of opinion is assumed to incorporate a more accurate assessment of future prospects.
- *Herd Behavior:* Relying on judgments of others, because average judgment is possibly better informed than individual judgment.

The reliance on the existing state of events, because it lacks objective basis, is nonetheless ephemeral and vulnerable to change as new information arrives. However, Keynes does emphasize that the state of long-term expectation, although not strictly calculable, is often steady because of the influence of conventions, as long as the belief in conventions is maintained (ibid., 162–63). The effects of long-term expectations will be felt for a long time, as equipment will continue to be used in production until it is worn out or becomes obsolete.

While there is an equilibrium level (or growth rate) of "long-period" employment associated with each state of long-term expectations, the economy is unlikely to reach equilibrium before expectations change again. The process of achieving the new equilibrium as changes in expectation work themselves out will take time, and in the period of transition there may be overshooting or undershooting (ibid., 49).[12]

As is well documented, Keynes argues that there is no basis for a mathematical expectation of the long-term performance of investments, and, even if there were, it would likely often suggest that investments should not be undertaken. The existence of animal spirits as an incentive to investment will overcome part of the problem of securing sufficient investment. However, because animal spirits have no objective basis, they are "easily dimmed" by economic and political uncertainty, and the volume of new investment will be unnecessarily dependent on "whim," "sentiment," and the "nerves," "digestion," and "hysteria" of business people. Thus, the fragility of the inducement to invest is compounded by the influence of animal spirits. This all suggests that, in Keynes's theory, uncertainty has a profound effect in depressing investment activity.

According to Keynes, in the past, investment depended on individual initiative and gambling instincts, and the results of investment were often disappointing. In addition, investment decisions were irrevocable, and this was a further impediment to new investment. More recently, investment activity has been encouraged by the development of organized investment markets in which the ownership of investments is separated from their management. If the rights to ownership of fixed assets can be traded in a stock market, individuals can revise their commitments to placements on a very short-term basis. This ability facilitates the transfer of old placements, making investors more willing to commit their funds. Furthermore, given no substantial basis upon which to estimate the marginal efficiency of capital, potential investors will look to stock-market valuations of investments in building new investments. If new investment is to be undertaken purely for profit, it will be governed by the average expectations as revealed in share prices rather than the genuine expectations of entrepreneurs. High share prices have the same effect as low interest rates. A high quotation will boost the marginal efficiency of capital by increasing the market valuation of a company, and, therefore, the company's estimates of its future prospective yields.[13]

However, problems emerge in that share prices themselves are not based on genuine expectations of the prospective yield of investments because there is little information on which to base such estimates. Therefore, investors will rely on the convention of assuming that the existing share price will prevail, unless they have reasons to expect a change. This convention is not based on rational judgments because there is limited information about future share prices. In reality, investors know that the share price is likely to change, but nonetheless believe that the existing market valuation is uniquely correct compared with existing knowledge, and will change only in proportion to changes in that knowledge. In addition, investors are able to form a judgment that the likelihood of changes in the market valuation in the short term is small because the only risk is of a change in news in the short term. Financial investments are therefore regarded as safe for short periods.

The fact that the convention is arbitrary and has no objective basis means that it is precarious and weak. This precariousness reflects a number of inter-related factors:

- Owners of capital assets have little real knowledge of the value of their investments, so ephemeral factors have disproportionate impacts.
- Mass psychology is volatile because there are no "strong roots of conviction to hold it steady," (Keynes 1936, 154) and thus the market will be subject to waves of optimism and pessimism.
- Experts will devote their skill to outwitting the market and predicting changes in mass psychology, and this leads to a whirlpool of speculative activity predominating over genuine entrepreneurship. Experts will devote their attention to beauty contests forecasting "what average opinion expects the average opinion to be" (ibid, 156) rather than genuine expectations of prospective yield. This is compounded by the fact that forecasting genuine changes in the prospective yield of investments over the long term is more risky, costly, difficult, and unconventional, and requires greater resources than simply trying to predict ephemeral changes in the market.

Organized asset markets allow investments, while fixed for the community as a whole, to become liquid for individuals. Keynes argues that this liquidity often facilitates investment activity by calming the nerves of investors. However, it will also impede investment. Keynes argues that the "fetish" with liquidity is a major destructive element in the capitalist system. The influence of conventionally based market valuations on new investment will mean that fluctuations in aggregate private investment will be unplanned, uncontrolled, and subject to the vagaries of the market. This predominance of speculative forces in modern capitalist economies compromises the development of economic potential:

> Speculators may do no harm as bubbles on a whirlpool of speculation. But the position is serious when enterprise becomes the bubble on a whirlpool of speculation. When the capital development of a country becomes a by-product of the activities of a casino, the job is likely to be ill-done. (ibid, 159)

Speculation has increased as the organization of investment markets has improved. However, the development of organized investment markets has not been "one of the outstanding triumphs of laissez-faire capitalism" (ibid, 159) because the "best brains" have focused their attention toward outwitting the market and anticipating changes in the market valuation of investment rather than directing new investment into the opportunities with the most potential. Therefore, organized investment markets, rather than increasing the volume of funds directed at new investment, have instead contributed to its increasing volatility.[14]

In Keynes's model, uncertainty and limited information play key roles: uncertainty prevents the assignment of precise numerical values to expectations. In particularly uncertain, times, when the state of confidence in the economy is very fragile, people will tend to rely on conventional behavior. They will fall back on the judgment of the rest of the world because the rest of the world is perhaps better informed about the prospects of investments. Herd behavior and crowd psychology will determine the movement of asset prices. Furthermore, because people realize that their estimates of the values of investments are based on precarious foundations, these conventions will be unstable and volatile. Speculative bubbles emerge as professional speculators in asset markets focus on forecasting average opinion of average opinion about the prospective prices of assets. This speculative activity will have a profound effect on entrepreneurial activity because "there is no sense in building up a new enterprise at a cost greater than that at which an existing one can be purchased" (ibid., 151).

While the existence of such asset markets provides much-needed liquidity, the market valuation of assets will have no tendency to coincide with the fundamental value of an asset. "Certain classes of investment are governed by the average expectation of those who deal on the Stock Exchange as revealed in the price of shares rather than by the genuine expectations of the professional entrepreneur" (ibid., 151). If speculative activity dominates asset markets, there will be substantial negative effects for real activity and output. During a bubble phase, entrepreneurial behavior is driven by subjective factors, such as animal spirits and spontaneous optimism. This subjectively driven level of activity cannot endure because the estimates of the marginal efficiency of capital that determine investment decisions are based on precarious and overoptimistic expectations. This overoptimism precipitates a crisis as disillusion sets in at the end of a boom: investors realize that their subjectively based profit expectations are not justified and errors of pessimism replace errors of optimism and the marginal efficiency of capital collapses.

For Keynes, investment plays a crucial role in the development of the business cycle. At the peak of a boom, relative to the objective factors affecting investment, overinvestment takes place. However, subjective factors will ensure that the marginal efficiency of capital remains high even when objective factors indicate that it should be decreased (ibid., 322). This subjectively driven level of investment is unlikely to endure because the precarious and overoptimistic expectations upon which estimates of MEK are based are bound to be disappointed. Overoptimism precipitates the crisis as disillusion sets in at the end of the boom. When, at the end of the boom, investors realize that their subjectively based profit expectations are not justified in terms of objective factors, errors of pessimism will replace errors of optimism.

The collapse in the MEK is so complete that decreased interest rates are not enough to offset falls in expected profitability (Keynes 1936, 316), doubt spreads rapidly, and the slump becomes intractable. The collapse in investment will be exacerbated by increased liquidity preference due to precautionary and speculative motives that are precipitated by the general instability associated with the onset of the crisis and the associated rise in the rate of interest. Liquidity preferences and the prospective yields of investments rest on insecure foundations, and fluctuations in one are unlikely to be offset by fluctuations in the other. Factors that aggravate pessimism about prospective yields will also increase the propensity to hoard, and vice versa. Therefore, the capitalist economic system will not be self-equilibrating. "Uncontrolled," "disobedient" business psychology and collapses in the state of confidence will mean that the MEK is insusceptible to control and purely monetary therapies will fail to raise investment. As Keynes emphasizes, "it is the return of confidence, to speak in ordinary language, which is so insusceptible to control in an economy of individualistic capitalism." (ibid, 317).

The slump phase of the cycle is more enduring than the boom phase because— although either a collapse in the state of confidence or a collapse in the state of credit is sufficient to precipitate crisis—recovery requires a recovery in both. Therefore, it will be three to five years before the recovery begins. The length of slumps is determined by the durable nature of capital assets and the carrying costs of holding stocks.[15] The durability of capital has an influence: as doubts spread about the profitability of capital, much of the capital stock will come to have an MEK of less than zero. Time is needed before depreciation and windfall losses deplete the capital stock to the levels associated with the higher MEKs that should encourage further investment.

Post Keynesian Analyses of Speculation, Uncertainty, and Investment

Post Keynesian investment theory evolves from the work of Keynes and Kalecki, and is distinguished from the mainstream neoclassical approach in the way that it treats expectations in an uncertain world (Mott 2003). The Post Keynesian literature focuses on the roles played by money and finance in times of uncertainty. This literature has developed along two broadly inter-related lines: the Kaleckian analyses and the Minskian analyses. Both parallel Keynes's analysis of the financial factors constraining investment decisions, and the refinements of his approach form an alternative to the Modigliani-Miller paradigm.[16]

In reaction against the neoclassical approach, Post Keynesians claim that money plays a crucial role in a world of uncertainty. Adopting Keynes's (1937) insight, Post Keynesians argue that, in an uncertain world, money is a "barometer of our distrust of our own calculations and conventions." This effect operates to affect investment decisions in two ways: first, via the supply of money; and second, via the impact on interest rates of the interactions between liquidity preferences and the "business motive" (or "finance motive"). This is the component of the transactions demand for money that captures businesses' demand for liquidity in bridging the gap between incurring costs and receiving revenues (Davidson 1965, 1967). Keynes points out that investors do not have limitless commands over money, and, therefore, investment is affected not only by the state of confidence, but also by the state of credit. The collapse in equity prices that precipitates a slump weakens the state of credit and the willingness of financial institutions to lend to potential investors. Given the importance of the finance motive, investment will be affected by the state of credit (the willingness of banks to lend) as well as by general business confidence. Equity collapses will precipitate slumps by undermining the state of credit and the lending behavior of financial institutions. Economic stagnation can be caused either by a collapse in the state of credit or by a collapse in the state of confidence, while general economic recovery requires a recovery in both. Financial factors will be a crucial determinant of investment, and, therefore, of fluctuations in output and employment over the course of the business cycle (Fried 1992, Vickers 1992).

Davidson explains that money, as an uncertainty barometer, will be affected, and speculative demands for finance will increase during uncertain times (Davidson 1978, Dymski 1997). This is because liquid reserves give decision makers thinking time during which they can assess and interpret market signals, meanwhile being able to meet existing commitments before having to make decisions (Davidson 1980). This endogenous creation of the money supply to satisfy business demands for liquidity means that instability can easily spread to lenders as well as to borrowers. Consequent declines in private-sector liquidity will limit the ability of companies properly to exploit investment opportunities. Aggregate demand, output, and employment will fall consequently (Davidson 1978).

Therefore, in opposition to the Modigliani-Miller paradigm of financial neutrality, Post Keynesians believe that the availability and type of finance is a crucial constraint on investment decision making. Money is created endogenously—by developments within the economy rather than by exogenous forces—and this is true not only of the demand for money, but, via credit creation, of the supply of money. Capitalist economies are characterized by inherent instability; uncertainty will spread easily from one sector to another and through the macroeconomy as a whole. Harcourt and Sardoni (1995) develop these ideas in arguing that the key sources of crisis and instability lie in the imbalances between finance capital and industrial capital. These ideas build upon two main traditions of analyzing links between investment and finance: the Kaleckian tradition and the Minskian tradition. These approaches will be explained below.

Kalecki was critical of Keynes's theory of investment because he thought that it did not properly address dynamic elements (Mott 2003). In contrast to the neoclassical-Keynesian synthesis, his explanation of investment focused on the role of monopoly and excess capacity in eroding profits and constraining investment (Sawyer 1985, Toporowski 2003). Kalecki (1954, 1968) focuses on the role of profits and financial factors in determining investment decisions. In his model of investment, the rate of investment decisions is increasing in gross corporate savings, decreasing in the rate of change in capital stock, and increasing in the rate of change in profits. In addition, Kalecki (1937) argues that the more entrepreneurs have to rely on outside finance rather than their own capital, the greater will be the level of risk involved with investments.

Laramie, Mair, and Miller (chapter 10) outline the factors that underlie Kalecki's investment theory: past profits, past changes in profits, and past investment. The dual-sided relationship between investment and profits is central to Kalecki's analysis. Kalecki constructed the following model to describe investment:

$$D = aS + b\frac{\Delta P}{\Delta t} - c\frac{\Delta K}{\Delta t} + d,$$

where D is the rate of investment decisions, S is gross savings, $\Delta P/\Delta t$ is the rate of change in profits, $\Delta K/\Delta t$ is the rate of change in capital stock, and d is a deterministic trend. Cycle and trend are caught up together. The latter is included in recognizing that "the long run trend is but a slowly changing component of a chain of short-period situations" (Kalecki 1968, 263). The two must be integrated if the impacts of uncertainty on investment are to be properly understood. Courvisanos (1996) develops these ideas in his analysis of "susceptibility," which provides a foundation for the cyclical instability observed within the process of investment.

These approaches are consistent with Kalecki's earlier insight that the availability of finance is a crucial constraint on investment decision making. Kalecki's (1937) "principle of increasing risk" describes the effects of debt buildup and declining liquidity on business willingness to invest. Kalecki (1968) develops this idea to show that uncertainty is affected by increasing risk, and it is via this that uncertainty depresses savings and dampens the investment cycle. Uncertainty will affect investment in two ways: semi-autonomous factors reflecting economic, social, and technological factors will introduce secular uncertainty; and, cyclical uncertainty will be affected by the increasing risks of rising debt, as explained above. These factors will operate to subdue investment for prolonged periods (Crotty 1992).

Mahdavi, Sohrabian, and Kholdy (1994) develop these ideas in arguing that sources of internal funds are a more crucial constraint on investment activity than are external funds. The volume of internal funds not only determines a business's ability to raise more funds, but also cushions them against adverse developments. As a business's ratio of debt to equity rises, lender and borrower risk will increase. The increased borrower's risk will be translated into an increased discount rate and a decreased demand price of capital. The increased lender's risk will be manifested in increased costs of borrowing.

The Minskian Approach

Minsky (1978, 1982, 1986) also focuses on financial factors as a crucial determinant of investment cycles. Minsky builds upon Keynes's analysis of the inefficient and perverse endogenous market processes and upon Keynes's insight that the state of credit can have as much influence on investment decisions as the state of confidence. If the money supply is not endogenously determined to satisfy business demands for liquidity, there will be decreased liquidity in the private sector, decreased ability to seize investment opportunities, and a consequent decline in aggregate output and employment (Davidson 1978). Minsky (1975) argues, therefore, that the banking system, in its ability to create money, holds the key to boosting investment. Minsky also argues that financial factors affecting the volume of investment exacerbate instability, with overoptimism of boom phases encouraging excessive reliance on debt financing. When businesses realize that the ability to service debt is lessening, they factor in the associated increase in borrower's risk. Therefore, the demand price of capital and the volume of investment fall sharply.

Minsky builds upon Keynes in developing an investment theory of the business cycle, but he focuses more closely on the role of endogenous money and finance in propelling bubbles and crises. The seeds of later financial crisis are planted during expansionary phases. In periods of tranquility there is a decline in the value of holding money; capital-asset prices and investment increase, and there is a portfolio shift toward relatively risk forms of finance. However, as the proportion of risky units dominate, the economy becomes increasingly sensitive to interest-rate variations. Investment demand increases the demand for finance, and interest rates tend to increase as the supply of finance and demand for finance become more inelastic. This promotes increasingly rapid rises in short-term interest rates, in turn leading to rises in long-term interest rates.

The rise in interest rates will lead to a fall in investment and, as profits are driven by investment, profits will fall. Lowered profit expectations will lead to decreases in the price of capital assets and a decreased ability to fulfill financial commitments. As "present-value reversals" take place, assets are sold in order to meet payment commitments, asset prices fall below their cost of production, and financial crisis is under way. As foreshadowed above, the seeds of crisis were planted in the beginning of an expansionary phase, and speculative bubbles are merely the catalysts of inevitable financial crises.

During phases of crisis and deflation, endogenous market processes are inefficient and perverse, so capitalist economies need robust financial institutions (such as a strong central bank) to guide finance and investment and to reduce the sensitivity of aggregate investment to the vagaries of private-sector investment.

Palley (2001), however, argues that Minsky is providing a "weak" alternative to the q theory of orthodox economics in his analysis. While Minsky disagrees with the efficient-markets hypothesis about the connection between the fundamental value of expected future returns with an asset's price, he does agree with Keynes's insight that stock-market activity is about outwitting the crowd rather than using share prices as efficient signals of the demand price of capital. For Minsky, changes in equity prices do not capture the expected long-term profitability of companies, but they do affect the cost of capital. When stock markets are doing well, and equity prices are high relative to output prices, investment will be buoyant and the costs of external financing will be low. In contrast, when equity prices are low, the costs of external financing will be high and investment will be depressed.

Minsky also develops Kalecki's principle of increasing risk by focusing on the role played by endogenous money and finance propelling bubbles and crises. Conventional theory cannot explain financial crisis—first, because of its emphasis on full-employment equilibria, and second, because the endogeneity of money is not properly explained in neoclassical economics.

Interaction between general economic confidence and the state of credit has an amplifying effect on deviations and propels deviations through the macroeconomy. The market interdependencies that emerge prevent the easy attainment of equilibrium positions. Minsky also reinforces the earlier Post Keynesian insight that just as profits determine investment, so investment determines profits. The ability of businesses to finance their debts in the future is determined by current investment decisions; in reaching equilibrium, short-period profit expectations must match financed investment, and profit flows must match debt obligations. Profits determine long-period business expectations and provide a dynamic link within a capitalist system. Profit expectations facilitate debt financing but future profits will only materialize if investment continues into the future. For Minsky, profits are both the carrot and the stick that make capitalism work (Minsky 1978).

Many of these ideas are developed by Minsky (1978, 1986) in his "financial instability hypothesis." Here Minsky argues that finance and investment are interdependent, with crucial impacts for the evolution of the business cycle. This emerges out of the debt profile, or "financial posture," that characterizes a company, and there are three types of business units, ranked according to their riskiness: hedge, speculative, and Ponzi finance units. The different forms of financing underlying these businesses involve different levels of borrower and lender risk, reflecting differing levels of expected returns.

Hedge finance units are relatively riskless and characterize safe investments. Investment in hedge finance units is relatively secure because the cash flows accruing from past investments exceed cash-flow commitments (i.e., for the repayment of borrowings) so the expected present value of hedge finance units is positive for finite interest rates. Speculative finance units are more risky because they are investments for which short-term sales cash flow exceeds short-term interest costs, and expected long-term cash flows are sufficient to fund the repayment of capital. Speculative financing, while more risky than hedge financing, is sustainable as long as economic conditions remain stable. Ponzi units finance the riskiest fixed investments. Ponzi financing gambles on profit bonanzas in the future. Current cash flows fall short of both the interest costs of debt and repayment commitments. Therefore, holders of Ponzi finance are in effect expecting increasing cash flows in the future and are hoping that these will enable them to repay their current debts.

According to Minsky, crisis is precipitated by the euphoria of expansionary phases; this is when capital-asset prices rise, investment increases, and portfolios shift toward Ponzi and speculative units. The mixture of finance units will change according to the state of expectations and the history of the economy. During stable times, with declines in the precautionary demand for money, uncertainty is less prevalent. Declines in interest rates will lead to a rise in capital-asset prices. The demand price of capital (which is the present value of expected future revenues) will rise as the present value of expected cash flows rises, and these rise in response to falling interest rates. Portfolio shifts toward Ponzi finance units will occur, and money will be created endogenously as banks issue more credit in response to booming conditions. The problem is that overoptimism encourages excessive reliance on debt financing, and as businesses realize that their debt-servicing ability is falling, the increasing risk of investment plans will lead to falls in volumes of new investment expenditure. In addition, while more investment takes place during a boom, initially at least, and as profits increase, this actually encourages not just more investment but rising capital-asset prices. With increases in inflationary pressure and rising uncertainty, banks will respond by constraining the supply of finance. The supply of finance will become increasingly inelastic, and demand for finance will become increasingly inelastic as well. Some investment projects will already be in process, and future stages of investment and investment financing cannot easily be abandoned. The combination of inelastic demand and inelastic supply promotes rapid rises in short-term interest rates.

As the cycle continues, the proportion of speculative and Ponzi units increases, promoting rapid rises in short-term interest rates, followed by rises in long-term interest rates. Rising interest rates engender lower investment. With profits being otherwise driven by investment, profits will thus fall. Asset prices will fall below the cost of asset production, and financial crisis will be under way. Interest rates rise, borrowing costs rise, profits fall, and investment falls. Falling profits reduce the ability to service debts, and create domino effects: hedge finance units are transformed into speculative finance units, speculative finance units become Ponzi finance units. The holders of Ponzi debt are forced to default. Revenues will fall as assets are sold. The present-value reversals mentioned above will take hold as the demand price of capital falls, reflecting falling revenues. Further falls in investment and profits will emerge. Finally, constraints on the ability to meet payments, even on relatively safe hedge finance, will affect outcomes, and as default increases, financial instability will be compounded. Minsky concludes that during deflationary crisis phases, endogenous market processes are perverse and inefficient. The policy implication is that capitalist economies should be supported by robust financial institutions (for example, strong central banks). These institutions can promote credit creation and investment in a way that will reduce the sensitivity of aggregate investment to the vagaries of private decision making.

An Empirical Analysis of the Relationship between Investment, Speculation, and Uncertainty

Previous empirical research on investment in a Post Keynesian setting has focused on the importance of developing empirical models within Keynesian-Kaleckian-Minskian models (for example, see Fazzari and Mott 1986–87; Fazzari, Hubbard, and Petersen 1988; Fazzari, Ferri, and Greenburg 2003) The empirical analysis here proceeds in three stages for two countries (the United States and United Kingdom). This replication of estimations was employed to establish how robust the findings are both to cross-sectional and temporal changes in data sets and variables. For both the United Kingdom and United States, the first stage involves the estimation of a q model of investment as an benchmark model in which the stock market plays a key role; q models were then tested, including cyclical and uncertainty variables. The second stage is the estimation of a Keynesian-Kaleckian model of investment in which profits, debts, and uncertainty play key roles. The third stage involved comparing the various models using nonnested testing procedures. In contrast to previous approaches, and to Kalecki's original analysis, an innovation is incorporated into the empirical analysis here in that the gearing/leveraging variable (i.e., net worth) is included because it captures movements in net worth relative to debt. This will capture susceptibility and "increasing risk" more effectively than Kalecki's entrepreneurial savings.

Purely cyclical factors are proxied via the inclusion of a capacity-utilization variable. Apart from that, the effects of secular versus cyclical uncertainty are measured using variables that represent a mixture of both, in recognition of Kalecki's insight that trend and cycle cannot easily be separated. For the United States, real-side uncertainty is captured using the volatility of both capital-goods prices and industrial production. The effect of speculative uncertainty, that is, uncertainty emerging via the stock market, is proxied by New York Stock Exchange data on stock-market turnover. In order to test the robustness of the empirical findings, different measures of uncertainty were used for the United Kingdom, which focused on price instability rather than volume instability. The effect of stock-market uncertainty within the United Kingdom was measured using share-price volatility (measured by the quarterly standard deviation in the All Ordinaries share price index on the London Stock Exchange). These measures of uncertainty are largely focused on financial-market uncertainty because, following Keynes (1936, 1937), the aim of this analysis is to assess the extent to which the destabilizing impacts of uncertainty emerge because of speculation on the stock markets. Data sources and full definitions of variables are listed in the Appendix.

Dickey-Fuller and augmented Dickey-Fuller tests for nonstationary were conducted on all the variables used in the analysis (with results available from author upon request) and all variables were found to be I(1), except for the capacity utilization and uncertainty variables, which were I(0). The models are estimated using an ARDL, top-down approach to cointegration (Banerjee et al. 1993). The

Cointegrating Regression Durbin-Watson (CRDW) statistics indicated that the variables within the models were cointegrated and the residuals were stationary in all models. In other ways, the models appear to be well specified. The tests for serial correlation (the Breusch-Godfrey LM test–BG test), for incorrect functional form (Ramsey's RESET test), and for heteroscedasticity (White's test) were insignificant at the 10 per cent significance levels.

Orthodox q-Models

From the theoretical section above, it can be seen that, in q theories, investment is a function of capital-goods prices and average q. Strictly speaking, the dependent variable is the investment rate (investment as a proportion of capital – I/K) but estimations using I/K as the dependent variable created significant econometric problems, and, therefore, in the following analysis the volume of net investment is used as the dependent variable. The estimations using q (in levels) were characterized by econometric problems, and, therefore, q was included in natural log form. The results from the q models are outlined in Table 8.1. In an initial, unrestricted q model, current logged q was insignificant, and so this variable was deleted in the restricted version. In the restricted version, all variables were significant and of expected sign; no significant econometric problems were detected within the regression. However, once cyclical and uncertainty factors were introduced into these models, the q variables became insignificant. Variable deletion tests confirmed that the q variables were insignificant and they were deleted from the final model. The stock-market-turnover variable was also insignificant, as were current and lagged capital-goods prices. However, lagged capital-goods prices were retained within the final model because the deletion of this variable created significant functional-form problems. Overall, the insignificance of q variables in the cyclical/uncertainty q model suggests that q is capturing aggregate uncertainty rather than a rational forecast of the prospects for future investment.

Post Keynesian Models

The empirical specification of the Kaleckian-Minskian model was constructed using the model outlined above, that is, investment was regressed on profits growth, capital growth, savings, and on a deterministic time trend. Savings was captured by using a net worth variable, where net worth is defined as the ratio of nonfinancial corporations' net worth to debt (see the Appendix for data sources). The results from the Kaleckian-Minskian model were good, and all the variables were significant at 5 percent (although the unlagged log of savings was insignificant and was therefore deleted in the restricted version of the model). All the coefficients were of the expected sign, except the coefficient on the long-run elasticity of investment with respect to capital growth is positive. This conflicts with Kalecki (1954) who hypothesized a negative relationship between investment and capital growth. The results from the Kaleckian-Minskian model are outlined in Table 8.2. Generally, the Kaleckian-Minskian model seems to be well specified, and it cer-

Table 8.1

q Models for the United States

Dependent variable: Logged investment
Estimation period: 1965–98, annual data

| | Models without uncertainty and cyclical variables | | | | Models with uncertainty and cyclical variables | | | |
| | Unrestricted model | | Restricted model | | Unrestricted Model | | Restricted Model | |
Variable	Parameter estimate	t-test (p-value)	Parameter estimate	t-test (p-value)	Parameter estimate	t-test (p-value)	Parameter estimate	t-test (p-value)
Log of $_{-1}$investment$_t$	0.5885	4.816 (0.000)	0.55288	4.723 (0.000)	0.8049	5.399 (0.000)	0.6526	6.835 (0.000)
Log of capital stock	2.340	6.0845 (0.000)	2.4774	6.8504 (0.000)	2.7807	4.8104 (0.000)	2.8136	5.4936 (0.000)
Log of capital$_{-1}$ stock$_t$	-2.167	-5.153 (0.000)	-2.261	-5.510 (0.000)	-2.595	-4.062 (0.001)	-2.569	-4.480 (0.000)
Log of q	-0.0270	-1.001 (0.321)	—	—	-0.0119	-0.4840 (0.633)	—	—
Log of q_{t-1}	0.0649	1.9255 (0.065)	0.03993	1.7371 (0.094)	-0.0144	-0.3759 (0.711)	—	—
Log of capital goods prices	-0.9407 —	-2.075 (0.046)	-1.064 —	-2.460 (0.021)	-0.2985 —	-0.5730 (0.573)	—	—

(continued)

Table 8.1 (continued)

| | Models without uncertainty and cyclical variables | | | | Models with uncertainty and cyclical variables | | | |
| | Unrestricted model | | Restricted model | | Unrestricted Model | | Restricted Model | |
Variable	Parameter estimate	t-test (p-value)	Parameter estimate	t-test (p-value)	Parameter estimate	t-test (p-value)	Parameter estimate	t-test (p-value)
Log of capital goods prices $_{t-1}$	1.375	3.3398 (0.003)	1.4896	3.7615 (0.001)	0.4911	0.95005 (0.353)	0.2932	1.624 (0.117)
Capacity utilization	—		—		0.00618	1.976	0.00569 (0.061)	2.8370 (0.009)
Volatility in capital goods prices	—		—		-0.0843	-2.896 (0.009)	-0.0731	-3.985 (0.001)
Stock exchange turnover	—		—		-0.1623	-1.216 (0.238)	—	—
Constant	0.63558	0.63885 (0.529)	0.51374	0.51996 (0.607)	-1.652	-1.440 (0.165)	-1.087	-1.228 (0.231)
Adjusted R²	0.9979		0.9979		0.9983		0.9984	
CRDW	1.4727		1.5596		1.6379		1.4396	
BG test	1.844 (p = 0.174)		1.3805 (p = 0.240)		1.151 (p = 0.283)		2.499 (p = 0.167)	
Ramsey's RESET	5.7153 (p = 0.025)		1.3522 (p = 0.255)		0.9869 (p = 0.332)		0.2925 (p = 0.594)	
White's test	0.174 (p = 0.677)		0.042 (p = 0.0838)		2.292 (p = .0130)		1.929 (p = 0.176)	

tainly presents a more robust estimation of investment activity than q theory for this data set.

Post Keynesian Models with Uncertainty Variables

The final restricted version of this Post Keynesian model is included in the final column of Table 8.2. Not all the cyclical and uncertainty variables were significant, and in the final restricted regression only the capacity utilization, price uncertainty, and stock-market-turnover variables remained. These variables were all of expected sign. The inclusion of these variables did affect the significance of lagged capital-growth, but this variable was retained for theoretical reasons and because its exclusion created significant signs of functional form problems.

The U.K. Evidence

To check the robustness of the results from the estimations of U.S. models using annual data, the models were also estimated for U.K. quarterly data over a different time period. The results from these regressions are reported in Tables 8.3 and 8.4. The signs and significance of the parameters in the U.K. estimations of q models were similar, suggesting that q models are robust not only to the changes in variable definitions but also to cross-sectional differences between the United States and United Kingdom. For the Post Keynesian models, while the diagnostic tests suggest that the U.K. model is well specified and the signs and significance of the profits variable are similar to the U.S. results, the signs and significance of the other variables are not comparable, suggesting that more complex mechanisms may be in operation in the United Kingdom. This empirical finding was investigated further via the use of a nonnested testing procedure, outlined below.

Nonnested Tests

For both the United States and the United Kingdom, the nonnested test results are recorded in Table 8.5. For the United States, excluding uncertainty and cyclical factors, the results from encompassing nonnested tests indicate that both the q and the Post Keynesian models contribute independent explanatory power in the specification of investment functions. However, as might be expected if the numerator of q is picking up stock-market volatility, the q variables become insignificant when the models include cyclical factors (captured by capacity utilization) and uncertainty (as measured by volatility in both stock-market turnover and capital-goods prices). This may be explained by the fact that q is proxying for uncertainty and/or movements in the business cycle. Overall, the Post Keynesian models outperform q theory in the nonnested tests including uncertainty/cyclical variables. This suggests that there are some useful complementarities between orthodox and Minskian approaches to empirical analyses of investment and the macroeconomy.

Table 8.2.

Post Keynesian Models for the United States

Dependent variable: Logged investment
Estimation period: 1962–98, annual data

Variable	Unrestricted		Restricted		With uncertainty variables	
	Parameter estimate	t-test (p-value)	Parameter estimate	t-test (p-value)	Parameter estimate	t-test (p-value)
Log of investment$_{t-1}$	0.85278	13.1688 (0.000)	0.86018	14.2405 (0.000)	1.1275	48.3934 (0.000)
Profits growth	0.12228	1.9436 (0.062)	0.13028	2.2515 (0.032)	0.10771	2.6493 (0.014)
Growth in capital stock	1.7294	5.6246 (0.000)	1.7611	6.0744 (0.000)	2.2707	5.3769 (0.000)
Growth in capital stock$_{t-1}$	−0.87203	−3.0176 (.005)	−0.86473	−3.0446 (0.005)	−0.39243	−1.5188 (0.142)
Logged corporate savings	0.024219	0.35454 (0.726)	—	—	—	—
Logged corporate savings$_{t-1}$	0.16315	2.4524 (0.020)	0.17083	2.7565 (0.010)	0.14080	4.0522 (0.000)
Time trend	0.015033	2.3823 (0.024)	0.014209	2.4581 (0.020)	—	—

(continued)

Table 8.2 (continued)

Variable	Unrestricted		Restricted		With uncertainty variables	
	Parameter estimate	t-test (p-value)	Parameter estimate	t-test (p-value)	Parameter estimate	t-test (p-value)
Capacity utilization	—	—	—	—	0.007826	3.6254 (0.001)
Volatility in capital goods prices	—	—	—	—	−0.07156	−4.0482 (0.000)
Stock-exchange turnover	—	—	—	—	−0.29127	−3.5105 (0.002)
Constant	1.3464	2.1447 (0.040)	1.2850	2.1612 (0.039)	−2.2628	−7.0857 (0.000)
Adjusted R^2	0.99817		0.99887			
CRDW	1.9660		2.0078			
BG test	0.00133 (p=0.971)	0.0021304 (p=.963)	0.16313 (p=.686)			
Ramsey's RESET	0.11332 (p=.739)	0.17024 (p=.683)	0.58072 (p=.454)			
White's test	.31480 (p=.575)	0.22845 (p=.633)	0.43123 (p=.511)			

Table 8.3

q Models for the United Kingdom

Dependent variable: Manufacturing investment (logged)
Estimation period: 1987Q2–2001Q2, quarterly data

| | Without uncertainty and cyclical variables | | With uncertainty and cyclical variables | | | |
| | Unrestricted/restricted[1] | | Unrestricted | | Restricted | |
	Parameter estimate	t-test (p-value)	Parameter estimate	t-test (p-value)	Parameter estimate	t-test (p-value)
Log of investment$_{t-1}$	0.9444	11.449 (0.000)	0.812971	9.146955 (0.000)	0.845380	12.51280 (0.0000)
Log of capital stock	0.7555	34.2034 (0.000)	0.787457	35.67807 (0.000)	0.764739	39.25554 (0.0000)
Log of capital stock$_{t-1}$	−0.7145	−10.325 (0.000)	−0.6424	−9.3075 (0.000)	−0.646815	−12.38260 (0.0000)
Log of q	8.1840	349.13 (0.000)	8.199567	379.0496 (0.000)	8.204681	399.3644 (0.0000)
Log of q_{t-1}	−7.722	−11.364 (0.000)	−6.6592	−9.1348 (0.000)	−6.926186	−12.54396 (0.0000)
Log of capital-goods prices	−0.0229	−2.0452 (0.046)	−0.0175	−1.6715 (0.1013)	—	—

(continued)

Table 8.3 (continued)

| | Without uncertainty and cyclical variables | | With uncertainty and cyclical variables | | | |
| | Unrestricted/restricted[1] | | Unrestricted | | Restricted | |
	Parameter estimate	t-test (p-value)	Parameter estimate	t-test (p-value)	Parameter estimate	t-test (p-value)
Log of capital-goods prices $t-1$	0.02374	2.1153 (0.039)	0.013016	1.198568 (0.2367)	—	—
Capacity utilization	—	—	0.0018	3.180000 (0.0026)	0.001748	3.400678 (0.0013)
Share-price volatility	—	—	−0.0002	−1.9964 (0.0517)	−0.000186	−1.695769 (0.0963)
Constant	0.1415	0.8156 (0.419)	0.384946	2.097357 (0.0414)	0.340607	2.211690 (0.0317)
Adjusted R^2	0.999987		0.999989		0.999990	
CRDW	2.266890		2.208274		2.064927	
BG test	1.038361 $p=0.397759$		0.923644 $p=0.458858$		1.151247 $p=0.344940$	
Ramsey's reset	0.231186, $p=0.632786$		0.543061 $p=0.464830$		281.2376 $p=0.000000\backslash$	
White's test	3.008711 $p=0.003759$		2.067380 $p=0.031811$		2.126934 $p=0.034556$	

[1]These models are the same because the parameters in the unrestricted model were significantly different from zero at the 5 percent level, apart from the constant, which is retained for econometric reasons.

Table 8.4

Post Keynesian Models for the United Kingdom

Dependent variable: Manufacturing investment (logged)
Estimation period: 1987Q2–2001Q2, quarterly data

Variable	Without cyclical and uncertainty variables				Includes cyclical and uncertainty variables			
	Unrestricted		Restricted		Unrestricted		Restricted	
	Parameter estimate	t-test (p-value)	Parameter estimate	t-test (p-value)	Parameter estimate	t-test (p-value)	Parameter estimate	t-test (p-value)
Logged investment$_{t-1}$	1.0362	22.571 (0.000)	1.0007	38.348 (0.000)	0.9240	12.25 (0.00)	0.891032	22.78818 0.0000
Logged profits	0.1203	1.5169 (0.13)	0.0974	3.523 (0.001)	0.0459	0.5235 (0.603)	—	—
Logged profits$_{t-1}$	–0.002	–0.028 (0.97)	—	—	–0.013	–0.165 (0.87)	—	—
Logged capital stock	–0.946	–0.753 (0.45)	—	—	–0.986	–0.799 (0.42)	—	—
Logged capital stock$_{t-1}$	0.8784	0.7009 (0.487)	—	—	1.051	0.8526 (0.398)	—	—
Net worth	–0.000	–1.153 (0.254)	—	—	–0.000	–1.103 (0.276)	–0.000	–1.919 (0.060)

(continued)

229

Table 8.4 (continued)

Variable	Without cyclical and uncertainty variables				Includes cyclical and uncertainty variables			
	Unrestricted		Restricted		Unrestricted		Restricted	
	Parameter estimate	t-test (p-value)	Parameter estimate	t-test (p-value)	Parameter estimate	t-test (p-value)	Parameter estimate	t-test (p-value)
Net worth$_{t-1}$	-0.000	1.0554 (0.296)	—	—	-0.000	1.1355 (0.262)		
Capacity utilization	—	—	—	—	-0.069	-1.772 (0.083)	-0.078	-3.799 (0.000)
Share-price Volatility	—	—	—	—	0.0071	1.1047 (0.275)	—	—
Constant	0.2052	0.1604 (0.873)	-0.209	-0.945 (0.349)	0.0778	0.0611 (0.952)	1.1870	3.274 (0.0019)
Adjusted R^2	0.9619		0.9635		0.9633		0.9653	
CRDW	2.009		1.988		2.046		2.049	
BG test	1.3020 p = 0.284		1.545 p = 0.204		0.4545 p = 0.768		0.8634 p = 0.493	
Ramsey's RESET	0.2718 p = 0.604		0.2720 p = 0.604		0.02421 p = 0.877		0.0768 p = 0.783	
White's test	1.367 p = 0.213		1.1080 p = 0.363		0.9415 p = 0.536		0.7858 p = 0.585	

Table 8.5

Nonnested Tests

Encompassing tests on models, excluding cyclical and uncertainty factors

	q vs. Post Keynesian		Post Keynesian vs. q	
	$F_{(4,45)} =$		$F_{(4,45)} =$	
Models without uncertainty				
U.S., 1965–88	2.7521	$p = 0.053$	5.3127	$p = 0.006$
Both models contribute independent explanatory power				
U.K., 1987Q2–2001Q2	2.1158	$p = 0.006$	38889	$p = 0.000$
Both models contribute independent explanatory power				
Models with uncertainty				
U.S., 1965–88				
Favors Post Keynesian	4.2207	$p = 0.019$	0.0786	$p = 0.971$
U.K., 1987Q2–2001Q2				
Favors q model	1.0638	$p = 0.3861$	40530	$p = 0.000$

However, substantive differences remain, and some of the key policy implications from Minsky, for example, are quite distinct from the policy implications addressed in mainstream analysis.

For the United Kingdom, the results from the nonnested tests are not dissimilar for the tests on models excluding capacity utilization and uncertainty (as measured by share-price volatility), with both models contributing independent explanatory power in the specification of investment. However, for the models including the uncertainty and capacity-utilization, the nonnested tests favor the q model, which is the opposite of the result for the United States. Overall, this confirms the above in suggesting that q models perform better for the United Kingdom than for the United States. It seems that the stock market may promote the development of unstable whirlpools in the United States, but more steady bubble behavior in the United Kingdom. These differences may be explained in terms of institutional structure and future research could focus on capturing institutional differences.

Conclusions and Policy Implications

This chapter examines the relationships between investment, the stock market, and uncertainty in the context of orthodox and Post Keynesian models. The empirical evidence presented supports the widely supported finding that uncertainty depresses aggregate investment. However, this study is distinct in that it presents a well-specified model of investment upon which to base this analysis of uncertainty. Keynes's emphasis on the role played by the stock market, and desires for liquidity under conditions of uncertainty, is in this way complemented by a Post

Keynesian model in which investment decisions are determined by profits growth, corporate savings, and growth in the capital stock. Orthodox specifications of q theory were found to have little empirical support once uncertainty and cyclical factors are included within the model.

The main policy implications to emerge from these analyses are centered on the significant links between investment activity and speculation/financial uncertainty. Given these influences, effective and strong institutions could be developed to moderate these forces of instability. Central banks could play a key role in coordinating economic activity and in moderating speculative activity (e.g., via a Tobin tax). The implementation of financial market controls could also be introduced to moderate destabilizing impacts of financial instability on investment. Given the problems of underinvestment created within a world of endemic uncertainty, the role of discretionary policy, e.g. focused on employment creation and public-sector investment, is crucial. And in a world in which increasingly large volumes of economic and financial activity are being globalized, the importance of macroeconomic policy coordination on a global scale must be recognized.

Notes

1. Although there are some parallels between the neoclassical concept of user cost of capital and Keynes's discussion of user cost, these two concepts should be regarded as quite distinct.

2. See also Baddeley (1995, 2003) and Chirinko (1993).

3. The rational-expectations theorists do not have sole claim on q theory: variants of q models are consistent with Keynes and Post Keynesian theory (e.g., Davidson's analysis).

4. Although Baddeley (1995) finds that, while Jorgensonian-style models were rejected outright, q theories provided some additional explanatory power beyond that provided in accelerator theory.

5. For example, Lucas and Prescott's (1971) article "Investment under Uncertainty" uses the rational-expectations approach to describe expectations formation by investors facing uncertainty, not nonexpectation reactions to uncertainty. In fact, uncertainty as a separate variable (independent of the expectation variables) is explicitly excluded from their analysis of investment.

6. Keynes (1921) does allow that "weight," a concept related to uncertainty, can be proxied by statistical measures of spread.

7. There are innumerable analyses, including those by Caballero and Pindyck (1992), Leahy and Whited (1995), Pindyck and Solimano (1993), Price (1995), Acemoglu (1993), Ferderer (1993), and Driver and Moreton (1992a, 1992b).

8. Keynes's theory of investment has been the target of many criticisms over the years (particularly as regards to his confusions of stocks and flows, objective and subjective factors, *ex ante* and *ex post* elements). For a fuller analysis of these issues, see Asimakopulos (1991).

9. In terms of associations with accelerator theory, while the emphasis on demand and output variables in accelerator theory could be seen as evidence in favor of Keynesian aggregate-demand-based models, a key insight from Keynes is that investment is the leading variable in the determination of macroeconomic outcomes.

10. This observation was probably more relevant to the time at which Keynes was writing. In the stagflation environment that characterized the 1970s and 1980s, inflationary risk had a significant, independent influence.

11. In Keynes's (1936) *General Theory*, the long-term expectations affecting investment and liquidity preference cannot be modeled accurately using existing data because individual decisions about investment and liquidity preference, decisions that have future consequences, are not quantifiable or even comparable. This insight has implications for arguments about the rationality of investor behavior in the *General Theory*. See also Keynes (1921).

12. The precariousness of expectations of the marginal efficiency of capital justifies a focus on short-term returns. This finding is compatible with Pindyck and Solimano's (1993) finding that uncertainty increases the discount rate and trigger rate of return, and thus focuses decision making on the short run. This hypothesis is confirmed by the results from the *CBI Industrial Trends Survey* (Confederation of British Industry, various years), which indicate that investment decisions tend to have shorter payoff periods and higher internal rates of return than would be expected from looking at the simple cost of borrowing as reflected in interest rates. Other factors mitigating the effects of the precariousness of expectations on the marginal efficiency of capital include the existence of contracts and risk sharing, monopoly privileges, and risks borne by public authorities undertaking activity for social purposes. Thus, not all classes of investment are affected by the volatility and complexity described above.

13. This is the basis of Tobin's (1969) q theory of investment, although the implications of Keynes's analysis are quite different from the orthodox developments of q theory outlined above.

14. In addition, Harcourt (1995) argues that the influence of speculation will mean cumulative processes rather than equilibrating tendencies will characterize the path of investment.

15. Liquid capital is another crucial time element. The initial contraction in investment will be offset by the accumulation of finished stocks and working capital. Once production decisions have adjusted to the onset of a slump there will be disinvestments in all liquid capital until the end of the slump, when working capital increases develop because production decisions adjust to expected increases in demand. This is initially offset by disinvestments in stocks of finished goods, as sales are greater than expected (Keynes 1936, 115–20). Changes in the stock of inventories, arising from mistaken short-term expectations, also play a role by contributing to minor fluctuations during the cycle (ibid., 332).

16. See Gordon (1992, 1994) and Davidson (1990) for more comprehensive criticisms of the neoclassical theory of finance and the associated Modigliani-Miller theorem.

References

Abel, A.B. 1983. "Optimal Investment under Uncertainty." *American Economic Review* 73(1): 228–33.
———. 1990. "Consumption and Investment." In B.M. Friedman and F.M. Hahn, eds., *Handbook of Monetary Economics,* 726–78. Amsterdam: North-Holland, 1990.
Acemoglu, D. 1993. "Learning About Others' Actions and the Investment Accelerator." *Economic Journal* 103(417): 318–28.
Akerlof, G.A. 1970. "The Market for Lemons: Quantity, Uncertainty and the Market Mechanism." *Quarterly Journal of Economics* 84(3): 488–500.
Arrow, K.J. 1968. "Optimal Capital Policy with Irreversible Investment." J.N. Wolfe, ed., *Value, Capital and Growth,* 1–19. Edinburgh: Edinburgh University Press.
Asimakopulos, A. 1991. *Keynes's General Theory and Accumulation.* Modern Cambridge Economics Series. Cambridge: Cambridge University Press.
Baddeley, M. 1995. "Rationality, Expectations and Investment: The Theory of Keynes Versus Neo-Classical Theory." Ph.d. diss., University of Cambridge.
———. 2003. *Investment Theories and Analysis.* London: Macmillan.

Baddeley, M., and J. McCombie. 2001. "An Historical Perspective on Speculative Bubbles and Financial Crisis: Tulip Mania and the South Sea Bubble." In P. Arestis, M. Baddeley, and J. McCombie, eds., *What Global Economic Crisis?* London: Macmillan.

Banerjee A., J.J. Dolado, J.W. Galbraith, and D.F. Hendry. 1993. *Co-integation, Error Correction and the Econometric Analysis of Non-Stationary Data.* Oxford: Oxford University Press.

Bernanke, B.S. 1983. "Irreversibility, Uncertainty and Cyclical Investment." *Quarterly Journal of Economics* 98(1): 85–106.

Bertola, G., and R.J. Caballero. 1994. "Irreversibility and Aggregate Investment." *Review of Economic Studies* 61(2): 223–46.

Blanchard, O.J., and M.W. Watson. 1982. "Bubbles, Rational Expectations and Financial Markets." In P. Wachtel, ed. *Crises in the Economic and Financial Structure,* 295–315. Lexington, MA: D.C. Heath.

Caballero, R.J. 1991. "On the Sign of the Investment-Uncertainty Relationship." *American Economic Review* 81(1): 279–88.

Caballero, R.J., and R.S. Pindyck. 1992. "Uncertainty, Investment and Industrial Revolution." National Bureau of Economic Research Working Paper 4160, Cambridge, MA.

Chirinko, R.S. 1993. "Business Fixed Investment Spending: Modeling Strategies, Empirical Results and Policy Implications." *Journal of Economic Literature* 31(4): 1875–911.

Courvisanos, J. 1996. *Investment Cycles in Capitalist Economies.* Cheltenham, UK: Edward Elgar.

Crotty, J.R. 1992. "Neo-classical and Keynesian Approaches to the Theory of Investment." *Journal of Post Keynesian Economics* 14(4): 483–96.

Cukierman, A. 1980. "The Effects of Uncertainty on Investment under Risk Neutrality with Endogenous Information." *Journal of Political Economy* 88(3): 462–75.

Davidson, P. 1965. "Keynes's Finance Motive." *Oxford Economic Papers* 17(1): 47–65.

———. 1967. "The Importance of the Demand for Finance." *Oxford Economic Papers* 19 (July): 245–52.

———. 1978. *Money and the Real World,* 2nd ed. London: Macmillan.

———. 1980. "The Dual-Faceted Nature of the Keynesian Revolution." *Journal of Post Keynesian Economics* 2 (Spring): 291–307.

———. 1990. *The Collected Works of Paul Davidson.* Basingstoke, UK: Macmillan.

Dixit, A.K., and R.S. Pindyck. 1994. *Investment under Uncertainty.* Princeton, NJ: Princeton University Press.

Driver, C., and D. Moreton. 1992a. *Investment, Expectations and Uncertainty.* Blackwell, UK: Oxford University Press.

———. 1992b. "The Influence of Uncertainty on UK Manufacturing Investment." *Economic Journal* 101(409): 1452–59.

Dymski G. 1997. "Money as a 'Time Machine' in the New Financial World." In P. Arestis, ed., *Keynes, Money and Exchange Rates: Essays in Honor of Paul Davidson.* Aldershot, UK: Edward Elgar.

Fazzari, S., P. Ferri, and E. Greenburg. 2003. "Cash Flow, Investment and Keynes-Minsky Cycles." Washington University in St. Louis, Department of Economics. Mimeographed.

Fazzari, S., G. Hubbard, and B. Petersen. 1988. "Investment, Financing Decisions and Tax Policy." *American Economic Review* 78(2): 200–205.

Fazzari, S.M., and T.L. Mott. 1986–87. "The Investment Theories of Kalecki and Keynes: An Empirical Study of Firm Data, 1970–1982." *Journal of Post Keynesian Economics* 9(2): 171–87.

Ferderer, J.P. 1993. "Does Uncertainty Affect Investment Spending?" *Journal of Post Keynesian Economics* 16(1): 19–35.

Fried, J. 1992. "Financial Theory and the Theory of Investment." *Journal of Post Keynesian Economics* 14(4): 465–82.

Gordon, M.J. 1992. "The Neoclassical and Post Keynesian Theory of Investment." *Journal of Post Keynesian Economics* 14(4): 425–43.

———. 1994. *Finance, Investment and Macroeconomics*. Aldershot, UK: Edward Elgar.

Harcourt, G.C. 1995. "A Modest Proposal for Taming Speculators and Putting the World on Course to Prosperity." University of Cambridge, Faculty of Economics and Politics. Mimeographed.

Harcourt, G.C., and C. Sardoni. 1995. "The General Theory of Employment, Interest and Money: Three Views." University of Cambridge, Faculty of Economics and Politics. Mimeographed.

Hartman, R. 1976. "Factor Demand with Output Price Uncertainty." *American Economic Review* 66(4): 675–81.

Ingersoll, J., and S.A. Ross. 1992. "Waiting to Invest: Investment and Uncertainty." *Journal of Business* 65(1): 1–29.

Jorgenson, D.W. 1963. "Capital Theory and Investment Behaviour." *American Economic Review* 53(2): 247–59.

———. 1971. "Econometric Studies of Investment Behaviour: A Survey." *Journal of Economic Literature* 9(4): 1111–47.

Kalecki, M. 1937. "The Principle of Increasing Risk." *Economica* 4(16): 440–47.

———. 1954. *Theory of Economic Dynamics*. New York: Rinehart.

———. 1968. "Trend and the Business Cycle Reconsidered." *Economic Journal* 78(310): 263–76.

Keynes, J.M. 1921. *A Treatise on Probability*. London: Macmillan.

———. 1936. *The General Theory of Employment, Interest, and Money*. London: Macmillan.

———. 1937. "The General Theory of Employment." *Quarterly Journal of Economics* 51(2): 209–23.

Leahy, J.V., and T.M. Whited. 1995. "The Effect of Uncertainty on Investment: Some Stylized Facts." National Bureau of Economic Research Working Paper No. 4986, Cambridge, MA.

Lucas, R.E. 1976. *Studies in Business Cycle Theory*. Cambridge, MA: MIT Press.

Lucas, R.E., and E.C. Prescott. 1971. "Investment under Uncertainty." *Econometrica* 39(5): 659–81.

Mahdavi, S.; A. Sohrabian; and S. Kholdy. 1994. "Cointegration and Error Correction Models: The Temporal Causality Between Investment and Corporate Cash Flow." *Journal of Post Keynesian Economics* 16(3): 478–98.

Manne, A.S. 1961. "Capacity Expansion and Probabilistic Growth." *Econometrica* 29(4): 632–49.

Minsky, H.P. 1975. *John Maynard Keynes*. New York: Columbia University Press.

———. 1978. "The Financial Instability Hypothesis." Thames Polytechnic Working Paper.

———. 1982. *Inflation, Recession and Economic Policy*. Brighton, UK: Wheatsheaf.

———. 1986. *Stabilizing an Unstable Economy*. New Haven: Yale University Press.

Mott, T. 2003. "Investment." In J.E. King, ed. *The Elgar Companion to Post Keynesian Economics*, 205–9. Cheltenham, UK: Edward Elgar.

Nickell, S.J. 1978. *The Investment Decision of Firms*. Cambridge: Cambridge University Press.

Palley, T. 2001. "The Stock Market and Investment: Another Look at the Microfoundations of q Theory." *Cambridge Journal of Economics* 25(5): 657–67.

Pindyck, R.S. 1982. "Adjustment Costs, Uncertainty and the Behaviour of the Firm." *American Economic Review* 72(3): 415–27.

———. 1988. "Irreversible Investment, Capacity Choice and the Value of the Firm." *American Economic Review* 78(5): 969–85.

———. 1991. "Irreversibility, Uncertainty and Investment." *Journal of Economic Literature* 29(3): 1110–48.

————. 1993. "A Note on Competitive Investment under Uncertainty." *American Economic Review* 83(1): 273–78.

Pindyck, R.S., and A. Solimano. 1993. "Economic Instability and Aggregate Investment." NBER Working Paper No. 4380, National Bureau for Economic Research, Cambrige MA.

Price, S. 1995. "Aggregate Uncertainty, Investment and Asymmetric Adjustment in the UK Manufacturing Sector." University of Essex, Discussion Paper, Series No. 441.

Roberts, K., and M.L. Weitzman. 1987. "Fundamental Criteria for Research Development and Exploration Projects." *Econometrica* 49(5): 1261–88.

Robinson J. 1962. *Essays in the Theory of Economic Growth.* London: Macmillan.

Sakellaris, P. 1994. "A Note on Competitive Investment under Uncertainty: Comment." *American Economic Review* 84(4): 1107–12.

Sawyer, M.C. 1985. *The Economics of Michal Kalecki.* London: Macmillan.

Shackle, G.L.S. 1967. *The Years of High Theory.* Cambridge: Cambridge University Press.

Simon, H.A. 1979. "From Substantive to Procedural Rationality." In F.H. Hahn and M. Hollis, eds., *Philosophy and Economic Theory,* 65–86. Oxford: Oxford University Press.

Tobin, J. 1969. "A General Equilibrium Approach to Monetary Theory." *Journal of Money, Credit and Banking* 1(1): 15–29.

Tobin, J., and Sumers, D. n.d. *Survey of Current Business* (various years). Washington, DC: Bureau of Economic Analysis.

Toporowski, J. 2003. "Kaleckian Economics." In J.E. King, ed., *The Elgar Companion to Post Keynesian Economics,* 226–29. Cheltenham, UK: Edward Elgar.

Vickers, D. 1992. "The Investment Function." *Journal of Post Keynesian Economics* 14(4): 445–64.

Viner, J. 1931. "Cost Curves and Supply Curves." *Zeitschrift für Nationalökonomie* 3:23–46.

Appendix 8.1. Data Sources

U.S. Data Sources

Capacity utilization:	Federal Reserve
Industrial production:	Federal Reserve
Federal effective interest rate:	Federal Reserve
Stock-market date on turnover:	New York Stock Exchange
Investment:	Bureau of Economic Analysis's *Survey of Current Business*
Depreciation:	Bureau of Economic Analysis's *Survey of Current Business*
Capital stock:	Bureau of Economic Analysis's *Survey of Current Business*
Price variables:	Bureau of Economic Analysis
Gross domestic product:	Bureau of Economic Analysis
Net worth ratios:	*Flow-of-Funds Accounts, Federal Reserve*
q:	From Tobin and Sommers, see "Note on Rates of Return," *Survey of Current Business*, various years.

U.K. Data Sources

Investment:	Manufacturing, 1995 prices, Office for National Statistics (ONS), *Economic Trends Annual Supplement*, various years.
q:	Ratio of market capitalization to capital stock (derived from data below)
Market capitalization:	from *Financial Times* (FT) all ordinaries shares: London Stock Exchange Website
Manufacturing capital stock:	*The Blue Book National Accounts*, ONS.
Capacity utilization:	Manufacturing Survey data, Confederation of British Industry (CBI)
Uncertainty:	Standard deviation on all ordinaries share price, London Stock Exchange
Profitability:	Gross rate of return for manufacturing, ONS
Net worth:	Total net worth of private, nonfinancial corporations, ONS

9

Lawrance L. Evans, Jr.

An Analysis of the Shrinking Supply of Equity and the U.S. Stock Market Boom: Does Supply Matter?

Introduction

From 1982 to the peak of the stock-market bubble in the first quarter of 2000, the nominal Standard and Poor's (S&P) composite index of 500 U.S. stocks rose roughly 1,150 percent, or nearly 600 percent in real terms. For most economic theorists, the dramatic increase in U.S. equity prices over the 1980s and 1990s is ultimately understood in terms of investor demand. Typically, the run-up is attributed to rational assessments of future prosperity, over-exuberant expectations, or the changing risk characteristics inherent in stock-market investing. To be sure, one popular view of the 1990 bull market holds that the revolution in information technology ushered in a high-growth, "new" era, and thus the appreciation in stock prices was rooted in economic fundamentals. The bursting of the dot-com bubble along with the rash of earning restatements and the uncovering of questionable accounting practices it divulged renders this theory untenable. Another popular view maintains that there was a substantial decline in the risk premium, and thus the required rate of return, over the period. While this theory might explain a portion of the variation in stock prices, it cannot explain the bulk of the escalation given investor survey data and other empirical evidence (Evans 2003). Also demand-centered, several speculative-market theories identify the market conditions of the 1990s as a bubble resulting from flows generated by either "irrational exuberance" (Shiller 2000) or fundamental uncertainty and an adaptive expectation process (Raines and Leathers 2000). Such speculative theories, although not complete, go a long way toward explaining the 1982–2000 run-up in stock valuations.

What is missing in the vast majority of such theories, however, is an analysis of supply pressures on equity prices over the period. Because supply dynamics are typically marginalized in the conventional theories of the recent stock-market boom, they are either highly implausible (those informed by the EMH) or incomplete (speculative-market theories). Between 1982 and 2000, U.S. corporations retired an unprecedented amount of equity from secondary markets through repurchases, leveraged buyouts, and merger activity. The EMH and the Modigliani-Miller theorem both imply that this shrinkage in the supply of corporate equity had no bearing on market valuations independent of economic fundamentals. The former theory maintains that the excess-demand curve for equity is horizontal at the full-information price, while the latter extends the EMH theory to suggest that the market value of the firm is independent of the manner in which it decides to finance investment or distribute profits. It is rarely acknowledged that the dramatic reduction in corporate shares during the last two decades may have abetted the burgeoning demand for equity in the escalation of equity prices.[1] As a result, an important force behind the unprecedented rise in U.S. stock valuations is generally omitted, and empirical works testing such hypothesis are sparse.

The marginalization of supply in equity markets begs the question why, in parallel asset markets, supply is coequal with demand in the determination of market prices. For example, macroeconomists and the general public readily acknowledge that the U.S. Federal Reserve can influence interest rates by tightening or loosening the supply of money—such is the *sine qua non* of monetary policy. Likewise, real-estate prices are held to be largely dependent on the local supply of housing—a relatively fixed supply of housing, or inadequate supply in the face of growing demand, is an important prerequisite in the formation of housing bubbles. Prior to 1982, the U.S. Securities and Exchange Commission (SEC) was concerned enough about the price effects of supply changes to assume a strong policy stance geared toward deterring companies from repurchasing their own shares. Although share repurchases were never explicitly prohibited, the SEC limited companies to repurchasing shares only during certain times during the trading day and effectively discouraged them (and discouraged repurchases by other market participants) with the threat of investigation and possible charges of market manipulation, illegal under the Securities and Exchange Act (SEA) of 1934 (Grullon and Michaely 2002, 1676–77).[2] As I discuss below, the reversal in the SEC's policy in 1982 unleashed a wave of stock buybacks and had far-reaching implications for the U.S. stock market.

The SEC's prior policy reflects a simple supply-and-demand theory and suggests that, similar to the markets for money and real estate, supply changes generate price-pressure effects irrespective of fundamentals. Correspondingly, more complex speculative-market theories, which place adaptive expectations at the center of the equity-price-determination process, suggest that supply changes can influence market valuations through various channels. Nevertheless, significant intellectual tension surfaces regarding the forces that move equity prices—on the one hand, some hold those forces to be only those relevant to economic performance, while on the other, some acknowledge forces independent of economic fundamentals. The issue of equity supply further exacerbates this theoretical debate and therefore complicates economic policies involving stock-market investment. This chapter provides an analysis of various theories of equity-price determination as it pertains to equity supply, and provides some empirical evidence from vector autoregressive and OLS techniques to support the often-ignored contention that the decline in the amount of outstanding corporate equity facilitated the movement of U.S. stock-market returns to levels unjustified by fundamentals, and, more generally, that the excess-demand curve for stock is not horizontal.

The chapter proceeds as follows. Section 2 chronicles the stylized facts and descriptive statistics as they pertain to the net issuance of corporate equity. In section 3 I briefly review various theories of equity price determination with respect to supply collectively with some corresponding literature. Additionally we unpack the reasons for a causal relationship and price-pressure effects both fundamental and nonfundamental. The remaining sections are devoted to examining the causal relationship between the inflow of funds due to negative net issuance of corporate equity and U.S. stock prices over the 1982–2000 period. Section 4 describes the data and defines the variables used in the econometric investigation. In section 5 we outline the VAR approach and present the empirical results. We find evidence of mutual causality between net issues of corporate equity and stock prices for the 1982–99 period on the basis of both bivariate, multivariate tests of Granger causality and also innovation accounting techniques.

Section 6 presents the structural model technique and corroborates the results documented in section 5. With the reduced form (VAR) approach we cannot address whether the causal relationship between net issues of market valuations is robust in the presence of variables that proxy for fundamental value of aggregate stock-market indices. Therefore, using a standard set of macroeconomic and financial variables popularized by Fama (1981, 1990) and Chen et al. (1986) to capture expected future dividend payouts, we reexamine the structural relationship between stock-market returns and net issues of corporate equity. I find that even when controlling for the fundamentals, lagged net issues remain a significant explainer of equity returns and yield an R^2 significantly larger than that obtained from regressions of stock returns on the variables assumed to determine the capture the fundamental variation in broad stock-market values alone.

The Shrinking Supply of Corporate Equity: The Stylized Facts

One reason for the neglect of the price effects of supply changes is that before 1981, quarterly new issues of corporate equity had been relatively small and positive, the exceptions being 1965 and 1979. However, since 1981, domestic corporations traded publicly in the United States have significantly reduced the amount of equity on the secondary market by way of mergers, leveraged buyouts, and stock buybacks (see Figure 9.1). During the stock-market boom years the decline in the volume of domestic shares outstanding averaged nearly $65 billion per year. In total, $1.2 trillion worth of corporate equity was removed from secondary markets. As illustrated in Figure 9.2, this unprecedented reduction originates with industrial companies, which retired $1.4 trillion; in distinction, financial companies issued, on net, $200 billion in real terms.[3] As a result, industrial corporate equity, as a percentage of the total domestic equity outstanding vis-à-vis secondary markets, fell from 90 percent in 1982 to 75 percent in 2002. This speaks to the "financialization" of the U.S. economy, a phenomenon that goes beyond the scope of this chapter (though see Epstein 2004).

The 1982–99 period can be divided into four separate phases: two phases of positive net issuance, 1982–83 and 1991–94, and two where net issuance was negative, 1984–90 and 1995–99. The 1984–90 phase is associated with intense merger and leveraged-buyout activity. However, stock buybacks also began to occur in large amounts following the implementation of SEC Rule 10b-18, which established a "safe harbor" for corporations that repurchased their own shares from the antimanipulative provisions of the SEA. This allowed firms to repurchase their own shares in record amounts, in part as a defensive strategy to prevent hostile takeovers (D'Arista 1994, 226). Just one year after the implementation of Rule 10b-18 the amount of cash spent on share repurchases tripled (Grullon and Michaely 2002, 1652). In 1989 alone, $165.3 billion in U.S. equity was removed from the market—an amount that was, in absolute value, roughly 42 percent of after-tax corporate profits, or 2.2 percent of the gross domestic product (GDP). It should be noted that this followed a year in which the volume of domestic equity was reduced by $155.5 billion, some 37 percent of net corporate profits, or 2.1 percent of GDP. In contrast, net domestic issues averaged $4.4 billion per annum in real terms, or approximately 8.9 percent of net corporate profits, from 1955 through 1981.

After the 1991–94 phase, where net issues were positive, 1995–99 saw a return to the negative-issuance phenomena prevalent in the 1980s. In 1998, an extraordinary $228 billion in domestic corporate equity was extracted from public markets. The consequent influx of funds amounted to 2.5 percent of GDP. This, in fact, made U.S. corporations themselves the largest net purchasers of corporate equity (larger than both mutual and pension funds), and thus the ultimate providers of liquidity to the market. With mergers undoubtedly still an important part of the story, stock buybacks, to provide stock options to employees or otherwise, made up a considerable portion of the reduction in the volume of outstanding corporate equities. During the 1995–99 phase, the largest 150 nonfinancial firms in the S&P 500 repurchased, on average, 2 percent of their stock per annum between 1994 and 1998 (1 percent of which made up stock options to employees) (Liang and Sharpe 1999). Share repurchases by all S&P 500 companies alone more than tripled between 1995 and 1998, and actually exceeded dividend payments to common shareholders in 1997 and 1998 (ibid., 1). Grullon and Michaely (2002) find that industrial firms spent more on share repurchase than dividends in 1999 and 2000, and the number of companies initiating buybacks rose to 84 percent by 2000.

Using data from the S&P's index, we have calculated the real price appreciation for the various subperiods, along with the figures for net issuance and earnings and dividend growth. The results, presented in Table 9.1, tell an interesting story, one worth further empirical scrutiny. The periods 1984–90 and 1995–99, when the volume of equities outstanding declined by $821 and $576 billion, respectively, saw the market appreciate significantly, by 9.5 percent and 28.0 per-

Figure 9.1 **Net Issuance of U.S. Corporate Equity** (in billions)

Source: Federal Reserve Board, Flow of Funds Accounts of the United States.
Note: Net issues in real dollars (inflation adjusted using the U.S. consumer price index).

Figure 9.2 **Net Issuance of U.S. Corporate Equity by Sector** (in billions)

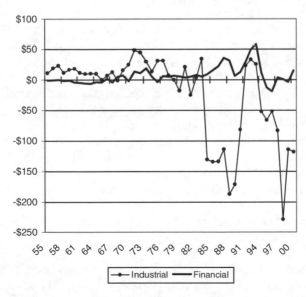

Source: Federal Reserve Board, Flow of Funds Accounts of the United States.
Note: Net issues in real dollars (inflation adjusted using the U.S. consumer price index).

Table 9.1

Real Net Issues, Stock Price, Earnings, and Dividend Growth

Interval	Net issues	Per annum S&P growth (%)	Per annum S&P earnings growth (%)	Per annum S&P dividend growth (%)
1982–83	50.6	13.6	6.9	−0.6
1984–90	−820.9	9.5	0.2	4.4
1991–94	177.4	2.6	25.5	−0.2
1995–99	−575.6	28.0	7.3	2.2

Sources: Federal Reserve Board, Flow of Funds Accounts of the United States; Shiller (2000).

Note: All figures adjusted for inflation using the U.S. consumer price index.

cent on average per annum, respectively. In contrast, for the period when the volume of equities increased, 1991–94, the real S&P index appreciated at approximately just 2.6 percent per annum. It is should also be noted that, in the 1982–99 sample, periods of positive issuance correspond not only to poorer stock-market performance but to lower dividend growth and higher earnings growth. The slight deviation from this trend is the 1982–83 period, when net issues were positive but S&P price growth was 13.6 percent.

Table 9.2 reports the correlation coefficients for changes in net issues ($\Delta Issue$), stock-price changes (ΔSP), changes in profits ($\Delta Profit$) and dividends ($\Delta Divid$) one period ahead, and interest rates ($Tbill$). The results indicate a negative pairwise relationship between net issues at time t and time $t–1$, and changes in the S&P index for 1953–99. While the correlation coefficients are not particularly sizeable (−.12 and −.21), they are larger than those between ΔSP and $\Delta Divid_{t+1}$, $\Delta Profit_{t+1}$ and the three-month T-bill rate. The relationship between ΔSP and net issues appears significantly weaker for 1953–81, and in the case of lagged issuance and ΔSP the relationship is positive. However, concentrating on the 1982–2000 period, what is noticeable is that both lagged and contemporaneous net issues exhibit strong negative correlation with changes in the S&P index.

Does Supply Affect Stock Prices? Conventional and Alternative Theories

That a correlation exists between equity issues and stock prices does not imply that a reduction in the supply of equity initiates unwarranted price increases. The reasoning is quite simple. Mergers and takeovers may send genuine signals about increased profitability, and thus the decline in equity supply conveys new informa-

Table 9.2

Correlation Coefficients

	ΔSP	ΔDivid$_{t+1}$	ΔProfit$_{t+1}$	ΔIssue	ΔIssue$_{t-1}$	Tbill
1953:1–2000:1						
ΔSP	1					
ΔDivid$_{t+1}$	0.10	1.00				
ΔProfit$_{t+1}$	0.11	0.10	1.00			
ΔIssue	−0.12	−0.21	−0.08	1.00		
ΔIssue$_{t-1}$	−0.21	0.12	−0.23	−0.43	1.00	
Tbill	−0.03	0.34	−0.01	0.00	−0.01	1.00
1953:1–1981:4						
ΔSP	1.00					
ΔDivid$_{t+1}$	−0.10	1.00				
ΔProfit$_{t+1}$	0.18	−0.01	1.00			
ΔIssue	−0.02	−0.13	−0.05	1.00		
ΔIssue$_{t-1}$	0.13	−0.14	−0.03	−0.13	1.00	
Tbill	−0.14	0.54	−0.05	−0.11	−0.11	1.00
1982:1–2000:1						
ΔSP	1.00					
ΔDivid$_{t+1}$	−0.08	1.00				
ΔProfit$_{t+1}$	0.04	0.02	1.00			
ΔIssue	−0.14	−0.27	−0.08	1.00		
ΔIssue$_{t-1}$	−0.24	0.17	−0.24	−0.43	1.00	
Tbill	−0.20	0.11	−0.08	0.00	0.00	1.00

Sources: Federal Reserve Board, Flow of Funds Accounts of the United States; Shiller (2000).

Note: Divid is aggregate dividends paid by S&P corporations, Profit is after-tax corporate profits, Issue is net issues of domestic corporate equity, and Tbill is the yield on the three-month U.S.Treasury bill.

tion about future dividend prospects. As it pertains to stock buybacks, there are two ways corporations can transfer income from their operations to shareholders, the most popular manner historically being the distribution of periodic dividend payments. However, as has been evidenced in the twenty years following the introduction of SEC Rule 10–b, profits can just as easily be distributed to shareholders via share repurchases. Breaking from the historic norm, companies have shifted in the recent era from dividend payments to repurchases. The consequent decline in dividend payout rates and the sharp rise in share repurchases have been documented in a number of studies (Fama and French 2001, 2002; Grullon and Michaely 2002; Liang and Sharpe 1999). Liang and Sharpe (1999) point out that, from 1994 to 1998, stock repurchases of S&P 500 corporations increased by over 200 percent, while dividend payments rose by only 35 percent. Analyzing S&P's industrial Compustat database, Grullon and Michaely (2002) find that industrial firms spent more funds on share repurchases than on dividends in 1999 and 2000.

This phenomenon has led some to conclude that the dividend discount model, the standard framework for evaluating stock prices, "has lost some appeal as an equity valuation tool" (Liang and Sharpe 1999, 1). However, it should be noted that although share repurchases are not explicitly accounted for within the dividend discount model, it is not an oversight that affects the validity of the model. Campbell et al. (1997, 256) aptly note that equity repurchases merely affect the time pattern of expected future dividend payments, with the respective totals remaining the same. Thus, when corporations pay dividends and repurchase shares, prices remain properly valued within the present-value framework, as is illustrated by Fama and French (2002), Jagannathan et al. (2001), and Wadhwani (1999). To be sure, a corporation with N shares outstanding at market price P, by repurchasing shares valued at S would initiate an increase in the per-share earnings growth of $s=S/NP$ (Campbell et al. 1997, 287; Liang and Sharpe 1999, 3). Consequently, the widely accepted Gordon growth model would simply reflect the higher growth rate of dividends: $P_t = D_t(1+g+s)/i+\rho-(g+s)$, where P, D, i, ρ, and g denote the price of stock, dividends paid, the risk-free interest rate, the risk premium, and the growth rate of dividends, respectively.[4]

Consistent with standard valuation analysis, dividend payouts to a collective of shareholders alters the pre-existing stock prices by forcing investors to consider the future, long-term stream of such payments. Likewise, it would appear on the surface that share repurchases function analogously by rewarding some shareholders immediately, buying back their stake in the firm, while others who were not inclined to sell are compensated by consequent price appreciation. The fact that this price appreciation is directly linked to growth in future dividend payments leads to the conclusion that share repurchases fit neatly within a standard valuation model, justifying fundamental changes in equity prices alongside dividends and discount rates. The implicit assumption here is that the funds used to repurchase shares would have been used to pay dividends. However, if dividend payments are maintained, and the share-repurchase funds otherwise used for investment purposes, shareholders should view the policy in an entirely different light. For this reason, the dynamic Gordon growth model (a dividend-ratio model) advanced by Campbell and Shiller (1988) is more appropriate for equity valuation since it holds price changes to be a function not only of expected dividend growth but also of whether the growth will be temporary or permanent.[5]

To some, repurchases should simply be incorporated into analyses of stock valuations by treating outflow of funds analogous to dividend payouts. In this manner, Cole et al. (1996), utilizing data on net share repurchases, which from 1986–95 were 48 percent of dividends, calculate a "share repurchases yield." Correspondingly, Lamdin (2000) augments the Gordon growth equation with a 40 percent increase in dividends at the beginning of 1999 to compensate for share repurchases. With justifiable assumptions about future growth rates and the risk premium, Lamdin deduces that the S&P 500 was not significantly overvalued in 1999. Unfortunately, share repurchases and dividend payouts are only superficially equivalent, and thus simply adding a "share-purchase yield" to the dividend growth rate is a precarious way to measure the fundamental value of the stock market.[6]

First, it must be emphasized that share repurchases to support employee stock-option programs cannot be likened to dividend payments. As Carlson (2001) notes, the stock-option payout is not a source of shareholder value because it does not accrue to other shareholders. Liang and Sharpe (1999) accurately point out that such payouts occur at the expense of retained earnings and, therefore, other shareholders. Clearly, a transfer of wealth from shareholders to employees does not warrant a justifiable increase in shareholder value like dividend payments do, and like some straight-up share repurchases can.

Second, a rational market should react differently to increases in dividend payments than to stock buybacks. Increases in dividends are derived from current profits signal to investor's higher future corporate profitability. The increase in stock prices is, therefore, premised on the expectation that new increases in payouts will be maintained. As a result, corporations generally do not increase dividends temporarily since wary investors penalize those that do. On the other hand, share repurchases, which are typically enabled by excess profits or temporary surpluses, are transitory and much more flexible, imposing no such requirement on corporations to buy back shares in the future (Liang and Sharpe 1999, 4; Carlson 2001, 1). Because dividends in all future periods enter the present-value formula underpinning equity valuations, an increase in payouts in one period is but a small component of price. What looms larger in the valuation of current stock prices is the expected growth rate of dividends. Thus, it is only when increases are held to be permanent that one should expect significant effects on the market price (Campbell et al. 1997, 253). Because share repurchases do not necessarily imply future repurchases, their effect on current prices should be related to future increases in dividend payments that come from a reduction in the amount of shareholders to share profits in the future.

Furthermore, new issues play an important role in economic growth. Arnott (2004) points out that GDP growth is engineered by the growth of existing firms and by the creation of new ones. Moreover, since more than half the growth in real GDP is due to "entrepreneurial capitalism," stock buybacks may result in lower earning and dividends, and in economic growth going forward. For this reason, some refer to the negative net issuance of corporate equity as "decapitalizing," while share repurchases have been likened to a "lizard lunching its own tail" (Lowenstein 1991, 145). Not surprisingly, Liang and Sharpe (1999) argue that for S&P 500 companies to maintain the current pace of share repurchases while maintaining current dividend payout rates, 90 percent of their earnings would be exhausted (52 percent and 38 percent, respectively). Therefore, share repurchases can be considered a permanent source of income to shareholders only if investing 10 percent of profits is sufficient to secure the future earnings that will enable the current payout rates to persist.

Fourth, it is clear that shareholders, trading solely on fundamentals, should not regard the two methods as indistinguishable if debt instruments or loans finance share repurchases. While there are several reasons why firms might borrow funds to repurchase equity, none of them justify an increase in share valuations if the purchase is unrelated to the future profitability of the firm. Moreover, there is a limit to the amount of debt a corporation can take on, and therefore *if* the market is a precise discounting machine it should not impute additional value to the shares of corporations who decrease the amount of their equity outstanding continually through increased leverage. After all, if it were uncovered that firms were borrowing to make dividend payments to shareholders, they would be accused of Ponzi financing, warranting a decline in their stock prices. Thus, the claim that share repurchases can be incorporated into the standard valuation model is in need of serious qualification.

Last, although Grullon and Michaely (2002) find that U.S. corporations have been substituting share repurchases for dividends, Fama and French (2001) and DeAngelo et al. (2000) find no evidence of a substitution effect. Grullon and Michaely (2002) and Jagannathan et al. (2000) show that dividend-paying companies have more stable earnings than those that rely on share repurchases, and the former also finds that dividend-paying firms are more profitable. Three studies, John and Williams (1985), Bernheim (1991), and Allen et al. (2000), argue that corporations use dividends to signal quality and are therefore not interchangeable with share repurchases. Despite the "earnings-stability" and "firm-quality" attributes of dividend-paying corporations, the 1990s rewarded share-repurchasing companies disproportionately.[7]

Thus, it is not immediately evident that investors should react to dividends and share repurchases in the same manner if we take the standard approach to asset pricing. However, if profits enable corporations to buy back shares and indicate a permanent increase in future dividend payouts, then share repurchases (a significant contributor to the negative net issuance during the 1990s) can be deemed an intrinsic part of the appreciation in market valuations. (The same is true for equity retirements due to merger and takeover activity.) Because fundamentals might explain the relationship between stock prices and the supply of equity, neither the standard valuation model nor the directives of the EMH can be completely ignored in empirical studies investigating the price-pressure effects of supply changes.

Efficient-Markets vs. Price-Pressure Hypothesis

It could be the case that the relationship between the amount of outstanding equity and equity prices has not garnered serious attention because net issues were generally positive before 1980. However, a more likely reason for the neglect is the influence of the theory of efficient capital markets (Fama 1970), which forms the cornerstone of modern financial theory and which consequently frames the debate over market valuations. An important prediction (or corollary) of the EMH is that the demand for equity is perfectly elastic at the full-information price. This outcome derives directly from the rational-expectations hypothesis, which guarantees that trade is objectively based on the conditional expectations of fundamentals, and from perfect markets, which ensures that the market processes information promptly and in a manner consistent with the absence of any arbitrage opportunities.

Further still, the high substitutability of stocks is assumed to render market prices independent of supply changes. The EMH holds that, with fundamentals unchanged, a decrease in supply would be negotiated by stockholders' willingness to sell without unjustified price increases. Thus, not only is the demand curve elastic, but with the supply of equity considered inconsequential for market valuation, the de facto *excess-demand* function for equity is perfectly (or nearly) horizontal as well (Shleifer 1986). Consequently, assuming away market failures, price-pressure effects should net out to zero. Given the mathematical complexity and intellectual appeal of the EMH, the notion that the supply and demand forces that govern the market do not interfere with the pricing of assets or efficiency of markets has therefore maintained a strong presence in the financial literature. Just as important is the Modigliani-Miller (1958) theorem, which assumes perfectly competitive and efficient capital markets, and consequently arrives at the notion that the market value of the firm, and, therefore, its investment decisions, are independent of financing policy. Within this framework, share repurchases and dividend payouts are perfect substitutes, and an investigation into the role of shrinking supply due to stock buybacks appears unproductive.

The "horizontalist" perspective dates back to Scholes (1972), who demonstrated that the selling of large blocks of stocks had a negligible impact on stock prices when these trades conveyed no private information about the true underlying value. This was taken as evidence in support of the efficient-markets contention that asset prices are unbiased estimates of intrinsic values, reflecting all publicly available information, and more importantly, that market valuations are largely independent of the number of shares the firm or a shareholder buys or sells. Several studies have scrutinized the demand side of the EMH corollary and successfully challenged the evidence documented by Scholes (1972). Using event-study methodology to study new inclusions into the S&P 500 index, both Schleifer (1986) and Harris and Gurel (1986) document evidence consistent with the price-pressure hypothesis, that is, that demand changes unrelated to economic fundamentals cause price increases. Although new purchases of stock occur purely for reasons of liquidity, the authors find prices increase by 3–4 percent with no evidence of price reversals—evidence that supports a downward-sloping excess-demand curve for equity.

More recently, the assumption of horizontal demand curves for stocks has been tested indirectly by analyzing mutual-fund flows into the stock market. Warther (1995) uncovers evidence that concurrent flows from mutual funds influence equity-price behavior using a two-step regression of stock returns on unexpected net sales of mutual-fund shares. Wermers's (1999) rigorous empirical study corroborates these results, finding evidence of herding behavior among equity mutual funds and whose activity in small stocks generates permanent changes in prices. Abnormal returns are found to be highest (lowest) for those stocks purchased (sold) in herds by mutual funds (ibid., 610–11). Edwards and Zhang (1998) document evidence that the mutual-fund flows affected prices for 1971–81 on the basis of Granger causality analysis and the instrumental-variable approach, which controls for economic and business fundamentals.

However, there has been very little work examining the supply side of the horizontal excess-demand curve for stock assumption; Brealey and Nyborg (1998) note that several studies on seasoned initial public offerings suggest the announcement of new equity issues results in a small, negative change in stock prices. However, it is not clear whether the price decline is a result of "temporary market indigestion" or simply the result of investors responding to the increase in net issues as a negative signal about firm cash flow (ibid., 71). An important study, although not a study of causality, is Baker and Wurgler's (2000), which finds that the proportion of equity in total new issues (equity issue plus debt issue) has stronger predictive power for market returns than other established predictors, such as divided yield. The authors document evidence that suggests stock returns tend to be high (low) following years in which the equity share of new issues was low (high). Consequently, firms that retire equity show above-average performances in subsequent years. This is interpreted as evidence of market inefficiency and, moreover, that the market value of the firm is dependent on the manner in which it decides to finance investment or distribute profits. Given the literature challenging the demand side of the excess-demand curve, and the work of Baker and Wurgler (2000), the marginalization of supply and demand forces in the equity market appears unwarranted.

Theoretical work exploring the supply side of the horizontal excess-demand curve for stock assumption is somewhat more evident. The theory of capital-market inflation as advanced by Toporowski (1999a, 1999b) is an extreme voting (supply/demand) theory of equity-price determination, which holds that the net inflow of funds into the stock market alone determines prices, irrespective of economic fundamentals.[8] He writes:

> The theory of capital market inflation is a nonequilibrium theory of capital markets. It argues that the actual value of capital markets . . . is determined by the inflow of funds into that market. . . . A large part of the inflow is taken out by securities issued by corporations. The balance is a net excess inflow which forms the liquidity of the market, circulating around until it is "taken" out by an additional stock issue. . . . When this inflow increases, brokers faced with rising purchase orders raise prices to induce stockholders to sell and maintain broker's stock balances. In this situation, turnover and prices rise in the market. (Toporowski 1999a, 2–3)

While most theories focus on the demand side of equity-price determination, Toporowski's theory pushes supply-side considerations to the fore. In focusing on "net inflows," it becomes clear that equity issuance can "take out" a portion of the excess inflow, which would then attenuate the incipient appreciation in equity values. Share repurchases, and retirements in general, will augment the appreciation in equity values by increasing buy demands and reducing the amount of equity on secondary markets with which to satisfy the remaining investor demand for equity. Indeed, Toporowski (1999a, 4) maintains that "share buyback places [additional] liquidity at the service of further capital market inflation." Within this framework, the excess-demand curve slopes downward and equity retirements have unambiguous price-pressure effects. However, the price-pressure effects of share retirements must be tempered with an understanding of the "fundamental" reasons the relationship might exist.

Expectations Theory

The effects of declining supply, by altering investor perceptions about future profitability, can be intensified by demand changes that encourage further net inflows and price appreciation. Once we move beyond the theory of efficient markets, investors may be seen to have short-term horizons, unconcerned about market valuations in the long term. That is, investors may purchase stock simply to reap gains by unloading it a higher price. This is the essence of J.M. Keynes's comments about the stock market approximating a game of "Old Maid," "Snap," or "Musical Chairs" (Keynes [1936] 1964, 156). This situation is enhanced by the rise of institutional investors, who are evaluated at a shorter frequency both by their managers and the public, thus leading to a bias toward the securing of short-term gains over the type of trading that would be deemed "rational" by EMH theorists. As such, the market may favor firms with high payout ratios since institutional and individual investors might not be expected to wait and see if the valuations prove correct.

Moreover, Keynes and Post Keynesians, such as Hyman Minsky in his theory of financial fragility (1975, 1982, 1986), emphasized fundamental uncertainty and the reliance of economic agents on adaptive or extrapolative expectations. These principles give rise to various rules of thumb and conventions, and a reliance on market prices as unbiased indicators of the present state of affairs as individuals attempt to discern the future value of corporations. Hence, even when investors attempt to focus on long-run prospects, they are apt to rely on tools to navigate the environment of certainty that ultimately leads to undue pessimism or to speculative bubbles.

McCauley et al. (1999) interpret 1984–90 as a period of financial-market mania that can be formally understood within Minsky's model of financial fragility. The authors note that leveraged buyouts (LBOs), especially those financed through the use of junk bonds, became a new source of profits during the 1980s, fixating many market participants. During the period, over 18,000 U.S. corporations "underwent leveraged buyouts, and the total dollar value of these deals exceeded $250 billion," and even the largest firms on the New York Stock Exchange became targets (ibid., 167). It is estimated that in the 1980s nearly one-half of the major U.S. corporations received "hostile" takeover bids, "where hostility is defined as bids pursued without the acquiescence of target management" (Holmstrom and Kaplan 2001, 124). One of the most important effects of this financial innovation is that it dramatically altered investors' perception of debt and of the relationship between risk and return. A convention emerged that highly speculative LBOs were value creating, thus supporting both debt-financed buyouts and share repurchases to thwart hostile takeover bids (McCauley et al. 1999, 158). This theory supports the price effects of equity retirements, although the effect ultimately surfaces from the interaction of supply with increased demand.

Within the Post Keynesian framework, share repurchases can generate indirect price effects as a result of an increase in the uncertainty inherent in the shift from dividends to stock buybacks as the primary form of payouts. As is evidenced in Figure 9.3, which illustrates the greater variability of earnings over dividends, earnings are less predictable that dividends. As dividend payments gave way to share repurchases, the focus of stock-price evaluation shifted from cash dividends and dividend yields toward earnings. This could serve to hasten a speculative bubble as investors with adaptive expectations rely on short-term forecasts of less predictable variables that may ultimately increase the reliance on average opinion. Moreover, while the value of cash dividends is straightforward, there is no unambiguously correct value of earnings. Prices based on prospects of dividends regardless of whether they were paid in the previous year are less tenuous than prices based on reported earnings, which may or may not reflect firm performance, and which may not reflect firm performance and the ability to pay dividends in the future. As a result, there are no discussions of dividend "quality," but "earnings quality" continues to be an important topic, especially in the wake of earnings restatements. In fact, Greenspan (2002, 3) maintains that the recent rise in earnings restatements reflects the rise in the importance of earnings and the uncertainties it poses for stock valuation:

> Not surprising then, with the longer-term outlook increasingly amorphous, the level and recent growth of short-term earnings have taken on especial significance in stock price evaluation, with quarterly earnings reports subject to anticipation, rumor, and "spin." Such tactics, presumably, attempt to induce investors to extrapolate short-term trends into a favorable long-term view that would raise the current stock price. CEOs, under increasing pressure from the investment community to meet short-term elevated expectations, in too many instances have been drawn to accounting devices whose sole purpose is arguably to obscure potential adverse results. . . .

Thus, it is quite plausible that the greater uncertainty created by the shift from dividends to share repurchases might explain some of the run-up in equity prices over the 1990s.

Figure 9.3 **Real Dividends and Earnings (1950–2001)**

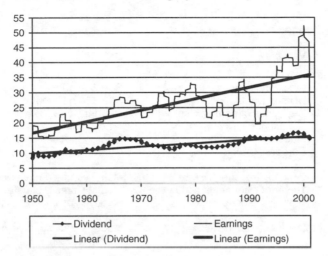

Source: Shiller (2000).
Note: All figures adjusted for inflation using the CPI.

Definitions of the Variables and Data Description

The financial and economic data used in our investigation is obtained from Shiller (2000), S&P's DRI database, and from the Federal Reserve Board's *Flow of Funds Accounts of the United States* (March 6, 2003).[9] All the variables and derived series employed in this paper are defined in Table 9.3. We examine the causal relations between aggregate net issuance of domestic corporations and broad stock-market performance from 1953:1 to 2000:1. The S&P 500 index is employed since it is considered the most accurate proxy for U.S. stock-market performance, with over 80 percent coverage of all U.S. equities. In turn, stock returns are calculated as the quarterly change in the S&P index plus the quarterly dividend yield.

The question of whether supply changes affect prices when controlling for fundamentals is made difficult by the fact that the true worth of a company's shares is unknowable. A macro-oriented approach permits us to focus on the issue of broad market valuation, thereby avoiding complex micro-details such as industry risk, investment strategies across firms, relative management efficiencies, and technical expertise. We closely follow Chen et al. (1986), Keim and Stambaugh (1986), Fama (1990), and Edwards and Zhang (1998) in our choice of variables to proxy for unobservable fundamentals. These variables, which include the term structure, risk premium, industrial production, and short-term interest rates, are specified in detail in the section titled "Structural Model Approach," below.

There are two long-term aggregate equity-issues series reported by the Federal Reserve that serve as possible candidates for observing changes in equity supply.

Table 9.3

Variables Defined

Symbol	Variable	Definition
Basic series		
SP	Stock price index	S&P 500 quarterly index
DY	Dividend yield	S&P 500 quarterly dividend yield
Issues	Net issues of domestic corporate equity	Quarterly flow, flow of funds accounts
IP	Industrial production	Monthly industrial production index
Profit	Corporate profits	Quarterly corporate profits after tax
Tbill	3-month Treasury bill rate	Monthly rates (annualized)
10yrB	10-year Government bond yield	Monthly rates (annualized)
Fyaaac	High-grade bond yield	Moody's AAA bond yield (annualized)
Fybaac	Low-grade bond yield	Moody's BAA bond yield (annualized)
Derived series		
Returns	Equity returns	$(SP_t - SP_{t-1}) + DY$
Uissues	Unexpected net issue of corporate equity	Unexpected net issues generated from an AR(3) model fit to series, issues
QIssues	Quarterly change in net issues	First difference of issues
QIP	Quarterly change in industrial production	First difference of IP
Qprofit	Quarterly change in after tax profits	First difference of Profit
Term	Term structure or term premium	$10yrb_t$–$Tbill_t$
Risk	Default spread or risk premium	fybaac–fyaaac

Sources: Federal Reserve Board, Standard and Poor's DRI database, and Shiller (2000).

One is the monthly gross total of equity issues reported in the *Federal Reserve Bulletin*. Although the use of monthly data is appealing, this series does not net out share repurchases. Consequently, it is useless for our study since it obscures the fact that net issues were negative during the 1980s and 1990s. Therefore, we utilize the net issues of domestic corporate-equity series reported in the Federal Reserve's *Flow of Funds Accounts* (Table F.213). Net issues are the dollar value of the increase in the amount of equity outstanding. As Baker and Wurgler (2000) point out, retirements due to merger activity comprise a significant portion of the flow of funds series. However, this is not a disadvantage for our purposes since we are concerned with the broad question of the effect of supply changes on stock prices, that is, supply changes due to mergers as well as repurchases.

It should be emphasized that net issues of corporate equity represent flows in and out of the stock market. Thus, negative net issuance, or share retirements, is equivalent to net purchases as far as the impersonal pricing mechanism is concerned—

both eventuate in an inflow of funds which places upward pressure on equity prices. Moreover, the net equity series is significantly serially correlated and, thus, predictable. Therefore, auto-correlated flows in one period may generate expectations of future flows. To the extent that stock prices are forward looking, it could be argued that market prices may very well predict future inflows. Additionally, Keim and Stambaugh (1986) and Fama and French (1988, 1989) document evidence that expected returns vary over time. Therefore, it could also be the case that the trending component of net issues and stock returns move together in a manner that induces the correlation. It is then appropriate to strip away the correlation between trending net issues and time-varying returns to address the relationship cleanly.

Chen et al. (1986) set the industry standard by using the residuals from an autoregressive model on a particular explanatory variable to represent unanticipated movements in that series. The authors hold that "the general impact of a failure adequately to filter out the expected movement in an independent variable is to introduce an errors-in-the-variables problem" (ibid., 386). Similarly, the predictable component is extracted from the net issue of the corporate-equity series to generate unexpected net issues for our investigation using OLS. This two-step procedure is also employed by Warther (1995) and Edwards and Zhang (1998) in their investigations of the impact of mutual-fund flows on asset returns. The data-generating process for the series was identified as an AR (3) model using the standard Box-Jenkins modeling procedure. A Portmanteau test on residuals from the AR (3) process suggest white noise, and over-fitting to an AR (4) model resulted in a deterioration in Akaike's information criterion. Consequently, unexpected net issues (*Uissues*) are estimated as the residuals from a regression of net issues on three lags of itself.

Granger Causality and VAR analysis

Granger causality analysis investigates causal relationships specifically by examining the forecasting power between variables (Granger 1969). Testing involves determining whether lagged values of variable x improve upon the prediction of y that is obtained from using lagged variables of y itself. Thus, $[x_t]$ is said to "Granger cause" $[y_t]$ if lagged variables of $[x_t]$ enter significantly into a regression of $[y_t]$ on lagged values of $[y_t]$ and $[x_t]$, or, following Hsiao (1979), if the inclusion of $[x_t]$ improves the final prediction error. In turn, the question of whether net issues of corporate equity Granger cause stock returns, or vice versa, can be determined by evaluating the null hypotheses, $B(L)x_{t-1}=0$ and $B(L)y_{t-1}=0$, in Equations (1a) and (1b).

$$y_t = \beta_0 + A(L)y_{t-1} + B(L)x_{t-1} = 0 + \varepsilon_t \qquad (1a)$$
$$x_t = \beta_0 + A(L)x_{t-1} + B(L)y_{t-1} = 0 + \varepsilon_t \qquad (1b)$$

where y_t and x_t denote stock returns and net issues, respectively. Evaluated on the basis of a standard F test, $B (L)x_{t-1} \neq 0$ implies that net issues are at least a proxy for unobservable Granger causal forces. In turn, if the null hypothesis is rejected for Equation (1a), and stock returns do not Granger cause net issues, the latter is said to be exogenous with respect to the former.

Granger's (1969) method of examining causality tests involves little more than ensuring the stationarity of the variables under consideration and selecting the appropriate lag length, $A(L)$ and $B(L)$. To properly conduct unit-root tests for stationarity, we first attempted to uncover the true data-generating process of the individual time series by over-fitting univariate autoregressive models for each, paring them down to the appropriate lag length using t-tests, Akaike's information criterion, and ensuring the residuals from the regressions were white noise. Table 9.4 presents the results of augmented Dickey-Fuller (ADF) (1979) and Phillips-Perron (PP) (1988) tests for stationarity. For the periods 1953–2000, the null hypothesis of a unit root is rejected at the 1 percent level for net issues and stock returns.

However, for the 1982–2000 period, nonstationarity cannot be rejected at the 10 percent level for either net issues series on the basis of the ADF testing procedure. Phillips-Perron tests, on the other hand, lead to a rejection of the null hypothesis at the 1 percent level of significance for net issues and stock returns. Given that the PP procedure corrects t-statistics for autocorrelation in the residuals and heteroscedasticity, and given that the autocorrelation function dies down relatively quickly, we could follow the directives of the PP tests and treat net issues as stationary (Enders 1995, 260–61). For completion, however, unexpected net issues and the first difference of net issues are also included in our examination. The advantage of utilizing these series is that, by PP and ADF criterion, both are stationary across all time periods and, therefore, eliminate any concerns about spurious results.

Table 9.5 presents the results of the Granger causality tests characterized by Equations 1a and 1b, treating stock returns and net issues symmetrically. The equations were estimated using the three equity-issuance variables for the entire sample and at various time periods within the sample. Additionally, several different lag specifications were investigated (two through eight). Table 9.5 documents the results of both tests of the joint hypothesis $B (L)x_{t-1}$, $B(L)y_{t-1}$. We arbitrarily report one specification for the entire sample and each subperiod since the results were not sensitive to the choice of lag length. In general, since the test of Granger causality is an investigation of all relevant, prior information, longer lag specifications are preferable. We would expect that equity issuance responds to market valuations with a lag since the issuing of new shares is subject to the corporate decision-making process. Correspondingly, changes in net issuance of equity can have substantial effects on market valuations in subsequent periods as the demand for equity reconciles with changes in supply.

For the entire sample, 1953:1–2000:1, evidence of mutual Granger causality between stock returns and net equity issuance is found. In contrast, there is no evidence that net issues Granger cause returns for 1953–81, regardless of the lag

Table 9.4

Stationarity Tests

Variable	ADF statistic	Lags	Phillips–Perron
1953:1–2000:1			
Issues	−3.54***	3	−6.35***
Qissues	−13.83***	1	−22.7***
Uissues	−8.43***	1	−12.17***
Returns	3.57**	4	−11.65***
IP	−1.52	4	1.11
QIP	−5.61***	3	−9.13***
Profit	1.86*	8	3.65***
Qprofit	−4.68***	8	−11.61***
Term	−4.27***	6	−5.57***
Risk	3.78**	1	−6.56***
Tbill3m	−2.23	4	−2.56
1982:1–2000:1			
Issues	−2.46	3	−4.38***
Qissues	−8.51***	1	−14.00***
Uissues	−5.34***	1	−7.61***
Returns	3.27*	4	−5.96***
IP	1.28	4	2.12
QIP	−3.34**	3	−6.25***
Profit	−2.14	4	−2.10
Qprofit	−4.65***	4	−7.80***
Term	−2.71*	6	−2.74*
Risk	−3.19**	1	−2.98**
Tbill3m	−2.34	4	−2.33

Notes: Tests for stationarity of the individual time series. See Table 9.3 for a full description of the variables.
   *Significant at the 10 percent level.
   **Significant at the 5 percent level.
   ***Significant at the 1 percent level.

length selected. If one accepts the conclusions of the ADF test, suggestive of the nonstationarity of the equity-issuance variable (in lieu of an "eyeball" test on the autocorrelation function and the formal PP test), the relevant variables to be examined are unexpected net issuances or the quarterly change in net issues (*Qissues*) and stock returns. Even in this case, the evidence still suggests that net equity issues do not Granger cause returns. This implies that the predictive power of issues for stock returns is largely driven by the strength of the relationship during the 1982–99 interval. Indeed, the null hypothesis that issues do not cause returns is decisively rejected for this interval. However, the null hypothesis that returns do not cause equity issues is rejected at the 5 percent level in each case.

Thus, in dissecting the 1953:1–2000:1 period, we find that the relationship is primarily driven by the 1982–2000:1 subperiod. There could be several reasons

Table 9.5

Bivariate Granger Causality Tests

Null hypothesis	F-statistics and significance levels
1953–2000	Four lags
Issues do not cause *Returns*	28.62***
Returns do not cause *Issues*	14.29***
Qissues do not cause *Returns*	11.44***
Returns do not cause *Qissues*	27.79***
Uissues do not cause *Returns*	13.92***
Returns do not cause *Uissues*	29.71***
1953–1981	
Issues do not cause *Returns*	1.09
Returns do not cause *Issues*	2.87**
Qissues do not cause *Returns*	0.31
Returns do not cause *Qissues*	3.39**
Uissues do not cause *Returns*	0.30
Returns do not cause *Uissues*	3.05**
1982–2000	
Issues do not cause *Returns*	5.20***
Returns do not cause *Issues*	11.27***
Qissues do not cause *Returns*	4.48***
Returns do not cause *Qissues*	10.85***
Uissues do not cause *Returns*	5.17***
Returns do not cause *Uissues*	11.90***

Note: See Table 9.3 for a full description of the variables.
*Significant at the 10 percent level.
**Significant at the 5 percent level.
***Significant at the 1 percent level.

for this finding. One plausible explanation is that while there is mutual causality, the lack of fluctuation in the net issues series during the 1953–81 period leads to a lack of information with which to assess the predictive power of supply changes for market returns. It is quite conceivable, moreover, that the effect of stock-market performance on equity issuance has changed significantly. Important institutional changes, such as SEC Rule 10b-13, investor acceptance of debt-financed buybacks as creating value value creating, and the payment of stock options has resulted in a dramatic shift in the relationship between stock returns and net issuance.

It is also quite plausible that the impact of equity issuances on market returns cannot be properly gauged by investigations built on quarterly data since net inflows are quickly impounded in prices. Thus, higher-frequency data (monthly or weekly) would allow us to better examine Granger causality. But this would suggest that the impact of shrinking supply on stock-market valuations during 1982:1–2000:1 is so strong that it overcomes the bias inherent in using lower-frequency data. This line of reasoning only strengthens the theory that net inflows effectively set prices. (Moreover, monthly data also introduces a greater noise component.) Nevertheless, the evidence from Granger causality analysis is consistent with the notion that net issuance has not historically been important for asset pricing, but net issuance has had a significant impact on returns during the 1982:1–2000:1 stock-market boom.

VAR and Multivariate Tests of Causality

The hypothesis that net issuance is a proxy for the effect of other more important variables or that stock returns and net issuance move together in response to an outside variable is also consistent with the results of the Granger causality analysis. On this note, Sims (1980) and others have argued that bivariate causality tests may not be reliable since other potentially important explanatory variables are not explicitly considered within the framework. In contrast, the multivariate approach provides unbiased tests of Granger causality and is part of the larger VAR procedure and innovation accounting techniques that serve as an alternative to the structural modeling approach. It therefore makes sense to include other variables that may influence the issuance of equity and the equilibrium value of stock prices in our investigation.

The VAR methodology advanced by Sims (1972, 1980) works with unrestricted reduced forms, treating all variables as potentially endogenous; it imposes no a priori structure on the data, instead allowing the existing causal relations between variables to emerge from the statistical procedure itself. The generalized vector autoregressive process can be written as:

$$\Phi(B)Y_t = \varepsilon_t,$$

where Y_t is a $k \times 1$ vector of constants, $\Phi(B)$ is a $k \times k$ matrix of coefficients, and ε_t is a vector of normally distributed, random shocks assumed to be white noise. Granger causality is said to exist within this framework if the corresponding elements off the diagonal of matrix $\Phi(B)$ (which characterize the relationship between a variable and lagged values of another) are nonzero.

The VAR process has the following moving-average representation:

$$Y_t = \mu_t + C(s)\varepsilon_{t-i},$$

where μ_t is a $k \times 1$ vector of the means of the constants in vector Y, $C(s)$ is an orthogonalized $k \times k$ matrix of errors, and ε_{t-i} is a vector of orthogonalized residuals (Enders 1995, 306). The vector moving-average (VMA) process, then, expresses current values of the variables in terms of current and lagged values of the error vector. Effectively, vector ε_{t-i} is a vector of innovations and $C(s)$ is a matrix of impact multipliers. The effects of shocks or innovations to one variable can be traced through the system and its impact on each of the other included variables can be examined. That is, we can produce impulse-response functions to examine the dynamic reaction of each of the endogenous variables to shocks to the system. To do so, however, the restrictions must be placed on the error matrix.

Similarly, the identified VAR system, Y_t, can be utilized to produce a forecast-error variance decomposition of each variable. Variance decompositions involve the calculation of the proportion of variation in one variable that is attributed to its own innovations and that which is initiated by the other variables in the system. More formally, we write:

$$\Sigma_{s=0...t-1} \, c_{ij}(s)^2 / \Sigma_{j=1...k} \Sigma_{s=0...t-1} \, c_{ij}(s)^2,$$

where $c_{ij}(s)$ is the (i,j) component of the $k \times k$ orthogonalized matrix $C(s)$ and, thus, the dynamic response of variable i to innovations in j. For the VAR with k variables, the equation above gives the variance of t-step-ahead forecasting errors of i, which is explained by shocks to variable j.

We employ the VAR modeling procedure and auxiliary innovation accounting techniques (impulse response and vector decomposition) in our investigation of the impact of shrinking supply on stock-market performance. For reasons of parsimony, we limit the examination to four variables—the S&P stock-market index, net issues of corporate equity, the nominal three-month T-bill rate, and corporate profits after taxes. Profits and interest rates are included as the fundamental factors that influence equity-price changes. Additionally, profits may explain a portion of the flow into the stock market from corporations, which purchase shares. Traditionally, econometric studies of stock-price changes using VAR methodology utilize industrial production as a proxy for general macroeconomic activity (Lee 1992, Gjerde and Saettem 1999). We estimated the model with industrial production in lieu of after-tax profits and the differences in the results were insignificant.

There is great deal of contention as to whether the variables under consideration need to be made stationary to obtain reliable results from the VAR methodology (see Enders 1995, 301). Sims (1980) argues that the purpose of the technique is not to estimate parameters but to uncover relationships between variables by examining their comovements. This means that differencing for stationarity purposes is akin to discarding useful information. For this reason we work with net issues and the actual level of the S&P index, estimating a truly unrestricted VAR without having to be concerned about the possibility of unit roots in all three periods: 1953:1–2000:1, and subperiods 1953:1–1981:4 and 1982:1–2000:1.[10]

The appropriate model was determined by initially estimating a VAR (10) model and then varying the lag structure, investigating the superiority of the different specifications using Akaike's information criterion, and running likelihood-ratio tests. In general, the results suggested that the VAR (3) and VAR (4) models were the best specifications. While Akaike's information criterion favored the former, we could not reject the null hypothesis that the restricted model characterized the interrelationship best. We nevertheless decided in favor of more lags and estimated the model with four lags and a constant—but again the results were not sensitive to this rather arbitrary selection. The results of the VAR modeling procedure, including F-tests for multivariate Granger causality, are documented in Table 9.6. For brevity's sake, only the results for net issues and our proxy for stock-market performance, the S&P index, are presented.

The results confirm our earlier findings that equity issues Granger caused market prices during both 1953:1–2000:1 and 1982:1–2000:1, but no evidence of Granger causal relationship in either direction is found for 1953:1–1981:4. This again emphasizes that the relationship between net issues and stock prices is driven primarily by the strength of the association in the most recent time period. Furthermore, the VAR (4) model indicates the first two lags on net issuance in the equation explaining stock prices are negative and significant for 1953–99 and 1982–99, while the first two lags on stock prices in the equation explaining net issuance are significant but alternate signs, from positive to negative. Thus, the cumulative effect of stock prices on net issuance is difficult to pin down.

The impulse-response functions and variance decompositions illustrated in Figure 9.4 and Table 9.7 shed more light on both these issues. For identification purposes, we ordered the variables in the models as follows: interest rates, stock prices, net issues, after-tax profits. We chose this ordering, or Choleski decomposition, since it gives causal priority to stock prices over net issues as reflected by the large F-statistics in prior Granger causality tests. However, changing the manner in which the errors are orthogonalized and giving priority to net issues yielded results that suggested that the response of stock prices to innovations in net issues was slightly stronger. The results are also robust to all other alternative rankings of the variables. The dynamic responses to innovations are traced over a two-and-a-half-year interval.

As Figure 9.4 illustrates, shocks to net issues have a strong negative impact on the time path of stock prices for both 1953:1–2000:1 and 1982:1–2000:1, albeit the response is significantly stronger during the latter period. Here, a one-standard deviation shock to net issues elicits a negative dynamic response of nearly twenty standard deviations in stock prices over a one-and-a-half-year period, with the effects lasting well over two years. On the other hand, the cumulative response of net issues to innovations in stock prices illustrates instability. In both periods, a one-standard deviation shock to stock prices generates a positive response from net issues over two quarters, but it generates a negative response over three quarters before turning positive again over five quarters. The instability continues as the impulse response becomes negative at one-and-a-half years and positive one quarter later. Thus, the cumulative impact of stock prices on the net issuance of new shares critically depends on the horizon at which the relationship is investigated. Again, the 1953–81 period shows little dynamic interaction between the variables.

The variance decompositions for net issues and the stock-price index, as to be

Table 9.6

1953:1–2000:1 S&P Index

	1953–2000		1953–1981		1982–2000	
	SP	Issues	SP	Issues	SP	Issues
SP(−1)	0.75	0.26	1.03	0.04	0.59	0.26
	(9.88)	(7.90)	(9.76)	(2.29)	(4.54)	(4.38)
SP(−2)	0.19	−0.43	−0.28	−0.04	0.19	−0.43
	(2.00)	(−10.21)	(−1.82)	(−1.73)	(1.26)	(−6.20)
SP(−3)	0.34	0.02	0.27	0.03	0.40	−0.02
	(2.81)	(0.36)	(1.72)	(0.94)	(2.03)	(−0.21)
SP(−4)	−0.26	0.19	−0.08	−0.02	−0.19	0.20
	(−2.53)	(4.22)	(−0.73)	(−0.86)	(−1.12)	(0.26)
Issues(−1)	−0.53	0.38	0.19	0.47	−0.53	0.32
	(−3.53)	(5.86)	(0.29)	(4.33)	(−2.18)	(2.89)
Issues(−2)	−0.71	0.61	0.22	0.21	−0.79	0.58
	(−3.74)	(7.39)	(0.29)	(1.70)	(−2.58)	(4.22)
Issues(−3)	0.52	0.05	−0.58	−0.05	0.37	0.02
	(3.42)	(0.80)	(0.81)	(−0.37)	(1.52)	(0.21)
Issues(−4)	0.32	−0.32	−1.56	0.07	0.557	−0.30
	(1.90)	(−4.31)	(−2.43)	(0.73)	(1.66)	(−2.43)

Causality tests

Null hypothesis	Issues do not cause SP	SP does not cause issues	Issues do not cause SP	SP does not cause issues
F–statistic	8.58***	22.96***	1.4	0.618	7.12***	4.65***

Notes: The numbers in parenthesis are t–statistics. The variables included in the unrestricted VAR (4) system are the S&P 500 index (SP), net issues of domestic corporate equity (Issues), after-tax corporate profits (Profit), and the three-month Treasury-bill yield (Tbill). A constant term was included.
*Significant at the 10 percent level.
**Significant at the 5 percent level.
***Significant at the 1 percent level.

expected, yield a similar conclusion concerning the dynamic interaction among the variables (Table 9.7). The percentage of the forecast-error variance in stock prices, explained by its own shocks, is substantial. This holds true even when we give issues causal priority in the system, although the latter explains a good portion of the variance as well. Nevertheless, even with the restriction we have placed on the error

Figure 9.4 **Impulse-Response Functions** (Panel A 1953:1–2000:1)

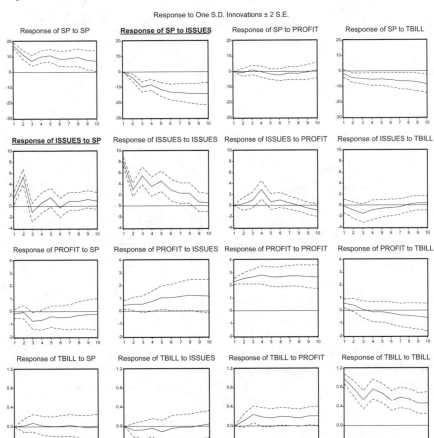

Response to One S.D. Innovations ± 2 S.E.

matrix, it is again clear that innovations to net issues explain a significant portion of the forecasting error variance at periods three through ten. Of course, this does not pertain to the 1953:1–1981 interval, where even in period ten innovations in net issues account for only 2.14 percent of the variation in stock prices (not shown).

The results for the VAR modeling procedure support the contention that the declining supply of equity was one of the driving forces behind the recent run-up in stock prices. This is an especially robust finding since announcements regarding mergers and repurchases activity at t-1 may immediately affect prices through increased demand for stock. This is important because share retirements due to merger activity is a significant component of the Federal Reserve's *Flow Funds* net issues series. Thus, the results are biased toward the finding that prices appear Granger-prior to net issuance of corporate equity. Even in this likelihood, we have

Figure 9.4 **Impulse-Response Functions** (Panel B 1982:1–2000:1)

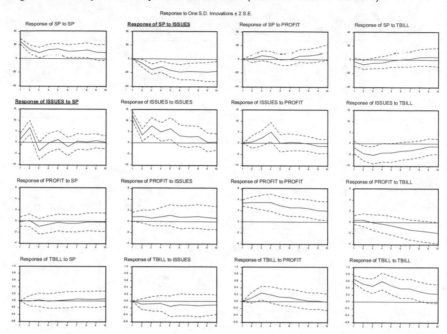

found evidence of a causal relationship running from net issues to stock prices. But what about the fundamental reasons why supply changes affect prices? Unfortunately, we cannot reject the hypothesis that supply of equity is merely a proxy for expected dividend payouts at this juncture.

Structural Model Approach

The VAR technique relies crucially on timing and on the use of lagged values of explanatory variables to model the evolution of the dependent variable. Consequently, the procedure precludes the investigation into whether the effects of the net issues of prices are robust when measures of future economic fundamentals are included. Because stock prices are forward-looking procyclical variables, a technique that relies exclusively on lagged explanatory variables to model the dynamics of stock prices over time, cannot appropriately control for fundamentals in a meaningful way. Thus, to consider whether price appreciation is warranted or unwarranted by objective economic considerations, contemporaneous forward-looking variables and leads of measures of expected profitability need to be included in the investigation. This is beyond the scope of any investigation within the VAR framework, and it is for this reason that we must turn to the structural-model approach. The methodology in this section is similar to Friedman's (1977, 1982) flow-funds approach to long-term bond yields.

Figure 9.4 **Impulse-Response Functions** (Panel C 1953:1–1981:4)

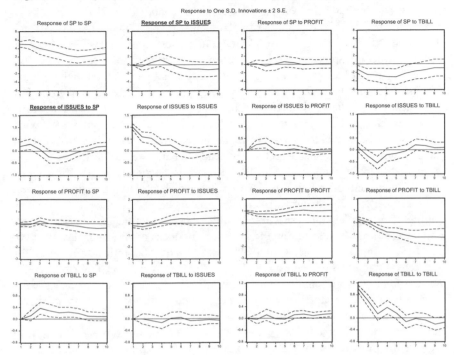

Note: The graphs plot the impulse functions of each variable. The impulse response is calculated from the parameters estimated by the VAR (4) model and obtained by shocking variable *i* and tracing the impact through the VAR (4) system using the Choleski decomposition ordering *Tbill*, *SP*, *Issues*, and *Profit*. The effects are traced over ten quarters (two-and-a-half years). The dashed lines represent the 90 percent confidence interval.

Financial economists seeking to explain equity prices usually depart from some version of the standard valuation model and therefore identify shocks to expectations of future income flows, the share of income accruing to corporations, and discount rates as the driving forces behind equity-price fluctuations. In principal, any systemic force that affects the economy's pricing operator or the expected dividend payments to shareholders can affect stock prices for reasons that can be considered fundamental or related to intrinsic value. Unfortunately, there is no direct measure for intrinsic values, and thus no precise or direct manner in which to control for fundamentals. Therefore, *ex ante* observable variables must be identified which might adequately proxy for the *ex post*, unobservable fundamentals in the formal econometric work. The downside is that the attempt to control for market fundamentals via alternative measures may introduce measurement error, with the results extremely sensitive to the choice of proxy, possibly under- or overstating the efficiency of the pricing mechanism.

The seminal econometric works of Fama (1990, 1981), Schwert (1990), and Chen et al. (1986) employ variables that are deemed appropriate proxies for shocks to expected cash flows to explain the fundamental variation in stock returns. Thus, these studies utilize leads of industrial production, short-term bond yields, as well as the term structure (spread between long-term and short-term interest rates) and risk premium (spread between low- and high-quality bond yields), implicitly holding them to determine the equilibrium value of aggregate stock-market valuations. For consistency, we follow Edwards and Zhang (1998) in their study of mutual-fund flows and employ these variables to proxy for the fundamental variables underlying aggregate stock-market indices as well. Similarly, we follow standard procedure in the literature, analyzing market returns instead of changes in the S&P index.

One should be skeptical about the ability to adequately proxy for *ex post* fundamentals and the possible omission of variables vital to the characterization of stock-market equilibrium. This must be balanced against the potential over-stating of the explanatory power stemming from the fact that the standard vari-ables were initially selected on the basis of goodness of fit (Fama 1981; 1990, 1107). In point of fact, Chen et al. (1986) develop no "theoretical foundation for the state variables," but suggest simply that their signs are plausible (ibid., 395). Furthermore, possible simultaneous equation bias, which arises from taking leads of real-economy variables as wholly exogenous with respect to stock prices, suggests that a relationship found to be suggestive of the efficiency markets could be further overstated. Nevertheless, we describe the variables thought to capture the fundamental variation in market returns as they are presented in the established literature (see Table 9.3).

An obvious candidate for inclusion in a study of stock valuations is interest rates, not only because the risk-free interest rate is directly related to market prices through the standard valuation model, but also because bonds are rival assets to equity. Additionally, interest rates are procyclical and thus sensitive measures of business-cycle changes. It should be mentioned that, because stock prices are also procyclical, this negative correlation between returns and interest rates might be significantly weakened. Because the yield on three-month Treasury bills was found to be nonstationary, we utilize changes in the variable, noted *Tbill* hereafter.

Industrial production is commonly used as the aggregate proxy for future prof-its because equity values are related to changes in long-term industrial activity (Chen et al. 1986, 387). Fama (1981, 555) notes that, "the stock market is con-cerned with the capital investment process and uses the earliest information from the process to forecast its evolution." It is acknowledged that industrial production contains more information about economic fundaments than actual profits. Changes in industrial production (*QIP*) are calculated as the first difference of the quarterly series. Because stock prices are understood to capture *future* developments in the real economy, we lead this variable by one period. Again, there is serious concern over the endogeneity of real economic variables with respect to the stock market given the wealth-effect and cost-of-capital channels.

Table 9.7

Variance Decompositions

Period	S.E.	SP	Issues	Profit	Tbill
Panel A. 1953:1–2000:1					
SP					
1	17.62639	99.02754	0	0	0.972459
2	22.28307	92.74478	2.359293	0.01675	4.879181
3	26.23248	77.48732	14.99524	0.308053	7.209394
4	30.35056	72.56246	18.25421	0.257179	8.926148
5	34.98586	67.67473	22.42426	0.265335	9.635678
6	39.31939	61.22185	27.95522	0.352177	10.47076
7	43.14554	57.27068	30.83994	0.294026	11.59535
8	47.27284	54.77394	32.79031	0.246409	12.18934
9	50.67282	52.14364	34.39427	0.219609	13.24247
10	53.94126	49.83982	35.27274	0.309411	14.57803
Issues					
1	7.469609	4.817675	95.16251	0	0.019814
2	9.175207	30.4232	68.98003	0.019556	0.577216
3	10.57931	24.03311	74.21188	0.289851	1.465154
4	11.50605	21.28665	73.26175	3.990969	1.460634
5	12.28497	21.03388	74.09032	3.509942	1.365861
6	12.8341	19.61054	75.40653	3.653824	1.329105
7	13.04134	19.9511	75.13599	3.603687	1.309224
8	13.32818	19.22016	76.04896	3.461667	1.269219
9	13.38383	19.57911	75.61602	3.488414	1.316453
10	13.45099	19.75787	75.00227	3.890524	1.349339
Panel B. 1982:1–2000:1					
SP					
1	25.15751	96.02287	2.065715	0	1.91142
2	30.55696	88.44423	3.302071	0.643345	7.610357
3	36.45557	72.21582	16.0591	4.242457	7.482627
4	41.44607	70.82799	17.14271	4.993523	7.035784
5	46.77974	68.88916	21.39379	4.01282	5.704236
6	52.13832	63.28478	28.6494	3.446208	4.619605
7	56.88475	60.29799	31.26049	4.557142	3.88438
8	62.02282	58.80788	32.52924	5.302664	3.360219
9	66.03982	56.0687	34.31023	6.553916	3.067161
10	70.10342	53.66357	34.47619	9.08442	2.775821
Issues					
1	11.1813	0	98.1621	0	1.837899
2	13.38211	15.80903	75.36756	0.005185	8.818225
3	16.25834	19.28217	67.47562	1.686365	11.55584
4	17.9858	15.76932	64.94231	7.061808	12.22657
5	19.19752	13.89941	66.9566	6.216374	12.92761
6	20.15832	16.01601	65.01296	5.923731	13.04731
7	20.44495	15.65997	64.83161	5.883661	13.62477
8	20.89756	15.39798	65.40525	5.638383	13.55839
9	20.91059	15.3862	65.32708	5.679121	13.6076
10	20.94496	15.35502	65.14973	5.80981	13.68545

Note: The table shows the percentage of the two-year forecast error variance of variable *i* explained by variable *j*. The forecast error variance is computed using the VAR (4) system described above. The variables SP, Issues, Profit, and Tbill are defined in Table 9.3. "S.E." denotes standard error.

It has been suggested that term and default spreads are informative business-cycle variables that lead turning points in real activity and capture information relevant to the evolution of the real side of the economy. Bernanke (1990) demonstrates empirically that the default spread has predictive power for several real-economy variables, such as industrial production, durable orders, the unemployment rate, personal income, capacity utilization, and consumption. Chen et al. (1986) argue that the default spread proxies for changes in the expected risk premium and document a relationship between contemporaneous default spread and stock returns. That is, when spreads are high, market conditions are poor and inherently more risky, warranting a higher rate of return. Keim and Stambaugh (1986) provide evidence that confirms that bond spreads proxy for changes in the risk premium. The risk premium (*risk*) is calculated as the spread between the credit-rating firm Moody's "Baa" and "Aaa" bond rates.

Likewise, the term structure or yield curve is reported to "capture cyclical variation in expected returns" or changes in the term premium (Fama 1990, Fama and French 1989). Estrella and Mishkin (1998) show that the slope of the yield curve impounds important business-cycle information; lower-than-average spreads are found to be associated with a higher possibility of recession, while higher-than-average spreads indicate a lower-than-average probability of a recession. Correspondingly, Keim and Stambaugh (1986) demonstrate that the term structure of interest rates has a shallow slope around business-cycle peaks and a steeper slope around business troughs. The term structure (*term*) is calculated as the spread between the twenty-year government bond rate and the yield on the three-month T-bill at time t.

Because of the time-varying nature of expected returns, it could be contended that the relationship between net issues and stock-market returns is spurious. This extends from the fact that net issues may be a proxy for the time variation in expected returns, and should therefore be capable of forecasting returns on that basis. This concern, along with the caveats expressed by Chen et al. (1986) mentioned earlier, lead us to extract the predictable component from the series to generate an unexpected net issue series. Again, this also deals adequately with the matter that stock prices may very well predict future inflows, prompting the relationship. As indicated by the VAR model and impulse-response functions, these flows show persistence, that is, the net equity series is significantly predictable. An AR (3) model is fit to the net issues of the corporate-equity series, and the resulting residuals make up the derived series, unexpected net issues (*Uissue*).

Empirical Results

The bivariate regression results in Table 9.8 show that contemporaneous unexpected net issues have no statistically significant explanatory power for stock returns for any time period except 1953:1–1981:4, where a positive relationship is found. However, lagged unexpected net issues for both 1953:1–1981:4 and 1982:1–2000:4 are significantly negative explainers of the variation in market returns. The

R^2s from the regressions of returns on $Uissue_{t-1}$ are .16 and .14, respectively. These results are consistent with the coefficients of determination, ranging from .12 to .16, attained by Baker and Wurgler (2000). The results from regressions of unexpected net issues on returns are documented in Table 9.9. Contemporaneous returns are significant only during the pre-1982 interval, while one-period-lagged returns are significant and positive in all periods.

The findings regarding contemporaneous returns and net issues could possibly be reflective of simultaneous equation bias. Typically endogenous variables tend to influence one another in the same direction (i.e., money supply and GNP), and thus a regression of one on another that does not properly account for endogeneity is likely to overstate the relationship. In our case, the forces work in opposite directions, and thus endogenous equations bias acts as a measurement error to obscure the relationship between contemporaneous unexpected net issues and stock returns. However, it could also be the case that the potential impact of the variables on each other is better captured with a lag, as indicated earlier by our examination of correlation coefficients. Thus, instead of estimating the relationship utilizing the two-stage least-squares procedure, we circumvent the endogeneity issue by addressing whether the influence-lagged unexpected net issues is robust in the presence of economic and business-cycle variables presumed to be fundamental determinants of market returns.

The results of the multivariate regressions for each time period are presented in Table 9.10. We estimated the models for the entire 1953:1–2000:1 period and for the subsamples within the period:

$$Returns_t = b_0 + b_1 QIP_{t+1} + b_2 Term_t + b_3 Risk_t + b_4 Tbill_t \qquad (2)$$

$$Returns_t = b_0 + b_1 QIP_{t+1} + b_2 Term_t + b_3 Risk_t + b_4 Tbill_t + b_5 Uissue_{t-1} \qquad (3)$$

White's test for heteroscedasticity revealed that the null hypothesis could be rejected at the 1 percent level for each of the subsamples. Consequently, standard errors and t-statistics were corrected for heteroskedasticity using White's procedure (White 1980). Regression 2 illustrates the explanatory power of the fundamental factors on stock returns. While the variables utilized to proxy for economic fundamentals show significance, collectively they explain only 11 percent of the variation for the 1953:1–2000:1 period.

Given that the sample combines two different time periods, one where share repurchases were constrained by SEC policy (1953:1–1982:3) and one where the SEC had reversed it stance on buybacks (via Rule 10b-13), we tested for a structural break in the fourth quarter of 1982, that is, when SEC Rule 10b-13 took effect. Chow's breakpoint test confirms the null hypothesis that no structural change took place in 1982:4 can be rejected at the 1 percent level of significance. Regression 2 illustrates that running the regression on the subperiods 1953:1–1981:4 and 1982:4–2000:1 yields results more consistent with the literature. For example,

Fama (1990) and Schwert (1990) report that "fundamentals" successfully explain 23 percent and 27 percent of the variation in returns, respectively. As Table 9.10 illustrates, the variables used to capture the rational variation in market returns in our experiment respectively explain 23 percent and 22 percent of the variation in quarterly returns during these two subperiods.

Regression 3 in Table 9.10 lends support to the claim that the decline in the volume of equity outstanding helps to explain the dramatic increase in equity values in the United States. The null hypothesis that lagged unexpected net issues has no explanatory power for stock returns is rejected at 1 percent for 1953:1–2000:1, with the proxies for fundamental value included. (The results were similar when we used the quarterly change in net issues in lieu of unexpected net issues.) Again, the relationship is driven by the strength of the causal relationship during 1982:4–2000:1 since no evidence of explanatory power is found for 1953:1–1981:4. This is consistent with the results obtained from the VAR analysis and Granger causality tests detailed above. For 1982:4–2000:1, the null hypothesis is strongly rejected, and the R^2 improves from 22 percent to 32 percent when unexpected net issues are included into the regression on stock returns. The results demonstrate that lagged unexpected net issues of equity is a significant explainer of stock returns even when *ex ante* variables believed to be proxies for the fundamental determinants of aggregate stock-market indices are included.

The failure to reject the null hypothesis during 1953:1–1981:4 and the decisive rejection of the null hypothesis during 1982:4–2000:1 indicate that something is meaningfully different about the last two decades. In fact, the finding of a structural break and the change in the responsiveness of market returns to net issues support the contention that SEC Rule 10b-13 fundamentally changed the market and lend credence to Post Keynesian expectation theories, notably the Minskian theory advanced by McCauley et al. (1999). Support for simple price-pressure effects of supply changes, however, appears weak since one would expect to find evidence of such effects in both subperiods. Finally, the results suggest that the notion that supply changes are irrelevant for asset pricing is supported by the data for the 1953:1–1981:4 period, but is not consistent with the period corresponding to the recent stock-market boom. This contradicts the EMH corollary that the excess-demand curve for equity is horizontal.

It is important to note that the strength of these results critically hinge on our treatment of fundamentals, which may have been inadequately proxied even though we employed variables commonly used by EMH proponents. However, when we included leads of after-tax profits and inflation, which, it could be argued, measure an economy's growth potential, the results remained unchanged. We conclude, then, that the relationship between the net issuance of corporate equity and stock-market returns is robust and helps to move returns above and beyond that which can be justified by economic fundamentals. Furthermore, the results suggest that fully dissecting the run-up in U.S. stock prices requires more than a theory of exuberant demand. Thus, stock prices cannot be viewed exclusively as indicators

Table 9.8

Bivariate OLS Results I

Equation: Return $s_t = b_0 + b_1 \text{Uissue}_{(t, t-1, t-2)}$

	(1)	(2)	(3)	(4)
Panel A 1953:1–2000:1				
Constant	7.54	7.46	7.46	7.32
	(4.23)***	(4.55)***	(4.54)***	(4.64)***
Uissues$_t$	−0.1		−0.02	−0.01
	(−0.60)		(−0.12)	(−0.09)
Uissues$_{t-1}$	−0.88	−0.88	−0.86	
		(−5.87)***	(−5.82)***	(−5.94)***
Uissues$_{t-2}$				−0.66
				(−4.49)***
R^2	0.002	0.16	0.16	0.24
Panel B 1953:1–1981:4				
Constant	−0.33	0.93	0.1	−0.34
	(−0.45)	−1.19	0.11	(−0.33)
Uissues$_t$	0.88		1.08	1.14
	(2.26)**		(2.54)**	(2.61)**
Uissues$_{t-1}$	−0.04	−0.5	−0.64	
		(−0.09)	(−1.14)	(−1.34)
Uissues$_{t-2}$			0.38	
				−0.75
R^2	0.04	0	0.05	0.06
Panel C 1982:1–2000:1				
Constant	18.1	16.2	16.3	14.57
	(4.19)***	(4.02)***	(3.99)***	(3.64)***
Uissues$_t$	0.002		0.05	0.04
	(−0.01)		(0.228)	(0.19)
Uissues$_{t-1}$		−0.78	−0.78	−0.78
		(−3.37)***	(−3.36)***	(−3.47)
Uissues$_{t-2}$				−0.56
				(−2.41)**
R^2	0	0.14	0.14	0.21

Note: Uissues denote unexpected net issues. Numbers in parentheses are t–statistics.
*Significant at the 10 percent level.
**Significant at the 5 percent level.
***Significant at the 1 percent level.

Table 9.9

Bivariate OLS Results II

Equation: $Uissue_t = b_0 + b_1 Returns_{(t, t-1, t-2)}$

	(1)	(2)	(3)	(4)
Panel A 1953:1–2000:1				
Constant	0.27	−1.04	−0.73	0.16
	(0.32)	(1.28)	(−0.89)	(0.84)
$Returns_t$	−0.02		−0.05	−0.03
	(−0.60)		(1.52)	(−1.01)
$Returns_{t-1}$		0.16	0.16	0.19
		(4.87)***	(5.08)***	(6.34)***
$Returns_{t-2}$				−0.18
				(−5.74)***
R^2	0.00	0.11	0.12	0.26
Panel B 1953:1–1981:4				
Constant	1.33	1.32	1.29	1.28
	(10.83)***	(11.00)***	(10.77)***	(10.52)***
$Returns_t$	0.05		0.04	0.04
	(2.26)**		(1.96)**	(1.96)*
$Returns_{t-1}$		0.07	0.07	0.69
		(3.54)	(3.33)***	(3.25)***
$Returns_{t-2}$				0.00
				0.86
R^2	0.04	0.10	0.13	0.13
Panel C 1982:1–2000:1				
Constant	−1.95	−5.36	−5.13	−2.88
	(−0.88)	(−2.64)***	(−2.33)**	(−1.32)
$Returns_t$	0.00		−0.01	−0.01
	(0.03)		(−0.28)	(−0.16)
$Returns_{t-1}$		0.20	0.20	0.22
		(3.93)***	(3.92)***	(4.41)***
$Returns_{t-2}$				−0.16
				(−3.31)***
R^2	0	0.17	0.17	0.27

Note: Uissues denote unexpected net issues. Numbers in parentheses are t–statistics.
*Significant at the 10 percent level.
**Significant at the 5 percent level.
***Significant at the 1 percent level.

Table 9.10

Multivariate OLS Results

Equation: Return $s_t = b_0 + b_1 QIP_{t+1} + b_2 Term_t + b_3 Risk_t + b_4 Tbill + b_5 Uissue_{t-1}$

	1953:1–2000:1		1953:1–1981:4	
	(2)	(3)	(2)	(3)
Constant	5.85	6.45	−2.60	−2.08
	(1.65)*	(1.90)*	(2.08)**	−1.49
QIP_{t+1}	8.63	7.98	2.46	2.6
	(3.94)***	(4.36)***	(3.27)***	(3.44)***
$Term_t$	−3.1	−2.49	0.16	−0.1
	(−1.54)	(−1.47)	(0.24)	(−0.13)
$Risk_t$	0.6	0.41	2.92	2.98
	(1.89)**	(0.17)	(2.38)**	(2.39)**
$Tbill_t$	−2.3	−2.2	−0.31	−0.3
	(−1.71)*	(−1.88)*	(−0.72)	(−0.68)
$Uissue_{t-1}$		−0.85		−0.39
		(−2.83)***		(−1.03)
R^2	0.11	0.24	0.23	0.24

	1982:4–2000:1	
	(2)	(3)
Constant	36.39	36.34
	(2.59)**	(2.42)**
QIP_{t+1}	11.92	11.75
	(2.64)***	(2.72)***
$Term_t$	−12.8	−10.08
	(−2.39)***	(−2.15)**
$Risk_t$	−5.86	−9.76
	(−0.77)	(−1.43)
$Tbill_t$	−2.98	−3.32
	(−0.56)	(−0.62)
$Uissue_{t-1}$		−0.67
		(−2.67)***
R^2	0.22	0.32

Note: Returns denote the return on S&P 500 stocks and Uissues denote unexpected net issues of domestic corporate equity. QIP is the quarterly change in industrial production, term is the term structure, risk is the default spread, and Tbill is the change in three-month treasury bill rate. Numbers in parentheses are t-statistics, which are adjusted for heteroscedasticity following White's (1980) procedure.

* Statistical significance at the 10 percent level.
** Statistical significance at the 5 percent level.
*** Statistical significance at the 1 percent level.

of future prosperity or the outcome of investor euphoria, but, rather, as partially due to transitory institutional dynamics. Because the present pace of share retirements is not likely to continue, U.S. investors should not expect to continually reap the large returns witnessed during the 1990s.

Notes

1. In some countries with thin equity markets (e.g., Norway), share repurchases are considered price manipulative and are therefore explicitly prohibited.

2. Notable exceptions are D'Arista (1994), Binswanger (1999), and Toporowski (1999a, 1999b). A few works, discussed herein, attempt to analyze share repurchases in a manner analogous to dividend payments.

3. Foreign companies apparently took full advantage of the stock-market boom, issuing roughly $713 billion over the period.

4. The original formulation of the Gordon equation is $P_t = D_t(1+g)/i+r-g$. The equation generates from the conventional dividend discount model, where the growth rate of dividends is assumed to be constant. See Myron J. Gordon (1962) and Campbell, Lo, and MacKinlay (1997).

5. Here the growth rate of dividends in not assumed constant, but when such an assumption is made the dynamic and static dividend growth models are equivalent.

6. Evans (2003, 88–89) illustrates that it would take an implausible combination of payout rates and required rates of return to justify the 1999 level of the S&P 500.

7. While a portfolio indexed to the S&P 500 returned 579 percent, a similar portfolio indexed exclusively to share repurchasing companies would have returned 1203 percent (Bailey 2000).

8. Graham and Dodd (1996), early pioneers of financial economics, conceived of the stock market as a "voting machine," in which prices are determined by the actions of "countless individuals [registering] choices, which are the product partly of reason and partly of emotion" (ibid., 27).

9. Shiller's data is available at www.econ.yale.edu/~shiller. It should be noted that the Federal Reserve revises data included in the *Flow of Funds Accounts* on a quarterly basis.

10. We also estimated the model using first differences of each of the variables. The results, while not reported here, did not differ meaningfully with respect to net issues and stock prices.

References

Allen, F.; A. Bernardo; and I. Welch. 2000. "A Theory of Dividends Based on Tax Clienteles." *Journal of Finance* 55(6): 2499–536.

Arnott, R. 2004. "Is Our Industry Intellectually Lazy." *Financial Analyst Journal* 60(1): 6–8.

Bailey, P. 2000. "How to Trade in Volatile Markets." http://wwww.Manhattanbaptist.org/Supertraders/ST10–06–01.htm (accessed January 2006).

Baker, M., and J. Wurgler. 2000. "The Equity Share in New Issues and Aggregate Stock Returns." *Journal of Finance* 55(5): 2219–57.

Bernanke, B. 1990. "On the Predictive Power of Interest Spreads." *New England Economic Review* (November–December), 51–68.

Bernheim, B.D. (1991). "Tax Policy and the Dividend Puzzle." *RAND Journal of Economics* 22: 455–476.

Binswanger, M. 1999. *Stock Markets, Speculative Bubbles and Economic Growth.* Cheltenham, UK: Edward Elgar Publishing.

Brealey, R., and K. Nyborg. 1998. "New Equity Issues and Raising Cash." In Wharton School, *The Complete Finance Companion: Mastering Finance.* London: Pitman Publishing.

Campbell J.; A. Lo; and A. MacKinlay. 1997. *The Econometrics of Financial Markets.* Princeton, NJ: Princeton University Press.

Campbell J., and R. Shiller. 1988. "The Dividend–Price Ratio and Expectations of Future Dividends and Discount Factors." *Review of Financial Studies* 1(3): 195–228.

Carlson, J. 2001. "Why Is the Dividend Yield So Low?" *Economic Commentary*, Federal Reserve Bank of Cleveland (April 1): 1–4.

Chen, N.; R. Roll; and S.A. Ross. 1986. "Economic Forces and the Stock Market." *Journal of Business* 59(3): 383–403.

Cole, K., J. Helwege; and B. Laster. 1996. "Stock Market Valuation Indicators: Is this Time Different." *Financial Analysts Journal* 52 (May-June): 56–64.

D'Arista, J. 1994. *The Evolution of the US Finance, Volume II: Restructuring Institutions and Markets.* Armonk, NY: M.E. Sharpe.

DeAngelo, H.; L. DeAngelo; and D. Skinner. 2000. "Special Dividends and the Evolution of Dividend Signaling." *Journal of Financial Economics* 57(3): 309–54.

Dickey, D., and W. Fuller. 1979. "Distribution of the Estimators for Autoregressive Time Series with a Unit Root." *Journal of the American Statistical Society* 74(366): 427–31.

Edwards, F., and X. Zhang. 1998. "Mutual Funds and Stock and Bond Market Stability." *Journal of Financial Services Research* 13(3): 257–82.

Enders, W. 1995. *Applied Econometric Time Series.* New York: John Wiley and Sons.

Epstein, G. 2004. *Financialization and the World Economy.* Cheltenham, UK: Edward Elgar Press.

Estrella, A., and F. Mishkin. 1998. "Predicting US Recessions: Financial Variables as Leading Indicators." *Review of Economics and Statistics* 80(1): 45–61.

Evans, L. 2003. *Why the Bubble Burst: US Stock Market Performance Since 1982.* Cheltenham, UK: Edward Elgar.

Fama, E. 1970. "Efficient Capital Markets: A Review of Theory and Empirical Work." *Journal of Finance* 25(2): 383–417.

———. 1981. "Stock Returns, Real Activity and Money." *American Economic Review* 71(4): 545–65.

———. 1990. "Stock Returns, Expected Returns, and Real Activity." *Journal of Finance* 45(4): 1089–108.

Fama, E., and K. French. 1988. "Dividend Yield and Expected Stock Returns." *Journal of Financial Economics* 22(1), 3–25.

———. 1989. "Business Conditions and Expected Returns on Stocks and Bonds." *Journal of Financial Economics* 25(1), 23–49.

———. 2001. "Disappearing Dividends: Changing Firm Characteristics of Lower Propensity to Pay?" *Journal of Financial Economics* 60(1), 3–43.

———. 2002. "The Equity Premium." *Journal of Finance* 57(2): 637–59.

Friedman, B. 1977. "Financial Flow Variables and the Short-run Determination of Long-term Interest Rates." *Journal of Political Economy* 85(4): 661–89

———. 1982. "Effects of Shifting Saving Patterns on Interest Rates and Economic Activity." *Journal of Finance* 37(1): 37–62.

Gjerde, O., and F. Saettem. 1999. "Causal Relations among Stock Returns and Macroeconomic Variables in a Small, Open Economy." *Journal of International Financial Markets* 9(1): 61–74.

Gordon, M. 1962. *The Investment, Financing, and Valuation of the Corporation.* Homewood, IL: Irwin.

Graham, B., and D. Dodd. 1996. *Security Analysis: The Classic 1934 ed.* New York: McGraw-Hill.

Granger, C. 1969. "Investigating Causal Relationships by Econometric Models and Cross-spectral Methods." *Econometrica* 37 (July): 424–38.

Greenspan, A. 2002. "Remarks on Corporate Governance." Speech delivered at Stern School of Business, New York University, New York (March 26).

Grullon, G., and R. Michaely. 2002. "Dividends, Share Repurchases, and the Substitution Hypothesis." *Journal of Finance* 57(4): 1649–84.

Harris, L., and E. Gurel. 1986. "Price and Volume Effects Associated with Changes in the S&P 500 Lists: New Evidence for the Existence of Price Pressures." *Journal of Finance* 41(4): 815–29.

Holmstrom, B., and S. Kaplan. 2001. "Corporate Governance and Merger Activity in the United

States: Making Sense of the 1980s and 1990s." *Journal of Economic Perspectives* 15(2): 121–44.

Hsiao, C. 1979. "Causality Tests in Econometrics." *Journal of Economic Dynamics and Control* 1(4): 321–46.

Jagannathan, M.; C. Stephens; and M. Weisbach. 2000. "Financial Flexibility and the Choice Between Dividends and Stock Repurchases." *Journal of Financial Economics* 57(3): 355–84.

Jagannathan, R.; E. McGrattan; and A. Scherbina. 2001. "The Declining US Equity Premium." *Federal Reserve Bank of Minneapolis Quarterly Review* 24(4): 3–19.

John, K., and J. Williams. 1985. "Dividends, Dilution, and Taxes: A Signaling Equilibrium." *Journal of Finance* 40(4): 1053–70.

Keim, D., and R. Stambaugh. 1986. "Predicting Returns in the Stock and Bond Markets." *Journal of Financial Economics* 17(2): 357–90.

Keynes, J.M. 1964 [1936]. *The General Theory of Employment, Interest and Money*. London: Harcourt Brace.

Lamdin, D. 2000. "New Results on Stock Prices and Fundamental Value." Social Science Research Network Working Paper Series, 2000. Available at http://papers.ssrn.com.

Lee, B. 1992. "Causal Relations Among Stock Returns, Interest Rates, Real Activity, and Inflation." *Journal of Finance* 47(4): 1591–603.

Liang, J., and S. Sharpe. 1999. "Share Repurchase and Employee Stock Options and Their Implications for S&P 500 Share Retirements and Expected Returns." Board of Governors of the Federal Reserve System, Finance and Economics Discussion Paper Series, 99/59 (November).

Lowenstein, L. 1991. *Sense and Nonsense in Corporate Finance*. Reading, MA: Addison-Wesley.

McCauley, R.; J. Rudd; and F. Iacono. 1999. *Dodging Bullets: Changing US Corporate Capital Structure in the 1980s and 1990s*. Cambridge, MA: MIT Press.

Minsky, H.P. 1975. *John Maynard Keynes*. London: Macmillan.

———. 1982. *Can It Happen Again*. Armonk, NY: M.E. Sharpe.

———. 1986. *Stabilizing an Unstable Economy*. New Haven, CT: Yale University Press.

Modigliani, F., and M. Miller. 1958. "The Cost of Capital, Corporation Finance and the Theory of Investment." *American Economic Review* 48(3): 261–97.

Phillips, P., and P. Perron. 1988. "Testing for a Unit Root in Times Series Regression." *Biometrica* 75(2), 335–46.

Raines, J.P., and C.G. Leathers. 2000. *Economists and the Stock Market: Speculative Theories of Stock Market Fluctuations*. Cheltenham, UK: Edward Elgar.

Scholes, M. 1972. "The Market for Securities: Substitution versus Price Pressure and the Effects of Information on Share Prices." *Journal of Business* 45(2): 179–211.

Schwert, W.G. 1990. "Stock Returns and Real Activity: A Century of Evidence." *Journal of Finance* 45(4): 1237–57.

Shiller, R. 2000. *Irrational Exuberance*. Princeton, NJ: Princeton University Press.

Shleifer, A. 1986. "Do Demand Curves for Stocks Slope Down?" *Journal of Finance* 41 (3): 579–90.

Sims, C.A. 1972. "Money, Income, and Causality." *American Economic Review* 62(4): 540–52.

———. 1980. "Macroeconomics and Reality." *Econometrica* 48(1): 1–49.

Toporowski, J. 1999a. "Monetary Policy in an Era of Capital Market Inflation." *Jerome Levy Economics Institute of Bard College*, Working Paper 279.

———. 1999b. *The End of Finance: Capital Market Inflation, Financial Derivatives and Pension Fund Capitalism*. London: Routledge.

Wadhwani, S. 1999. "The US Stock Market and the Global Economic Crisis." *National Institute Economic Review* 167 (January): 86–105.

Warther, V. 1995. "Aggregate Mutual Fund Flows and Security Returns." *Journal of Financial Economics* 39(2–3): 209–35.

Wermers, R. 1999. "Mutual Fund Herding and the Impact on Stock Prices." *Journal of Finance* 54(2): 581–622.

White, H. 1980. "A Heteroskedasticity-consistent Covariance Matrix and a Direct Test for Heteroskedasticity." *Econometrica* 48(4): 817–38.

Part III

Empirical Studies of
International Economic Relations

10

ÖZLEM ONARAN AND ENGELBERT STOCKHAMMER

The Effect of Distribution on Accumulation, Capacity Utilization, and Employment: Testing the Profit-led Hypothesis for Turkey

Introduction

The impact of distribution on growth, accumulation, and employment remains a focus of debate within macroeconomics. Does a procapital redistribution of income stimulate growth, accumulation, and employment?

Current economic orthodoxy, which perceives wages merely as a cost, would expect lower wages to be associated with a higher level of economic activity and employment. Post Keynesian macroeconomics challenges this position by pointing out the dual function of wages: wages are a component of aggregate demand as well as a cost. Depending on the relative magnitude of these dual effects, Marglin and Bhaduri (1990) distinguish between profit- and wage-led regimes, where the latter leads to a high profit share accompanied by a low rate of accumulation.

The dominant economic policies since the end of the Golden Age have assumed that higher profits will automatically transform into higher investment, growth, and employment. However, the hypothesis of profit-led growth needs to be verified empirically.

For developing countries, the last two decades have brought little more than misery.[1] The orthodox structural-adjustment programs implemented in most developing countries—beginning in the late 1970s and early 1980s, and continuing into the twenty-first century—sought to integrate individual countries into the global economy, shifting the source of effective demand from the home to the foreign market. Regulation of the labor market to achieve a procapital redistribution has been a major component of this process, with the promise that greater openness and higher profits will stimulate growth and employment. However, many developing countries ended up with high profit shares, low accumulation rates, and little growth in employment, despite massive increases in exports and greater labor-market flexibility.

This chapter seeks to evaluate structural-adjustment programs from a Post Keynesian viewpoint. It presents an empirical analysis of the impact of distribution on accumulation, capacity utilization, and employment for Turkey. As Turkey has followed the standard recipes of the International Monetary Fund (IMF) and the World Bank, it is an interesting case that illustrates some of the unexpected results of orthodox policy prescriptions. High profits have not stimulated investment and employment after more than two decades following IMF policies. The case of Turkey is similar to that of Latin American countries, which liberalized their economies substantially, but is different from that of Southeast Asian countries, where liberalization was always subject to active state industrial policy, and where export promotion was mostly mixed with import substitution.[2] The IMF and World Bank view Turkey as a case of the successful application of their liberalization approach with a clear procapital bias (Celasun and Rodrik 1989). Unlike in Latin America, where political change caused breaks in the continuity of their policies, in Turkey there have been no reversals in the economic-policy stance for almost twenty years (Boratav 1990, Boratav, Türel, and Yeldan 1994).[3]

The chapter tests whether accumulation and employment are profit-led in Turkey. This is done by means of a Post Keynesian open-economy model in structural vector autoregression (SVAR) form. Our estimates are a novel application within the Post Keynesian literature.

An Overview of Post Keynesian Growth Theory

Post Keynesian growth theories have been correctly classified as demand-constraint growth theories (Foley and Michl 1999). Unlike neoclassical growth theory, investment and savings are separate functions for Post Keynesians. Changes in income and in income distribution equilibrate the two. Thus, the goods market is at the center of the analysis. The labor market is assumed to follow passively, and unemployment is allowed to exist in the long run. Financial markets are thought to be flexible, with the money supply adjusting endogenously (Moore 1988), although there is an ongoing debate as to whether this is due to accommodating central-bank policy or financial innovation. The former position is often called "horizontalist," the latter "structuralist" (Pollin 1991). Technical change and substitution between input factors play a secondary role in Post Keynesian growth theories. Technological progress is important to Kaldorian models, which are discussed below.

The core of Post Keynesian growth theory is the interaction of investment and savings in the long run. The precise form of the investment function is subject to debate (see Davidson 1993), but as Marglin (1984) has pointed out, the crucial assertion is that there is an independent investment function. In its basic versions, this function consists of an accelerator term and a profit term, both of which are confirmed by empirical research on investment (Chirinko 1993). The savings function is assumed to depend on income distribution, because saving propensities differ between wage income and profit income, with the savings propensity of the latter exceeding that of the former.

A first group of Keynesian models assumes that the economy operates at full capacity. Kaldor (1957, 1960) assumed that accumulation would be governed by the natural rate of growth, so that full employment would be guaranteed. Robinson (1956, 1962) assumed that investment was a function of the profit rate. While the two models obviously differ with respect to labor-market outcomes, they have important similarities. In equilibrium, accumulation and income distribution are determined simultaneously. Income distribution adjusts to the pace of accumulation so that the required savings are provided through an inflationary process that undermines the real value of nominal wages (see Harris 1978, Marglin 1984, Marcuzzo 1996). While these models are of historical interest, the assumption of constant and full capacity utilization has been thought to be overly restrictive (Nell 1985, Dutt 1987).

A second group of Keynesian models, sometimes labeled "stagnationist," goes back to the work of Kalecki (1971) and Steindl (1952). Here capacity utilization is assumed to vary over longer periods through the price-setting power of oligopolistic companies. Hence, there is no assumption of perfect competition. Because capacity utilization is allowed to vary, there is no a priori trade-off between wages and profits, and wage increases can foster growth (Rowthorn 1981, Dutt 1984, Taylor 1985). Marglin and Bhaduri (1990) have clarified when such a wage-led growth regime can arise—it depends on the relative strength of the profit effect and the demand effect in the investment function.

A third family of Post Keynesian growth models stems from the later writings by Kaldor (1966) and the ensuing debate (collected in King 1994). The major innovation is the endogenous growth of labor productivity. Dynamic returns to scale are deemed realistic (Kaldor [1972] 1989). Simultaneous feedback from output growth to productivity growth (the effective demand function), and from productivity growth (the technical progress function) to output growth is allowed for in these models (see Boyer 1988; Boyer and Petit 1981, 1991; Targetti 1992).

The Model

We present here a Post Keynesian open-economy model, based on Bhaduri and Marglin (1990). It consists of behavioral functions for investments, savings, and international trade that define the goods market; a producer equilibrium curve, which relates capacity utilization and labor market pressures to the distribution of income; and an employment equation.

For the sake of simplicity, the public sector is left out of the analysis. This makes sense in the case of Turkey, given the structural changes in public spending, which has become increasingly dominated by interest payments, and by tax exemptions to promote exports, which breaks the link between growth and public-sector income. Given the constraints on degrees of freedom, and the difficulty of estimating public-sector behavior, we present a model and results only for the private sector.

The goods-market part of the model extends the work of Bhaduri and Marglin (1990) by examining employment and its effect on income distribution. Producer equilibrium is determined not only by the pricing behavior of companies, but also by a reserve-army effect, reflecting the bargaining power of workers. Employment is modeled by a version of Okun's law (as in Stockhammer 2004a, 2004b). These two extensions include the labor market in the analysis, allowing an interaction between distribution, accumulation, capacity utilization, and employment, rather than implicitly defining labor demand as a passive outcome of the system. Table 10.1 summarizes the model.

Equation 1 defines the investment decision of private companies. The rate of accumulation (investment/capital stock) is a function of expected profitability, which is proxied by the profit share and capacity utilization. This follows Bhaduri and Marglin (1990), who decompose the profit rate (r) into the profit share (π), capacity utilization (z), and (technical) capital productivity (k).

$$r = \frac{R}{K} = \frac{R}{Y}\frac{Y}{\bar{Y}}\frac{\bar{Y}}{K} = \pi z k. \tag{1}$$

The expected profit rate will thus be composed of expected profit share and capacity utilization, assuming that capital productivity is not expected to change.[4] We assume that expectations are formed on the basis of past values. This is a profit and accelerator model, where both capacity utilization and the profit share are expected to have a positive effect on investment. This function separates the demand effect of wages on investment from the cost effect, making the end result of a change in distribution ambiguous. High capacity utilization (high demand) does not necessarily increase investment, which is determined by savings behavior as well as domestic and foreign demand. Bhaduri and Marglin (1990) have pointed out that including the profit rate along with capacity utilization imposes a stagnationist regime. By using the profit share rather than the profit rate as the measure of profitability in the investment function, along with the rate of capacity utilization, Bhaduri and Marglin (1990) present a more general formulation that includes the earlier stagnationist models as special cases.

What is missing compared to standard formulations of the investment function is the interest rate. It is excluded because in our model the financial sector is not treated explicitly; for this reason, changes in the interest rate may show up as shocks to accumulation.

Equation 2 (Table 10.1) models private savings behavior. Private domestic savings, normalized by the capital stock, is a positive function of profit share and capacity utilization. It is assumed that a constant fraction, s, of profit income is saved, whereas there is no saving out of wages.

Table 10.1

Summary of the Model

Accumulation	$I/K = g^I(\pi, z)$ $\quad\quad + \,\, +$	(1)
Private savings	$S_p/K = s\pi z$	(2)
Exports	$X/Y = x(\pi)$ $\quad\quad +$	(3)
Imports	$M/Y = m(\pi, z, I/K)$ $\quad\quad\quad - \,\, + \,\, +$	(4)
Producer's equilibrium	$\pi = p\,(z, E/N)$ $\quad\quad\quad + \quad -$	(5)
Employment (Okun's law)	$\Delta E/N = e(I/K, \Delta z)$ $\quad\quad\quad\quad + \quad +$	(6)
Goods–market equilibrium	$g^I = g^{Sto}s\pi z\_(X/Y-M/Y)z$	(7a)
Capacity utilization implied by the goods–market equilibrium	$z = z(V, I/K, (X/Y-M/Y))$ $\quad\quad\quad - \quad + \quad\quad +$	(7b)

Where:
I/K = investment/capital stock
π = profit share
z = capacity utilization
S_p/K = Private savings/capital stock
s = marginal propensity to save out of profits
X/Y = Exports/output
M/Y = Imports/output
E/N = employment rate (employment/working-age population)
g^{St} = growth rate of total savings (private and foreign)

Equations 3 and 4 (Table 10.1) add international trade to the model by defining the export intensity of production (exports/output) as a positive function of profit share, and import penetration (imports/output) as a negative function of profit share and a positive function of the level of domestic activity, which is determined by the rate of accumulation and capacity utilization. The profit share is taken as an indicator of international competitiveness, and thus global market share.[5] Due to the limitations of the VAR model, we need a variable to serve both as an indicator of distribution and international competitiveness. Although domestically we assume procyclical markups, we take the markup as fixed at the international level, so that export prices change due to changes in input costs. As the profit share is affected by unit labor costs, which is conventionally taken as an indicator of competitiveness, the profit share and exports should be positively related. However, an increase in the profit share caused by an increase in the markup would not indicate improved competitiveness. As it is widely argued that redistribution of income at the expense of wage earners is moderated in open economies by increased export competitiveness, estimating export performance as a function of distribution makes sense in a model relating accumulation, distribution, capacity utilization, and employment. Nevertheless, the impact of distribution on import demand is ambiguous since a rise in profit share might also increase the demand for imported consumption goods. Additionally, the real exchange rate, which is also affected by international capital flows and policy decisions, is an important component of international competitiveness.

Equation 5 (Table 10.1) represents the supply side of the model, or producer equilibrium. The profit share is a positive function of the rate of capacity utilization and a negative function of the rate of employment. The former follows Marglin and Bhaduri (1990), who assume that companies use a markup over unit labor costs to set prices and that the markup varies procyclically with the rate of capacity utilization. The effect of the employment rate is similar to the reserve-army effect in a Marxist framework. It extends the Marglin and Bhaduri model because it allows labor market outcomes to affect the distributional struggle. Marglin and Bhaduri (1990), like Bowles and Boyer (1995), assumed that employment moves in parallel with capacity utilization. Thus the modification of the producers' equilibrium only becomes important in conjunction with our different view of the labor market.

The labor market is portrayed by Equation 6 (Table 10.1). The change in the rate of employment is a positive function of accumulation and changes in capacity utilization, which is a variation of Okun's law.[6] Bhaduri and Marglin (1990) take the short-term view that employment depends on capacity utilization. Because we are interested in a medium-term model, the creation of capacity, as well as capacity utilization, determines employment.

Finally, Equation 7a (Table 10.1) represents the goods-market equilibrium, where the growth rate of private capital stock equals the growth rate of total savings, where $s\pi z$ is the private domestic savings and $-NX/Y.z = -(X/Y - M/Y).z$ is foreign savings, both normalized by the capital stock.[7]

Solving Equation 7a for z gives us the capacity utilization rate implied by the goods-market equilibrium. Equation 7b (Table 10.1) separates the relative impact of accumulation, distribution, and net foreign demand on the capacity-utilization rate. Accumulation is expected to have an immediate positive effect on capacity utilization, via increased demand, which dominates the negative effect via increased capital stock. An increase in the profit share is expected to have a negative impact, assuming that the propensity to consume out of profits is lower than that out of wages. An increase in net exports is expected to have a positive impact.

The relationship between capacity utilization and profit share distinguishes two types of growth regimes—stagnationist and exhilarationist. In a stagnationist regime, lower profit share is associated with a higher level of capacity utilization. In contrast, when a higher profit share goes along with higher capacity utilization, we have an exhilarationist regime.

Finally, the relationship between accumulation and the profit share defines the regime of accumulation. When a high rate of accumulation accompanies a low profit share, the regime is wage-led; in the opposite case it is profit-led. Depending on the relative magnitudes of the direct positive effect of profit share on accumulation (the partial derivative $\partial g^I/\partial \pi$), its indirect effect via the positive international-demand effect ($\partial g^I/\partial z \cdot \partial z/\partial nx \cdot \partial nx/\partial \pi$),[8] and the negative domestic consumption effect ($\partial g^I/\partial z \cdot \partial z/\partial \pi$), the sign of the total derivative, $dg^I/d\pi$, is either positive or negative. If the direct profit effect and the international demand effect of a lower wage share are high enough to offset the decline in domestic consumption, accumulation is profit led, otherwise it is wage led.[9]

Empirical Literature on the Relationship Between Distribution and Accumulation

The empirical literature on Kaleckian models has focused mainly on the goods market. Bowles and Boyer (1995) focus on the question of how distributional changes affect output. They find that France, Germany, and Italy are weakly profit-led, whereas the United Kingdom and the United States are wage-led. The domestic sector is wage-led in all countries. Similarly, the world economy as a whole is wage-led. Their work differs from ours because they focus exclusively on the goods market and use a single-equation approach, while we use a systems approach.

Gordon (1995a, 1995b) argues that the profit function is nonlinear in capacity utilization and includes an index of capitalist power as an explanatory variable. For the demand function, he estimates a two-stage least-square model, that is, a systems approach, of savings, investment, and net exports. The lagged interest rate and the lagged profit rate are used as shift variables and capacity utilization is endogenous. Gordon finds that demand is profit-led in the United States.

Taylor (1996, 156) concludes from the evidence that "aggregate demand tends to be profit-led in industrialized economies and wage-led in developing countries." However, Hein and Krämer (1997) claim that advanced capitalist countries have been wage-led.

Stockhammer and Onaran (2004) estimate a model similar to the one estimated here for the United States, United Kingdom, and France. They find that the effects of changes in the profit share are not statistically different from zero and that employment is demand driven, while changes in real wages have little if any effect on unemployment.

In the case of developing countries, Yentürk (1998) analyzes the relationship between profitability and investments for tradable and nontradable sectors, while Onaran and Yentürk (2001) analyze the response of investment to demand and profitability for Turkey. Sarkar (1992) questions the empirical validity of the stagnationist thesis for India, but does not present a formal test. Furthermore, these studies do not develop a complete macroeconometric analysis of the overall inter-action between distribution, demand, accumulation, and employment.

Method of Estimation

The main motivation behind this study is to model the dynamic relationship be-tween distribution, accumulation, capacity utilization, and employment consider-ing both lagged and contemporaneous interactions within a systems approach. To do this, we employ a SVAR analysis.

The general form of a vector autoregression (VAR) model is:

$$B.y(t) = Dd(t) + A(i)y(t-i) + e(t), \tag{8}$$

where y is a vector of variables, $i = 1, \ldots, p$ denotes the number of lags to be used in the model, and $d(t)$ is a vector of deterministic variables, which may include a time trend as well as a constant. The $e_j(t)$'s are $i.i.d.$ $N(0, I)$ innovations. Matrix B represents the contemporaneous interaction among the variables. This general form cannot be estimated, since matrix B is not known. Thus, the VAR is estimated in Equation 9 as:

$$y(t) = B^{-1}Dd(t) + B^{-1}A(i)y(t-i) + u(t). \tag{9}$$

This formulation can readily be estimated, since it only relies on lagged values as explanatory variables. Intuitively, each variable is assumed to depend on lagged values of all other variables in the system. When referring to a VAR estimation below, we refer to an estimation of Equation 9. It is crucial to note that in Equation 9 contemporaneous interactions among variables are suppressed and surface in the error term.

The vector $u(t)$ of the reduced form errors is related to the vector $e(t)$ of innova-tions by the following system of structural equations:

$$u(t) = B^{-1}e(t), \tag{10}$$

where $u_j(t)$ are assumed to have zero mean, constant variances, and are serially uncorrelated; but, because of matrix B^{-1}, there has to be a contemporaneous corre-lation between innovations.

The structure of matrix B distinguishes between two types of VAR models—standard VAR and structural VAR. In standard VAR, B^{-1} is a lower triangular ma-trix, according to the so-called standard Choleski decomposition (Sims 1980). In structural VAR (SVAR), B is specified on the basis of economic theory, where, without loss of generality, the diagonal elements of B can be normalized to unity (Bernanke 1986, Sims 1986). The specification of B corresponds to specifying the zero off-diagonal elements.[10] The structural parameters are estimated by maximum likelihood.

SVAR allows for richer interaction because it does not impose restrictions on the contemporaneous interaction among the variables by imposing a triangular structure on the covariance matrix of the error terms. Standard VARs are a special case of SVAR.

An alternative estimation technique would be to develop a system of simultaneous equations. However, this raises the problem of defining proper instrumental variables to deal with endogeneity. The approach usually ends up using lagged values of the endogenous variables. SVAR is superior to simultaneous equations because it incorporates the contemporaneous interaction among the variables.

Two further comments on VAR models are in order here. First, because of the systems approach, exogenous shift variables have little meaning in VARs unless they have strong effect. In our case, the variables that are relevant to investment decisions (such as the rate of return in financial markets, risk factors, the cost of capital, and the real exchange rate) could be among these exogenous variables. However, since our focus is on the interaction of the endogenous variables, we do not include exogenous variables.

Second, VAR analysis is a systems approach. It traces effects through an entire system rather than looking at one equation at a time. Because VARs involve lagged values of all dependent variables, multicollinearity problems are inevitable. Therefore, inference in a VAR model does not focus on t-values and their significance, but on impulse-response functions. Impulse functions trace the dynamic impact of a shock to one of the variables on all other variables in the system.

The Data

Here we concentrate on some data problems. Definitions of variables and data sources are contained in Appendix 10.1.

One major problem is the absence of data for capital stock in national statistical sources. For this reason we use a ratio of private investment to Gross Domestic Product (GDP).[11] Consequently, the growth rate of GDP is used as a proxy for capacity utilization instead of the output/capital ratio. In order to check for robustness, the ratio of GDP to potential GDP is also used, although we recognize that there are problems with the notion of potential GDP.[12]

Another data problem concerns the measurement of employment. Given the nature of unpaid family work, and the significance of underemployment in the agricultural sector, we exclude the agricultural sector from our analysis. We define the employment variable as the rate of employment in order to capture labor-market pressure on profits via the reserve-army effect, as well as to reflect the employment-creation capacity of the economy. In this sense, the share of employment in the total working-age population in the nonagricultural sector is the appropriate variable, rather than the share of employment in the labor force.

Taking the labor force as the denominator limits the pressure exerted on the bargaining power of labor to people actively looking for work. This ignores a significant portion of the population not employed and not actively looking for work, either because they are discouraged or involved in nonmarket work. The distinction between nonemployment and unemployment is particularly important in developing countries with declining participation rates, particularly for the female working-age population, following increased rates of urbanization. However, measuring the potential labor supply for the nonagricultural sector is a nontrivial problem. Although agriculture is almost totally a rural occupation, the opposite is not true. Almost 20 percent of nonagricultural employees reside in rural areas. Therefore the denominator cannot be limited to the urban population. The alternative, using the whole working-age population to measure the potential work force, creates an additional problem. The ratio of nonagricultural employment to the total working-age population also reflects the sectoral transformation of employment from agriculture to industry. As a result, we use nonagricultural employment (in logarithms), abstracting from the demographic trends about changes in the working-age population, as well as the sectoral changes in employment. While the level of employment is not as good a measure of the labor-market pressure as the employment rate, it can be a better measure to evaluate the employment-creation capacity of an economy.

Investment, profit share, growth, and exports are also adjusted to exclude the agricultural sector. It is not possible to exclude imports of agricultural goods due to data limitations; however, the share of agricultural imports in total imports is negligible.

Except for the logarithm of employment, our variables are already defined in ratios, and it is unlikely that these variables exhibit a unit root. And since VAR is by nature an autoregressive distributed lag model (ADL), which has desirable properties even in the face of unit roots, we do not need to worry about spurious correlations between unit-root variables.

Stylized Facts

Turkey experienced a major structural change in 1980. It moved from an import-substituting industrialization strategy to an export-led growth model. It also implemented the structural-adjustment program prescribed by the IMF and the World Bank. Figure 10.1 plots the variables for distribution, investment, growth, international trade, and employment (i.e., the growth rate of employment) both before and after the structural adjustment.

The period of import substitution created a mass-consumption market for national production under a protectionist trade regime. Given improvements in productivity, wages were able to sustain the level of effective demand while profits remained high enough to maintain the level of investments. This inter-class consensus reached its limits slowly. As productivity increases slowed down, current-

Figure 10.1 **Plots of Variables** (1965–97)

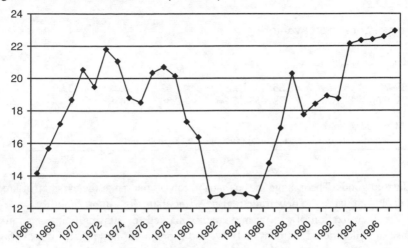

I/Y: Private investment/GDP in non-agricultural sector (%).

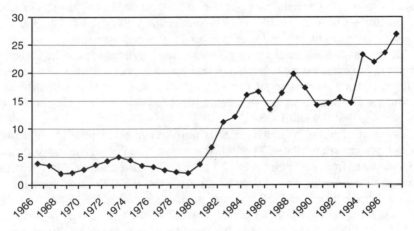

X/Y: Exports of goods and services/GDP in non-agricultural sector (%).

account deficits and industrial investment became increasingly harder to sustain.

In the years after 1980, Turkey tried to overcome the severe foreign-exchange crisis of 1977–79 through export-led growth based on a structural-adjustment program.[13] The beginning of the period was characterized by a repression of labor rights, accompanied by a military coup. The new institutional setting was retained by the subsequent civil administrations. Export-oriented trade policies, import liberalization, and deregulation of financial and product markets necessitated upward adjustments, particularly in the prices of foreign exchange, energy, and

Table 10.2

Summary of Period Averages

	I/Y	π	X/Y	M/Y	z*	ln(E)	Growth (E)**
1965–79	18.54	68.55	3.27	11.02	6.09	8.59	4.84
1980–97	17.70	71.79	15.98	22.86	5.33	9.17	2.83

*Growth rate of nonagricultural GDP.
**Growth rate of nonagricultural employment, memo item.

industrial goods. The change in the distribution of income at the expense of labor let capital adjust to the new trade regime without any loss in profitability.

The liberalization of capital movements marked the starting point of another phase of structural adjustment in 1989, and it prepared the ground for real wage increases via increased public spending and currency appreciation, which led to a decline in nonlabor input costs. However, these unsustainable fiscal and monetary policies soon led to a significant increase in the twin deficits. When this process was interrupted by a severe crisis in 1994, the economy was stabilized through real wage declines, eroding the gains of the post-1989 period.

The export-led industrialization policy shifted industrial capacity towards international markets via a contraction of real wages, export subsidies, and real devaluations. But this strategy of export promotion was unable to stimulate new productive investments in industry. Table 10.2 shows the average figures for two subperiods, 1965–79 and 1980–97.

The share of profits in GDP increased from 68.5 percent in the 1965–79 period, to 71.8 percent in the 1980–97 period, whereas the ratio of private investment to GDP declined from 18.5 percent to 17.7 percent. The investment/GDP ratio in the nonagricultural sector was 19.4 percent during the 1977–79 crisis period, and, after a sharp decline after 1980, the investment ratio reached the historically high levels of the import-substituting period only in the mid-1990s. The low and volatile investment ratios in the post-1980 period are striking, especially given the large increases in profitability and exports.

Exports boomed in the post-1980 period, with the ratio of exports of nonagricultural goods and services to GDP (nonagricultural) increasing from 3.3 percent in the 1965–79 period to 16 percent during 1980–97. Imports also doubled in the same period. Consequently, the trade deficit declined from 7.8 percent to 6.9 percent of GDP.

Despite improvement in export performance, the average annual growth of nonagricultural GDP in the 1980–97 period was 5.3 percent, lower than the 6.1 percent rate for the 1965–79 period. More importantly, variation of the growth rate was greater in the post-1980 period. The average annual growth rate of nonagricultural employment dropped even more steeply, from 4.8 percent in the 1965–79 period to 2.8 percent in the 1980–97 period.

These stylized facts provide some evidence about wage-led regimes. Investment has been stagnant despite a rising profit share. The export boom has not been enough to raise growth rates. This illustrates the demand aspect of wages. Finally, the stagnation in accumulation can be an important factor behind the slow employment growth in the 1980s, drastic declines in real wages, and increased labor-market flexibility. Based on this evidence, three main questions need to be addressed: What is the relative responsiveness of accumulation to distribution and growth? What is the impact of distribution on growth? How does procapital redistribution affect employment?

Specification of the SVAR Model

Defining a SVAR model is a matter of specifying the contemporaneous relations between the variables, namely matrix B. According to our theoretical model, our matrix of endogenous variables, y, and matrix B are defined as follows:

$$y = \begin{vmatrix} I/Y \\ \pi \\ X/Y \\ M/Y \\ z \\ E \end{vmatrix} ; \qquad B = \begin{vmatrix} b_{11} & 0 & 0 & 0 & 0 & 0 \\ 0 & b_{22} & 0 & 0 & b_{25} & b_{26} \\ 0 & b_{32} & b_{33} & 0 & 0 & 0 \\ 0 & b_{42} & 0 & b_{44} & b_{45} & 0 \\ b_{51} & b_{52} & b_{53} & 0 & b_{55} & 0 \\ 0 & 0 & 0 & 0 & b_{65} & b_{66} \end{vmatrix} ,$$

with the expected signs being $b_{25}, b_{32}, b_{45}, b_{51}, b_{53}, b_{65} > 0$ and $b_{26}, b_{42}, b_{52} < 0$. All the diagonal elements are positive by definition. Note that the zeros in matrix B depict no contemporaneous interaction, but a lagged interaction between the variables will still be at work.

We assume that investment decisions respond both to profit share and capacity utilization with a lag, due to a time lag between the investment decision and the investment expenditure. Also, since our capacity utilization variable is the growth rate, imports are only a function of z, not of I/Y. The same holds true for the employment equation. In addition, the employment variable has to be introduced in difference form in the employment equation, and it has to be used in level form in the profit-share equation to reflect labor-market pressures. The autoregressive-distributed-lag (ADL) specification of the VAR model will make the necessary transformations. Finally, the equation for the contemporaneous interactions for z does not include imports. This equation reflects the components of demand, and the effect of imports is assumed to be captured via the profit share, which is one of the determinants of imports. This modification has the additional advantage of decreasing computational complexity by decreasing the number of simultaneous interactions in the system. Without imposing this restriction, the model would be unsolvable.

The model includes two lags to control for problems that might arise from autocorrelation and nonstationarity in the time series. VARs give consistent results, even in the presence of unit roots (Sims, Stock, and Watson 1990), if more than one lag is employed. Using more lags will not add much in the case of annual data, and will further reduce the degree of freedom.

Our main focus will be on the responses of investment, growth, and employment to a one-time shock to the profit share. Impulse-response functions offer an advantage in interpreting results within a systems approach. The response of a variable to an innovation to another variable is not equivalent to the partial derivatives that are the outcomes of standard regression models. Unlike comparative statics, the response to an innovation incorporates the combined response of the variable to all changes in the system following a shock to one of the variables. VAR models also help trace these interactions through time.

Estimation Results

The VAR results of OLS estimations are presented in Appendix 10.2. VAR estimations tend to suffer from multicollinearity problems that lead to low t-statistics. This is why impulse responses are of interest. Our VAR results are consistent with the model at acceptable levels of statistical significance.

According to our VAR results, the accelerator term in the accumulation function is confirmed. Both the first and second lags of growth are significantly positive. The profit term is also statistically significant and positive, and the results suggest that it enters the accumulation equation in difference form.

The first lag of employment enters the profit function with a negative sign and is statistically significant, confirming the reserve-army hypothesis. Growth also has the expected positive sign, indicating the procyclical behavior of the profit share.

There is a high degree of persistence in the employment function, though less than perfect persistence, with the coefficients of the lagged employment variables summing up to 0.82. The ADL structure has nearly converted employment into difference form, consistent with Okun's law.

The greatest problems are with the growth function, where the lagged values of the components of demand usually do not have the expected sign. However, if capacity utilization adjusts quickly, the contemporaneous interaction may be more pronounced. The SVAR results below support this argument.

A trend is included in the VAR model to capture long-term effects such as structural shifts in trading relationships, or domestic and international financial markets that are not causally affected by variations in the system. The trend is significant in most equations. Models were also estimated with and without a trend. Excluding a trend does not make any significant contribution but adversely affects the impulse-response functions, resulting in higher standard errors. As a result, we conclude that a trend is important in capturing some long-term effects that are not included in the system. The discussion below refers to the estimations with a trend.

Table 10.3 presents the SVAR estimation results—the entries in matrix B^{-1} of contemporaneous correlations among error terms.

Model 1 (Table 10.3) shows the SVAR results according to the specification in the preceding section. The contemporaneous effect of growth on the profit share has the expected positive sign, although it is not significant. The contemporaneous effect of employment is neither significant nor has the expected sign, showing that the reserve-army effect becomes operative only with a lag. However, in the case of growth, the insignificant sign may result from the inability of the model to capture simultaneity between growth and the profit share. Problems with the structural parameters may be limiting when modeling contemporaneous effects. The standard errors of the model increase significantly in this specification.[14] An alternative model, where profits depend contemporaneously on growth, but not on employment, was also tested. In that specification, growth is not only insignificant, but also has a negative sign.[15] To simplify the model, we assumed that the profit share responds to growth, as well as to employment, with a lag.

We also tested for the contemporaneous effects of the profit share and growth on investment, and found them both to be insignificant. Moreover, the sign of the profit share was negative. Although insignificant, a negative sign for the profit share, even when modeled as the only variable that has a contemporaneous effect on investment, points to mechanisms other than demand leading to low investment in a time of high profits.

In Model 2 (Table 10.3), b_{25} and b_{26} in matrix B are set to zero; thus, in addition to investment, distribution is also contemporaneously exogenous. In this new specification, the coefficients have the expected signs and are mostly significant.[16] The positive demand effect on investment, and the negative consumption effect of profits on growth, are confirmed. Exports have a positive demand effect, although it is statistically insignificant. The strong positive contemporaneous relationship between growth and employment is in line with Okun's law. The profit share has a significant positive contemporaneous effect on exports, capturing the competitiveness of Turkish exports. The equation for imports is the only one that does not perform well. The coefficient of growth is not significant and, more importantly, the coefficient of the profit share is positive, but insignificant. Various factors can explain this result. First, profits might be unable to capture the price competitiveness of imports. Second, if the propensity to demand imported goods out of profit income is higher than out of wage income, the competitiveness effect of a higher profit share may be offset by the increased demand for imported luxury goods. Finally, the price elasticity of imports can be rather low in Turkey, which has a

Table 10.3

Structural VAR Results: Contemporaneous Interaction among Error Terms
(the elements of B^{-1}, where $u = B^{-1}e\,(t)$)

	Model 1	Model 2
I/Y		
Innovation	1.526 [0.82634]	0.927 [0.00000]
π		
Z	117.123 [0.99808]	—
E	1185.438 [0.98928]	—
Innovation	175.669 [0.99596]	1.843 [0.00000]
X/Y		
π	−3.385 [0.00058]	0.323 [0.01171]
Innovation	2.821 [0.00077]	1.068 [0.00000]
M/Y		
π	−0.705 [0.90521]	0.320 [0.41630]
z	0.240 [0.95145]	0.047 [0.82585]
Innovation	5.822 [0.75589]	1.664 [0.00004]
z		
I/Y	5.355 [0.00000]	0.910 [0.11339]
π	−0.720 [0.00000]	−0.940 [0.06098]
X/Y	0.994 [0.00000]	0.111 [0.87742]
Innovation	0.706 [0.00000]	2.397 [0.00001]
E		
z	0.167 [0.99995]	0.002 [0.03836]
Innovation	1.325 [0.99992]	0.010 [0.00000]

Note: *p*-values in brackets. A trend and a constant is added to the VAR model. The estimation period is 1965–97, after adjusting for lags.

Figure 10.2a **Impulse Response of *I/Y* to a One-Standard-Error Shock in Profit Share**

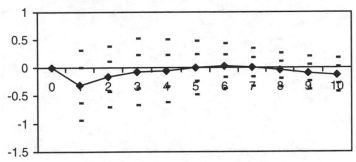

Note: The dots represent +/– 2 standard errors.

Figure 10.2b **Impulse Response of *I/Y* to a One-Standard-Error Shock in *z***

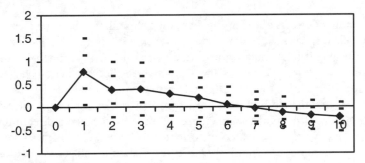

Note: The dots represent +/– 2 standard errors.

high degree of import dependency, not only for capital goods, but also for intermediate inputs.

Figures 10.2a and 10.2b show the impulse response functions of accumulation to the profit share and growth. The impulse response of accumulation to the profit share incorporates the direct profit effect, as well as the indirect effects of the change in the profit share on the system via international and domestic demand. The results of the impulse responses are suggestive, although the confidence intervals are large in many cases.

An innovation to the profit share creates a negative accumulation response in the next period; the shock continues for another period, and then dies without leading to any significant improvement in accumulation. These results are in line with the empirical evidence about the stagnant accumulation rates and increasing profit share. However, the standard errors are high, and although the results show that accumulation is not profit-led, they do not indicate strong wage-led growth. On the other hand, the response of accumulation to growth is significantly posi-

Figure 10.3 **Impulse Response of z to a One-Standard-Error Shock in Profit Share**

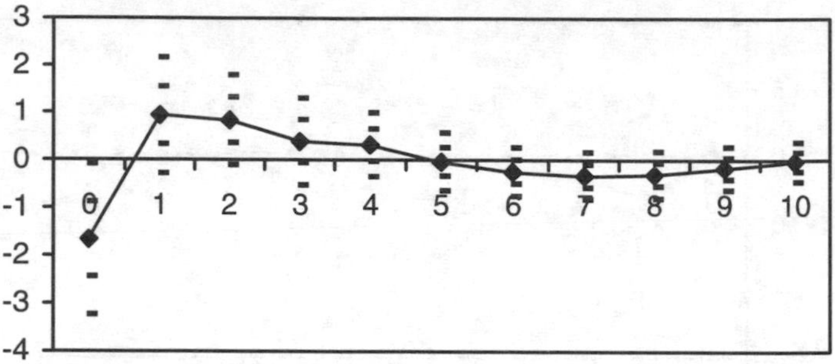

Note: The dots represent +/– 2 standard errors.

tive, verifying the Post Keynesian emphasis on demand in determining investment decisions.

The indirect effects of the profit share on accumulation become clearer from the impulse response of growth to the profit share in Figure 10.3. An increase in the profit share is immediately transformed into a decline in growth, indicating a stagnationist regime. The effect turns positive in the next period; however, it takes three periods for the growth rate to return to its initial level.[17] The recovery of the growth rate is due to the improvements in exports. Analyzing the overall impact of the profit share on growth incorporates the indirect impact of export demand, which is expected to lower the probability of a stagnationist regime. An increase in the profit share creates a positive and persistent impact on exports, as can be seen in Figure 10.4, and exports eventually have a positive effect on demand. However, it is only in the medium run that a higher profit share is capable of increasing export demand enough to compensate for the initial decline in consumption out of wages.

The immediate decline in growth due to an increase in the profit share explains the decline in accumulation in the second period; and the demand effect persists into the next periods, offsetting the profit effect. Investment decisions are highly path dependent; a slowdown in accumulation tends to be long lasting. Nevertheless, other factors lead to a stagnation in accumulation despite higher profits, factors that are different from the indirect effect of the profit share via consumption out of wage income and lower capacity utilization. Increased rates of return in financial markets, higher volatility and uncertainty, and higher costs of capital goods have been identified as contributing to the accumulation slowdown during the 1980s and the 1990s, in both developed and developing countries.[18] Adding the financial sector to the model could fill this gap. Unfortunately, the limitations of SVAR and the lack of data to measure these effects do not allow us to explore this possibility. Adding the real interest rate to the model did not lead to any significant improvement.[19] Real interest rates were unable to capture the full com-

Figure 10.4   **Impulse Response of X/Y to a One-Standard-Error Shock in Profit Share**

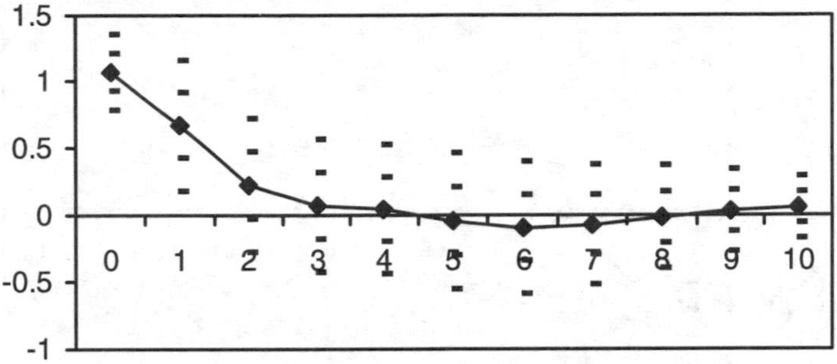

Note: The dots represent +/– 2 standard errors.

plexity of the structural change in the financial system. Another critical point is that the profit-share variable used in the analysis is gross profits, which does not decompose the differences in the sources of capital income. Finally, our use of two lags may be unable to capture the dynamics behind the build up of profit expectations and business confidence.

One consequence of the inability of profits to enhance growth and accumulation is that employment is wage-led in the short run. Figure 10.5a shows the impulse response of employment to the profit share. An increase in the profit share reduces employment immediately, and the decline persists during the next period as well. The cumulative negative effect dies away only five periods later. Contrary to the arguments of neoclassical economics, a lower wage share does not stimulate employment. The initial decline in growth and accumulation provides a coherent explanation for the stagnation in employment. Figures 10.5b and 10.5c show the impulse-response functions of employment to growth and accumulation. These results show that demand is the main driving force behind employment, but that accumulation is also important for job creation.

An interesting finding about labor demand is the negative and persisting impact of exports on employment. Figure 10.5d shows the impulse response of employment to exports. It provides counterevidence to the expectation that labor intensity would increase following an increase in export orientation. It also shows that in a global economy it is harder for developing countries to increase their competitiveness by using labor-intensive technologies. Although their exports may be more labor intensive than advanced countries, the capital intensity of most export-oriented sectors are increasing (Günçavdi and Küçükçiftçi 1999, Wood 1997, Yentürk 1997). Another important consequence of this finding is that the increase in competitiveness, which is maintained by low wages, does not transform into higher employment.

A final point that needs to be highlighted is the response of distribution to growth and labor-market pressures. Although distribution does not immediately adjust to

Figure 10.5a   **Impulse Response of *E* to a One-Standard-Error Shock in
Profit Share**

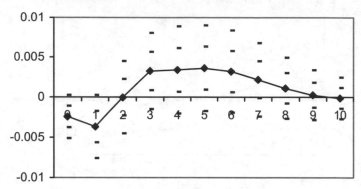

Note: The dots represent +/– 2 standard errors.

Figure 10.5b   **Impulse Response of *E* to a One-Standard-Error Shock in *z***

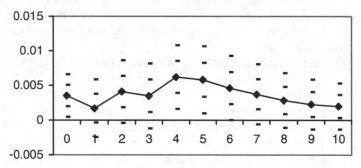

Note: The dots represent +/– 2 standard errors.

changes in demand and balance-of-power relations, the lagged effects are significant. Figures 10.6a and 10.6b show that the profit share responds procyclically following innovation in growth, indicating an increased markup and greater economic
power by companies. Labor-market pressures also become effective in the second
period, as implied by the strong negative response of the profit share to a change in
employment.

Conclusion

This chapter presents an empirical analysis of the impact of distribution on accumulation, growth, and employment based on a Post Keynesian open-economy model
for Turkey. The intention was to test the profit-led accumulation and employment
hypothesis. In Turkey, accumulation and employment are not profit-led, and the

Figure 10.5c **Impulse Response of *E* to a One-Standard-Error Shock in *I/Y***

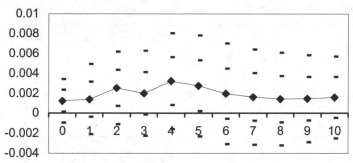

Note: The dots represent +/– 2 standard errors.

Figure 10.5d **Impulse Response of *E* to a One Standard-Error-Shock in *X/Y***

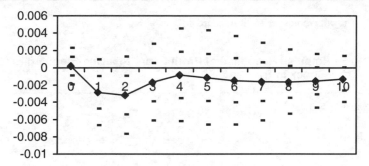

Note: The dots represent +/– 2 standard errors.

growth regime is stagnationist, at least in the short run. Although, the results do not point to a strong wage-led accumulation regime, a high profit share does not increase investment. The results also indicate that only in the medium run can a high profit share increase export demand enough to compensate for the decline in consumption out of wages. The inability of high profits to create high growth rates explains part of the stagnation in accumulation in conjunction with greater profitability. However, the reasons behind the stagnation in accumulation go beyond the indirect effect of the profit share on consumption out of wage income. Our inability to incorporate some significant exogenous variables within the SVAR framework, such as the rise in financial returns and the increase in risk and uncertainty, limits the ability of the model to account for some other crucial sources of stagnation in accumulation. Although our estimation method was not capable of capturing all the interactions within the system, our results suggest why higher profit levels in the export-led growth period do not generate a higher rate of accumulation and employment.

Finally, a few policy implications need to be highlighted. First, the results suggest that a procapital incomes policy is neither a necessary nor a sufficient

Figure 10.6a **Impulse Response of Profit Share to a One-Standard-Error Shock in *z***

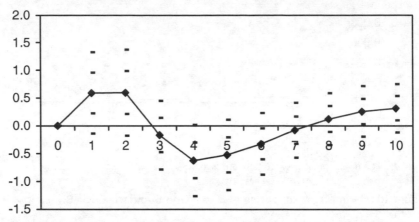

Note: The dots represent +/– 2 standard errors.

Figure 10.6b **Impulse Response of Profit Share to a One-Standard-Error Shock in *E***

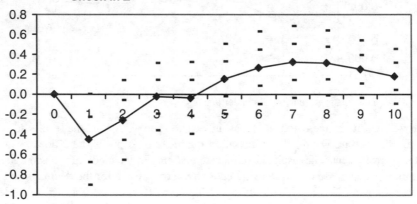

Note: The dots represent +/– 2 standard errors.

condition to achieve higher accumulation and growth. On the contrary, the decline in domestic demand can have negative effects on growth if the improvements in international competitiveness are not strong and sustainable. Second, demand is the driving force behind employment, and wage suppression is unable to improve the growth of employment. The limits in creating employment via low wages and a growth regime based on the use of existing capacity (rather than new investment) highlight the importance of economic policies to stimulate accumulation and suggest that enhancing productivity is the way to develop international competitiveness.

Notes

We have benefited from comments by Minqi Li, James Crotty, Robert Pollin, David Kotz, Samuel Bowles, Amit Bhaduri, Ric Holt, and Steve Pressman on an earlier version of this paper. The usual disclaimer applies. The paper was presented at the 27th Annual Conference of the Eastern Economic Association, February 23–25, 2001, New York, and the Middle East Technical University International Conference in Economics 5, September 10–13, 2001, Ankara.

1. See Taylor (1988), Amsden and Hoeven (1996), Akyüz (1995), Toye (1995), Boratav, Türel, and Yentürk (1996), and Amadeo (1996) for a review of the growth patterns in developing countries during the implementation of structural-adjustment policies.

2. A companion study compares Turkey with South Korea (Onaran and Stockhammer 2005). We discuss the results of this study in more detail below.

3. In 1989 the strict procapital policies reached its socio-economic limits, and wage increases became inevitable. However this short deviation was reversed after the economic crisis of 1994. The stylized facts of the country are discussed in depth below.

4. In order to abstract from the changes in potential output/capital ratio (Y^*/K), we define capacity utilization, z, by capital productivity, thus $z=Y/K=(Y/Y^*)(Y^*/K)$. Capacity utilization is proxied by output/capital ratio (Y/K).

5. Bowles and Boyer (1995) also use the profit rate as an indicator of international competitiveness.

6. According to Okun's law, change in the rate of unemployment is a function of growth. We are using the change in the employment rate rather than the unemployment rate in our model, due to the reasoning discussed in the section on data. Growth is then broken down into its sources, namely change in capacity utilization and change in capacity, that is, growth rate of capital stock.

7. In the empirical estimations, public savings are assumed to be captured by the constant term.

8. $\partial nx/\partial p = \partial x/\partial p - \partial m/\partial p$

9. See Bhaduri and Marglin (1990), Blecker (1989, 1999), and Bowles and Boyer (1995) for an analytical discussion about wage- and profit-led regimes in open economies.

10. The number of moment restrictions is equal to the number of nonzero parameters in B^{-1}. But, even if the number of free parameters equals the number of nonzero elements of matrix B^{-1}, identification is not guaranteed due to the existence of simultaneity in the system.

11. The Penn World Tables, developed by the United Nations International Comparisons Project, provide data about capital stock. But comparing the net change in capital stock (after depreciation) with the investment figures available in national data sources, in terms of trend and correlations, highlights serious differences in the measurement of investment variables in this database. Yet, in order to check for robustness, the initial year of capital/output ratio in the Penn World Tables was used as a benchmark to construct the capital stock series. The main results of the estimations are quite robust to the use of the rate of accumulation as opposed to the investment/GDP ratio. Nevertheless, we prefer to base our analysis with the existing data on investment/GDP; the results of various other specifications are available upon request.

12. The estimation results are robust to the use of gap as the measure of capacity utilization. The results are available upon request.

13. See Senses (1989), Boratav, Türel, and Yeldan (1994), Yeldan (1995), Yentürk (1997),

Onaran (2002), Onaran and Yentürk (2003), Yentürk and Onaran (2000), Metin-Özcan, Voyvoda, and Yeldan (2001) for a discussion of the dynamics of macroeconomic adjustment in Turkey.

14. Even some of the coefficients of the innovations to the variables itself have insignificant signs, indicating the significance of the problems regarding identification when simultaneity in the model increases.

15. The correlation between the residuals of the OLS estimations also verifies this result. The correlation coefficient between the profit share and growth is significantly negative, indicating the immediate negative effect of an increase in profit share on growth.

16. When the limiting effect of imports on growth is also modeled explicitly (including imports in the contemporaneous interaction equation for z), the model was unable to capture the simultaneity between growth and imports. The sign of growth in the import equation was negative, whereas that of imports in the growth equation was positive. Moreover, the sign of exports in the growth equation was also negative, which is counterintuitive.

17. Note that the impulse-response graphs shown here are not cumulative—rather, they show the response to the initial shock in each period.

18. See Akyüz (1991, 1995) and Boratav, Türel, and Yentürk (1996) for developing countries, and Davidson (1998), Dumenil and Levy (2000), and Stockhammer (2004a) for advanced capitalist countries.

19. For the period before 1989, the interest rate on a one-year time deposit is used; after 1989, the average annual compound interest rate on government debt instruments is used, since after 1989 the interest rate on government debt instruments increased significantly compared with the deposit rates, becoming a more realistic measure of financial returns.

References

Akyüz, Y. 1991. "Financial Liberalization in Developing Countries: A Neo-Keynesian Approach." UNCTAD Discussion Paper no. 36. New York: United Nations Conference on Trade and Development.
———. 1995. "Financial Liberalization in Developing Countries: Keynes, Kalecki and the Rentier." In G. Helleiner, ed., *Poverty, Prosperity and the World Economy: Essays in Memory of Sidney Dell*, 149–66. New York: St. Martin's Press.
Amadeo, E.J. 1996. "The Knife-Edge of Exchange-Rate-Based Stabilization: Impact on Growth, Employment and Wages." *UNCTAD Review:* 1–25.
Amsden, A.H., and R.V. Hoeven. 1996. "Manufacturing Output, Employment and Real Wages in the 1980s: Labor's Loss until the Century's End." *Journal of Development Studies* 32(4): 506–30.
Bernanke, B. 1986. "Alternative Explanations of the Money-Income Correlation." In Brunner and Meltzer, eds., *Real Business Cycles, Real Exchange Rates, and Actual Policies*, Carnegie-Rochester Conference Series on Public Policy 25 (May): 49–100.
Bhaduri, A., and S. Marglin. 1990. "Unemployment and the Real Wage: The Economic Basis for Contesting Political Ideologies." *Cambridge Journal of Economics* 14(4): 375–93.
Blecker, R. 1989. "International Competition, Income Distribution and Economic Growth." *Cambridge Journal of Economics* 13(3): 395–412.
———. 1999. "Kaleckian Macromodels for Open Economies." In J. Deprez and J.T. Harvey, eds., *Foundations of International Economics: Post Keynesian Perspectives*. London and New York: Routledge.
Boratav, K. 1990. "Inter-Class and Intra-Class Relations of Distribution Under Structural Adjustment: Turkey During the 1980s." In T. Aricanli and D. Rodrik, eds., *The Political Economy of Turkey*, 199–229. London: Macmillan.
Boratav, K., O. Türel, and E. Yeldan. 1994. "Distributional Dynamics in Turkey Under

'Structural Adjustment' of the 1980s." *New Perspectives on Turkey* 11 (Fall): 43–69.

Boratav, K., O. Türel, and N. Yentürk. 1996. "Adjustment, Distribution and Accumulation." Research paper prepared for United Nations Conference on Trade and Development, Geneva, January 1996.

Bowles, S., and R. Boyer. 1995. "Wages, Aggregate Demand, and Employment in an Open Economy: An Empirical Investigation." In G. Epstein and H. Gintis, eds., *Macroeconomic Policy after the Conservative Era: Studies in Investment, Saving and Finance.* New York: Cambridge University Press.

Boyer, R. 1988. "Formalizing Growth Regimes." In G. Dosi, C. Freeman, and R. Nelson, eds., *Technical Change and Economic Theory.* London: Pinter.

Boyer, R., and P. Petit. 1981. "Progrès Technique, Croissance et Emploi: Un Modèle D'inspiration Kaldorienne Pour Six Industries Européennes." *Revue Economique* 32(6): 1113–54.

———. 1991. "Kaldor's Growth Theories: Past, Present and Prospects for the Future." In E. Nell and W. Semmler, eds., *Nicholas Kaldor and Mainstream Economics: Confrontation or Convergence?* London: Macmillan.

Bulutay, T. 1995. *Employment, Unemployment and Wages in Turkey.* Ankara: State Institute of Statistics and International Labor Office.

Celasun, M., and D. Rodrik. 1989. "Debt, Adjustment, and Growth: Turkey." In J. Sachs and S.M. Collins, eds., *Developing Country Debt and Economic Performance, Country Studies,* 615–808. Chicago: University of Chicago Press.

Chirinko, R. 1993. "Business Fixed Investment Spending: Modeling Strategies, Empirical Results and Policy Implications." *Journal of Economic Literature* 31(4): 1875–911.

Davidson, P., ed. 1993. *Can the Free Market Pick Winners? What Determines Investment?* Armonk, NY: M.E. Sharpe.

Davidson, P. 1998. "Post Keynesian Employment Analysis and the Macroeconomics of OECD Unemployment." *Economic Journal* 108(448): 817–31.

Dumenil, G., and D. Levy. 2000. "Costs and Benefits of Neoliberalism: A Class Analysis." Paper presented at the Rethinking Marxism conference, Amherst, MA, September 21–24, 2000.

Dutt, A. 1984. "Stagnation, Income Distribution and Monopoly Power." *Cambridge Journal of Economics* 8(1): 25–40.

———. 1987. "Alternative Closures Again: A Comment on Growth, Distribution and Inflation." *Cambridge Journal of Economics* 11(1): 75–82.

Foley, D., and T. Michl. 1999. *Growth and Distribution.* Cambridge: Harvard University Press.

Gordon, D. 1995a. "Growth Distribution, and the Rules of the Game: Social Structuralist Macro Foundations for a Democratic Economic Policy." In G. Epstein and H. Gintis, eds., *Macroeconomic Policy after the Conservative Era: Studies in Investment, Saving and Finance.* New York: Cambridge University Press.

———. 1995b. "Putting the Horse (Back) Before the Cart: Disentangling the Macro Relationship between Investment and Saving." In G. Epstein and H. Gintis, eds., *Macroeconomic Policy after the Conservative Era: Studies in Investment, Saving and Finance.* New York: Cambridge University Press.

Günçavdi, Ö., and S. Küçükçiftçi. 1999. "The Calculation of Sectoral Labor Intensities in an Open Economy (in Turkish)." *Ulusal Ekonometri ve Istatistik Sempozyumu,* Antalya, Turkey, May 14–16, 1999.

Harris, D. 1978. *Capital Accumulation and Income Distribution.* London: Routledge.

Hein, E., and H. Krämer. 1997. "Income Shares and Capital Formation: Patterns of Recent Developments." *Journal of Income Distribution* 7(1): 5–28.

Kaldor, N. 1957. "A Model of Economic Growth." *Economic Journal* 67 (December): 591–624.

————. 1960. "Alternative Theories of Distribution." *Review of Economic Studies* 23(2): 83–100.

————. 1966. *Causes of the Slow Rate of Economic Growth of the United Kingdom.* Cambridge: Cambridge University Press.

————. 1989 [1972]. "The Irrelevance of Equilibrium Economics." Reprinted in F. Targetti and A. Thirlwall, eds, *The Essential Kaldor.* New York: Holmes and Meier.

Kalecki, M. 1971. *Selected Essays on the Dynamics of the Capitalist Economy 1933–1970,* Cambridge: Cambridge University Press, 1971.

King, J., *Economic Growth in Theory and Practice: A Kaldorian Approach.* Aldershot, UK: Edward Elgar.

Marcuzzo, M., ed. 1996. *The Economics of Joan Robinson.* London: Routledge.

Marglin, S. 1984. *Growth, Distribution, and Prices.* Cambridge: Harvard University Press.

Marglin, S., and A. Bhaduri. 1990. "Profit Squeeze and Keynesian Theory." In S. Marglin and J.B. Schor, eds., *The Golden Age of Capitalism: Reinterpreting the Postwar Experience,* 153–86. Oxford: Clarendon Press.

Metin-Özcan, K., E. Voyvoda, and E. Yeldan. 2001. "Dynamics of Macroeconomic Adjustment in a Globalized Developing Economy: Growth, Accumulation and Distribution in Turkey 1969–98." *Canadian Journal of Development Studies* 21(1): 219–25.

Moore, B. 1988. *Horizontalists and Verticalists: The Macroeconomics of Credit Money.* New York: Cambridge University Press.

Nell, E. 1985. "Jean Baptiste Marglin: A Comment on Growth, Distribution and Inflation." *Cambridge Journal of Economics* 9(2): 173–78.

Onaran, Ö. 2002. "Measuring Wage Flexibility: The Case of Turkey Before and After Structural Adjustment." *Applied Economics* 34(6): 767–81.

Onaran, Ö, and E. Stockhammer. 2005. "Two Different Export Oriented Growth Strategies: Accumulation and Distribution in Turkey and South Korea." *Emerging Markets Finance and Trade* 41(1): 65–89.

————. 2003. "The Mark-Up Rates in Turkish Private Manufacturing Industry During Trade Liberalization." *Journal of Income Distribution* 11(3–4): 21–41.

Onaran, Ö., and N. Yentürk. 2001. "Do Low Wages Stimulate Investments? An Analysis of the Relationship between Distribution and Investments in Turkish Private Manufacturing Industry." *International Review of Applied Economics* 15(4): 359–74.

Özmucur, S. 1996. *Income Distribution, Taxes and Macroeconomic Indicators in Turkey* (in Turkish). Istanbul: Bosphorus University Publications.

Pollin, R. 1991. "Two Theories of Money Supply Endogeneity: Some Empirical Evidence." *Journal of Post Keynesian Economics* 13(3): 366–98.

Robinson, J. 1956. *The Accumulation of Capital.* London: Macmillan.

————.1962. *Essays in the Theory of Economic Growth.* London: Macmillan.

Rowthorn, R. 1981. "Demand, Real Wages and Economic Growth." *Studi Economici* 18: 3–53.

Sarkar, P. 1992. "Industrial Growth and Income Inequality: An Examination of 'Stagnationism' with Special Reference to India." *Journal of Quantitative Economics* 8(1): 125–38.

Senses, F. 1989. "The Nature and Main Characteristics of Recent Turkish Growth in Export of Manufacturing." *The Development Economics* 27(1): 19–33.

Sims, C. 1980. "Macroeconomics and Reality." *Econometrica* 48(1): 1–48.

————. 1986. "Are Forecasting Models Usable for Policy Analysis?" *Federal Reserve Bank of Minneapolis Quarterly Review* 10(1): 1–16.

Sims, C., J. Stock, and M. Watson. 1990. "Inference in Linear Time Series Models with Some Unit Roots." *Econometrica* 58(1): 113–44.

State Institute of Statistics (SIS). 1998. *Statistical Indicators.* Ankara: SIS.

State Planning Organisation (SPO). 1998. *Economic and Social Indicators: 1950–1998.* Ankara: SPO.

Steindl, J. 1952. *Maturity and Stagnation in American Capitalism.* New York: Monthly Review Press.

Stockhammer, E. 2004a. "Explaining European Unemployment: Testing the NAIRU Story and a Keynesian Approach." *International Review of Applied Economics* 18(1): 3–24.

———. 2004b. "Is There an Equilibrium Rate of Unemployment in the Long Run?" *Review of Political Economy* 16(1): 59–77.

Stockhammer, E., and Ö. Onaran. 2004. "Accumulation, Distribution and Employment: A Structural VAR Approach to a Kaleckian Macro Model." *Structural Change and Economic Dynamics* 15(4): 421–47.

Targetti, F. 1992. *Nicholas Kaldor: The Economics and Politics of Capitalism as a Dynamic System.* Oxford: Clarendon Press.

Taylor, L. 1985. "A Stagnationist Model of Economic Growth." *Cambridge Journal of Economics* 9(4): 383–403.

———. 1988. *Varieties of Stabilization Experience.* Oxford: Clarendon Press.

———. 1996. "Stimulating Global Employment Growth." In J. Eatwell, ed., *Global Unemployment: Loss of Jobs in the 90s.* Armonk, NY: M.E. Sharpe.

Temel, A., and M.A. Kelleci. 1995. "Developments in the Functional Distribution of National Income in Turkey, 1980–1994" (in Turkish). *New Turkey* 6: 172–76.

Toye, J. 1995. *Structural Adjustment and Employment Policy: Issues and Experience.* Geneva: International Labour Office.

Wood, A. 1997. "Openness and Wage Inequality in Developing Countries: The Latin American Challenge to East Asian Conventional Wisdom." *World Bank Economic Review* 11(1): 33–58.

Yeldan, E. 1995. "Surplus Creation and Extraction Mechanism Under Structural Adjustment in Turkey, 1980–1992." *Review of Radical Political Economics* 27(2): 38–72.

Yentürk, N. 1997. *Wages, Employment and Accumulation in Turkish Manufacturing Industry* (in Turkish). Istanbul: Friedrich Ebert Stiftung Research Results.

———. 1998. "Ajustement et accumulation: la Turquie." *Canadian Journal of Development Studies* 19(1): 55–77.

Yentürk, N., and Ö. Onaran. 2000. "Industrial Growth Patterns in Turkish Manufacturing Industry." Working paper, Birmingham Business School, February 2000.

Appendix 10.1. Definition of Variables and Data Sources

Y: Real GDP in nonagricultural sector, State Institute of Statistics (SIS) 1998.

I/Y: Private nonagricultural investment/Y, State Planning Organization (SPO) 2000.

π: Gross profits/Y in nonagricultural sector, Özmucur (1996) and Temel and Kelleci (1995).*

z: Annual growth rate of real GDP in nonagricultural sector (growth rate of Y).

X/Y: Exports of goods and services excluding agricultural exports /Y, SIS (1998).

M/Y: Imports of goods and services /Y, SIS (1998).

E: Nonagricultural employment in natural logarithms, SIS (1997) and Bulutay (1995).

*The data after 1994 and before 1968 do not exist in these studies; therefore, the percentage increase in profit/value-added ratio in the private manufacturing industry is used to extend the existing time series.

Appendix 10.2

VAR Results (OLS estimations)

	I/Y_t	π_t	X/Y_t	M/Y_t	z_t	E_t
I/Y_{t-1}	0.462 [0.01289]	−0.528 [0.11715]	0.051 [0.84425]	−0.495 [0.11795]	0.368 [0.52973]	0.001 [0.68861]
π_{t-1}	0.245 [0.02652]	0.933 [0.00000]	0.031 [0.83912]	0.218 [0.24690]	0.095 [0.78635]	−0.001 [0.57583]
X/Y_{t-1}	−0.015 [0.92081]	0.416 [0.11613]	0.610 [0.00283]	0.317 [0.20296]	−0.212 [0.64615]	−0.003 [0.10458]
M/Y_{t-1}	−0.370 [0.00130]	−0.098 [0.63824]	0.193 [0.23048]	0.550 [0.00503]	0.714 [0.04923]	0.001 [0.57064]
z_{t-1}	0.331 [0.00001]	0.314 [0.02209]	0.208 [0.04919]	0.142 [0.27195]	−0.427 [0.07380]	0.000 [0.97249]
E_{t-1}	6.946 [0.56117]	−43.292 [0.04569]	−51.656 [0.00198]	−11.956 [0.55683]	77.384 [0.04006]	0.434 [0.00181]
I/Y_{t-2}	0.261 [0.09986]	0.179 [0.53403]	−0.292 [0.18880]	0.439 [0.10467]	−0.128 [0.79864]	0.001 [0.77928]
π_{t-2}	−0.151 [0.10457]	−0.390 [0.02050]	0.059 [0.64969]	−0.037 [0.81603]	0.069 [0.81363]	0.003 [0.01063]
X/Y_{t-2}	0.093 [0.45563]	−0.499 [0.02703]	−0.348 [0.04520]	−0.330 [0.11952]	0.306 [0.43519]	0.000 [0.87985]
M/Y_{t-2}	−0.062 [0.63401]	−0.230 [0.32954]	−0.166 [0.36169]	−0.250 [0.25796]	0.129 [0.75357]	0.002 [0.30460]
z_{t-2}	0.139 [0.09010]	0.225 [0.12822]	0.024 [0.83654]	−0.027 [0.84437]	−0.321 [0.21284]	0.001 [0.32255]
E_{t-2}	−27.827 [0.02295]	34.087 [0.12429]	19.967 [0.24291]	−15.600 [0.45393]	−70.681 [0.06696]	0.394 [0.00573]
constant	167.058 [0.00441]	112.787 [0.28889]	254.172 [0.00194]	216.122 [0.03049]	−67.216 [0.71637]	1.300 [0.05689]
trend	1.032 [0.00511]	0.600 [0.36919]	1.641 [0.00143]	1.457 [0.02020]	−0.819 [0.48085]	0.005 [0.22514]
s.e.	1.357	2.460	1.897	2.311	4.280	0.016
R–Square	0.899	0.754	0.964	0.938	0.407	0.998

Note: p-values are in brackets. A trend and a constant is added to the VAR model. The estimation period is 1965–97, after adjusting for lags.

Frederico Jayme, Jr.

Growth Under External Constraints in Brazil: A Post Keynesian Approach

Introduction

During the late 1980s, Latin American countries committed themselves to structural economic reforms. The new reforms were designed to enhance economic efficiency and integrate Latin American countries into international markets. The reforms included constraints on government spending and taxation, the removal of trade barriers, along with incentives for new foreign investment and stable exchange rates and prices.

Despite these structural economic changes and increased capital flows, the economic and welfare outcomes of these reforms have been poor.[1] Bluntly put: liberalization policies of the 1980s did not lead to economic stability and growth in Latin America as predicted.

Some of the most striking aspects of the 1990s, after these reforms were put into place, were the overvaluation of the exchange rates, high interest rates, as well as trade and current-account deficits in many Latin American countries. These episodes led to balance-of-payments (BOP) crises in Mexico (1995), Brazil (1999), and Argentina (2001).[2]

In the case of Brazil, the country's economic performance during the 1990s and into 2000 was far less than what it achieved in the 1970s. In spite of the world economic crisis of 1974, Brazil enjoyed an annual gross domestic product (GDP) growth rate of 7 percent in the 1970s. After the debt crisis of the 1980s, the Brazilian economy stagnated, with sharp increases in unemployment and income concentration. Even after price stabilization in 1994, which had a positive short-term effect on income distribution, the current situation in Brazil is far from stellar.

Neoclassical economists argued that the market reforms in the 1980s would lead to economic growth because of increases in labor productivity and total factor productivity. They saw participation in world markets and the importing of technology leading to faster growth in the long run, following the mainstream literature on endogenous growth models (Ben-David and Kimhi 2000; Edwards 1992, 1993, 1998; Krueger 1997; Sachs and Warner 1995; Srinivasan and Bhagwati 1999). However, empirical studies have failed to find a clear relationship between these reforms and growth (Hanson and Harrison 1995, Rodriguez and Rodrik 1999).

Throughout its history, Brazil has sought to carry out import-substitution industrialization (ISI) in order to avoid fiscal, external, and savings constraints. The last major attempt was in the mid-1970s, and it failed because of the structural problems related to the interest-rate shock in 1979, its development strategy, and the collapse of capital flows during the 1980s. After capital flows resumed in the 1990s, Brazil stabilized its economy. Nevertheless, exchange-rate appreciation, increasing external debt, and trade liberalization left the Brazilian economy highly vulnerable to external forces. Persistent trade and current-account deficits confirm this assertion. In response to the neoclassical view, this chapter aims to show that external constraints strongly influence the pattern of economic growth in Brazil by testing Thirlwall's BOP-constrained economic-growth model.

An examination of Thirlwall's framework is useful in attempting to understand the pattern of Brazilian economic growth during this period since his demand-pull approach demonstrates that increasing returns are essential to analyzing economic development. Thirlwall's model differs from the new endogenous growth models in that it shows that aggregate demand and financial constraints are essential determinants for long-term economic growth. Thirlwall shows that productive resources are not always fully utilized and that their supply tends to be dictated by their demand.

The basic idea of Thirlwall's approach highlights how the BOP affects the growth performance of countries. In fact, mainstream versions of economic growth generally neglect not only the demand side of the economy, but also external constraints. Keynesian models along Kaldorian lines, such as Thirlwall's BOP-constrained growth model, link trade to growth because exports pull demand. Indeed, trade represents a crucial constraint to economic growth when there are BOP problems. Static trade models suggest that movements toward openness can temporarily increase the rate of growth as a result of short-term gains from the reallocation of resources, which would imply a positive relationship between changes in openness and GDP growth.

Several authors argue that if GDP and exports do cointegrate in the long term, Thirlwall's law is valid. (Atesoglu 1993, 1994, 1997; Hieke 1997; López and Cruz 2000; Moreno-Brid 1999). This chapter, however, claims that further tests have to be carried out to confirm this assertion. The test used here is a vector error correction (VEC) representation of the variables, thus we can also check the direction of causality.

Also, the cointegrated equation has statistical significance when exports are considered as an independent variable. All the same, the short-term behavior of these variables in the form of a VEC representation suggests that the causal relationship between exports and GDP comes from GDP to exports. Hence, Thirlwall's law, as a sense of an empirical regularity in the long term, under some restrictive assumptions (such as the absence of price effects), is valid for Brazil. The direction of causality, however, is ambiguous since lag variables of exports do not have significance in explaining GDP in the VEC representation.

Alexander and King (1998) argue that it is important to be cautious when analyzing econometric results in models relating variables such as exports and GDP. Because exports are part of GDP, it is highly probable that the endogeneity of these variables affects the results, and that we should be cautious as we analyze the econometric results of Thirlwall's law. The authors do not deny, however, the possibility that a country's rate of economic growth may be subject to a long-term BOP constraint. What they suggest is that the simple rule of Thirlwall's law may have oversimplified the nature of the relationship. This is an important issue that one has to keep in mind, and it is clear that the parameter of the equation, as well as its validation, has to be examined cautiously since this model is simple in that it intends to look for any BOP constraints in the Brazilian economy. Other factors, such as financial or institutional aspects, would require a more sophisticated model. With these caveats, what are important are the results of this chapter, which support Thirlwall's law that states that exports, income elasticities of imports, and GDP have a long-running relationship. Indeed, from 1955 to 2002 and selected subperiods, there has been cointegration between exports and GDP.

Some Features of the Brazilian Economy, 1955–2004

Beginning at mid-century, 1955 to 1963 is notable as a period of profound structural change in Brazil, as well as being an era of robust economic growth. Afterward, following a period of poor economic development between 1964 and 1967, Brazil's GDP rose by more than 10 percent per annum from 1968 to 1973, in what has come to be known as the Brazilian economic miracle. Between 1973 and 1981, the average annual growth rate still remained high, at around 7 percent a year, and until 1973 the inflation rate was relatively stable, with a moderate fiscal deficit. (see Figure 11.1) . After 1974, however, inflation accelerated, and the current account and fiscal deficits increased.[3] In the 1980s, a combination of high fiscal deficits and an exchange-rate crisis led to poor economic growth as well as high inflation, and this continued into the 1990s, with per capita GDP in 1998 only 3.5 percent higher than in 1980.[4] The central question for policy makers in Brazil in this period was how to stabilize inflation, which was finally answered in the mid-1990s, when the new-currency "Real Plan" succeeded in steadying inflation.

Another concern was the financial account of the BOP, with Ponta (1996) showing the unsustainable intertemporal path of the external debt. The empirical evidence was undeniable: current-account deficits became impossible to manage in the long term. After 1991, however, capital inflows to Brazil increased dramatically. The capital-account surplus rose from $4.148 billion in 1991 to $29.820 billion in 1995, whereas short-term capital increased from a deficit of $2.9 million to $17.554 million between 1991 and 1995, leading to a fast and dangerous accumulation of external debt.[5] This path changed considerably after

Figure 11.1   **Brazilian GDP and GDP Per Capita (1955–2003)**

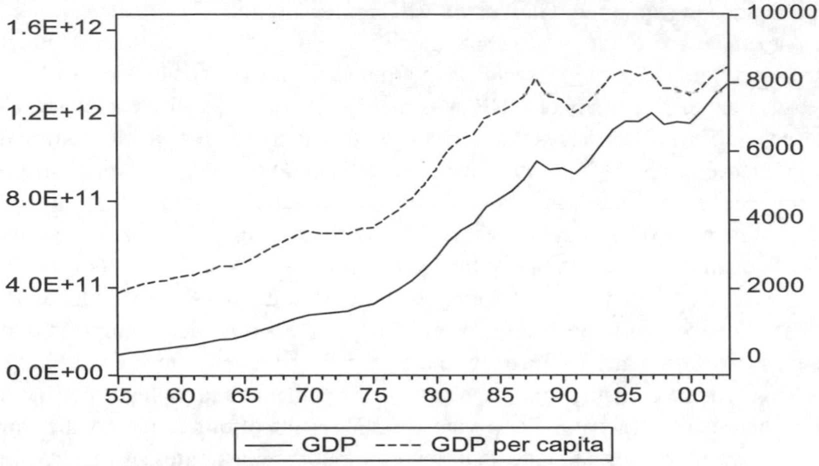

Source: Central Bank of Brazil *Bulletin* (several issues).

2002, when Brazil enjoyed a healthy trade and current-account surplus as well as a stable exchange rate.

As Sampaio (2000) has pointed out, after trying to reduce the external debt in the 1980s, 1990 saw the net external debt in Brazil reach $123 billion, or 26 percent of GDP. By the end of 1999 this amount reached $237 billion, or more than 40 percent of GDP. On top of this, during the 1990s, Brazil spent $117 billion on interest payments alone. Figure 11.2 illustrates the pattern of the gross and net external debt in Brazil. The trajectory was stable until 1992, when there was a slight shift, followed in 1998 by a more apparent change in the slope of the curve. After 1992, the level of debt is closely related to the deepening involvement with the financial liberalization policies carried out by structural reforms under former president Fernando Collor (1990–92). The principal feature of these reforms was the attempt to increase trade and financial liberalization by lowering imports tariffs as well as breaking down barriers to short-term and speculative capital flows. As a result, greater capital inflows allowed for a rapid accumulation of foreign reserves, but at the cost of increasing the foreign debt. The net foreign debt remained almost stable until the Asian crisis of 1998, when Brazilian policy makers implemented new rules for external capital, thus intensifying economic liberalization. Again, the foreign debt increased, even though the loss of external reserves had been less dramatic.[6] The behavior of external accounts after 2002, however, is clearly not enough to conclude that Brazil has changed its external vulnerability (Jayme and Crocco 2005).

In fact, external vulnerability for Brazil has become even worse due to policies that have allowed a fast and systematic accumulation of foreign reserves by giving

Figure 11.2 **Gross and Net External Debt in Brazil (1980–2003)**

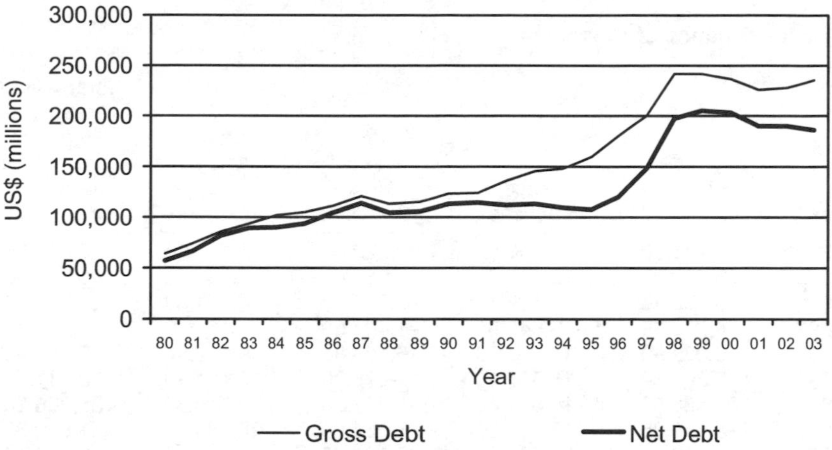

Source: Central Bank of Brazil *Bulletin* (several issues).

facilities to short-term foreign capital. The consequences of these actions included a denationalization of firms as well as a fast accumulation of external debt. Brazil's political-economic strategy after the Mexico crises in 1982 was to improve the external balance, since it was impossible to finance current-account deficits. By calibrating monetary and exchange-rate policy, successful results were achieved with respect to trade-balance surpluses and, soon after, narrower current-account deficits. Although the results were convincing on the external front, the side effects included high inflation and a high internal disequilibrium, which led to an unsustainable course of national debt in the long term.

After 1981, the ratio of the national debt to GDP increased and continued on a steady upward trend, as borrowing from international financial markets became virtually impossible after Mexico's pronounced economic crisis in September 1982. The central government's borrowing requirements increased from 4.8 percent of GDP in 1983 to 12.5 percent in 1985, and from 26.6 percent of GDP in 1988 to 48.3 percent in 1989. These unique deficits were strictly correlated to the indexation process in the Brazilian economy and the difficulty in financing the domestic debt. Indeed, Brazil started an indexation process in its economy after 1965. There were two sides to this indexation. On the one side, indexation prevented losses for debtors and gains for creditors when inflation was moderated, as well as avoiding the classic hyperinflation that occurred in interwar Germany in 1922 and in Argentina at the end of the 1980s. But, it also meant it was more difficult to control the high inflation process. Inflation rates soared during the 1980s, with the annual rate ranging from 110 percent in 1981 to 2740 percent in 1990. There was little doubt that the source of the problem in the 1980s was strongly related to the exter-

Table 11.1

Brazil's Balance of Payments: Selected Items

Year	Trade balance ($ million)	Balance of services	Current-account balance ($ million)	Capital-account balance ($ million)	International reserves ($ million) international liquidity (end of period)
1980/84*	3,743.00	−13,400.00	−9,529.00	6,531.00	6,501.00
1985/89*	13,453.00	−13,936.00	−355.00	−2,084.00	8,929.00
1990	10,752.40	−15,369.10	−3,783.70	4,591.30	9,973.00
1991	10,580.00	−13,542.80	−1,407.50	162.70	9,406.40
1992	15,238.90	−11,336.20	6,108.80	9,910.40	23,754.30
1993	13,298.80	−15,577.10	−675.90	10,411.90	32,211.20
1994	10,466.50	−14,691.80	−1,811.20	8,518.30	38,806.20
1995	−3,466.00	−18,541.00	−18,384.00	28,744.00	51,840.30
1996	−5,599.00	−20,350.00	−23,502.00	33,514.00	60,110.10
1997	−6,753.00	−25,522.00	−30,452.00	25,408.00	52.172.71
1998	−6,575.00	−28,299.00	−33,416.00	29,381.00	44,556.44
1999	−1,199.00	−25,825.00	−25,335.00	16,981.00	36,342.28
2000	−698.00	−25,048.00	−24,225.00	19,053.00	33,011.50
2001	2,642.00	−27,503.00	−23,213.00	27,088.00	35,866.42
2002	13,121.00	−23,148.00	−7,718.00	7,571.00	37,823.00
2003	24,801.00	−23,652.00	4,051.00	4,606.00	49,296.00
2004	33,693.42	−23,292.00	11,668.87	−8,013.40	52,935.00

Source: Central Bank of Brazil *Bulletin* (various issues), and Rocha and Bender (1999) for the two first rows.

*Annual averages of the period.

nal crisis and to the impossibility of financing investment by external debt, as was the case in the 1970s.

As previously mentioned, the success of the external adjustment came on the back of exports, which created vast trade surpluses. Exports increased sharply after the devaluation of the exchange rate in 1983, and imports remained almost constant. This allowed for an accumulation of trade surpluses until 1994 (Table 11.1). This was the most important component for the success with respect to the trade balance after 1983. The close relationship between exchange rate policies and trade balances is evident when looking at the behavior of the trade surpluses during the 1980s. After the financial liberalization in 1992 and the explicit actions to allow the Brazilian real to over-appreciate after 1994, trade surpluses were reduced. There were intense debates in Brazil about these surpluses during the 1980s, and it is reasonable to assume that the import-substitution policies in the 1970s, after the first oil shock, produced productivity gains for some industries. This, in turn, allowed Brazilian industry to compete on international markets under better

Table 11.2

Brazil's Balance of Payments: Selected Items (percent of GDP)

Year	Trade balance	Balance of services	Current-account balance	Capital-account balance
1990	2.29	−3.27	−0.81	0.98
1991	2.61	−3.34	−0.35	0.04
1992	3.93	−2.93	1.58	2.56
1993	3.10	−3.63	−0.16	2.42
1994	1.93	−2.71	−0.33	1.57
1995	−0.49	−2.63	−2.61	4.07
1996	−0.72	−2.62	−3.03	4.32
1997	−0.84	−3.16	−3.77	3.15
1998	−0.83	−3.59	−4.24	3.73
1999	−0.23	−4.81	−4.77	3.16
2000	−0.12	−4.15	−4.08	3.17
2001	0.52	−5.39	−4.61	5.31
2002	2.60	−5.04	−1.68	1.65
2003	5.00	−4.79	0.82	0.94
2004	5.60	−3.83	1.91	−1.32

Source: Central Bank of Brazil *Bulletin* (various issues).

conditions. Those gains in productivity led to an impressive performance of exports in the early 1980s. On the other hand, the short-term exchange rate, and wage as well as monetary and fiscal policies, were organized jointly to guarantee external equilibrium. A huge decrease in internal absorption as a result of recession represented the other side of these policies.[7]

Tables 11.1, 11.2, and 11.3 show the behavior of external accounts mainly after 1990. The strong fall in the current-account and trade balance after 1990 can be explained by the strategy to expose the Brazilian economy to the external environment. As part of the structural reforms carried out under the umbrella of the so-called Washington consensus, Brazilian policy makers launched rapid and intense trade and financial liberalization, as well as large-scale privatization and other liberal policies. The results in terms of GDP and per capita growth were somewhat disappointing, although high inflation was brought under control after the successful exchange-rate-based stabilization plan of mid-1994.[8] The consequences of the stabilization and Washington consensus–based reforms were high current-account deficits, an interest-rates trap to warrant capital inflows, an overvalued exchange rate until the 1999 crisis, unprecedented rates of unemployment, and modest economic growth.[9] The strategy of the Brazilian central bank to keep the exchange rate overvalued brought about a BOP that was highly vulnerable, so the 1999 crisis was no surprise. The current-account deficit as a percentage of GDP varied from −0.30 percent in 1994 to −4.4 percent in 1998. Indeed, the literature

Table 11.3

Index of Foreign Vulnerability

Year	International reserves/ current account	International reserves/ imports (FOB)	Openness (X + M)/PIB	Net public debt (% GDP)
1990	−2.64	0.48	0.11	N/A
1991	−6.68	0.45	0.13	38.58
1992	3.89	1.16	0.15	35.12
1993	−47.66	1.28	0.15	31.16
1994	−21.43	1.17	0.14	30.38
1995	−2.82	1.04	0.14	30.83
1996	−2.56	1.13	0.13	33.23
1997	−1.71	0.87	0.14	34.33
1998	−1.33	0.77	0.14	41.73
1999	−1.43	0.74	0.18	49.39
2000	−1.36	0.59	0.19	49.43
2001	−1.55	0.65	0.22	52.60
2002	−4.90	0.80	0.23	55.50
2003	12.17	1.02	0.25	57.20
2004	4.54	0.84	0.26	51.80

Source: Central Bank of Brazil *Bulletin* (various issues).

on the currency crisis has pointed out that one important indicator of the weakening of the external front, as well as the basic determinant of speculative attack, is the deficit and its proportion to GDP.[10]

In January 1999, the central bank changed its monetary and exchange-rate policies, first with the devaluation of the real, and, second, by letting the currency float.[11] Bonomo and Terra (1999) showed a historical relationship between political cycles and the exchange rate, and it seems reasonable to suppose that the decision to keep the real overvalued was made with the explicit purpose of reelecting President Cardoso in November 1998.[12]

The Model of BOP-constrained Growth

Thirlwall's model emphasizes that the dynamic Harrod foreign-trade multiplier determines long-term economic growth. It stresses that demand factors induce economic growth. In an open economy, the dominant constraint upon demand is the BOP.

The new growth literature also identifies a number of avenues through which openness might affect long-term growth.[13] Some of these channels are technological change and technological gaps. The idea behind these new growth models is that countries that are more backward actually have more opportunities to absorb new ideas and will converge on international norms more quickly, allowing them to benefit from technological change. Nevertheless, even open new endogenous growth models, such as that of Grossman and Helpman (1990, 1991), focus only on trade and growth, neglecting BOP constraints. On the other hand, a one-gap model in the Keynesian and structuralist traditions reveals the demand and external constraints in an open economy.

Indeed, Thirlwall's approach stresses that neither trade and financial liberalization nor strategies of export promotion necessarily lead to better growth performance. The Keynesian and structuralist traditions take into consideration both current- and capital-account equilibrium. Therefore, one should consider not only exports of goods and services, but also—and very importantly—the income elasticity of demand for imports. Export performance and income elasticity of demand for imports imply that trade and capital-account liberalization do not necessarily lead to economic growth through technological gains or through an increase in total factor productivity (TFP). Furthermore, export-led growth does not necessarily lead to better economic performance.

A traditional version of Thirlwall's (1979) model can be presented in Equations 1, 2, and 3:

$$x = \phi (p_d - p_f) + \rho z, \tag{1}$$

$$m = a (p_d - p_f) + \pi y, \tag{2}$$

$$x + p_d = m + p_f, \tag{3}$$

where $\rho, \pi, \alpha > 0$, and $\phi < 0$. Income elasticity of exports and imports are ρ and π, respectively; price elasticity of exports and imports are, respectively, ϕ and α; x is the growth rate of real exports; m is the growth rate of real imports; z is the growth rate of the-rest-of-the-world real income; y is the growth rate of real domestic income; $(p_d - p_f)$ is the rate of growth of relative prices (rate of growth of domestic prices less the rate of growth of prices in the rest of the world). Equations 1 and 2 are, respectively, export- and import-demand functions, whereas Equation 3 is current-account equilibrium.

Solving Equation 3 for the growth of real income:

$$y^* = [(1 + \phi - \alpha) / \pi] (p_d - p_f) + (\rho/\pi) z, \tag{4}$$

or, substituting for the growth rate of the world real income, z, from Equation 1, yields:

$$y^* = [(1/\pi) (1 - \alpha)] (p_d - p_f) + (1/\pi) x. \tag{5}$$

Supposing that the Marshall-Lerner condition holds, or that relative prices are constant if measured in a common currency, then $(p_d - p_f) = 0$, (5) becomes:

$$y^* = (1/\pi)\ x. \tag{6}$$

Equation 6 is BOP-constrained growth, a version of the Harrod foreign-trade multiplier. This equation, or Thirlwall's law, states that we should expect a higher income elasticity of demand for imports (π), the lower the BOP equilibrium growth rate.[14]

Empirical evidence for developed countries shows that this model is an efficient framework for analyzing economic growth in relation to a country's international payments position.[15] However, the model presented above takes into consideration only the current-account position. Although in the long term, current-account equilibrium is extremely important for the BOP position, many developing countries are affected by capital flows. The model must be modified in order to introduce capital flows. Indeed, as McCombie and Thirlwall (1994, 241) point out, "The growth experience of the developing countries over the last thirty years has been even more diverse than that of the developed countries, and can hardly be explained by reference to differences in the autonomous rate of growth of factor supplies." As long as these characteristics are considered, for countries in which capital inflows are important for BOP equilibrium, it is important to include current-account imbalance in the model. Clearly, capital flows affect the simple version of Thirlwall's law, leading to differences between the growth the law predicts and the effective growth of a country.[16]

Estimating Growth Constrained by the BOP for the Brazilian Economy, 1955–2000

As Hieke (1997) and Atesoglu (1997) stressed, traditional econometric procedures are not sufficient predictors of BOP-constrained growth, even if one estimates equations by means of the first difference. In fact, as the cointegration literature emphasizes, estimation of a time series under ordinary-least-squares (OLS) regression may lead to a spurious regression, and furthermore does not show the long-term relationship between the variables. Therefore, a cointegration technique is important because it yields results that are more realistic. Using augmented Dickey-Fuller (ADF) tests, Hieke (1997) demonstrated that for some periods after World War II, Thirlwall's law was not valid for the U.S. economy. Atesoglu (1997) showed that, with the exception of the period between 1943 and 1947, the growth rates of exports and GDP always move together.

Because a cointegration test yields complementary results, I will use it to analyze Brazil's economic growth.[17] Our purpose is to determine the order of integration in time series using ADF and Phillips-Perron (PP) tests for variables in Equation 6. Because this long-term relationship is verified, we would not reject the hypothesis that Thirlwall's law holds for time-series data on Brazil.

Empirical Results

As pointed out above, since the model proposed presents nonstationary variables, cointegration regression will be used toward its estimation. If the variables do cointegrate, the cointegrating regression allows us to estimate the long-term regression coefficients, which are consistent regardless of the dynamic structure of the model and whether any variables are correlated with the disturbance.[18] These estimates are super consistent since they converge to their true values at a faster rate than normal OLS estimates. If, however, two series of different orders are integrated, they cannot be cointegrated. Therefore, the first step in testing a time-series model is to determine the order of integration by means of testing for unit roots. The two tests most often used for this purpose are Dickey-Fuller (DF) and PP tests.

DF and ADF tests admit that the error term is nonspherical. If it is suspected that the errors are autocorrelated or heteroskedastic, PP tests have to be carried out. This procedure consists in calculating the DF statistics, obtaining a t-value by running an auxiliary regression, and or adjusting these statistics before consulting the critical values appropriate for that version.

Once the order of integration of the time-series data is determined, the cointegration test can then be performed if integrated variables are of the same order. If variables are found to be $I(1)$, as it may happen in the exercises that follow, cointegration requires the residuals from cointegrating regression to be $I(0)$, that is, it requires the residual series from the OLS regressions of the variable in level form to be stationary. The ADF and PP tests must reject the hypothesis of a unit root in the residual series.

Therefore, the first step is to test for unit roots in each series. The ADF and PP tests will be used to find the presence of unit roots. Holden and Perman (1994) suggest estimating equations to test for trend and intercept, including sufficient lags to eliminate serial correlation in the regression residual. The null hypothesis is that the time series is nonstationary, against the alternative hypothesis that the series is stationary.

Unit-root tests, using both PP and ADF tests, were carried out for both variables in Equation 6, that is, for the growth of gross national product and exports in Brazil between 1955 and 2000, both for levels and first differences of the variables.[19] As used in empirical macro-econometrics, these tests have to be performed using (i) trend and intercept, (ii) no trend and intercept, and (iii) no trend and no intercept.[20] ADF tests included different lags, while PP tests included only three truncation lags, since the Newey-West test suggests this number. The tests are highly responsive to the number of lags included. Indeed, on one hand, PP tests do not reject the null hypothesis that the variables being considered are $I(1)$, against the alternative that they are $I(0)$, nor do they demonstrate time-trend significance. ADF tests, on the other hand, tend to be responsive to the number of lags included (admitting no time trend, since this variable does not show significance different

Table 11.4

Test of the Unit Roots: Intercept and Trend (1955–2000)

Variable	ADF (1)	ADF (2)	ADF (3)	PP (3)
LnY	−3.47246	−3.26432	−3.03255	−2.77793
ΔLnY	−4.23048*	−3.89245**	−5.09848*	−5.08121*
LnX	−3.13943	−2.16370	−2.28024	−2.65794
ΔLnX	−9.43123*	−4.15695**	−3.76376**	−6.69603*

*Significant at 1 percent level.
**Significant at 5 percent level.
***Significant at 10 percent level.
MacKinnon critical values for rejection of hypothesis of a unit root: 4.18 (1%), −3.52 (5%), −3.19 (10%).
ADF (d) Augmented Dickey-Fuller test, null of unit roots, lag (d).
PP (d) Phillips-Perron test, null of unit root, lag truncation (d). As the Newey-Nest test suggests, PP tests were carried out with only three truncation lags.
AIC and SC suggest one lag at ADF.

from zero, only with two lags is GDP integrated of order (1). Nevertheless, one can admit that both series are I(1) based on PP (3) and ADF (2) tests without a time trend. Because the evidence indicates the presence of a single unit root in all the series tested, it is possible to perform a cointegration test for the relationship between exports and GDP in Brazil—see Tables 11.4, 11.5, and 11.6.

The Johansen cointegration test between LnY and LnX was carried out admitting a drift (intercept) and no time trend since this exogenous variable does not show significance different from zero. Holden and Perman (1994) started considering large lags in cointegration tests in order to avoid autocorrelation in the residuals of the cointegrated regression. The optimum lag length is obtained after progressively reducing the lag length based on the significance tests of the parameters. Indeed, the reason for using cointegration is to reduce the lag length to the shortest possible in order to make the model more parsimonious in the VAR estimation. After reducing the lag length, the choice of two lags is based on the significance of the parameters, since after the reduction the parameters do not demonstrate significance at the 10 percent level. Table 11.7 presents the results of Johansen cointegration tests for different samples using two lags for each cointegration sample and assuming no deterministic trend in the data.[21] In all the different periods, the Johansen cointegration test presents positive cointegration between the log of the GDP and the log of exports. The residual tests not reported showed no autocorrelation in the residual series, and they showed nonstationarity.[22]

Table 11.5

Test for Unit Roots: Intercept (1955–2000)

Variable	ADF (1)	ADF (2)	ADF (3)	PP (3)
LnY	−1.12442	−0.69908	−0.52698	−1.02444
ΔLnY	−4.28783*	−3.97114*	−4.98448*	−5.14851*
LnX	0.56468	2.07523	1.23099	1.36148
ΔLnX	−8.44543*	−3.66329*	−3.22832**	−6.27596*

* Indicates significance at the 1 percent level.
** Indicates significance at 5 percent level.
*** Indicates significance at 10 percent level.
MacKinnon critical values for rejection of hypothesis of a unit root: 3.59 (1%), −2.93 (5%), −2.60 (10%).
ADF (d) Augmented Dickey-Fuller test, null of unit roots, lag (d).
PP (d) Phillips-Perron test, null of unit root, lag truncation (d). As the Newey-West test suggests, PP tests were carried out with only three truncation lags.
AIC and SC suggest one lag at ADF.

Table 11.6

Test for Unit Roots: No Intercept or Trend (1955–2000)

Variable	ADF (1)	ADF (2)	ADF (3)	PP (3)
LnY	0,15961	0,62767	0,90608	0,33676
ΔLnY	−4,05610*	−3,59869*	−4,16158*	−5,07981*
LnX	2,26667	4,77623	2,77593	3,86527
ΔLnX	−6,09152*	−2,27086**	−1,76961	−5,28128*

*Indicates significance at the 1 percent level.
**Indicates significance at the 5 percent level.
***Indicates significance at the 10 percent level.
MacKinnon critical values for rejection of hypothesis of a unit root −2.62 (1%), −1.94 (5%), −1.62 (10%).
ADF (d) Augmented Dickey-Fuller test, null of unit roots, lag (d).
PP (d) Phillips-Perron test, null of unit root, lag truncation (d). As the Newey-West test suggests, PP tests were carried out with only three truncation lags.
AIC and SC suggest one lag at ADF.

Table 11.7

Johansen Cointegration Equation for the Relationship Between Growth in Exports and Growth in GDP

Sample	Coefficient LnX	Intercept
(1955–2000)	0.419857	−2.590466
	(0.01616)	(0.16042)
	(25.9742)	(−16.1477)
(1981–2000)	0.399278	−2.278520
	(0.02709)	(0.27847)
	(14.7390)	(−8.18239)
(1955–89)	0.419875	−2.599530
	(0.02175)	(0.20220)
	(19.3018)	(−12.8560)
(1955–80)	0.387033	−2.274516
	(0.03748)	(0.30038)
	(10.3272)	(−7.57205)
(1966–2000)	0.411229	−2.473456
	(0.00678)	(0.06958)
	(60.6940)	(−35.5502)
(1966–2000)	0.451559	−2.911429
	(0.00690)	(0.06988)
	(65.4275)	(−41.6626)

All samples show significant cointegration at 5 percent.

The values in parentheses are the standard errors of normalized cointegrating coefficients, and t-statistics.

All of the residuals are integrated of order zero.

Correlation Coefficient of LnX and LnY: 0.975727.

Two lags were used in the cointegration equation.

LnY is the dependent variable.

No deterministic trend in the data.

The use of different samples in assessing the BOP-constrained model for the Brazilian economy enables us to make some comparisons among different economic-policy and exchange-rate-policy regimes. The implicit long-term income elasticity of demand for imports found in every sample is similar to other studies that estimate the income elasticity of demand in Brazil.[23] For the whole period (1955–2000), the implicit income elasticity of demand for imports is 2.38 (representing a coefficient of 0.42), and the results show positive and significant cointegration between the GDP and exports. For 1955 to 1989, the results do not present a difference from the total sample since the implicit income elasticity of demand for imports is also 2.38. This behavior suggests that trade liberalization in Brazil after 1990 did not imply changes in the income elasticity of demand for imports, and further studies should attempt to investigate why. A comparison between the periods of 1955 to 1980 and 1981 to 2000 shows that the implicit income elasticity of demand for imports decreased from 2.58 to 2.50, and one might argue that BOP-constrained economic growth in Brazil could not be a result of income elasticity of demand for imports. Nevertheless, if one compares the shorter period of 1966 to 1980 with 1981 to 2000 one finds that, in the former, the parameter was 2.21, and, in the latter, a period in which the Brazilian economy was relatively more open, it was 2.58.[24] This result suggests that the increased income elasticity of demand for imports explain part of the slowdown in Brazilian economic growth after 1981.

López and Cruz (2000) applied Thirlwall's law to four Latin American countries (Argentina, Brazil, Colombia, and Mexico) and, for Brazil, found an implicit income elasticity of demand for imports of 1.6 from 1965 to 1995. They also showed a cointegration between exports and the GDP in this period. Like other studies, they claimed that this result is sufficient to confirm the validity of Thirlwall's law. As will be shown later, however, it is necessary to analyze the short-term behavior based on a vector-error-correction (VEC) model to confirm this hypothesis. In order to establish a causality relation between exports and GDP, they tested a Granger causality model. The results show Granger causality from exports to the GDP, which is another condition for claiming that Thirlwall's law is valid. In this analysis, however, I achieve different results using a VEC representation. Indeed, as shown above, the causality has not run in the same order demonstrated by López and Cruz (ibid.). Because a VEC representation allows an analysis of impulse-response functions, the technique is more complete.[25]

López and Cruz proposed not only to show the validity of Thirlwall's law for some Latin American countries, but also to examine the role that exchange rates have on trade equations. Their results for Brazil, however, were problematic since they found that exchange-rate depreciation appears to deepen the trade balance. The mega-surpluses in the trade balance during the 1980s show the opposite behavior, though. They also claim that the Marshall-Lerner condition was not fulfilled from 1965 to 1995, which is not a reasonable assumption for a small country. Moreover, the behavior of trade surpluses after 1983 in Brazil does not support the hypothesis that the Marshall-Lerner condition was not valid.

Using the implicit income elasticity of demand for imports obtained from the cointegrated equation in the whole sample and applying it to Equation 6, and taking into account that the Marshall-Lerner condition holds, it is possible to find the predicted long-term growth in the present model. Figure 11.3 shows a comparison between predicted and effective growth from 1970 to 2000. The results suggest an excellent adjustment between estimated and effective growth using Thirlwall's law.

Figure 11.3   **Growth Predicted by Thirlwall's Law and Effective Growth (1970–2000)**

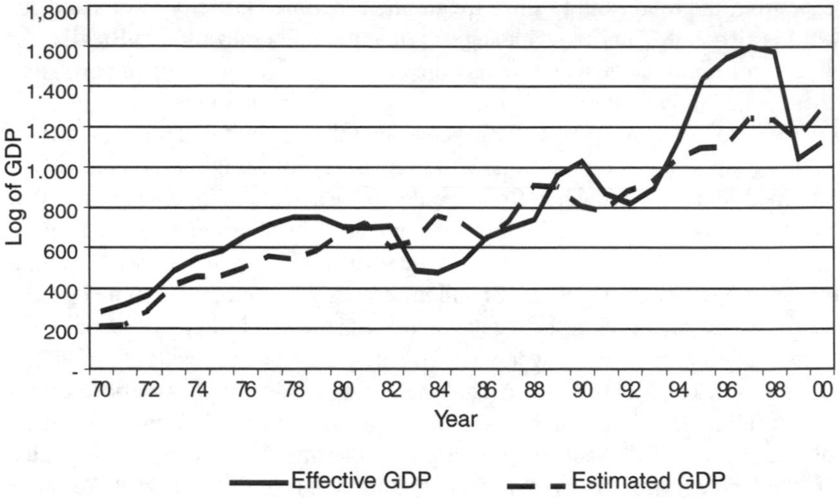

——— Effective GDP   — — Estimated GDP

Source: Brazilian Central Bank *Bulletin* (several issues) and our estimations.

The differences can be explained by the capital inflows, as shown in Figure 11.4.[26]

Having performed cointegration tests, both for the whole sample and selected subperiods, and having found the existence of at least one vector of cointegration in each sample between the GDP and exports, there is room to suppose that Thirlwall's framework is suitable for understanding external constraints upon growth in Brazil's economy. Some authors, in fact, consider the existence of a single vector of cointegration a sufficient condition to show the validity of Thirlwall's law (Atesoglu 1997, Moreno-Brid 1999, among others). If, however, cointegration does not hold between these variables, as Hiecke (1997) found in the U.S. economy, the law is not valid. Although cointegration can help us analyze the relationship between GDP and exports, as well as the implicit income elasticity of demand for imports, it seems insufficient since there is no causal relation involved in the cointegration equation. Therefore, a VEC specification for the same model not only helps to establish a short-term relationship between these variables, but also the impulse-response functions following an exogenous shock in the error terms of both variables. This fact allows us to better estimate the causal relation involved among the variables.[27] Furthermore, the variance decomposition of a VEC gives the relative contribution of an innovation to the means-squared error of the forecasted variable h periods ahead. These methods can therefore give results that are more accurate, mainly because the relationship between exports and income elasticity of demand for imports related to GDP likely has bidirectional causality. Yet,

Figure 11.4   **Net Foreign Capital in Brazil (1970–2000)***

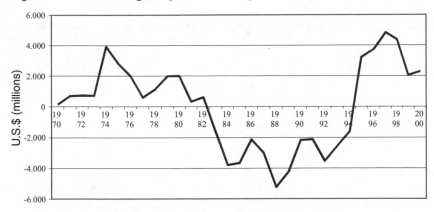

Source: Brazilian Central Bank *Bulletin* (several issues) and our estimations.
*Difference between net capital flow and net services.

assuming that the Harrod foreign multiplier determines the growth of GDP, it seems fair to assume that growth in GDP also leads to better export performance, thus generating a virtuous cycle.

Because the estimated coefficients in the VEC are difficult to interpret, the results can be better summarized by the impulse-response functions and variance decomposition of the error covariance matrix. After performing the VEC for both directions and assuming two lag lengths, as explained, the results are presented in Table 11.8. The VEC parameter shows no significance different from zero in the equation where GDP is the dependent variable. When exports are the dependent variable, 74 percent of the discrepancy between the short-term values of exports is corrected in the first period. This result suggests that, at least in the short run, lagged values of exports do not present the robust behavior needed to explain the growth of the GDP (ΔGDP in Table 11.8). On the other hand, the lagged values of the GDP present statistical significance in explaining the direction of exports in the whole period analyzed (i.e., 1955–2000). This result also reveals that, over a short period of time, the causality relation between GDP and exports demonstrates the opposite direction suggested by Thirwall's framework.

Price effect in the short term can explain this behavior since, particularly in Brazil, the exchange-rate policy represented an important aspect in macroeconomic policy principally after the debt crisis in the early 1980s (as described above). Further research should be carried out to analyze in greater depth the short-term behavior of the variables.

With regard to the impulse-response functions and variance decomposition, the ordering of the variables affects the results and should therefore be chosen carefully. For the sake of this exercise, the choice of order is from exports to GDP, since the

Table 11.8

Vector Error Correction Estimates for Δ GDP and Δ Exports, 1955–2000

Error Correction	ΔGDP	ΔExports
Cointegration Equation	−0.041748	0.743441
	(0.05491)	(0.14304)
	(−0.76025)	(5.19748)
ΔGDP(−1)	0.547280	0.990885
	(0.15274)	(0.39787)
	(3.58300)	(2.49050)
ΔGDP (−2)	0.330682	0.122103
	(0.16166)	(0.42108)
	(2.04557)	(0.28997)
ΔExports (−1)	0.042345	0.136272
	(0.04878)	(0.12707)
	(0.86802)	(1.07241)
ΔExports (−2)	−0.030887	−0.346761
	(0.04697)	(0.12234)
	(−0.65763)	(−2.83446)
R–squared	0.281189	0.528857
Adj R–squared	0.201322	0.476508
Sum sq residuals	0.046112	9.312864
S.E. equation	0.035789	0.093224
Log likelihood	81.02388	41.77247
Akaike AIC	−6.546359	−4.631656
Schwarz SC	−6.337387	−4.422684

Note: Standard deviations and *t*-statistics in parentheses.

aim is to define the pattern of the short- and long-term effects of exports on growth. The results were seen in Figures 4 and 5, as well as Tables 11.6, 11.7, 11.8, and 11.9.

Tables 11.9 and 11.10 and Figure 11.4 indicate the dynamic responses of exports and GDP. The results illustrate their bi-directional causality. Indeed, as expected, exports affect GDP and GDP affects exports. Table 11.6 shows that, on one hand, GDP's initial response to innovations in exports is positive and tends to increase in intensity, while being absorbed after ten periods. On the other hand, GDP's responses to its own innovations are low at one lag, but tend to increase

Table 11.9

Impulse Response to Innovations to the One-standard-deviation: Response of GDP

	Ordering exports—GDP	
Response period	GDP	Exports
1	0.032342	0.008869
2	0.048692	0.018582
5	0.099912	0.035972
10	0.144915	0.056889

Table 11.10

Impulse Response to Innovations to the One-standard-deviation: Response of Exports

	Ordering exports—GDP	
Response period	GDP	Exports
1	0.000000	0.087355
2	0.056092	0.087373
5	0.160805	0.080770
10	0.293616	0.119122

rapidly and with high intensity until being absorbed after ten to fifteen periods. This behavior is compatible with the Keynesian and structuralist traditions, which show that demand pulls economic growth, and that BOP problems have constrained growth in Brazil's economy. Table 11.9 shows the effects of innovations on GDP and exports to exports. It has been verified that the innovations effect displayed a similar pattern on GDP. Indeed, the initial innovations' dynamic response in GDP over exports is zero, increasing in intensity after the second period. At the same time, exports, responding to its own innovations, initially decreases in intensity, then reverses this behavior and is finally absorbed after ten to fifteen periods. Once more, the theoretical hypotheses of the model developed in this chapter seem to be in accord with the empirical pattern in the Brazilian economy.

The variance decomposition of a VEC, as previously stated, gives the relative contribution of an innovation to the mean-squared error of the forecasted variables h periods ahead. On the one hand, Table 11.11 shows that after ten periods, 87.5 percent of the forecast error of GDP is accounted for by its own innovations, whereas 12.45 percent is accounted for by innovations in exports. It is worth noting that innovations in exports tend to increase quickly in the first two periods until being absorbed after ten periods. Table 11.12, on the other hand, shows the variance decomposition of exports. It reveals that 100 percent of the forecast error in the first period is accounted for by its own innovations. After twelve periods, however,

Table 11.11

Variance Decomposition of GDP

Period	S.E.	GDP	Exports
1	0.033536	93.00657	6.993430
2	0.061975	88.96215	11.03785
5	0.169802	88.75774	11.24226
10	0.355561	87.54266	12.45734

Table 11.12

Variance Decomposition of Exports

Period	S.E.	GDP	Exports
1	12.45734	0.000000	100.0000
2	0.135688	17.08914	82.91086
5	0.291807	66.88366	33.11634
10	0.671431	81.88697	18.11303

82 percent of the forecast error in exports is accounted for by GDP, and 18 percent by its own innovations.

The VEC, impulse response, and variance decomposition of the model presented show the relevance of the short-term behavior in GDP and in exports for the long-term relationship presented in the cointegrated regression for 1955–2000. Indeed, these results confirm the importance of BOP-constrained economic growth for long-term economic growth in Brazil. Moreover, it shows that Thirlwall's model, using only cointegration, neglects short-term behavior, and is, therefore, insufficient for demonstrating its empirical validity. The relationship between short- and long-term behavior allows us to make a better connection in the model, demonstrating the importance of the relationship between exports and income elasticity of demand for imports (in this case, represented implicitly by the parameter in the cointegrated equation) with growth, and, of course, with growth to exports.

Conclusion

In this chapter, BOP-constrained economic growth in Brazil was tested on the Brazilian economy. BOP-constrained growth was tested using the cointegration technique and a VEC representation. The findings provide a satisfactory explanation of the variations in the long-term economic growth of Brazil. The Keynesian approach to economic growth predicts economic development in Brazil. This is important not only because it can help foster long-term growth, but also because, in recent history, Brazil and other Latin American countries have faced episodes of hyperinflation as a result of deficits in the current account and breaks in capital flows.

Although the results demonstrate the importance of BOP-constrained economic growth in Brazil, both for the whole period and for selected subperiods, one has to be cautious with econometric results, as Alexander and King (1998) pointed out. Furthermore, one cannot guarantee strategies toward persistently high economic growth. Indeed, achieving sustainable and stable economic growth depends on strategies that relate to institutional and technological policies. This chapter only shows the importance of external constraints for economic growth in the long term. In addition, the results suggest that a policy of export promotion, combined with an import-substitution strategy, could be rational in terms of policy prescriptions, since both strategies lead to moderate BOP constraints in the long term.

Notes

A grant from the CNPQ (Brazilian Council of Research) is gratefully acknowledged.

1. The first wave of reforms concerns the well-known southern cone liberalization programs. For a recent assessment of these programs, see Frenkel (1998). For a critical review of the structural reforms in developing countries, see Taylor (1997).

2. Argentina suffered the consequences of every currency crisis of the 1980s and 1990s under its currency-board system. See Frenkel (1998).

3. A good study of the period from 1974 to 1979 and the external consequences is found in Castro and Souza (1985).

4. The value of GDP per capita in U.S. dollars can be slightly different if we adjust for purchasing-power parity (PPP).

5. Cardoso and Goldjfan (1998).

6. It is worth noting that the net foreign debt remained constant from 1992 to 1998, since the accumulation of external reserves was larger than debt. Nevertheless, the loss of foreign-denominated reserves in 1999's currency crisis led to a rapid deepening of the foreign debt.

7. See Castro and Souza (1985) for this debate.

8. Similar behavior occurred in other Latin American countries. See Frenkel and Rozada (1999) for Argentina and Ros and Lustig (1999) for Mexico.

9. See Taylor (1997) for a critique of the Washington Consensus–based reforms.

10. See Blecker (1992) and Rodrik and Velasco (1999), among others.

11. After unsuccessfully controlling the exchange rate in January and February 1999, the central bank imposed a flexible exchange-rate regime.

12. Bonomo and Terra (1999) pointed out the effects over government popularity of keeping the currency overvalued, since real wages in an open economy tend to be higher than real wages under the equilibrium exchange rate.

13. For the special relationship between trade and growth using endogenous growth, see Grossman and Helpman (1990, 1991). For an empirical estimation of economic growth across countries, see Barro (1997).

14. As Anwar Shaikh correctly pointed out, Thirlwall's approach does not need to work under current-account equilibrium. It is enough that the relationship between exports and imports keeps constant, even if trade balance is in disequilibrium. See Shaikh (1999).

15. See, for example, Atesoglu (1993, 1994, 1997) for the U.S. experience, McCombie and Thirlwall (1994) for a sample of developed countries, Hieke (1997) for the U.S. experience, and Atesoglu (1993–94) for Canada, to cite a few.

16. Brazil is a good example of capital inflows from 1966 to 1979, as well as after 1990.

17. Jayme (2003) estimated this model for Brazil from 1955 to 1998. This is a new version of that estimate.

18. There is an extensive literature about cointegration and its results for time-series regressions. See, for example, Rao (1994), Maddala and Kim (1998), and Hamilton (1994) among others. A discussion about this technique is outside the scope of this chapter.

19. Y is the domestic income measured by the GDP in Brazil. Until 1992, the data was taken from Maddison (1995). After that, the source of the data was *Conjuntura Econômica*, FGV, Brazil, several issues. X is the volume of exports in current U.S. dollars (*Conjuntura Econômica*, FGV, Brazil). Maddison (1995) has been chosen because it has a large span of data from the GDP and GDP per capita in dollars using PPP. After 1992, I use the GDP index from *Conjuntura Econômica*. Although it has used a different source of data, Maddison is the only available work that presents a large span of data in dollars using PPP. The compatibility of both sources has been made by using an index of GDP after 1992 from *Conjuntura Econômica*. Despite the tribulations of such methodology, it gives the advantage of allowing us to work in dollars in a long time series.

20. All these tests were performed using Microsoft E-views 4.1.

21. The results using a linear trend in the data are similar to no deterministic time trend.

22. The Johansen co-integration test carried out using E-views 4.1 presents the cointegrated normalized coefficients after certifying that residuals are white noise. In order to confirm the results, the residuals of each cointegrated equation have been submitted to the Engle-Granger procedure. This procedure consists of testing for unit root and autocorrelation for the residual series. Both the Breusch-Godfrey serial correlation LM test and unit-root tests have showed there is no correlation in the residuals series of the cointegrated equation. Besides, the presence of a unit root in the residuals was rejected.

23. See Ferreira (1992) and Azevedo and Portugal (1998).

24. In fact, between 1955 and 1965, the Brazilian economy was relatively more closed than in the subsequent period.

25. It is plausible, however, that a different source as well as a different span of the data can explain these different results.

26. We used data from 1970 to 2000 because only after 1970 did we find accurate statistics from capital flows in Brazil.

27. The causal relation can be also tested by means of Granger causality tests. In fact, Mehra (1994) pointed out, as per Granger (1986), that if a pair of series is cointegrated, then there must be Granger causation in at least one direction. In a bivariate case, this follows from the observation that such series satisfy an error-correction specification.

References

Alexander, R., and A. King. 1998. "Growth and the Balance of Payments Constraints." Research Paper No. 622, Department of Economics, University of Melborne, Australia.

Atesoglu, H.S. 1993. "Balance of Payments Constrained Growth: Evidence from the United States." *Journal of Post Keynesian Economics* 15(4): 507–14.

———. 1993–94. "Exports, Capital Flows, Relative Prices and Economic Growth in Canada." *Journal of Post Keynesian Economics* 16(2): 289–98.

———. 1994. "An Application of a Kaldorian Export-led Model of Growth to the United States." *Applied Economics Letters* 2(1): 91–94.

———. 1997. "Balance of Payments Constrained Growth Model and Its Implications for the United States." *Journal of Post Keynesian Economics* 19(3): 327–35.

Azevedo, A.F.Z., and M. Portugal. 1998. "Abertura Comercial Brasileira e Instabilidade da Demanda por Importacoes." *Nova Economia* 8(1): 20–32.

Barro, R.J. 1997. *Determinants of Economic Growth: A Cross-Country Empirical Study.* Cambridge: MIT Press.

Ben-David, D., and A. Kimhi. 2000. "Trade and the Rate of Income Convergence." National Bureau of Economic Research (NBER) Working Paper 7642 (April). Cambridge, MA: NBER.

Blecker, R. 1992. "Structural Roots of U.S. Trade Problems: Income Elasticities, Secular Trends and Hysteresis." *Journal of Post Keynesian Economics* 13(3): 321–46.

Bonomo, M., and M. Terra. 1999. "The Political Economy of Exchange Rate Policy in Brazil: 1964–1997." Working Paper, Fundação Getulio Vargas. Rio de Janiero: Fundação Getulio Vargas.

Cardoso, E., and Ilan Goldfajn. 1988. "Capital Flows to Brazil. The Endogeneity of Capital Controls." IMF Staff Papers, (45): 161–202.

Castro, A.B., and F.E. Souza. 1985. *A Economia Brasileira em marcha forçada.* Rio de Janeiro: Paz e Terra.

Conjuntura Economica, several issues. Rio de Janiero: Fundação Getulio Vargas (FGV).

Edwards, S. 1992. "Trade Orientation, Distortions, and Growth in Developing Countries." *Journal of Development Economics* 39(1): 31–57.

———. 1993. "Trade Policy, Exchange Rates and Growth." National Bureau of Economic Research (NBER) Working Paper 4511 (February). Cambridge, MA: NBER.

———. 1998. "Openness, Productivity, and Growth: What Do We Really Know?" *Economic Journal* 108(1): 383–98.

Ferreira, A. 1992. "Trade and Growth: Three Exercises Using Brazilian Data." Ph.D. diss., New School for Social Research, New York.

Frenkel, R. 1998. *Capital Market Liberalization and Economic Performance in Latin America.* CEPA Working Papers 1998-06, Center for Economic Policy Analysis (CEPA). New York: The New School.

Frenkel, R., and M. Rozada. 1999. *Balance of Payments Liberalization: Effects on Growth and Employment in Argentina.* Paper prepared for Center for Economic Policy Analysis (CEPA), The New School Conference on Globalization and Social Policy (January). New York: The New School.

Granger, C. 1986. "Developments in the Study of Cointegrated Economic Variables." *Oxford Bulletin of Economics and Statistics*, (48): 213–28.

Grossman, G., and E. Helpman. 1990. "Comparative Advantage and Long-Run Growth." *American Economic Review* 80(4): 796–815.

———. 1991. *Innovation and Growth in the Global Economy.* Cambridge: MIT Press, 1991.

Hamilton, W. 1994. *Time Series Analysis.* Princeton, NJ: Princeton University Press.

Hanson, G., and A. Harrison. 1995. "Trade, Technology, and Wage Inequality." National Bureau of Economic Research (NBER) Working Paper 5110. Cambridge, MA: NBER.

Hieke, H. 1997. "Balance of Payments-Constrained Growth: A Reconsideration of the Evidence for the U.S. Economy." *Journal of Post Keynesian Economics,* spring, 10(3): 313–25.

Holden D., and R. Perman. 1994. "Unit Roots and Cointegration for the Economist." In B.B. Rao, ed., *Cointegration for the Applied Economist,* 47–112. New York: St. Martin Press.

Jayme, F.G., Jr. 2003. "Balance of Payments Constrained Economic Growth in Brazil." *Brazilian Journal of Political Economy* 23(1): 62–84.

Jayme, F.G., Jr, and M. Crocco. 2005. "Vulnerabilidade Externa e Saldos Comerciais no Brasil." In J. Sicsú et al., eds, *Novo Desenvolvimentismo,* 145–64. São Paulo, SP: Manole.

Krueger, Anne O. 1997. "Trade Policy and Economic Development: How We Learn?" *American Economic Review* 87(1): 1–21.

López, Julio G., and A.B. Cruz. 2000. "Thirlwall's Law and Beyond: The Latin American Experience." *Journal of Post Keynesian Economics,* 22 (3): 477–96.

McCombie, J., and A. Thirlwall. 1994. *Economic Growth and the Balance of Payments Constraint.* New York: St. Martins.

————. 1999. "Growth in an International Context: A Post Keynesian View." In J. Deprez and John Harvey, eds., *Foundations of International Economics: Post Keynesian Perspectives*, 35–90. London: Routledge.

Maddala, G.S., and I.M. Kim. 1998. *Unit Roots, Cointegration, and Structural Change*. Cambridge: Cambridge University Press.

Maddison, A. 1995. *Monitoring the World Economy: 1820–1992*. Paris: OECD.

Mehra, Y.P. 1994. "Wage Growth and the Inflation Process. An Empirical Approach." In R.B. Rao, ed., *Cointigration for the Applied Economist*. New York: St. Martin's Press.

Moreno-Brid, J.C. 1999. "Mexico's Economic Growth and the Balance of Payments Constraint: A Cointegration Analysis." *International Review of Applied Economics* 13(2): 149–59.

Ponta, A.F. 1996. A sustentabilidade do endividamento externo no Brasil: uma análise de co-integração. *Pesquisa e Planejamento Econômico* 26(3): 399–416.

Rao, B.B. 1994. *Cointegration for the Applied Economist*. New York: Saint Martins Press.

Rocha, F.F., and S. Bender. 1999. "Present Value Text of the Brazilian Current Account." Unpublished manuscript.

Rodríguez, F., and D. Rodrik. 1999. "Trade Policy and Economic Growth: A Skeptic's Guide to the Cross-National Evidence." National Bureau of Economic Research (NBER) Working Paper 5791. Cambridge, MA: NBER.

Rodrik, Dani, and André Velasco. 1999. *Short-Term Capital Flows*. National Bureau of Economic Research (NBER) Working Paper 7364 (September). Cambridge, MA: NBER.

Ros, J., and N. Lustig. 1999. "Trade and Financial Liberalization with Volatile Capital Inflows: Macroeconomic Consequences and Social Impacts in Mexico During the 1990's." Paper prepared for Center for Economic Policy Analysis (CEPA), The New School Conference on Globalization and Social Policy (January). New York: The New School.

Sachs, J., and A. Warner. 1995. "Economic Reform and the Process of Global Integration." *Brooking Papers on Economic Activity* 1: 1–117.

Sampaio, P.A., Jr. 2000. "A Armadilha das Dívidas Eternas." In *Folha de S.Paulo*, 9/11/2000.

Shaikh, 1999. *Real Exchange Rates and the International Mobility of Capital*. New School Working paper N. 265 (March). New York: The New School.

Srinivasan, T.N., and J. Bhagwati. 1999. "Outward-Orientation and Development: Are Revisionists Right?" Unpublished manuscript.

Taylor, L. 1991. *Income Distribution, Inflation, and Growth*. Cambridge: MIT Press.

————. 1997. "The Revival of the Liberal Creed—The IMF and the World Bank in a Globalized Economy." *World Development* 25(2): 145–52.

Thirlwall, A. 1979. "Balance of Payments Constraint as an Explanation of International Growth Rate Differences." *Banca Nazionale del Lavoro Quarterly Review* 128(791): 45–53.

About the Editors and Contributors

Carolyn B. Aldana is Associate Professor of Economics and Assistant Dean of the College of Social and Behavioral Sciences at California State University, San Bernardino. She has published papers on inequality, economic performance and well-being, minority bank performance, and health care for nonstandard workers. Her current research focuses on wealth accumulation issues for people of color.

Michelle Baddeley is Fellow, College Lecturer and Director of Studies in Economics at Gonville and Caius College, Cambridge University, UK, and Teaching Associate, Faculty of Economics, Cambridge. She has published a wide range of papers in a number of journals and is the author and editor of many books including *Investment: Theories and Analysis*.

Jerry Courvisanos is Senior Lecturer in Innovation and Entrepreneurship, University of Ballarat, Australia. His research seeks to understand the processes of innovation and how they affect investment spending, business cycles, and the long-term development of businesses and the economy. He is the author of *Investment Cycles in Capitalist Economies* (Edward Elgar, 1996) as well as many articles in journals and books.

Gary A. Dymski is Professor of Economics at the University of California, Riverside. His publications include *The Bank Merger Wave* (1999), several edited books, and *Reimagining Growth: Toward a Renewal of Development Theory*, which he co-edited with Silvana De Paula. He has written many articles and chapters on banking, financial fragility, urban development and poverty, credit-market redlining and discrimination, the Latin American and Asian financial crises, exploitation, and housing finance.

Lawrance L. Evans, Jr. is a Senior Economist in the Applied Research and Methods Group at the US Government Accountability Office (GAO). Prior to his position at GAO, Evans was a research fellow in the Economics department at Amherst College. He has several publications including the book *Why the Bubble Burst*.

James K. Galbraith holds the Lloyd M. Bentsen, Jr., Chair in Government/Business Relations at the LBJ School of Public Affairs, University of Texas at Austin. He is a Senior Scholar of the Levy Economics Institute and Chair, Economists for Peace and Security. He is the author of *Created Unequal* and *Balancing Acts*.

Enrique Garcilazo is a graduate student at the Lyndon B. Johnson School of Public Affairs, University of Texas at Austin. His research interest lies primarily in unemployment and inequality and at the regional level during the European integration process.

Richard P.F. Holt is Professor of Economics at Southern Oregon University. He has authored and edited a number of books, book chapters, and journal articles including *A New Guide to Post Keynesian Economics* (with Steven Pressman) and *The Changing Face of Economics: Conversations with Cutting Edge Economists* (with David Colander and Barkley Rosser, Jr.).

Frederico G. Jayme, Jr. is Associate Professor of Economics, Economics Department, UFMG, Brazil, and Vice President, Brazilian Economic Association (ANPEC).

Anthony J. Laramie is a Professor of Economics at Merrimack College, USA. He is co-author (with Douglas Mair) of numerous papers on Kaleckian public finance, which have been published in such journals as the *Cambridge Journal of Economics, the Journal of Post Keynesian Economics*. He is also co-author (with Douglas Mair) of *A Dynamic Theory of Taxation: Integrating Kalecki into Modern Public Finance*.

Douglas Mair is Professor Emeritus at Heriot-Watt University, Edinburgh, Scotland. With A.J. Laramie he has developed a Post Keynesian approach to taxation based on the work of Kalecki. He has numerous publications on public finance including such journals as *Cambridge Journal of Economics, Metroeconomica* and *Regional Studies*.

Anne G. Miller is a former lecturer in economics at Heriot-Watt University, Edinburgh, Scotland. She is co-editor with Douglas Mair of *A Modern Guide to Economic Thought.* Her main research interest is basic income and its policy implications.

Özlem Onaran is an Associate Professor at Istanbul Technical University. She has published various articles in journals and books in the areas of labor and development economics, particularly on the macroeconomics and political economy of distribution, growth, accumulation, and employment.

Steven Pressman is Professor of Economics and Finance at Monmouth University in West Long Branch, NJ. He also serves as co-editor of the *Review of Political Economy*, and as Associate Editor and Book Review Editor of the *Eastern Economic Journal*. He has published approximately 100 articles in refereed journals and as book chapters, and has authored or edited ten books, including *A New Guide to Post Keynesian Economics* and *50 Major Economists* (2nd ed.).

Robert H. Scott, III is Assistant Professor of Economics at Monmouth University. His main research interests are credit cards, microcredit, and environmental economics.

Engelbert Stockhammer is Assistant Professor at the Vienna University of Economics and Business Administration. He is the author of *The Rise of Unemployment in Europe*, and he has published articles on financialization, unemployment, and growth theory in journals such as *Cambridge Journal of Economics*, *Structural Change and Economic Dynamics* and the *International Review of Applied Economics*.

Index

Abel, A.B., 203, 204
Abramson, A., 91n13
Acemoglu, D., 231n7
accumulation and distribution, 6, 15–16, 285–86
Akerlof, G.A., 205
Akyüz, Y., 302n18
Aldana, Carolyn, 11–12, 85
Alexander, R., 305
Allan, J., 20
Allen, F., 246
Amadeo, E.J., 301n1
American institutionalism, 90n2
Amsden, A.H., 301n1
anti-poverty policies, views, 24–27
Arestis, P., 4, 168n16, 178
Arnott, R., 246
Arrow, K.J., 205
Asimakopulos, A., 148
Atesoglu, H.S., 308, 316, 322
Atkinson, A., 29
Australia (1984–1994)
    econometric analysis, 144–67
    industrial development, stages, 163–64
    See also innovation-investment
Ausubel, L.M., 111

Baddeley, Michelle, 14, 198, 203, 206
Bailey, P., 271
Baker, D., 44
Baker, M., 248, 252, 267
balance of payment constrained growth model,
    307–9, 314–27
Banerjee, A., 219
Baran, P., 146
Barro, Robert J., 8, 9, 327n13
Becker, G., 25
behavioral economics. *See* Courvisanos, Jerry;
    Kalecki, Michal
Ben-David, D., 307
Bernanke, B.S., 204, 265, 280
Bernheim, B.D., 246
Bertaut, C.C., 125
Bertola, G., 204
Bhaduri, A., 277, 278, 280, 284

Bhaduri-Marglin open economy model, 279–85
Bhagwati, J., 307
Binswanger, M., 271n2
Blanchard, O., 44, 206
Blecker, R., 327n10
Blundell, R., 198
Boatwright, J.W., 168n16
Boland, L., 8
Bond, S., 198
Bonomo, M., 314, 327n12
Boratav, K., 278
Boskin, M., 25
Bowles, S., 284, 285
Boyer, R., 284, 285
Bradford, P., 49
Brazil, economy (1955–2004)
    balance of payment constrained growth model,
        307–9, 313, 314–16
    capital flows, 307, 308, 310, 316, 327
    central bank (1999), 313–14, 327
    co-integration test, 16, 308, 317, 321
    currency crisis (1999), 307, 310, 313–14, 327
    current accounts, 307, 308, 309, 310, 311, 313,
        315–16
    debt crises (1980s), 307, 308, 309, 310, 311,
        313, 323
    exports and GDP, 308–9, 316, 318, 321, 324–26
    external constraints limit growth, 308, 322, 327
    external debt, 308–12
    growth performance, 308, 315
    import substitution industrialization, 308
    income elasticity of demand for imports, 315,
        320, 321–22, 326
    indexation process, 311
    inflation, 309, 311–13
    market reforms (1980s), 307–8
    structural reforms, 307, 310, 313
    Thirlwall's model. *See* Thirlwall
    trade surpluses, 312, 321
    Washington consensus, 313
Brealey, R., 248
Brito, D.L., 111
Brocket, P., 111
Brown, C., 26, 72

Index prepared by Donna Reeder.